child care policy at the crossroads

child care policy at the crossroads

gender and welfare state restructuring

edited by sonya michel and rianne mahon

ROUTLEDGE
New York • London

Published in 2002 by
Routledge
29 West 35th Street
New York, NY 10001

Published in Great Britain by
Routledge
11 New Fetter Lane
London EC4P 4EE

Routledge is an imprint of the Taylor & Francis Group.

10   9   8   7   6   5   4   3   2   1

Library of Congress Cataloging-in-Publication Data

Child care policy at the crossroads : gender and welfare state restructuring / edited by
Sonya Michel and Rianne Mahon.
       p. cm.
     Includes bibliographical references and index.
     ISBN 0–415–92704–8 — ISBN 0–415–92705–6 (pbk.)
       1. Child care— Government policy. 2. Sex discrimination against women. 3. Family
     policy. 4. Welfare state. I. Michel, Sonya, 1942– II. Mahon, Rianne, 1948–

HQ778.5 .C494 2002
362.71'2—dc21   2001040371

Printed on acid-free, 250-year life paper.
Manufactured in the United States of America.

CONTENTS

Part 3. The Impact of Neoliberalism

Part 4. Preserving/Creating Universalism

ACKNOWLEDGMENTS

We have been thinking and writing about child care for many years, and it has been a great pleasure to work with other scholars who share our conviction that this is one of the most crucial issues in the struggle for gender equality. Our special appreciation goes to Jane Jenson, who worked with us in the early stages of conceptualizing this project, and whose own collection on child care has contributed significantly to research in this field.

In the spring of 1999, the Belle van Zuylen Institute for Multicultural and Comparative Gender Studies at the University of Amsterdam arranged for us to hold a workshop on comparative child care policy, where many of us met face-to-face for the first time. We would like to thank Professor Frances Gouda of the Institute for graciously making this possible.

We also thank Elizabeth Blount, a graduate student in French at the University of Illinois at Chicago, who has contibuted to this project in many ways. She ably translated one of the chapters, did a thorough job of proofreading, and prepared the index.

At Routledge, Eric Nelson supported this project from the outset and Hope Breeman has patiently guided it to fruition. Victoria Pope of *U.S. News and World Report* alerted us to the photograph by Ken Jarecke that appears on the cover.

In working on this book, we frequently had occasion to recall the many wonderful care providers we and our children (and grandchildren) have encountered over the years. We would like to acknowledge the fine work they do, and to express our hope that in the future, they and their colleagues everywhere will receive the recognition and compensation they so richly deserve.

Sonya Michel, Chicago

Rianne Mahon, Ottawa

Gender and Welfare State Restructuring: Through the Lens of Child Care

Rianne Mahon

The erosion of the male breadwinner/female homemaker family form constitutes one of the critical challenges confronting contemporary welfare states. Whereas other important challenges—such as those posed by "globalization" (economic and political) or the postindustrial "trilemma"[1]—are usually associated with pressures for retrenchment, the decline of the male-breadwinner family challenges states to take on new responsibilities. As it can no longer be assumed that mothers/wives/daughters are at home, ready and able to care for young children, the sick, the disabled, and the elderly, alternative arrangements are called for. Of the various measures to reconcile work and family life, child care policies are especially important as they can also help to solve the demographic problem posed by an aging society. Quality early childhood care and education can also contribute to greater social equality and provide the foundations for lifelong learning.

The pressures created by the erosion of the male-breadwinner/female-homemaker model exist in all countries in the Organization for Economic Cooperation and Development (OECD), and in many they have existed for some time. Yet the responses are by no means everywhere the same. Different patterns of response, reflecting different roles to be played by states, markets, and families, in turn hold different implications for equality. A public guarantee of universal access to high quality child care, provided by caregivers earning equitable wages, is critical to any solution aimed at simultaneously pursuing gender and class equality. Some countries have laid the foundations for such systems; others favor market-based solutions that deepen class, and often racial, inequality; still others try to shore up the male breadwinner family. All, however, are in a state of flux.

This volume examines a range of examples, drawn from postindustrial societies across the world, that illustrate these divergent patterns of response. In addition to Anglo-American and Western European cases more typically examined in such comparative studies, we include cases from Japan and Poland. The inclusion of these cases enriches the basis of comparison, offering new angles from which to consider dominant assumptions about the welfare state and the sociocultural relations in which it is embedded. Each chapter outlines the main features of current child care policy in a particular country, asking to what extent the pattern of provision advances the goals of access, quality, and equity. In addition, a central goal for all authors is to illuminate the political forces at play in generating a new structure of challenge and choice in contemporary polities. What rationales have been advanced to support or impede policy initiatives? What have been the positions, alliance patterns, and influence of major political forces? Have feminists been able to place their stamp on issues, or have other voices been paramount?

This introduction provides an overview, highlighting the themes and issues that run through this volume. It seeks to locate our questions and findings in relation to broader debates on welfare state restructuring. We argue that a comparative analysis of early childhood care and education policies offers a privileged window into the gender implications of restructuring processes. Public support for the provision of nonparental child care is central to the solution of the "care crisis" induced by the decline of the breadwinner family. How and whether nonparental child care is provided, moreover, is indicative of whether and how states are able to tackle the question of full employment in a postindustrial era. More broadly, analysis of child care policies can tell us a lot about how gender, class, and racial equality are faring as welfare states restructure.

Welfare State Restructuring and the Decline of the Male-Breadwinner Family

The literature on contemporary welfare states has been dominated by the debate over whether globalization or postindustrialism should be seen as the primary force driving the restructuring process.[2] Both sets of pressures are important and, as we shall see, both are implicated, in various ways, in the formation of contemporary child care policies. Yet no account is adequate that does not also include the challenge(s) posed by the decline of the male-breadwinner model.[3] As one detailed study of European employment patterns concluded, "Governments may create or perpetuate contradictions or inconsistencies, and choose to ignore for political expediency the breakdown of the male-breadwinner family as the single or even the most important family form. Nevertheless, it is becoming increasingly difficult for governments to cling to a simple model of household and family organization in framing welfare policy or to maintain the notion that the labor market consists primarily of male full time continuous participants" (Rubery et al. 1997, 5).

The welfare regimes consolidated in the postwar era focused on the male breadwinner and the risks—unemployment, ill health, industrial accidents, retirement—that could jeopardize his capacity to support himself and his dependents. They also assumed the domestic presence of a housewife and her capacities to provide primary care—for young children, the sick and the injured, and aging parents. Elder care and care of the very young and the infirm were often provided largely as an unpaid "labor of love" by mothers, sisters, and daughters. Of course, the male-breadwinner family represented an ideal, never the reality for all families. In some societies, like Japan, it never fully took hold. In others, like Italy, it was only in the 1960s that women's labor-force participation began to decline—just as it began to rise in North American and many northern European countries.[4] Over the last twenty years, however, the continued rise in labor force participation by women, including mothers of young children, has come up against attempts at welfare state retrenchment that seek to increase reliance on this form of unpaid labor.

That is, changes in labor markets (the shift to postindustrial employment, the declining ability of a single wage to provide for a family) and in families (rising rates of divorce, separation, and lone parenthood) are everywhere undermining the male-breadwinner family form. At the same time, medical advances have prolonged life expectancy and enabled greater control over childbirth. In many countries, this is giving rise to a demographic crisis, as people are living longer while women are choosing to have smaller families, often later, or to avoid childbirth entirely (Castells 1997, chap. 4). These developments reflect the lack of supportive child care arrangements which in turn contributes to a broader "crisis of care" (Daly and Lewis 2000). While states have been under pressure to rethink assumptions underlying the way all forms of care have been provided (and provided for), the population replacement crisis makes child care an especially important concern.

There is another strong reason for welfare states to consider taking on greater responsibility for the provision of care: the restoration of full employment. Gøsta Esping-Andersen (1999) has provided the best-developed argument for a "post-industrial Keynesian strategy" (1999, chaps. 4 and 6). That is, the time-pressed dual-earner (or lone-parent) household can be seen as a potential source of demand for job-rich personal and social services. Such families face time constraints, making it more difficult to avoid substituting external sourcing for self-provision. They are also more likely to have the disposable income to purchase at least some services. The full flowering of postindustrial jobs can come about, however, only if the state is prepared to facilitate access to services by all dual-earner and solo-parent families, either through direct provision or some form of subsidy.[5]

Of course, as feminists have long argued, state support for the development of an ample social care infrastructure is not just about job growth or demographics. It is also a necessary, if not sufficient, condition for achieving gender equality. As Janet Gornick argues, "One of the most entrenched and consequential components of gender differentiation is in the provision of unpaid care for children and other family members. . . . In the industrialized countries, the primary responsibility for dependent care work remains delegated to women. The gendered nature of standard patterns of unpaid work affects women throughout the life cycle, since adult work roles are long anticipated and have enduring consequences. The sexual division of unpaid labor, in turn, shapes gender-linked patterns of labor market investments and attachments, and consequently claims on welfare resources as well" (1999, 2). In other words, only with appropriate child care policies can progress toward greater equality between the sexes be achieved. This is not, unfortunately, the aspect that particularly interests Esping-Andersen.

In fact, Esping-Andersen is prepared to endorse a level of service sector

wages—including those of child care workers—that would generate a certain inequality "in the here and now." This assumes that these are low-skilled jobs, requiring little more than the "talents" women deployed within the home, and fails to
recognize the *skills* required, especially in child care systems that emphasize early
childhood education.[6] For Esping-Andersen the social democrat, this is justified as
long as governments offer training and educational opportunities to allow those
stuck in poor jobs today to get off the "poverty bus" in the future. In addition, he
sidesteps the whole question of power relations within the family, finding in Gary
Becker's model of household joint decision making an adequate explanation for the
fact that it is still women who bear the primary responsibility for care work in and
around the home (Esping-Andersen 1999, 58; Becker 1981). Others, like Manuel
Castells, however, are prepared to recognize that "the massive incorporation of
women into *paid* work increased women's bargaining power vis-à-vis men, and undermined the legitimacy of men's domination as providers of the family" (1997,
135). Indeed, the power implications associated with the erosion of the male breadwinner family form are laying the groundwork for one of the important forces in favor of greater socialization of the responsibility for care, the contemporary feminist
movement—but that is to get ahead of our story.

For Nancy Fraser, these views suggest that Esping-Andersen has succumbed to
the "postsocialist" condition, convinced that the egalitarian and democratic—even
"revolutionary"[7]—reforms he earlier championed are no longer feasible.[8] Fraser,
however, holds to an egalitarian agenda, and is prepared to take on the postsocialist
challenge: "the trick is to imagine a social world in which citizens' lives integrate
wage earning, caregiving, community activism, political participation, and involvement in the associational life of civil society—while also leaving time for some fun.
This world is not likely to come into being in the immediate future, but it is the only
imaginable postindustrial world that promises true gender equity. And unless we are
guided by this vision now, we will never get any closer to achieving it" (1997, 62).
She thus rejects the "universalized breadwinner" model that underlies Esping-Andersen's argument, because it fails to secure genuine equality among all citizens. Instead, she advocates the universalization of caregiving.[9]

According to this model, carework should be organized in such a way as to yield
the status and pay attached to primary sector work (Fraser 1997, 42). This demand
need not be considered utopian. There are ways of raising productivity in the caring
services that improve the terms of the equality-jobs tradeoff (Mahon 2000) even
while they improve the quality of the service provided.[10] High-quality early childhood care and education, in turn, offer important developmental benefits that establish the foundations for greater equality of opportunity and even outcome
(McCain and Mustard 1999). Universal access to quality child care, *irrespective of the
parents' labor force status*, is thus important to the extent that it can contribute to
equality as well as "social inclusion."[11] As we shall see, this is an issue that has arisen
in Sweden, which has one of the most advanced systems of child care arrangements
(Bergqvist and Nyberg, in this volume). The issue of democratic control also has to

be addressed. In this regard, Fraser sees an important role for locally organized, self-managed carework activities of the sort envisioned by advocates of the "social economy."[12]

Clearly the achievement of gender and class equality requires more than universally accessible, high-quality child care. As Fraser and others have argued, it requires reasonably paid parental leave,[13] pay and employment equity provisions (either through legislation or through an encompassing collective bargaining system), access to appropriate education and training, good urban transportation systems, and so on. Our focus, however, is on child care systems and, as readers will see, child care arrangements vary substantially across the thirteen cases we have selected. We need a way of assessing these in terms of their potential contribution to equality. Such arrangements can thus be expected to promote equality to the extent that:

1. they include universally-accessible, affordable, high-quality non-parental care, thereby mitigating existing gender inequalities in domestic care work;
2. nonparental child care work is organized so as to require skilled providers, and the value of such skills is recognized through equitable wages and good working conditions;
3. such care facilities are open to all, including the children of parents who are neither working nor taking some form of training; and
4. provision is made for democratic control, including parental and community "voices."

These criteria admittedly set the bar high. The decline of the male-breadwinner family form has opened up the possibility of establishing the institutional conditions for the flowering of postpatriarchal relations. This can only come about, however, if there is an adequate measure for assessing current arrangements—and the strategies for reform advanced by those seeking to change them—in terms of their implications for gender equality.[14]

Understanding Divergent Patterns of Response

Thus far we have dealt with the challenge posed by the decline of the male breadwinner family at a fairly general and abstract level. When we move to consider particular welfare regimes, it is clear that some have begun to lay the foundations for a postindustrial welfare state that has much in common with Fraser's utopia. Some have looked largely to markets for provision while others seem to be trying to shore up the old breadwinner model. In this section I examine these divergent patterns of response. Following Esping-Andersen, I ask whether differences in the form of welfare regime affect the capacity to respond to the challenges posed by the decline of the male-breadwinner family (including falling birthrates) as well as those associated with the emergence of a postindustrial economy.

The cases chosen allow us to explore the possible links between regime types and forms of child care provision. Here and in chapters to follow we examine five "liberal" (Australia, Britain, Canada, including Quebec, and the United States), six "conservative" (Belgium, France, Italy, Japan, the Netherlands, and Spain), and two "social democratic" (Denmark and Sweden) regimes, as well as one from the former Soviet bloc (Poland). We argue that while Esping-Andersen's typology—and its associated hypothesis of "path-dependent" restructuring—offers some insight, it is not sufficient to explain developments in the area of child care. The "irresistible" pressures facing all welfare regimes—including those generated by changing family forms—mean that all regimes are experiencing a certain instability. Under these circumstances, it is especially important to analyze the complex of social forces attempting to reshape the system and the universe of political discourse in which they operate.[15]

In developing the original "three worlds of welfare capitalism," Esping-Andersen (1985; 1990) focused on two key variables: the degree to which policies fostered citizen solidarity versus segmented and stratified systems, and commodification versus decommodification (the degree to which the system of social entitlements mitigates the cash nexus). Although his original interest was in the implications of each regime for class power relations, the focus on postindustrial employment patterns also brought gender to the fore. This opened the way to an at least partial incorporation of feminist arguments regarding the salience of families as well as markets and states. Thus to his original regime-defining characteristics Esping-Anderson added defamilialization, "the degree to which households' welfare and caring responsibilities are relaxed—either via welfare state provision, or via market provision" (1999, 51).

Liberal regimes, which rely on a residual "safety net" supplemented by measures that reinforce dependence on the market, tend to be open to defamilialization, albeit in a manner that is primarily reliant on the market. In terms of child care, liberal regimes tend to favor the market on both the demand (parent fees) and supply (commercial or employer provision) side. To the extent that public support is forthcoming, it most often takes the form of tax deductions or credits, though special provisions may be made for those "at risk" or with particularly low incomes. This regime form allows for greater gender equality and postindustrial job growth at the expense of deepening class and racial inequality. These are clear in the typical forms of child care provision—"nannies" for those better off, the positions being filled (at low wages) by immigrant women workers or "transnational mothers" (Hondagneu-Sotelo and Avila 1997); informal or gray-market arrangements (such as unregulated family or home-based child care, also at low [or no] wages) for the rest.

Social democratic regimes offer generous and comprehensive protection from market-generated and other risks (decommodification) on an inclusive or solidaristic basis. They have also been supportive of defamilializing measures. This form of regime is associated with strong postindustrial employment growth, especially in the (public) social services. Jobs in this sector tend to require a skill range reminiscent of Fordist industry and, like the latter, have often been unionized jobs, offering a reasonable degree of employment security.[16] Publicly provided and financed child care constitutes an important component of this regime's social infrastructure. The social democratic regime form, Esping-Andersen argues, favors (class and gender) equality and postindustrial full employment—within certain limits. His prescription here coincides with that of the OECD, for whom job growth in "sclerotic" Europe depends on the elimination of payroll taxes and other "demand inhibitors." Tax-financed social services can only expand to a certain point. Beyond that, job growth can be fostered only by relaxing the equality ("in the here-and-now") stipulation, in order to permit growth in personal services, especially in the private sector (1999, 179–80).

Conservative or "Bismarckian" regimes offer generous protection but do so in a way that reinforces status differences. They have also tended to be the most resistant to defamilialization. Their work-based social insurance systems, often biased toward older workers (early retirement), and underdeveloped social service sectors prop up the male-breadwinner family form. This holds true for child care, where families (mothers, grandparents, or even fathers in their "free" time) are assumed to be the dominant source of such care. Provision may, however, be made for quality preschool education—on a part-day basis. In these regimes, women who wish or need to work often have to seek (short) part-time or "off-hours" (weekends and evenings) employment.[17]

As various studies suggest, this typology offers insight into divergent patterns of response to what can be seen as a common set of challenges. Nevertheless, it is not unproblematic. First, there are significant intraregime differences that warrant consideration; these are especially visible in the area of child care. Second, there are problems of periodization—the moment of consolidation of regime types—and, more broadly, the associated hypothesis regarding path-dependent responses to change is open to question. The path-dependency thesis becomes particularly problematic when it slides from prediction to prescription.

In terms of child care provision, none of the liberal regimes fare well, especially in terms of provision of quality care for children under three and only moderately for children three and over (Gornick and Meyers 2001, figure 3). Although women's labor force participation is relatively high in all four, poor performance in terms of men's real wage growth provides an important inducement in lieu of positive supports for maternal employment.[18] Nevertheless, there are important differences in the "gender logics" underlying the four key liberal regimes, as Julia O'Connor, Ann Shola Orloff, and Sheila Shaver (1999) have argued. Thus, whereas the United States and Canada fit Esping-Andersen's thesis regarding the openness of liberal regimes to the dual-earner family (an androcentric "gender sameness" stance), Australia and Britain have been more actively supportive of the male breadwinner family (the logic of "gender difference"). This pattern did not, however, carry forward neatly into child care provision; here the United States and Britain conform to what one might expect to find in a liberal regime, maximizing private (market and family) responsibility. As we shall see, however, both systems are undergoing transformation as a result of welfare reform, with the changes envisioned for Britain, and already in place in the United States, marking a potential departure from the family-focused system of the past (Randall, and Levy and Michel, in this volume.)

Australia and Canada have deviated, to some extent, from the market and/or family-centered liberal pattern. In the 1980s, Australia moved to recognize child care as an element of the social wage, although more recent developments bear a markedly neoliberal imprint (O'Connor, Orloff, and Shaver 1999, 79; Brennan 1998, and in this volume). From the 1970s through the 1990s, the Canada Assistance Plan provided important public subsidies to low and middle-income families (Mahon and Phillips, in this volume). In the 1970s and 1980s, moreover, both countries favored locally organized, not-for-profit forms of provision. The really striking departure from the liberal mold, however, is that taken by the francophone province of Quebec, which has recently launched an ambitious five-dollars-a-day child care program (Jenson, in this volume).[19]

There are also differences among the Nordic social democratic welfare regimes, and these, too, are visible in the sphere of child care (Bergqvist et al. 1999). The chapters by Anette Borchorst, and by Christina Bergqvist and Anita Nyberg in this volume explore these differences as they are reflected in Danish and Swedish child care policy. Both countries nevertheless come out especially well in terms of availability and affordability of early childhood education and care for children from birth to age six. Nearly half of Danish children from birth to age two receive publicly financed care, and that figure climbs to 82 percent for children from three to five. Sweden provides publicly financed care for one-third of children from birth to two, and as much as 72 percent of those ages three to five (Gornick and Meyers 2001, table 4). In considering the difference in provision rates, however, it should be noted that in Sweden, due to provision of parental leave at relatively generous rates of compensation, most infants in fact spend all or most of the first year at home with one of their parents (usually their mothers[20]). Parental leave is a more recent innovation in Denmark (1984), and it is shorter—ten weeks added onto a fourteen-week maternity leave.[21] It also remains less flexible than the Swedish (Rostgaard and Fridberg 1998, 43).

The differences among the "conservative" or "Bismarckian" regimes are particularly striking, especially when it comes to child care. Esping-Andersen's own work shows that with regard to state-supported expansion of family services such as child and elder care, Belgium and France were close on the heels of the pathbreaking Danish and Swedish states (1999, 55). This is apparent in patterns of child care provision. Belgium provides publicly financed care for 30 percent of children from birth to age two while 23 percent of the children in that age group in France are in publicly supported day care. Both countries fare even better than Sweden and Denmark for three- to five-year-olds (95 and 99 percent, respectively) due to the development of comprehensive, full-day preschools (Jenson and Sineau 2001; Gornick and Meyers 2001, table 4). The labor-force participation rates of French and Belgian women are also higher than in the other conservative regimes.[22] While Germany and Austria have thus far proved as resistant to change, as Esping-Andersen suggests, the Dutch welfare regime has undergone significant changes (Daly, 2001). Monique Kremer's comparison of the Dutch and Flemish cases in this volume not only probes the reasons behind the early divergence of them, but also reflects on the implications of recent changes for child care provision in the Netherlands. Nearly three-fourths of children ages three to five were registered in preschool, but for most this only offered part-time care. Moreover, only 8 percent of children from birth to age two were in publicly financed care (Gornick and Meyers 2001, table 4). Women's labor-force participation rates have risen in the Netherlands, but the predominant pattern—89 percent of mothers with preschool children—is (short) part-time work (Gornick 1999, table 2).

The very applicability of Esping-Andersen's "conservative" label to southern European countries like Spain, Italy, and Greece has been challenged by Maurizio Ferrera (1998; 2000). While these countries' welfare regimes share certain features with their northern "Bismarckian" cousins, all the southern European states have developed universal health care systems modeled on the British National Health Service. More broadly, southern welfare regimes are unevenly developed relative to their northern counterparts. In particular, they exhibit marked imbalances—notably, overprotection against the risks associated with old age and a serious underdevelopment of family benefits and services like child care. Concomitant with this (and high income taxes) is a substantial black market in personal services. Under these circumstances, of course, wages are very low and social security nonexistent. Both Italy and Spain have a well-developed public preschool system that covers the vast majority of three- to five-year-olds, however. In this sense, they match the French and Belgian "deviants" in the northern part of the continent. Celia Valiente in this volume focuses on the forces behind the development of preschool care in post-Francoist Spain. Family (supplemented by the black market) seems to be the main form of care provision for children under the age of three as public provision in Italy, as in Spain, is minimal. Vincent Della Sala in this volume examines the reasons for this in the Italian case.

This volume includes two countries that are less easily placed within Esping-Andersen's typology: Poland, formerly part of the Soviet bloc, and Japan. Clearly the latter ranks among the leading postindustrial countries and should be included in any comparative analysis that seeks to be reasonably comprehensive. Similarly, the former Soviet bloc countries of Eastern Europe are poised to enter the European Union, and whether they are admitted or not, they do form part of contemporary Europe. Most were countries that relied on a high rate of women's labor-force participation during the Soviet era. It is therefore useful to consider how the transition process is affecting child care arrangements.

Although "communist" in form, the former Soviet bloc countries had certain features in common with the conservative or Bismarckian regimes in that the workplace operated as the key access point to social security and social service benefits.

The financing mechanism differed, however. Through a centralized state budget, the government would allocate the national product between the "accumulation fund" used by collective enterprises (for wages, social services, and the like) and the "consumption fund" that included social insurance (Deacon 2000, 147). More importantly from the standpoint of our concerns, these regimes also differed from their conservative counterparts in the treatment of women. As Gillian Pascall and Nick Manning argue, a woman's place in the labor market was "supported by a bridge of social investment in child care and other services. High labor force participation was achieved, with women spending most of their adult lives in paid work, at a much earlier period than in the West—by 1980 half of the labor force of Eastern Europe consisted of women, compared with 32 percent in Western Europe. . . ." (2000, 245). In this sense, the former Soviet bloc countries come closest to the French and Belgian models, which aimed to combine women's labor force participation with demographic concerns (Lohkamp-Himmighofen and Dienel 2000, 65). In some countries, like the former Czechoslovakia and Poland, however, neither maternity/parental leave insurance nor child care arrangements were anywhere near adequate (Ferge, 2001, table 7.4; Heinen 1993, and in this volume).

Of all of the postwar welfare regimes, those of the former Soviet bloc are facing the strongest pressures to restructure as part of the process of implanting capitalist economies, especially in the form of neoliberal prescriptions for reform. The pace of change is uneven and the future form of welfare regime is difficult to predict. Frequently, however, women's rights to child care benefits are being seriously eroded while the role of housewife-mother is lauded (Deacon 2000). Nor are women easily marshaled to the defense of the old order, for the latter usually left women with a double—even triple, given the time consumed by normally simple tasks like shopping—burden (Pascall and Manning 2000; Heinen, in this volume). Zsuzsa Ferge thus concludes that "the essence of the 'European model'—an attempt to control inequality, to pay increased attention to ethnic and gender issues, to strengthen social rights so as to assure the emancipatory potential of the welfare system, to underpin social rights by labor rights, to put social integration on the agenda—is almost totally absent" (2001, 162–63). In this context, both class and gender inequalities are deepening.

The Japanese case presents a special set of challenges, appearing to be a kind of hybrid of all the other systems (Esping-Andersen 1997). It shares with the Nordic social democratic regimes a strong commitment to full employment. The rudimentary safety net and heavy reliance on private, especially corporate, welfare, is reminiscent of the liberal regime, especially the American variant. The scope of corporate benefits, including service provision, for core (male) workers, however, is more reminiscent of the *ancien régime* in Eastern Europe (Esping-Andersen 1997, 185). Like the Bismarckian regimes, it has a status-segmented social insurance system and shows a marked familialism. As Ito Peng's contribution to this volume shows, however, Japanese child care policy has been rather more contradictory, caught between official familialism and the need for women in the labor market, and, more recently, in the demographic crisis.

From the standpoint of broader status of the classificatory schema, however, perhaps the most interesting point is the conclusion Esping-Andersen draws: "it is arguably the case that the Japanese welfare system is still in the process of evolution; that it has not yet arrived at the point of crystallization" (1997, 188). This raises the whole question of when a welfare regime becomes sufficiently "crystallized" to generate the path dependencies associated with this theoretical approach. In his 1997 article, "Hybrid or Unique? The Distinctiveness of the Japanese Welfare State," Esping-Andersen seems to locate the moment of regime formation rather early in the twentieth century: "while most welfare states found their institutional expression around the turn of the century or, at least, before the Second World War, the Japanese is a rather ad hoc postwar construct" [23] (1997, 187). In *Social Foundations of Postindustrial Economies*, however, Esping-Andersen clearly argues that the 1960s and 1970s, not the immediate postwar decades, represent the moment of "consolidation" (1999, 2). Thus he suggests that while welfare policies in countries like Britain and Sweden may have looked remarkably similar in the 1950s, the real regime-dividing developments took place in the 1960s and 1970s (1999, 173). If it is the latter date, Japan seems little different from the others in terms of the relative fluidity of arrangements.

In itself, the issue of periodization is of less concern to us here than the associated hypothesis regarding the conditions for generating path-dependent responses to contemporary challenges. That is, Esping-Andersen's main reason for arguing the fluidity of the Japanese welfare regimes is the "absence of fierce political opposition to welfare reforms or cutbacks," which suggests that Japan "has not yet cultivated powerful institutionalized interests in favor of itself as have the European welfare states" (1997, 188). This takes us to the thesis that lies at the heart of the path dependency argument that Esping-Andersen shares with Paul Pierson (1994; 1998) and others. That is, regimes tend to respond to contemporary challenges—globalization, postindustrialism, the erosion of the male-breadwinner family—via incremental reforms largely because the beneficiaries of the existing regime are many and are readily mobilized to defend their interests. More broadly, welfare institutions, with their characteristic norms of conduct and incentive systems, are said to reproduce a predominance of liberal, conservative, or social democratic *homines* and *femines* within each country (Esping-Andersen 1999, 172).

Clearly there is considerable merit in the path-dependency argument: existing institutions do affect the nature and intensity of the challenges faced, the values and ideas held by social actors, and the strength of diverse interests. Yet regimes also change, at times quite dramatically. Nor is it only the Japanese and East European systems that are in flux. As Esping-Andersen admits, in the 1980s Australia and New Zealand recently veered away from the social democratic—or "wage-earner" (Castles and Mitchell 1993)—path toward a markedly liberal system. Apparently incremental changes to the Danish (Esping-Andersen 1999, 88, n.16) and French (Palier 2000) regimes could similarly result in systemic shifts.

Adherence to the path-dependency thesis may limit the predictive capacity of this approach, but a more serious problem arises when these theorists slide from prediction to prescription. For instance, Esping-Andersen concludes that "any blueprint for reform is bound to be naïve if it calls for a radical departure from existing welfare regime practice. The IMF [International Monetary Fund] is naïve when it asks that European welfare states adopt, lock, stock, and barrel, the Chilean pension system; American leftists, or emergent democratic governments in ex-communist countries, are equally naïve when they call for the importation of the 'Swedish model'" (1999, 173).[24] Even if we assume the predominance of social democratic, liberal, or conservative homines and femines within particular countries, each of these normative orientations admits of greater variety than is often suggested. Here the work of O'Connor, Orloff, and Shaver on changes in the meaning of liberalism is instructive.

Classical liberalism, which emphasized individual freedom in a market economy, tended to deny such rights to women while leaving the (male-headed) family to fend for itself in that market. The "new" or social liberalism characteristic of the postwar era enlarged the notion of individual freedom from state interference to include "the positive freedoms of opportunity and personal development" (O'Connor, Orloff, and Shaver 1999, 50). The family also came into view as an institution that warranted support, albeit largely through the family wage system. Neoliberalism returns to the market individual of the classical epoch, but this time women, too, may be included. In other words, liberalism is an elastic concept and the boundary between "liberal" and "social democratic" regimes has at times been thin indeed.[25] This is important to bear in mind in assessing prospects for change.

Theorizing change is, in fact, one of the admitted weaknesses of the historical-institutionalist version of political economy (Thelen and Steinmo 1992, 15). In this respect, historical institutionalists tend to ignore one of the key challenges facing social scientists—the human capacity for learning (and therefore *changing*). As Andrew Sayer (1992) has argued, "One of the main reasons for openness of social systems is the fact that we can interpret the same material conditions and statements in different ways and hence learn new ways of responding, so that effectively we become different people" (123). It is especially in periods like the present, which are marked by the clash of "irresistible forces" and "immovable objects" (Pierson 1998), that such learning is most likely to occur. Times like these are moments when the universe of political discourse is open to new understandings (Jenson 1986), enabling the formation of new coalitions around reform agendas that imply a significant departure from the path previously followed. In other words, in periods marked by intense pressures to restructure, new ideas and changing relations of power among contending interests can result in substantial institutional transformation.

The Politics of Child Care

The argument in this book is that it is important to analyze not only past patterns and the interest configurations associated with these, but also to look for the emergence of new representations of child care. In this volume we examine the various forces contesting the most appropriate forms (if any) of nonparental child care. As we are especially interested in the possibility of outcomes that favor gender (and class) equality, we pay particular attention to the role played by feminists:[26] Have they been able to construct an alliance in favor of child care as a necessary component of a broader policy for institutionalizing sexual equality?

As various theorists recognize, feminism constitutes an important contemporary social force. Thus, sociologist Manuel Castells recognizes that although feminism is not new, it has become a central force in contemporary societies across the globe. He writes that "only in the last quarter of this century have we witnessed what amounts to a mass insurrection of women against their oppression throughout the world, albeit with different intensity depending on culture and country. The impact of such movements has been felt deeply in the institutions of society, and, more fundamentally, in the consciousness of women. In industrialized countries, a large majority of women consider themselves equal to men, entitled to their rights, and to women's control over their bodies and their lives. This is the most important revolution because it goes to the roots of society and to the heart of who we are. And it is irreversible" (1997, 135). To many contemporary feminists, the demand for accessible, high-quality child care is seen as indispensable to women's economic independence. The struggle for universal child care can, in turn, strengthen the women's movement by fostering cross-class solidarity and by helping feminists to establish alliances with other progressive forces.

While the presence and strength of mobilized women among the forces debating child care policy may affect the possibility for adoption of equality-promoting child care, it is important to remember that their interests are not monolithic. Certainly the kind of maternalism that was so prominent earlier in the twentieth century and has its echoes today favored measures that made it feasible for women to stay home and care for their children (see Michel 1999, chap. 3). The contemporary variant of this takes the forms of various types of "care allowances," many of them proposed in gender-neutral terms. Its liberal feminist counterpart, which defended an abstract view of sexual equality, often tended to avoid the issue entirely out of a fear that it would call attention to the child care responsibilities that differentiated women from men. While "social liberal" or socialist feminists may recognize that sexual equality in the labor market is dependent on the existence of universally accessible child care as a public service, New Left elements within second-wave feminism often favored local, community-controlled services. Although both of these approaches eschew for-profit child care, contemporary neoliberal feminists would be quite prepared to accept the latter as a new zone for women entrepreneurs. The story becomes even more complex when the ideas of third-wave feminism, which challenge a monolithic representation of women's interests, are added. Thus, in multiethnic and multiracial societies—the reality in most OECD countries today— feminists might well be divided over the choice between an integrationist model and one that allows for difference without sacrificing equality.[27]

Nor do feminists operate in a vacuum. They confront allies and opponents of variable strength and strategic orientation. Opponents can include traditional groups as well as the New Right, but the relationship between feminists and neo-liberals can be more complex, as O'Connor, Orloff, and Shaver suggest (1999, chap. 2). As all the chapters in this volume show, moreover, feminists have to choose their allies from among those available and, in forging these coalitions, may have to present the case for child care in ways that obscure their own objectives. The terrain on which they operate is also being (re)shaped by broader processes of welfare state restructuring in response to diverse pressures. Thus demographic and "employabil-ity" concerns, calls for greater "choice," and/or the projected demands of an emer-gent "knowledge-based economy" jostle with gender equality as possible rationales for new child care initiatives. How the issue is understood in turn affects the range of conceivable solutions and their implications for women.

In various ways, then, the stories told in the following chapters explore the im-pact of these patterns of alliance and opposition on existing child care arrange-ments. Ultimately, the analyst may be able to show, ex post facto, how, in most cases, the paths taken followed regime-specific path dependencies. Often, however, there is sufficient turmoil to make outcomes uncertain.

Among the liberal regimes, the United States appears to be headed down the most predictable path, one that deepens the existing (class and racial) divide be-tween a public system of state-subsidized places designed to rationalize pushing poor mothers off social assistance, and a "semiprivate" system where better-off par-ents look to the market to choose the form of child care that they can afford.[28] Denise Urias Levy and Sonya Michel explore in this volume what happened when the Clinton administration replaced the Aid to Families with Dependent Children program with a workfare program that will dramatically increase needs within the public system. The associated Temporary Assistance to Needy Families potentially makes federal funding available for child care, but the decentralized way in which the program is designed will make its impact highly uneven at best. Faced with a program that threatens to turn child care into "a lever of a harsh social policy and punitive control for women who are compelled to work," Levy and Michel conclude that "perhaps the best that feminists can hope for—and certainly should work to-ward—is a greatly improved system of public child care . . . that provides poor and low-income families with convenient, affordable, high-quality care of the types they prefer."

Vicky Randall's analysis in this volume of the treatment of the child care issue in Britain explores the impact of Margaret Thatcher's brand of neoliberalism on the horizons of feminists and others involved in the decades-long campaign for child care. Whereas in the 1970s and early 1980s the debate was over state versus community provision, by the end of the 1980s neither of these options seemed realistic, except perhaps for older preschool children. With the election of the government of Tony Blair, the prospects seemed brighter. Blair's New Labour government may have shared the Thatcher Tories' (and the OECD's) commitment to "activation" rather than "passive" welfare dependency, but it was also committed to public measures to enhance equality of opportunity. In addition, its ranks included a substantial number of female members of Parliament and one of them combined the office of Minister of Social Security with that of Minister for Women. The government's main achievement has been the expansion of preschool education, through locally constructed "early years" partnerships.

The Australian case is interesting first for the way it began to challenge the parameters of the liberal (and familialist) welfare regime. As Deborah Brennan shows in this volume, in the 1970s and 1980s, Australian feminists were able to construct an alliance with leading elements in the trade union movement and the Labour Party. This permitted the forging of a policy centered on the provision of quality community-based child care, with the national government providing substantial subsidies to enable working- and middle-class families to afford such care. Yet in negotiating the precise terms of support, the child care alliance had to compromise—accepting a formula for funding operational costs that sacrificed staff wages—with traditionalists within the party. This served to drive a wedge between parents and child care providers that, in turn, made it more difficult to oppose the government's later decision to extend subsidies to users of for-profit facilities. The conservative government, encouraged by the antifeminist Lyons Forum, took the "choice" theme further, with its tax measures aimed at helping single-breadwinner families.

Like Australia's in the 1970s Canada's child care policy began to deviate from the liberal mold. In this volume, Susan Phillips and I show how the growth of second-wave feminism contributed to the incremental expansion of the terms of a federal shared-cost program for child care, to permit its extension well into the middle class. Since the mid-1980s, a growing preoccupation with fiscal austerity, combined with a deepening crisis of federalism, have made it increasingly difficult for child care advocates to advance their case. They were able to mount effective opposition to a bill that would have separated child care from the general social assistance plan,[29] but at the price of including commercial centers. When the bill died in the House of Representatives, what survived was a tax credit program inspired by the conservative Family Caucus, a group markedly similar to Australia's Lyons Forum. Despite a change of government, during the 1990s child care activists operated in an environment where universally accessible care was made to seem increasingly utopian. To keep the issue alive, they joined forces with a broader coalition under the banner of fighting child poverty. The new Social Union Framework Agreement, which has shifted the site of negotiations to departments of intergovernmental affairs, makes it harder for the coalition to influence policy development.

As in the United States, the trend in Canada has been toward greater decentralization. Thus the various provinces are following different trajectories. The most interesting case is that of the francophone province of Quebec, which boldly launched its universal five-dollars-a-day child care program in 1997. Jane Jenson in this volume shows that this was not the move of a beleaguered independentist government eager to restore its fortunes with its social base. The main breakthrough was made in the late 1980s by feminists and their allies (antipoverty activists, social workers, specialists in early childhood development), who managed to place their stamp on the issue. As Jenson concludes, "Quebec shares with other liberal welfare states a concern with employability and fostering parents' labor force participation. . . . Yet . . . it has developed universal social programs and avoided putting children at risk of poor quality child care. Therefore, rather than a story of path dependency, this is a story of how a determined reform coalition sensitive to children's developmental needs, as well as to gender and class equality, can row against the neoliberal tide, saving some values in the general process of welfare state redesign."

Child care provision in the two social democratic countries we examine—Denmark and Sweden—shares the broader features of the regime within which it is embedded. In Sweden in the 1960s, a group of feminists, cutting across parties both left and center (especially the liberals) and across the blue-collar/white-collar divide, helped to establish public child care as a program to promote class and gender equality (Daune-Richard and Mahon 1998; Bergqvist et al. 1999). While support from the left and center parties also helped the cause of child care in Denmark, Anette Borchorst in this volume argues that the (largely female) early childhood "pedagogues" played a critical role. Despite mounting pressure for welfare state restructuring, in both countries child care provision remains clearly within the social democratic mold.

Denmark was first to experience the pressure as it was affected by growing unemployment and by the rise of a right-wing antitax party in the 1970s. Yet, as Borchorst shows, the policy established in the 1960s—universal child care, with a strong pedagogical component, financed jointly by the national government, municipalities, and parents—was defended by the union, parents, and the feminist movement. Their efforts met with success in part because the policy enjoyed support not only of the parties of the left and center but also the conservative Christian People's Party. In the 1990s, a number of changes were made. Democracy was enhanced by the introduction of "user boards" made up of parents. The national government also introduced a child care guarantee, although to get the municipalities to cooperate it had to allow parent fees to rise. At the same time, more room was made for private and family-based solutions, but within a broader framework that retained the core features of the model.

Strong pressure to restructure came later in Sweden. It was only in the 1990s that unemployment hit with a vengeance. At the same time, a bourgeois coalition government, determined to engineer a "system shift," was elected. In this volume Bergqvist and Nyberg look at five key features of the Swedish model of child care:

generous public finance, high-quality service, limited scope for the private sector, universalism, and egalitarianism. They find that more room has indeed been made for private provision (still, however, publicly financed) and staff-child ratios have increased. Nonetheless, the core features have been retained, even strengthened. Of particular note is that responsibility for child care has been transferred to the Ministry of Education. With this comes a commitment to introduce universal preschool for four- and five-year-olds as well as the introduction of a right of the children of unemployed parents to at least three hours of preschool care per day.

If the social democratic examples have held up rather well, the same cannot be said for the Soviet model, at least in Poland. As Jacqueline Heinen shows in this volume, since 1989 there has been a substantial drop in the number of child care centers and, to a lesser extent, preelementary "nursery schools," but there has been little protest. Part of the explanation lies in the inadequacies of the old system of support in Poland. Unlike the former East Germany or Hungary (and in contradiction to its own constitution), the Polish Communist regime displayed at best an ambiguous stance toward gender equality in general and women's labor market participation in particular. This was reflected in child care provisions that were never adequate. Moreover, the administration of Edward Gierek restored the position of the Catholic Church, which fostered traditionalist responses to the problems of "reconciling work and family" in the crumbling *ancien régime*. The Church's influence in postcommunist Poland is all the greater. Nonetheless, as Heinen argues, younger women seem to be engaging in a silent "womb strike" and have career aspirations very much like their Western counterparts. This could provide the basis for a renewed push to realize the earlier dream "of creating a society based on the model of the Nordic countries—a task that now seems immense."

France is generally subsumed under the rubric of the conservative-corporatist welfare state regime, but with regard to child care, the French system—especially the *écoles maternelles* for preschool children—deviates markedly from the regime norm; Kimberly Morgan in this volume explains why. It is not only that French women have long been a necessary part of the labor supply; as early as the 1880s, preschool became part of an education system charged with the mission of developing secular *citoyens* for the republic. This secular, modernizing ideology was also central to the Gaullists who oversaw the expansion of the French welfare regime in the 1960s. When social movements associated with "May '68," not least the French women's movement, demanded universal child care, moves were made to expand the crèche system for children under three. France, like Denmark, began to come under pressure to restructure in the 1970s. As in Denmark, support for the *écoles*, which appealed to traditional and nontraditional families, was strong enough to protect the system. The crèches, however, felt the brunt of fiscal austerity. This part of the system has remained the most malleable. In the 1980s and 1990s, various French governments opened the way to more at-home care—by nannies as well as registered family child care providers for mothers who continue to work—and through long "parental" leaves, usually taken by low-income women. This increasingly class-divided system has in turn undermined the potential basis of support for expansion of the publicly funded crèches.

Italy, too, has a well-developed preschool system for children ages three to six, launched as part of a broader effort to modernize the Italian school system in the 1960s. In the early 1970s, an act was also passed committing the central government to raise funds via the allocation of 0.1 percent of income taxes to enable regional governments to develop care for younger children. As Della Sala argues in this volume, neither act was motivated by a concern to promote women's labor-force participation, much less gender equality. Moreover, public support for infant and toddler care remained modest and highly uneven in its distribution. Globalization, especially in the form of the European Union, has helped to stimulate a renewed effort at welfare state reform, including a bill to reform the child care system. Although the reform falls well short of providing the kind of financial support needed to expand early childhood care, for the first time, its educational value is recognized as well as its importance for women's employment. Nevertheless, Della Sala remains pessimistic about the possibilities for developing a regime that recognizes child care as an indispensable component of women's social citizenship rights.

Welfare regime redesign was launched in Spain following the end of Francisco Franco's dictatorship. Preschool education formed a part of the newly elected socialist party's project for achieving greater class equality, as Valiente argues. Since then preschool child care has expanded under the sponsorship of the Ministry of Education. Given the limited hours of operation, however, it does not support Spanish women's labor-market participation, which remains the lowest in Western Europe. Spain's provision for younger children is even less developed than Italy's. None of the parties have taken up the cause of child care, nor has the Spanish feminist movement tried to challenge this. As Valiente argues here and elsewhere (1995), after Franco's fall, the Spanish women's movement had a full agenda and child care, with its associated links to women's maternal roles, was not a high priority. There is little sign of change, although one might ask what effect, if any, the European Union's promotion of measures to "balance work and family" might have (Hantrais 2000).

Kremer's chapter in this volume compares two cases in the same "family of nations"—the Dutch and the (Flemish) Belgian—which provide a marked contrast, at least in the sphere of child care.[30] As early as the 1960s, Belgians embraced a policy of public support for both early childhood care and preschool education. With regard to the latter, the Belgian system is very much like the French and arguably shaped by similar forces. With regard to early childhood care, however, Kremer argues that it was facilitated by the emphasis that Belgian policy accorded family child care. This "surrogate mother" model required a limited break with the familialism typical of conservative regimes. It enabled many married women to care for their children as well as those of others, at the expense of gender equality. Family child care providers are legally protected and do get tax exemptions, but they remain completely dependent on their husbands' social insurance, including pensions. There are, however, signs that the agency in charge of Flemish child care is prepared to push for the transition to a professional care model—though still within the family child care mold. In this sense, the educational as well as labor-market value of early childhood care is gaining a certain recognition.

Unlike most of the cases we have examined, the Dutch welfare state actively supported the male-breadwinner family right into the 1980s. Child care facilities remained highly undeveloped, and there was no consensus on the issue on the part of the broader women's movement. The Dutch regime began to undergo substantial transformation in the late 1980s, as the corporatist ("pillarized") institutions that had sustained it went into crisis. The new themes of cutting the costly welfare state and the "activation/breaking dependency" model resonated well with a discourse that pointed to housewives as wasted human capital. In this context, the government launched a program to stimulate the expansion of child care facilities—to be funded primarily by employers and employees. For the most part, however, the entry of mothers into the labor market has been on a part-time basis.[31] Kremer argues that the emergent model is understood as a "shared-parenting" model, quite different from the Nordic. Whereas the latter focuses on shared parental care in the first year combined with center-based care from ages one to six, the new Dutch ideal would reduce the need for nonparental care entirely. There have been campaigns to increase fathers' participation in child care. While it is true that a significantly greater share of Dutch men are involved in part-time work than in other OECD countries, it is unclear that this reflects a greater commitment on their part to shared parental care. Women still account for the lion's share of (short) part-time work and most men remain full-time breadwinners.

Despite the homage paid to the male breadwinner/female housewife model in postwar Japan, actual practice has been more contradictory. As Peng argues, corporate needs for female labor supply have combined with the lobbying efforts of women's groups to provide support for the development of a system that currently provides care for 22 percent of preschool children. Recognition of the scope of the current demographic crisis has added to the pressures for further expansion imposed by the career-orientation of the younger generation of women. The Angel Plan, launched in 1994, aims to increase the number of child care centers, and the 1999 version is even more ambitious. Peng is skeptical of the plan's ability to lay the foundations for a genuinely equitable society. As she argues, "Child care extension as a pronatalist tool has limited effect today when the main reason for the declining fertility is the lack of gender equality." To succeed, the state needs to launch a social dialogue with men and women on the outlines of a new gender order.

Preliminary Conclusions

Child care arrangements in none of the cases that we examine meet the criteria for generating equality laid out above, although some (like Sweden's) come closer than others. Our results thus concur with those of Gornick, who provides a quantitative assessment of the relation between the kind of employment support system available and women's labor market support in fifteen OECD countries (1999). Her data suggest that there is a link between women's share of total labor market earnings and employment support policies. Thus, mothers of young children fare best in countries like Sweden, Denmark, Belgium and France, and worst in Germany and the Netherlands (Gornick 1999, table 4). In none, however, do mothers of young children account for more than 35 percent of total labor market earnings, which suggests that none have gone far enough toward equalizing the division of unpaid care. This accords with Fraser's argument; in other words, the best have only managed to universalize the breadwinner model. Genuine gender equality can only come about when arrangements are in place that encourage and enable both parents to combine breadwinning and caregiving.

What all of these chapters suggest, however, is that change—path-dependent and otherwise—is indeed on the agenda today. For those who hope that the decline of the male-breadwinner family is creating space for the emergence of a genuinely postpatriarchal family form, there are grounds for cautious optimism. The optimism and the caveats both stem from the way in which responses to changes in gender relations have come to be entwined with other major challenges (not the least of which are postindustrial full employment and demographic balance) and debates about how best to meet these. Gender equality is but one of the objectives that may be advanced for providing public support for nonparental child care and feminists often choose to present the case in ways that stress these other objectives in order to gain new allies and thus to win the battle for public support.

Of these other representations, *education* seems to be the most encompassing and the least problematic, as the French, Italian, Spanish, Danish and Swedish cases suggest. Preschool education serves traditional as well as dual-earner (or lone-parent-earner) families. It can also be seen as an important national investment in future "knowledge-based economy" workers. On its own, however, it can result in a pattern of provision that does little to support women's economic emancipation. The "demographic time bomb" is opening space for new child-care initiatives in countries as diverse as Britain and Japan. Here, too, all can be seen to benefit to the extent that care provisions make it easier for families to choose to have children—and thus help to offset the aging of society. Again, however, the absence of a strong commitment to thoroughgoing gender equality, such measures are at best likely only to alleviate women's burden under existing arrangements, as Peng argues.

The concern with class equality, especially in a knowledge-based postindustrial economy, can also offer an avenue for women. When, however, this is articulated within a discourse centered on relieving child poverty, as it has been in the Canadian and American cases, it simply reinforces the liberal bias in favor of targeted programs. "Employability" or "activation" discourses also create room to demand child care as a prerequisite to getting lone mothers off social assistance. As Levy and Michel argue, however, under these circumstances, child care can easily become part of an arsenal of measures aimed at forcing poor mothers to take low-paid jobs.

Finally, decentralization is on the agenda of many states. This can serve to increase opportunities for greater local democratic control and diversity in child care programs. When decentralization is associated with a shift from funds targeted to child care to block funding arrangements, however, child care provision may be eroded, in the absence of the kind of national supports that the Danish and Swedish governments have provided. Greater decentralization may also result in patterns of provision designed to enhance gender equality, in that women have often been more actively engaged in local politics. Yet local politics can also become a site for the mobilization of antifeminist backlash or neoliberal forces determined to privatize social services. The latter has happened in certain Swedish municipalities, a move that the social democratic national government has found difficult to counter.

All of these themes will be explored in greater depth below. Each chapter locates national child care arrangements in relation to the broader welfare regime within which they are embedded.[32] At the same time, all acknowledge that these regimes have experienced and continue to experience major shocks: globalization, postindustrialism, aging, and, of course, the erosion of the male breadwinner family norm. In some instances, these shocks have induced the path-dependent adjustments that regime theory would lead us to expect. In other cases, they have resulted in more dramatic changes. In all, they have induced a certain instability that leaves room for the introduction of alternative projects, both reactionary and egalitarian.

Notes

1. Iversen and Wren (1998) argue that, because of a stubborn productivity gap between most services and goods production, the postindustrial economy confronts states with a "trilemma." They can successfully pursue two, but not all three, of their classic (postwar) objectives: full employment, social equality, and fiscal balance.

2. See for example Cerny (1997), Mishra (1999), Rhodes (1996 and 1998), Garrett (1998), Pierson (1998), Iversen and Wren (1998), Scharpf and Schmidt (2000), and Sykes, Palier, and Prior (2001).

3. Although we stress the model's decline, it is important to recognize that this family form was never equally well-entrenched in all societies nor all social classes. As Esping-Andersen notes, we may come to see the male-breadwinner family as a "fleeting mid-twentieth century interlude" (1999, 53).

4. On Japan, see Peng (in this volume). On Italy, see Della Sala (in this volume).

5. His argument here rests on the assumption, shared with Iversen and Wren (1998) and Pierson (1998), that productivity growth in the service sector remains a stubborn problem, driving up costs—at least if those providing the service are to earn a living wage. For these authors, this means that contemporary states are faced with a necessary tradeoff between equality "in the here and now" and full employment.

6. See Jenson (1989, 5) for a critique of this tendency to see women's jobs as relying on gender-specific "talents."

7. In *Politics against Markets* (1985), Esping-Andersen foresaw the possibility of moving toward economic democracy, through the enactment of revolutionary reforms like the Swedish "wage-earner funds."

8. For Fraser, the postsocialist condition refers to the collapse of leftist utopian energies in the late 1980s and early 1990s, as well as the challenge posed by the emergence of a new politics focused on claims for recognition, which seems to fit poorly with the redistributive focus of industrial social movements.

9. Whereas Esping-Andersen is content to accept continued gender inequality in the distribution of household tasks, Fraser argues the necessity of adopting a set of social arrangements—including a shorter work week for all—that make it possible for both men and women to combine paid work and domestic care responsibilities. Her ideal is closer to the one Swedish feminists advocated in the 1960s. For more on the latter, see Scott (1983).

10. This is a complicated argument that we cannot go into in any depth here. Based on their analysis of various ways of organizing work in the service sector, Herzenberg, Alic, and Wial (1998) have developed an argument for improving performance in personal and social services in a way that generates numerous jobs with skill levels that can command a decent wage. This is in contrast both to the "professionalization" route that Esping-Andersen associates with limited post-industrial job generation and to the proliferation of routinized, low paid jobs characteristic of the American "fun, food and wine" sector.

11. Since the 1960s, an important part of the argument for quality child care has been its potential contribution to early childhood development, especially for disadvantaged children. In the context of the debate over the "lifelong learning" requirements associated with the postindustrial or "knowledge-based" economy, this argument can be extended to include all children.

12. The "social economy" has aspects in common with the "third sector" or "community" discussed in the literature on voluntarism to the extent that it stresses local community initiatives. At the same time, it is not seen as a substitute for state involvement. Rather the latter is understood to provide critical supports. See Jenson (1998), Lévesque and Mendell (1999), and Shragge and Fontan (2000) for a discussion of the conditions under which the third sector/social economy can flourish in a manner consistent with egalitiarian aims.

13. Parental leave can, of course, have a negative effect on one's career trajectory. Thus it is important to promote an equitable sharing of that leave as between parents. In addition, longer leave provisions, such as those found in France, are more likely to have a negative impact than shorter ones (e.g., that of Sweden).

14. In the afterword, Sonya Michel will discuss some of the complex ways in which feminist rationales for child care intersect with other discourses concerning child care.

15. Jane Jenson developed this concept, which helps to grasp the parameters of debate—the limits to what is considered possible at any particular juncture. See, for example, Jenson 1986.

16. That is, a blend of professional to semiskilled occupations.

17. Gornick, Meyers, and Ross (1998) and Gornick (1999) have assessed the link between policies supporting maternal employment and women's position in the labor market.

One of the aspects they consider is the rate of women's (versus men's) involvement in part-time employment. They fail, however, to distinguish between countries where women are involved primarily in short part-time employment (e.g., the Netherlands and the United Kingdom) and those where "part-time" employment usually means three-quarters or more of the "normal" forty-hour week (e.g., Sweden).

18. As Gornick argues, men's real wage growth in Australia, Canada, and the US "has been well below that found in most other OECD countries in recent years" (1999, 24). She does not suggest that this is the sole explanation, however.

19. The province of British Columbia, under a social democratic government, has launched an ambitious child care scheme. Although the first step focused on provision of before and after care for school-aged children, the NDP has made the extension of this to preschool children part of its 2001 election campaign.

20. For some years, Swedish fathers have taken less than 10 percent of parental leave. As Bergqvist and Nyberg note, however, since the early 1990s, one month of that leave has been reserved for fathers. When the income replacement rates fell to 75 percent as part of the deficit-reduction measures adopted in the mid-1990s, the rate for the reserved months (one for each parent) was kept at the higher level (80 percent).

21. In addition, in 1993, an additional six months—at a 70 rather than 90 percent replacement rate, and less advantageous with regard to pension points—was introduced.

22. Sixty-two percent of Belgian mothers with young children and 55 percent of French mothers are employed—well above the rates for Italy (42 percent), the Netherlands (37 percent), and Spain (26 percent) and even higher than liberal countries like Australia (49 percent), the United Kingdom (53 percent), and the United States (55 percent). Canada's was just below Belgium's, at 61 percent, while Danish (77 percent) and Swedish (86 percent) women are clearly the leaders. See Gornick 1999, table 1.

23. Japan in fact began to construct a welfare regime, along Bismarckian lines, in the pre-war period. The pension scheme was first introduced in the 1920s for government employees and military servicemen and then extended to general workers well before the end of the war. Health care insurance was also established in this period. The "hybrid" character comes from the postwar reconstruction, when the American pattern was superimposed on top of the earlier system, and the "pragmatic" approach subsequently taken in responding to new challenges. Written communication with Ito Peng, February 23, 2001.

24. Esping-Andersen is far from alone here. The "varieties of capitalism" school of political economy (Kitschelt et al. 1999) exhibits a similar predilection.

25. Thus for instance, Esping-Andersen notes that the postwar equality agenda involved a mix of collectivism and individualism: "On the one side, social citizenship prevails over old class solidarities. On the other side, the raw *laissez-faire* call for individual self-reliance was pushed aside and liberals linked arms with social democrats in a battle for equal opportunity. In effect, welfare capitalism was often a synthesis of liberal and social democratic egalitarianism." (1999, 8).

26. Here our approach parallels Esping-Andersen's earlier (1985) work when he sought to assess why some outcomes were more favorable for class equality (and working-class

power) by analyzing the relative strength of workers' and employers' organizations. Like O'Connor, Orloff, and Shaver (1999) and Bergqvist et al. (1999), we argue that the relative strength and strategic orientation of feminists is important, if not decisive, to the outcome.

27. An integrationist perspective sees universal child care as contributing to social cohesion "uniting families of all social strata and cultural origins in common activites related to the well-being of their children and by demonstrating that cooperation among racial groups and social classes is possible and valued" (Friendly 1997, 5). Fincher finds an alternative approach in New Zealand where Maori children had their own child care system based on their own language and culture (1996, 156).

28. As Levy and Michel note, the so-called private system is also publicly subsidized through various forms of tax credits or deductions.

29. The Canada Assistance Plan, adopted in 1966, opened the door to federal contributions to child care on a cost-shared basis.

30. Although Kremer provides information on Belgian child care, she chose to focus on the Flemish side because (1) responsibility has been devolved to the Flemish and Walloon communities respectively and (2) the Flemish community has a lot in common with the Dutch in terms of language, religion, and culture.

31. Gornick places Dutch women at the top among fifteen OECD countries in terms of the percentage of women working part-time (59 percent of all women and 89 percent of mothers with a child under six years of age; Gornick 1999, table 2).

32. In the Kremer and Jenson chapters, these are subnational arrangements in the form of the Flemish half of the Belgian state and Quebec, a distinct regime within the broader "liberal" Canadian welfare state.

References

Becker, Gary. 1981. *A Treatise on the Family*. Cambridge, Mass: Harvard University Press.

Bergqvist, Christina, Anette Borchorst, Ann-Dorte Christensen, Nina Raanen, Viveca Ramstedt-Silen, and Audur Styrkarsdóttir. 1999. *Equal Democracies: Gender and Politics in the Nordic Countries*. Oslo: Scandinavian University Press.

Brennan, Deborah. 1998. *The Politics of Australian Child Care: Philanthropy to Feminism and Beyond*. Cambridge: Cambridge University Press.

Castells, Manuel. 1997. *The Power of Identity*, vol. 2 of *The Information Age: Economy, Society and Culture*. Oxford: Basil Blackwell.

Castles, Frances, and Deborah Mitchell. 1993. "Worlds of Welfare and Families of Nations." In *Families of Nations*, ed. F. Castles. Hants, Aldershot, Eng.: Dartmouth.

Cerny, Philip. 1997. "Paradoxes of the Competition State: The Dynamics of Political Globalization." *Government and Opposition* 32, no. 2: 251–74.

Daly, Mary. 2001. "Globalization and the Bismarckian Welfare States." In *Globalization and European Welfare States: Challenges and Changes*, ed. Robert Sykes, Bruno Palier, and Pauline Prior. London: Macmillan.

Daly, Mary, and Jane Lewis. 2000. "The Concept of Social Care and the Analysis of Contemporary Welfare States." *British Journal of Sociology* 51, no. 2: 281–98 .

Daune-Richard, Anne-Marie, and Rianne Mahon. 1998. "La Suède: le modèle égalitaire en danger?" (Sweden: The Egalitarian Model in Danger?). In *Qui doit garder le jeune enfant? Les répresentations du travail des mères dans l'Europe en crise* (Who Should Care for the Young Child? Images of Mothers' Work in a Europe in Crisis), ed. J. Jenson and M. Sineau. Paris: LGDJ Droit et Societé.

Deacon, Bob. 2000. "Eastern European Welfare States: The Impact of the Politics of Globalization." *Journal of European Social Policy* 10, no. 2: 146–61.

Esping-Andersen, Gøsta. 1985. *Politics against Markets: The Social Democratic Road to Power*. Princeton, N.J.: Princeton University Press.

_____. 1990. *The Three Worlds of Welfare Capitalism*. Cambridge: Polity Press.

_____. 1997. "Hybrid or Unique? The Distinctiveness of the Japanese Welfare State." *Journal of European Social Policy* 7, no. 3: 179–89.

_____. 1999. *Social Foundations of Postindustrial Economies*. Oxford: Oxford University Press.

Ferge, Zsuzsa. 2001. "Welfare and 'Illfare' Systems in Central-Eastern Europe." In *Globalization and European Welfare States: Challenges and Changes,* ed. Robert Sykes, Bruno Palier, and Pauline Prior. London: Macmillan.

Ferrera, Maurizio. 1998. "Welfare Reform in Southern Europe: Institutional Constraints and Opportunities." In *Challenges to the Welfare State*, ed. H. Cavanna. Aldershot: Elgar.

_____. 2000. "Reconstructing the Welfare State in Southern Europe." In *Survival of the European Welfare State*, ed. S. Kuhnle. London: Routledge.

Fincher, Ruth. 1996. "The State and Child Care: An International Review from a Geographical Perspective." In *Who Will Mind the Baby? Geographies of Child Care and Working Mothers,* ed. Kim England. London: Routledge.

Fraser, Nancy. 1997. *Justice Interruptus: Critical Reflections on the "Postsocialist" Condition*. New York and London: Routledge.

Friendly, Martha. 1997. "What Is the Public Interest in Child Care?" *Policy Options* 8, no. 1: 3–6.

Garrett, Geoff. 1998. *Partisan Politics in the Global Economy*. Cambridge: Cambridge University Press.

Gornick, Janet C. 1999. "Gender Equality in the Labour Market: Women's Employment and Earnings." Luxembourg Income Study Working Paper no. 206.

Gornick, Janet C., and Marcia K. Meyers. 2001. "Public or Private Responsibility? Inequality and Early Childhood Education and Care in the Welfare State." Unpublished manuscript.

Gornick, Janet C., Marcia K. Meyers, and Katherin E. Ross. 1998. "Public Policies and the Employment of Mothers: A Cross-National Study." *Social Science Quarterly* 79, no. 1: 35–54.

Hantrais, Linda, ed. 2000. *Gendered Policies in Europe: Reconciling Employment and Family Life*. London: Macmillan.

Heinen, Jacqueline. 1993. "Le poids du passé sur un présent incertain. L'exemple de la

Pologne et de l'ex-RDA" (The Weight of the Past on an Uncertain Present: The Case of Poland and the Ex-GDR). In *Le sexe des politiques sociales* (The Sex of Social Politics). Paris: Côté-femmes.

Herzenberg, Stephen, John Alic, and Howard Wial. 1998. *New Rules for a New Economy.* Ithaca, N.Y.: Cornell University Press.

Hondagneu-Sotelo, Pierette, and Ernestine Avila. 1997. "I'm Here, but I'm There: The Meanings of Latina Transnational Motherhood." *Gender and Society* II, no. 5: 548–71.

Iversen, Torben and Anne Wren. 1998. "Equality, Employment and Budgetary Restraint: The Trilemma of the Service Economy." *World Politics* 50: 507–46.

Jenson, Jane. 1986. "Gender and Reproduction, or, Babies and the State." *Studies in Political Economy* 20: 9–46.

_____. 1989. "The Talents of Women, the Skills of Men: Flexible Specialisation and Women." In *The Transformation of Work?* ed. Stephen Wood. London: Unwin Human.

_____. 1998. "Mapping Social Cohesion: The State of Canadian Research." Canadian Policy Research Network #F:03. Available online at http://www.cprn.com/cprn.html.

Jenson, Jane, and Mariette Sineau, eds. 1998. *Avi doit garder le jeune enfant? Les répresentations du travail des mères dans l'Europe en crise* (Who Should Care for the Young Child? Images of Mothers' Work in a Europe in Crisis). Paris: LGDJ.

Kitschelt, Herbert, Peter Lange, Gary Marks, and John D. Stephens. 1999. *Continuity and Change in Contemporary Capitalism.* Cambridge: Cambridge University Press.

Lévesque, Benoit and Margie Mendell. 1999. "L'économie sociale au Québec: Éléments théoriques et empiriques pour le débat et la recherche" (The Social Economy of Quebec: Theoretical and Empirical Factors for Debate and Research). *Cahiers du CRISES* #9908.

Lohkamp-Himmighofen, Marlene, and Christiane Dienel. 2000. "Reconciliation policies from a comparative perspective." In *Gendered Policies in Europe: Reconciling Employment and Family Life,* ed. L. Hantrais. London: Macmillan.

McCain, Margaret and Fraser Mustard. 1999. *Report from the Early Years Study.* Toronto: Children's Secretary, Government of Ontario.

Mahon, Rianne. 2000. "Swedish Social Democracy: Death of a Model?" *Studies in Political Economy* 63: 27–60.

Michel, Sonya. 1999. *Children's Interests / Mothers' Rights: The Shaping of America's Child Care Policy.* New Haven, Conn.: Yale University Press.

Mishra, Ramesh. 1999. *Globalization and the Welfare State.* Cheltenham: Edward Elgar.

O'Connor, Julia, Ann Shola Orloff, and Sheila Shaver. 1999. *States, Markets, Families: Gender, Liberalism and Social Policy in Australia, Canada, Great Britain and the United States.* Cambridge: Cambridge University Press.

Palier, Bruno. 2000. "'Defrosting' the French Welfare State." *West European Politics* (special issue: "Recasting European Welfare States," ed. Maurizio Ferrera and Martin Rhodes) 23, no. 2: 113–36.

Pascall, Gillian, and Nick Manning. 2000. "Gender and Social Policy: Comparing Welfare States in Central and Eastern Europe and the Former Soviet Union." *Journal of European Social Policy* 10, no. 3: 240–66.

Pierson, Paul. 1994. *Dismantling the Welfare State? Reagan, Thatcher and the Politics of Retrenchment*. Cambridge: Cambridge University Press.

_____. 1998. "Irresistible Forces, Immovable Objects: Post-industrial Welfare States Confront Permanent Austerity." *Journal of European Public Policy* 5, no. 4: 539–60.

Rhodes, Martin. 1996. "Globalization and West European Welfare States: A Critical Review of Recent Debates." *Journal of European Social Policy* 6, no. 4: 305–27.

_____. 1998. "Globalisation, Labour Markets and Welfare States: A Future of Competitive Corporatism?" In *The Future of European Welfare: A New Social Contract?* ed. Martin Rhodes and Yves Mény. London: Macmillan.

Rostgaard, Tina and Torben Fridberg. 1998. *Caring for Children and Older People: A Comparison of European Policies and Practices* (Social Security in Europe 6). Danish National Institute of Social Research 98:20.

Rubery, Jill, Mark Smith, Colette Fagan, and Damian Grimshaw. 1997. *Women and European Employment*. London: Routledge.

Sayer, Andrew. 1992. *Method in Social Science: A Realist Approach*, 2nd ed. London: Routledge.

Scharpf, Fritz. 2000. "Globalization and the Welfare State: Constraints, Challenges and Vulnerabilities." Paper presented at the workshop on European Welfare States: Domestic and International Challenges, Max Planck Institute, Cologne, October.

Scharpf, Fritz, and Vivienne Schmidt. 2000. *From Vulnerability to Competitiveness: Welfare and Work in the Open Economy*. Oxford: Oxford University Press.

Scott, Hilda. 1983. *Sweden's "Right to be Human": Sex Role Equality, the Goal and the Reality*. Armonk, N.Y: M. E. Sharpe.

Shragge, Eric, ed. 1997. *Community Economic Development: In Search of Employment*. Montreal: Black Rose Books.

Shragge, Eric and Jean-Marc Fontan, eds. 2000. *Social Economy: International Debates and Perspectives*. Montreal: Black Rose Books.

Sykes, Robert, Bruno Palier, and Pauline Prior, eds. 2001. *Globalization and European Welfare States: Challenges and Changes*. New York: St. Martins.

Thelen, Kathleen, and Sven Steinmo. 1992. "Historical Institutionalism in Comparative Politics." In *Structuring Politics: Historical Institutionalism in Comparative Analysis*, ed. Kathleen Thelen, Sven Steinmo, and Frank Longstreth. Cambridge: Cambridge University Press.

Valiente, Celia. 1995. "Children First: Central Government Child Care Policies in Post-Authoritarian Spain (1975–1994)." In *Childhood and Parenthood: Proceedings of the ISA Committee for Family Research on Children and Families, 1994,* ed. Julia Brannen and Margaret O'Brien. London: Institute of Education, University of London.

the consequences of weak feminism

CHAPTER 1

Gender and Generation:
Japanese Child Care and the Demographic Crisis

Ito Peng

Introduction

Throughout the postwar era, the Japanese state has used women as a point of adjustment to negotiate varying social, economic, and political imperatives; this is probably most clearly reflected in family and child care policies. Ever since the introduction of the child welfare law in 1947, which laid the legal foundation for the state to provide public child care to "children lacking in care" at home, interpretations of what constitutes "a child lacking in care" have vacillated in response to the market demands for women's labor, political demands to strengthen the family's welfare obligations, and public pressures for more social care. Hence, a simple overview of family and child care policies shows a continuous shift in government positions vis-à-vis the social care of children. For example, the first decade after the introduction of the legislation saw enthusiastic state support for the idea of public child care, but by the mid-1950s that position was reversed as the state began to endorse the idea of mother-centered child care. However, with economic growth, increased demand for women's labor, and public pressure from working mothers for more child care, the 1960s saw another shift toward more flexible and expansionary public child care. Then, with the economic downturn of the mid-1970s, the state's formal policies shifted once again. This time child care provisions were rolled into the state's social welfare restructuring plan, which strongly favored reinstating the family's traditional obligations. The extension of public child care and many other family support programs were thus brought to a halt, as the state sought ways to cap its social welfare expenditures amid a rising tide of public demand for child care.

Yet by the early 1990s, family and child care policies were back again on the government's expansion list. This time, social and demographic shifts in Japan had become such that the state had to rethink its policy strategies vis-à-vis women and the family. The main issue was the aging of the society, exacerbated by what seemed to be an inexorable decline in the fertility rate. Key indicators revealed that the Japanese population was aging much more quickly than initially thought and, given the declining fertility rate, Japan would soon face serious social and economic problems. The public was put on notice that the soaring dependency ratio, economic slowdown, and eventual population decline resulting from the current demographic trajectory would seriously undermine Japan's political and economic position in the world.

In addition, it also became clear that the aging trend was directly connected to existing gender relations. Studies showed that the lack of gender equality within both the home and the labor market had left Japanese women with little option but to defer or forgo marriage and/or childbearing, thus contributing to the decline in the total fertility rate and accelerating the aging process. In response to these imperatives, state policies since the early 1990s have begun to encourage childbirth. To this end, the Japanese welfare state has embarked on what appears to be the beginning of a "family-friendly/woman-friendly" welfare expansion. This has led to a marked extension in public child care and reforms in parental and family care leave policies.

Throughout such postwar policy fluctuations, women's groups have also been very important in shaping the Japanese family and child care policies. While often regarded as largely a conservative, prohousewife force aligning itself behind the state machinery (Garon 1997), the postwar women's movement has not always been in agreement with the state. In fact, its role in social policy formulation, as we shall see in this chapter, has been much more complex. True, the political interests of mainstream women's organizations have often coincided with those of the state; however, with regard to child care, many women's groups have also pushed the state hard for more public services in order to protect the interests of working mothers. Hence throughout the postwar era, while the dominant women's groups worked to protect the social status of full-time housewives, working mothers and lone mothers' groups lobbied for public child care as the basis for women's right to work and children's right to social education.

This chapter examines family and child care policy in Japan within the context of gender and welfare state restructuring. Child care policy is an excellent lens through which to examine Japanese welfare state restructuring because it has been at the center of important policy debates throughout most of the postwar era and is becoming salient once again. For the purpose of understanding Japanese social policy, the recent child care reform is important because it illustrates how the constraints of a highly gendered system have compelled individuals to opt out of the traditional family structure and forced the state to accept a greater role in social care.

Throughout this chapter, I pursue two lines of discussion: first, I provide an overview of the developmental trajectory of family and child care policies in postwar Japan; and second, in the process of the discussion, I highlight the role of the women's movement in shaping the state's family and child care policies. The first part of the chapter sets Japan within a comparative framework, while in the second, I discuss the development of family and child care policy in Japan since 1945. Here I illustrate how family and child care policies intersect with changes in gender relations, and how the women's movement has contributed to policy development. Finally, in the third part I consider in more detail current child care policies and assess their effectiveness in dealing with the problem of fertility decline.

The Postwar Japanese Welfare State

Numerous attempts have been made to locate Japan within existing comparative welfare state models, but so far none has been very satisfactory. At the moment views on the Japanese welfare state are split between those who consider it to be a hybrid welfare regime (Esping-Andersen 1997; Miyamoto 1997) and those who attempt to explain it in terms of a unique and possibly East Asian–type welfare regime (for example, Goodman and Peng 1996; Peng 2000b). However, regardless of their differences, most proponents agree on two particular features of the Japanese welfare state: a strong emphasis on the family and the importance of corporate or occupational welfare.

It is widely accepted that the Japanese welfare state is strongly family centered— that is, the family has always taken on the central role in social welfare—and that the state has always expected the family to take on this role.[1] The state's reliance on the family is most clearly reflected in Japan's comparatively high level of coresidency and low level of institutional care for the elderly and disabled. For example, the proportion of people over the age of sixty-five who are living with children was 50.3 percent in 1998 (of whom 31.2 percent were living with their married children, while 19.1 percent were living with their unmarried children), which is significantly higher than Western welfare states (Ministry of Health and Welfare 2000). On the other hand, the level of institutional support for elderly people in Japan is also extremely low. In 1998, the proportion of elderly people who were living or being cared for in institutions amounted to only 3.6 percent, even though an estimated 13 percent of all elderly people were in need of such care.[2] Given these figures, it is clear that a large proportion of Japan's elderly are being cared for by their families, and that the family constitutes an important form of social security for this group.

In addition to the family, the corporate sector also performs an important social security function in Japan. What many Japanese refer to as the country's corporate-centered welfare system (*kigyo-chushin shakai fukushi*) is a product of the postwar social consensus forged among the state, the corporate sector, and labor unions. This system enabled employers to institutionalize corporate prerogatives over workers and their families in exchange for job security and rapid economic growth. This welfare regime mandated highly gendered household and labor market arrangements: the corporate demand for long working hours, and hence men's long absence from home, required women's housewifery and caring roles within the home, and the system of lifetime employment and automatic seniority-based wage raises were predicated upon a peripheral role for women in the labor market. To facilitate such domestic arrangements, the state introduced a variety of positive and negative labor market and social policies. Some of the policy tools used to reinforce women's dependence on their husbands and discourage marital dissolution included legal hiring practices that discriminated against women and ethnic minorities, mandatory retirement for women upon marriage or childbirth, a married-women's tax credit, and punitive policies and inadequate income assistance for divorced and unmarried

lone mothers. To male workers who form the core of the labor force, lifetime employment, automatic seniority wage raises, productivity-indexed wages, and generous company welfare benefits were offered as rewards for company loyalty. A wage
structure based on a family's life cycle rather than skills and work experience has
also discouraged labor mobility, and employee benefits such as family, housing, and
transportation allowances, low-interest loans for home purchase, and large lump-
sum retirement allowances also served to encourage family formation, promote
home ownership, discourage married women's full-time employment, and increase
worker dependency on the company.

The result of such institutional arrangements is a package of social security measures centered on the needs of the corporate sector. It includes a set of fairly comprehensive but occupationally and status-separated social insurance schemes
favoring male corporate employees and their families, and a modicum of income
support and social services for the family, women, children, and the elderly. Here it
is important to underline that one outcome of the corporate-centered welfare system in Japan has been the state neglect of its social welfare responsibilities and the
overloading of those responsibilities on the family (i.e., women). This arrangement
has enabled the Japanese state to maintain an exceptionally low level of social security expenditure. For example, from 1955 to 1970 the Japanese state expenditure
on social security remained steady at about 6 percent of the total gross domestic
product (GDP), approximately half the level of the United States, a third of Britain's,
and less than a quarter of Sweden's at the same time. Even when Japan's social security expenditure began to rise after 1970, it remained one of the lowest among the
nations involved in the Organizaton for Economic Cooperation and Development.
Currently Japan's spending in this area stands at about 17 percent of the total GDP,
slightly higher than that of the United States.

Gender Politics and the Development of Family and Child Care Policies in Japan

Given the assumptions of Japan's corporate-centered welfare system about women's
domestic roles, it would seem logical that there would be little state interest or support for public child care. Yet despite this orientation, the postwar Japanese welfare
state has not always opposed the idea of public child care. In fact, throughout most of
this period, the Japanese government tried to assert prohousewife policies while implicitly, and sometimes quite explicitly, supporting public child care in order to enable working mothers to enter the labor market. Indeed, data show that the number
of preschool children attending public child care centers rose steadily from the 1950s
to the 1980s, even though the state's formal policies toward the family admonished
middle-class mothers to stay home and care for their young children (see tables 1.1
and 1.2). Today, the proportion of preschool-age children who are in public child
care in Japan is about 22 percent (Ministry of Health and Welfare 1998), which puts
the country between what are often considered "women-friendly" welfare states such

TABLE 1.1: NUMBER OF PUBLIC AND PRIVATE CERTIFIED CHILD CARE CENTERS,* 1947–1995

YEAR	PUBLIC CENTERS	PRIVATE CENTERS	PUBLIC/PRIVATE RATIO
1947	395	1,223	0.32
1952	1,855	3,268	0.57
1957	4,951	4,187	1.18
1960	5,571	4,221	1.32
1965	6,907	4,292	1.61
1970	8,817	5,284	1.67
1975	11,545	6,693	1.72
1980	13,311	8,725	1.53
1985	13,590	9,309	1.46
1990	13,371	9,332	1.43
1995	13,184	9,304	1.42

TABLE 1.2: NUMBER OF AVAILABLE SPACES AND CHILDREN REGISTERED
IN CERTIFIED CHILD CARE CENTERS, 1949–1995

YEAR	NUMBER OF CHILD CARE SPACES			NUMBER OF CHILDREN REGISTERED		
	PUBLIC	PRIVATE	TOTAL	PUBLIC	PRIVATE	TOTAL
1949			195,377			216,887
1952			380,989			502,345
1957			700,815			657,010
1960	424,092	309,553	733,645			689,242
1965	546,096	330,044	876,140	503,259 (92.2)	326,481 (98.9)	829,740
1970	752,710	442,222	1,194,932	690,344 (91.7)	441,017 (99.7)	1,131,361
1975	1,090,653	690,028	1,699,681	1,012,290 (92.8)	618,735 (89.7)	1,631,025
1980	1,321,677	815,051	2,136,728	1,188,340 (89.9)	807,742 (99.1)	1,996,082
1985	1,247,306	831,459	2,078,765	1,046,060 (83.9)	797,490 (95.9)	1,843,550
1990	1,171,637	807,822	1,979,459	957,249 (81.7)	766,526 (94.9)	1,723,775
1995	1,128,074	794,761	1,922,835	912,659 (80.9)	766,207 (96.4)	1,678,866

Numbers in ( ) represent the enrollment rate.

Source for both tables: Zenkoku Hoikudantai Rengokai and Hoikukenkyusho, eds. 1997. *Hoiku Hakusho: 1997 (White Paper on Child Care: 1997)*. Tokyo: Sodo Bunka.

*In Japan, both the public and private child care centers listed here are public child care. That is, they are all registered and state-regulated child care centers.

as Sweden and Denmark and not so "women-friendly" regimes like those of the United Kingdom and the United States. Also, because of the legacy of the child welfare law, the only eligibility criterion for public child care in Japan is proof of need, which does not take family income into account, as is the case for countries such as the United States or Canada. Hence, if Japanese parents can prove that their child lacks care at home—and in most cases this implies a proof of both parents' full-time employment and the absence of any possible family care arrangement—the state is by law obliged to place the child in a child care center. State subsidies for public child care fees are also relatively generous. Fees are calculated on a sliding scale based on the combination of family size and total family income,[3] with the remainder shared between the central and the local governments through a general tax.[4]

The reasons the idea of full-time housewife and public child care could coexist in postwar Japan are twofold. First, while Japan's corporate-centered welfare system idealized women's domestic role, in reality women's labor was also needed in order to sustain the country's postwar economic growth. Also, a significant portion of families were excluded from the corporate sector and thus needed two incomes to support their households. During the transitional period of the 1950s, for example, a large number of women were engaged in agricultural work and in family businesses. After the 1960s, women were increasingly channeled into low-wage peripheral work as the service sector expanded. In response to these shifts, the state made public child care available as a part of its economic policy, while its formal family policy urged mothers to stay home and care for small children.

The second reason for the coexistence of these seemingly conflicting ideas is that at least until the early 1980s, there was also steady public and political pressure to expand child care. These came from two groups of working women: lone mothers and women in skilled professions such as teachers and nurses. For lone mothers, the state regarded achievement of economic self-sufficiency through employment as being more desirable than dependence on income support, and hence made child care available to them. With regard to the other group of working mothers, the state made child care available in response to their political lobby. In previous years, labor unions and women's groups also actively supported public child care. For example, the women's section of the Sohyo (the National Council of Workers' Unions), the main umbrella group representing most of the labor unions in Japan, as well as large women's groups such as the National Alliance of Women's Groups, often joined the Working Mothers' Committee (Hataraku Haha no Kai) and lone mothers' groups to lobby for state-supported services. These groups called for the protection of women's social identities as mothers but also pressed for a variety of employment and social policies to protect working mothers' right to work and their children's right to social education.

It should be pointed out here that not all the postwar women's groups took on the cause of public child care. One of the largest of these, the National Federation of Regional Women's Organizations (NFRWO; Zenkoku Chiiki Fujin Dantai Renraku Kyogikai), for example, strongly supported protecting and legitimating women's primary roles as full-time mothers, housewives, and consumers. There was, however, little direct conflict between these groups, partly because, despite their differences, they shared a similar political position. Both sought to advance women's social and economic status within Japan's male-dominated system and both applied a maternalist approach to push for women's rights. Hence in principle they both agreed on the need for social protection for women as mothers, regardless of whether they were full-time care providers or wage earners. Indeed, after the 1960s, the mainstream women's groups made a decisive move away from issues that would put them in direct confrontation with working mothers. As maternal employment grew, these organizations gradually shifted their activities to broader social issues such as environmental protection and the peace movement.

Within the context of postwar gender politics, the Japanese welfare state developed increasingly dualistic family and child care policies: while formal policies extolled the primacy of women's housewifery and family care roles, in practice, public child care continued to grow in relation to the increasing number of working mothers. For the corporate-centered welfare system, this did not present a serious problem either. In fact, as this system became more entrenched, the inherent dualism began to surface here as well. Because of its preference for corporate sector employees and their families, the system had in fact created a two-tiered structure in which formal welfare programs served to protect and benefit those who belonged to the core sector, while informal measures accommodated the welfare needs of those on the periphery. In this manner, formal policies continued to valorize housewifery for the wives of core sector employees, while marginalizing women who did not fit that pattern—lone mothers and women in low-income families. It was only in the late 1980s that this contradiction became clearly untenable. Faced with economic globalization, large firms began to abandon their commitment to the corporate-centered welfare system. In addition, with the steady decline in fertility and rise in maternal employment, the Japanese welfare state was faced with a demographic imperative that called for rethinking the institutional framework for social welfare vis-à-vis the family.

To more fully understand postwar Japan, however, it is important to examine the development of gender politics and family and child care policies from a historical perspective. I divide this process roughly into four periods: 1) 1947 to the mid-1950s; 2) the mid-1950s to the late 1960s; 3) the 1970s to the mid-1980s; and finally 4) the second half of the 1980s to date.[5] I shall, however, emphasize the last two periods, as these are more relevant to the current debate on gender and welfare restructuring in Japan.

The Postwar Development of Gender Politics and Child Care Policies

From 1947 to the Mid-1950s: The Reemergence of Women's Public Roles and the Notion of Public Child Care as a Way to Resuscitate the Family and the Nation

The current child care legislation in Japan has its roots in the Child Welfare Law, which was introduced in 1947. At the time, the legislation was intended to address the pressing social welfare issues of thousands of war orphans and the children of lone-mother families; however, the law was eventually expanded to provide universal welfare for all children.[6]

The early postwar era was also a moment of (re)emergence for women's movements in Japan. During the first decade after the war, many of the prewar and interwar women's groups reestablished themselves, often under the leadership of their original leaders.[7] Carrying on with the work they had undertaken before and during the war, most of these organizations sought to advance women's interests in national and local politics by advocating their vision of a "distinctively female politics." They sought to connect politics and the kitchen by focusing on promoting better family life and, in the context of postwar social and economic reconstruction, they worked actively in conjunction with the state to promote economic nationalism and maintain stable family life (Garon 1997). A good example of such collaborative relationships between women's groups and the state was the New Life Campaign (Shin Seikatsu Undo), the aim of which was to "build a new Japan" through such activities as promoting personal savings and supporting the state's national reconstruction efforts.

In terms of the family and social welfare policies, the state urged individuals to help themselves and to cooperate with the state in rebuilding the country's economy. A 1946 government policy paper called "The Basic Issues Concerning Japanese Economic Reconstruction" (Nihon Keizai Saiken no Kiso Mondai), for example, urged families to maintain themselves through hard work and mutual assistance until the national economy had regained its strength and a social security system was established (Shakai Hosho Kenkyujo 1975).

The state's expectation of women's multiple roles as family care providers, social mobilizers, and workers was also evident in child care policy. The Child Welfare Law of 1947 led to the creation of child care centers that were to be accessible to all children in need of care, regardless of family income. The eligibility criteria, based on the notion of "a child lacking in care," also included mothers who were not formally engaged in the labor market employment. Those who were engaged in "constructive social activities" such as volunteer work, national reconstruction work (i.e., community work), and self-education, for example, also qualified. As illustrated in a parliamentary debate in 1947, the state saw public child care as an integral part of national reconstruction and an important basis for the promotion of children's welfare and positive family life. As was noted, "Child care is an important basis for promoting the welfare of small children because, by relieving ordinary working mothers of their child care duties, they can engage themselves in the nation's economic, cultural and/or political activities, or can gain time for self-education or respite, all of which will in the end lead to the betterment of family life (Jido-fukushiho Kenkyukai 1978, vol. 2, 871).

The state's support for public child care also coincided with the demands of the labor unions and new women's groups like the Democratic Women's Club (Fujin Minshu Kurabu). In 1946, the Democratic Women's Club formed the Democratic

Child Care Federation (Minshu Hoiku Renmei) in alliance with the Mothers' Committee (Haha no Kai), labor unions, agricultural cooperatives, and consumers' cooperatives (*seikatsu kyodokumiai*), to push for state-sponsored services. In response to economic hardship and the needs of a large number of working mothers, they lobbied the government, employers, and local communities. Given the fact that women's labor-market participation rate was over 55 percent at the time and that they represented close to a quarter of the labor union membership, the federation sought to advance public child care as a way to protect women's right to work and ensure social protection and education for children of working mothers (Minshu Hoiku Renmei 1946).

The Democratic Child Care Federation not only lobbied for the expansion of public child care; they also mobilized workers and community members to set up workplace and community-based child care centers. Between 1947 and 1952 the federation organized child care centers in local housing complexes and company housing areas, as well as setting up their own cooperative child care in areas where the local governments were slow to respond (Minshu Hoiku Renmei News 1947–1952).

In summary, the first decade after the introduction of the Child Welfare Law saw positive state support for public child care, a position that coincided with public opinion. The result was a rapid expansion of state-sponsored services. In fact, the state could not keep up with the pace of the expansion. The growth of public child care was so urgent that the state opted to build public child care centers as well as contracting out child care services to private nonprofit organizations.[8] As is illustrated in tables 1.1 and 1.2, from 1947 to 1952, the total number of child care centers (public and private) increased more than threefold from 1,618 to 5,153, while the total number of children being cared for in these centers rose from 216,887 to 502,345, more than double. Although public demand for more child care seemed to have moved in conjunction with state objectives, it is important to underline here that there was a clear difference between the state and groups such as the Democratic Child Care Federation with regard to the rationales behind their support. From the state's perspective, child care served as a policy lever for channeling women into the nation's postwar social and economic reconstruction activities; the federation, on the other hand, saw it as a necessary means of protecting mothers' right to work and children's rights to social education.

The Mid-1950s to the End of the 1960s: A New Vision of the Western Middle-Class Family and the Beginning of Policy Fragmentation

In the 1950s, the Japanese state's formal family and child care policies began to shift away from those of its earlier position. At the same time, the women's movement, too, found itself increasingly polarized between those interested in enhancing the social status of full-time housewives and those wanting to protect a mother's right to work. On the one hand, for example, the cooperation between the state and women's groups such as NFRWO in the New Life Campaign continued throughout this period. In the aftermath of the 1955 social contract, the New Life Campaign shifted its focus to educating middle-class housewives, a goal that was often advanced in concert with the state and business to reinforce the legitimacy of the corporate-centered welfare system (Kimoto 1997).

On the other hand, women's organizations representing lone mothers and wage-earning mothers were also becoming increasingly vocal in their calls for social welfare reforms. The National Council of War Widows' Organizations (NCWWO; Zenkoku Mibojin Dantai Kyogikai)[9] and the National Organization of Widows of Car Accident Victims (NOWCAV; Kotsu Iji Ikueikai), for example, were two groups that became increasingly visible and assertive in claiming public child care during this period (Yamataka 1978). Since the labor-market participation rate of lone mothers was over 80 percent, child care was vital for the economic survival of their families (Peng 1995). As war victims and victims of the rapid industrialization, they also commanded a great deal of moral authority. The cooperation between lone mothers' groups and other working mothers' groups like the Working Mothers' Committee thus became a powerful voice for better labor conditions, more protective welfare policies, and, in the case of widowed lone mothers, also some public compensation.[10]

The government's response to the different demands from women's groups was to adopt separate policies. With the NFRWO representing a burgeoning population of middle-class, full-time housewives, the state continued to provide funds and attempt to draw them into various state-funded projects. In response to the demands of the lone mothers' and working mothers' groups, by contrast, the state made available public child care spaces. For lone mothers, the state also extended special low-interest loans, skill training and employment assistance programs, counseling services, and housing support in an effort to help them achieve economic self-sufficiency (Peng 1995).

In summary, this period marks the beginning of policy dualism as the state tried to advance two separate objectives at the same time. During the 1950s and the 1960s, formal state policies shifted away from public child care and toward home-based child care by mothers. However, with regard to wage-earning mothers, many of whom were lone parents, the state continued to provide child care as a preferred option over income support. In reality, the state's own policy positions concerning the family and child care simply reflected a similar divide within the government bureaucracy. For example, while the Family Life Issues Council (Katei Seikatsu Mondai Shingikai), supported by the Prime Minister's Office and representing broader political interests, was advocating policies to strengthen "traditional" family responsibilities, the Central Child Welfare Council (Chuo Jido Fukushi Shingikai), supported by the Ministry of Health and Welfare, advocated the expansion of public child care on the ground that it would help lone mothers and low-income working-parent families gain economic self-sufficiency (Shobi 1986).

The 1970s to the Mid-1980s: The Emergence of the Japanese-Style Welfare Society and Intensification of the State's Dualistic Policies toward the Family and Child Care

Toward the end of the 1960s, just as the effect of the postwar economic growth began to show in terms of a real increase in individual income, the social cost of the rapid economic surge also began to surface. For example, pollution problems resulting from unrestrained industrial waste and an increase in traffic accidents due to rapid and often unplanned urban growth began taking their toll, with annual increases in health risks and fatal automobile accidents. A rise in the divorce rate was also beginning to cause public and policy outcry, particularly as many feared that it would undermine the "traditional Japanese family" and its functions.

Meanwhile, the Working Mothers' Committee and lone mothers' groups, joined by newly emergent feminist groups, began to press for more gender equality in the labor market and social support for women. These groups rallied at both local and national levels for public child care, universal child allowances, and special child allowances for divorced and unmarried mothers.[11] In terms of their political strength and mass support, the NCWWO had a membership of over 870,000 by the end of the 1960s, including a growing number of divorced or separated lone mothers, while the NOWCAV had a membership of about 50,000. Notwithstanding their large memberships and well-organized national networks, the lone mothers' political lobbies for public child care were also joined by a growing number of working mothers from two-parent households. In one of the most successful national campaigns, called As Many Child Care Centers as There Are Post Boxes (Posto on Kazu dake Hoikusho), for example, an estimated one million women took to the street to demand more services.

The lobbying bore fruit: state policies began to shift in favor of social welfare and public child care expansion. Starting in 1970, both the Economic Planning Agency and the Ministry of Health and Welfare issued policy papers calling for economic development and community building through an extension of social welfare (Economic Planning Agency 1970; Central Council of Social Welfare 1971). Arguing that Japanese families were becoming more "nuclear" and that the population was beginning to age, they pointed to the need to strengthen the social security system as well as the (traditional) family support and community network.

The state's policy on public child care was now more supportive to families headed by two working parents or by single mothers, though in principle they continued to assert the importance of mother-centered child care. Earlier restrictions to public child care were temporarily relaxed, as the "child lacking in care" clause became once again open to liberal interpretation. As a result the number of child care centers and spaces continued to expand throughout the seventies, in keeping with public demand and the rise in the number of working mothers.

This period of social welfare expansion did not last long, however. With a sudden onset of economic crisis in 1973–74, the country's political sentiment quickly shifted back to conservatism and the state's formal social and welfare policies took a similar turn. The most important outcome of this shift was the emergence of the concept of the so-called Japanese-style welfare society, whose rhetoric attempted to recast the Japanese welfare state in its earlier, leaner form, characterized by smaller government and a greater individual and family share of social welfare responsibilities. The government was not able to implement this reversion immediately due to its minority position in the parliament; however, once it secured an electoral victory in 1980, it immediately began making widespread cuts in the state's welfare expenditures. Throughout the following decade, the state welfare provisions contracted visibly.

With respect to family life, the state attempted to strengthen the traditional family structure by fostering three-generational living arrangements (Ministry of Health and Welfare 1978; Liberal Democratic Party 1979) and reasserting the value of the family's (i.e., women's) caring responsibilities. For example, a special tax credit was introduced in 1983 to encourage three-generation coresidency and assist families who were caring for their elderly relatives. At the same time, the income assistance program called Seikatsu Hogo, or general welfare for lone mother families, was systematically cut to weed out the "welfare frauds." [12]

The decline in the real income of middle-class households also affected married women's employment patterns. The employment rate of married women, which had been declining throughout the 1960s, began to rise again in the 1970s. For example, while overall employment rate of married women rose from 45 percent to 51 percent between 1975 and 1985 (Ministry of Finance 1997), that of salaried men's wives—the middle-class women who formed the very base of the corporate-centered welfare system—surged from 38 percent in 1970 to 49.2 percent in 1985. Rather than discouraging their labor market participation, as would have been the case a decade earlier, this time the Japanese state actively sought to facilitate their economic activities by channelling married women into part-time employment. A special tax exemption was introduced in 1987 to allow married women to earn up to one million yen, approximately 20 percent of the average male annual income, in part-time income. This not only limited married women's economic activities to part-time work but further entrenched their caring role within the home. The combined effect of the married women's tax exemption and policies of family care was an increase in women's double burden: married women's part-time employment continued to rise while public support for care of the elderly and the young remained negligible.

Notwithstanding the increase in married women's labor-market participation, the 1980s also saw a curtailment of the child care expansion and a gradual move toward contracting out services to private child care centers as a way of lowering public expenditure. As shown in tables 1.1 and 1.2, starting in 1980 the number of child care centers and levels of enrollment began to decline, despite the fact that the demand for public services was great. The reduction in child care spaces was particularly visible in centers run by public agencies such as prefectural and municipal governments, where the operating costs were higher than in those run by the private sector. Between 1980 and 1995 the number of children registered in publicly run child care centers dropped by about 280,000 and the actual enrollment rates in these centers fell from about 90 to 81 percent, while the decline in the spaces and enrollment rate in private child care centers was much less dramatic.[13]

Falling enrollments were not, however, a reflection of public demand; rather, they were the result of the greater restrictions placed on eligibility criteria. While local governments were responsible for assessing child care needs, they were not required to fill all the child care spaces. During the fiscal retrenchment phase of the 1980s, these authorities systematically restricted the interpretation of the "child lacking in care" clause to make it harder for families to qualify for public child care. Indeed, the gap between the stated decline in child care registration and the actual need for child care could be seen in rising numbers of children on waiting lists and enrolled in nonregistered child care (that is, private child care for parents who could not get their children in public child care).

Thus, the early 1970s saw a brief period of welfare extension that was soon reversed due to economic crisis. By the 1980s the Japanese welfare state had shifted its policies in line with the Japanese-style welfare society discourse. This was marked by attempts to reduce state welfare expenditures and push the welfare burden back onto the family and individuals. Married women, caught between the family's need for a second income and reductions in the state's social welfare support, were now expected to manage the dual task of work and care. With the introduction of the married women's tax exemption, part-time work became the most obvious option for married women. The result was a steady increase in married women's labor market participation *and* of their "double burden." In terms of child care, this was also a particularly difficult period for working parents and lone-mother families, as many local governments made child care eligibility more difficult, while at the same time low-income women and lone mothers were told to work to maintain their families.

The Late 1980s to the Present: The "1.57 Shock" and the Resurgence of Public Child Care

In practice, Japanese-style welfare society rhetoric did not last long. By the end of the 1980s it had become plainly obvious that such policies were simply unsustainable. The state's policy attempt to shift the care burden of the young and the elderly to the family came under increasing public criticism as more married women entered the labor market. In addition to this, however, major demographic shifts were also beginning to affect social policy and bring into question the soundness of the conservative rhetoric.

First, the 1980s saw a rather sharp rise in the elderly population. Between 1980 and 1990, the proportion of people over the age of 65 rose from 9.1 to 12.1 percent. At the same time, the proportion of three-generation households continued to decline (from 54.4 percent in 1975 to 39.5 percent in 1990), while elderly-only households rose from 15.0 to 28.6 percent. Such demographic shifts challenged not only the effectiveness of the government's family policy measures but also the capacity of the family to care for its elderly members.

Public anxiety about the family's (women's) care burden was also reflected in the emergence of new public pressure groups. For example, by the end of the 1980s, women's groups like the Japan Federation of Women's Groups (Nihon Fujin Dantai Rengokai) were beginning to voice their concerns about women's double burden in Japan's aging society. Special-interest groups like the Committee to Consider Social Care (CCSC; Kaigo wo Kangaeru Kai), organized by women who were caring for family members, soon became a powerful lobby for socialized care. Through its national campaign, the Ten Thousand Citizens' Committee to Realize a Public Elder-Care System (Kaigohoken no seitoka to Kaigo no Shakaikawo Motemeru Ichiman, known as the 10,000 Citizens' Committee, Ichiman'ninshimin Iinkai), CCSC successfully lobbied politicians and gained significant public support for the introduction of the Long-Term Care Insurance Scheme in 1997.

Meanwhile, the attitudes of young Japanese women had also changed in the 1980s. Government surveys found that women as a whole, but particularly those in their twenties and thirties, were becoming increasingly more work oriented and less willing to accept traditional gender arrangements either at work or within the home. For example, according to the prime minister's office, public opinion surveys found that the proportion of women who claimed that they considered paid work as the most significant part of their life rose from 35.9 percent in 1975 to 43.6 percent in 1992. The same surveys found that the proportion of women who thought that "women should continue to work after they have children" had increased from 11.5 percent in 1972 to 32.5 percent in 1995 (Ministry of Finance 1997). These attitudinal shifts were presumed to be linked to the rise in women's average age at first marriage (from 24.2 in 1970 to 26 in 1990), longer career pattern (from 6.1 years in 1980 to 8.2 years in 1997), and an increase in the divorce rate (from 1.0 in 1970 to 1.6 in 1997; Ministry of Labor 1998).

The attitudinal changes of young women did not, however, translate into political activism. Rather, the women's political lobby in the 1980s continued to be dominated by activists who were at the scene in the 1960s and '70s. By this time, however, child care was no longer their first priority. To be sure, most indications pointed to a general decline in public interest in child care at this time; although a large number of families were clearly in need of child care they were often too pressed for time to become involved in political activities. But the women's groups that had traditionally formed the backbone of the campaign for public child care had shifted their focus to the issue of elderly care, since most of their members had reached an age when they now had to be concerned about their own aging parents. This in turn alienated younger women and discouraged them from joining the women's groups. The state, too, was more concerned with the problems of aging, as illustrated by the plethora of policy and research papers on this topic throughout the decade. Given the public and policy climate at the end of the 1980s, it seemed that child care policy would gradually fade from public consciousness.

By 1990, however, public child care had once again reemerged as a key policy topic. Interestingly, this time the state had become the main factor in pushing for family and child care reforms. The cause of this policy shift was the drop in the fertility rate; in 1989, Japan's total fertility rate fell to an "unprecedented low" of 1.57, causing a wave of panic referred to as the "1.57 shock" (*1.57 shokku*). In reality, the fertility rate in Japan had been declining steadily since 1950, but the figure of 1.57 broke the psychological barrier 1.58 had established in 1966, which was considered a particularly bad year for childbirth (see fig. 1.1; Kashiwame 1997).[14]

The state's main concern about the declining fertility rate had to do with its long-term implications for the aging of Japanese society. This problem had been a topic of discussion since the 1960s and had been used at different times to argue for welfare state expansion as well as retrenchment. Until this point, however, the debate had mainly focused on welfare state responses to what was considered a natural demographic phenomenon in an industrialized society; no attempt had been made to halt, let alone reverse, this trend. The fall of the fertility rate below 1.57, however, brought into sharp focus the link between aging and low fertility and highlighted the macro social and demographic impacts of women's life choices. In the process, it opened a new set of debates interlocking issues of gender relations with the state's vision of welfare state restructuring.

Initially the issue was defined largely in terms of the "women's problem": low fertility was explained by the fact that women were deferring marriage and childbirth or not marrying at all in order to realize their career aspirations and/or desire for personal freedom. Such social phenomena were in turn attributed to women's high educational attainment, their propensity to work after completing education, and their lack of desire to take on traditional family responsibilities. For example,

FIGURE 1.1: TOTAL FERTILITY RATE, 1950–1995

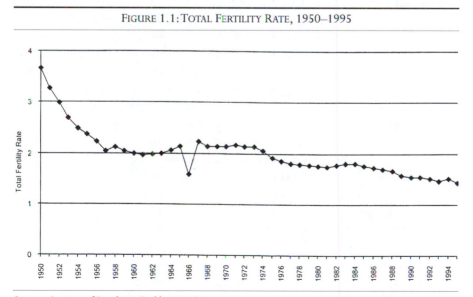

SOURCE: Institute of Population Problems (1996).

survey reports from the Institute of Population Problems in the early 1990s pointed out that a noticeable proportion of young people were claiming that they did not intend to ever marry. Moreover, among those who want to marry, the desired age at marriage was about two years higher for all age groups compared to their cohorts in the early 1980s (Institute of Population Problems 1993; Atoh et al. 1994; Kaneko 1994; Nakano and Watanabe 1994).

Correspondingly, the policy discourse at the time focused on ways to get women to marry young. In fact, some Liberal Democratic Party politicians, like then finance minister Rytaro Hashimoto (who later became the Prime Minister), even went as far as proposing limits on the number of women entering the four-year universities in order to redirect them to early marriage, while the Health and Welfare minister's personally appointed Discussion Group to Think about the Future of the Family and Child Rearing (Korekara no Kazoku to Kosodate ni Kansuru Kondaikai) took a more reflective tone, expressing concern about the "grave and quiet crisis" (*shinkoku de shizukanaru kiki*) that would lead to the "attrition and erosion of the family and community's [traditional] functions" and urging the state to develop policies to raise the national fertility rate (Korekara 1990).

As the policy debates shifted to the root causes of the problem, however, the inherent tension within gender relations began to emerge. Evidence showed that the gender division of labor that had underpinned the postwar Japanese welfare state had been directly responsible for the fertility crisis: namely, that the strict gender roles prescribed by the existing welfare regime were forcing women to choose either marriage (and assumption of traditional gender roles) or career (which meant remaining single), and this had prompted many young women to defer their choice as long as possible.

The policies formulated in response to the new findings thus sought to offer more positive incentives for marriage and childbirth. This time the government attempted to draw policy lessons from more successful Western welfare states like Sweden and Denmark. A series of 1992 white papers and policy statements highlighting the government's commitment to harmonizing work and family and promoting a healthy environment for childbirth set the tone for the new family and child care policies to follow (Sukoyakani 1992; Ministry of Health and Welfare 1994).

The new pronatalist policies instituted since the 1990s have resulted in a significant expansion of public child care. In 1994 the Angel Plan was launched to address the problems of the declining fertility by widening the net for social care through welfare state extension. The plan included an overhaul of the entire child care system and expansion of support services for families and women with small children. Specifically, the plan proposed to increase, between 1995 and 2000, the number of public child care centers for children under the age of two from 470,000 to 600,000 and the number of multifunctional day care centers from 200 to 1,500. The number of temporary child care programs for mothers who work part-time or need child care on an emergency basis would also be increased from 600 to 3,000; the number of extended-hour services from 2,530 to 7,000; local child rearing support centers for full-time stay-at-home mothers with preschool-age children from 354 to 3,000; and finally, the number of after-school programs from 5,220 to 9,000, all within the same time frame (Ministry of Health and Welfare 1994). More recently the government reset these numbers in its effort to further extend child care services. In 1999 the government introduced the New Angel Plan, which raised the numerical targets further, as shown in table 1.3.

In addition to expanding child care services, the government also increased eligibility for the child allowance from the previous age limit of three years to six and raised the income cut-off for this benefit so that an estimated 80 percent of families with small children will qualify. The New Angel Plan also locates itself firmly within the context of a comprehensive welfare state restructuring that sees pronatalism as a solution to the aging of the Japanese society. To that end, promoting well-functioning, self-supporting, and (re)productive families, as well as an active and deregulated labor market is considered paramount.

In concert with the expansion of child care services, the administrative processes related to public child care have also been reformed. The mandatory placement system (*sochi seido*), which involved total state control over the placement of children in public child care centers, was replaced by an individual contract system as of the spring of 1998. This has technically allowed parents to choose child care centers and services. The child care centers and services, too, have been deregulated, and the principle of market competition has been introduced in the new system. (For further discussion on the deregulation of child care services in Japan, see Peng 2000a.)

In addition to direct services and financial incentives for families with small children, a number of new employment laws have been implemented since 1994 to assist working mothers. The parental leave law introduced in 1994 allowed parents to take up to one year of unpaid child care leave with job guarantee. In 1998, an income replacement of 25 percent of the salary and coverage for the cost of social in-

TABLE 1.3: THE NEW ANGEL PLAN

TARGET ACTIVITIES/SERVICES	1999	2004 TARGET
No. of spaces for children from birth to two years of age	580,000	680,000
No. of extended hour child care centers	7,000	10,000
No. of child care centers operating during weekends and holidays	100	300
No. of temporary child care centers	In 450 local communities	In 500 local communities
Multifunctional child care centers	1,600	2,000
Child care support centers for stay-at-home mothers	1,500	3,000
Temporary child care support for stay-at-home mothers	1,500	3,000
After-school programs for elementary school age children	9,000	11,500
Treatment and counseling centers for infertile couples	24	47

SOURCE: Ministry of Health and Welfare (1999).

surance was added to this legislation to encourage takeup; in the spring of 2000, the income replacement was increased to 40 percent of the salary. A family care leave was also added in 1996, allowing workers to take up to four months to care for family members. All of these measures reflect the state's effort to encourage childbirth. It is worth pointing out here that the new family policy reform in Japan as illustrated by the Angel Plan and the New Angel Plan is highly reminiscent of the pronatalist policy of early twentieth-century France (Jenson 1986). Here, as in France, the state has accepted the fact of women's employment and is thus seeking to use child care as an incentive to women workers to also bear children.

Toward a New Discourse in Gender and Welfare State Restructuring in Japan

As can be seen from the most recent family and child care policy reform, the issue of changing gender relations is now at the center of the welfare state restructuring in Japan. The new policies seem to indicate a departure from the earlier path. Does this mean that the Japanese welfare state's thinking about gender relations and its own relationship with women has shifted fundamentally?

In pursuing work and family reconciliation policies, the Japanese state seems fully aware that the existing system of gender relations is not sustainable in the long run. For example, the Basic Law Pertaining to the Low Birth Rate (Shoshika Shakai Taisaku Kihon Ho), introduced in 1999, clearly identified the existing corporate-centered welfare system as the main cause of the weakening of the family and community and, ultimately, of the decline in fertility in Japan. The 1999 Ministry of Health and Welfare's white paper stated,

> The Japanese-style employment system's control over male workers who form the main labor power has not only denied men the time and psychological space to participate in the family and community activities, but also, as a result, forced women to take on an undue burden of child care and childrearing, which furthermore has led to the decline of community activities. . . . Moreover, because the Japanese employment system assumes that men will fully devote themselves to their work and will be free of any family and child care responsibilities, and because the system has been supported by the gender division of labor, it has made the harmonization of work and family responsibilities extremely burdensome and difficult for women.
>
> Finally, because Japanese employment is customarily a male-centered system, it has made women's long-term employment difficult. Once a woman leaves her job for child care reasons, the reentry into the labor market is difficult, and even if she returns, working conditions are worse than before. Given that marriage and childbirth often lead to a decline in income, not only because of forced retirement but also because of a decline in working conditions and pay after the return, it is reasonable to think that this has been a fac-

tor behind the decrease in the marriage rate (Ministry of Health and Welfare 1999, 176).

The statement clearly shows a very different kind of gender analysis from that offered in earlier periods, when the gender division of labor went unquestioned and the disintegration of the family and community was explained by external forces such as industrialization and urbanization. Hence, until now the government's policy responses were often aimed at preventing the family and community from fragmenting by reinforcing "traditional" gender roles. The new perspective, however, identifies traditional gender relations as the main factor undermining the family and community, and seeks to reform the corporate-centered employment system in order to make it more gender sensitive and family friendly.

However, while the state's new gender analysis represents progress, the actual policy responses have been disappointing. First, while the policies focus mainly on providing care services for children and the elderly and allowing care leaves as a means of reducing a woman's double burden, they leave virtually untouched another important part of this issue—namely, the promotion of gender equality. To be precise, while the effort to expand public child care to enable working mothers to harmonize work and family responsibilities has been significant, very little attention has been paid to problems such as women's unequal and vulnerable positions within the labor market and the lack of women's representation in almost every sector of the society except for voluntary activities. Although in 1996 the prime minister's office initiated policymaking for a gender-equal society (Danjo Byodo Shakai Sankaku) by establishing an advisory committee on gender issues, the committee's status has been limited to an advisory one. Moreover, not only is most of the public unaware of this project, but very few corrective measures have actually filtered into public policy. For example, much-needed employment legislation like discrimination and sexual harassment laws have yet to be introduced. The Japanese government only publicly began to recognize the problem of sexual harassment in the workplace as of 1999, but many of the measures introduced to deal with it have been limited to public education and setting up rudimentary mechanisms such as counseling and support services for women to report and discuss infringements. No specific measures have been introduced to actually stop harassment or discrimination in the workplace. Women's representation in politics and government is also extremely low.

With so little attention to advancing gender equality, there has been little substantial change. While child care services have been expanded, women's overall fertility rate continues to decline: in 1999 it sank to 1.38. This underscores the fact that despite the existence of child care services and parental leave, women continue to feel insecure about their work and are unable to harmonize the demands of their work and family life.

Second, despite the extension of social care and policy support for family and work harmonization, the lack of enforcement power attached to new legislation has undermined the public confidence in policy reforms. This is most apparent in the low number of people taking parental leave. According to the government's own survey in 1996, only about 60 percent of employers had actually implemented parental leave programs. Among eligible women workers employed at firms that offered parental leave programs, only 44.5 percent had actually taken leave, while for men that rate was merely 0.16 percent (Ministry of Labor 1998). Such data underscore the huge gap between stated policy objectives and actual outcomes. Part of the reason for this is the state's reluctance to enforce the policy. As in the case of the Equal Opportunity Law of 1986, the government has consistently refused to introduce penalties for employers who fail to comply with the legislation. However, under public pressure, it has recently announced that it will publish the names of noncompliant employers in the hope of shaming them into compliance.

Given the lack of policy enforcement, women workers continue to feel unable to take advantage of their legal right to leave. Surveys show that the two main reasons for the low rate in leave taking are (1) job insecurity (i.e., fear that taking leave will cause personal frictions at the workplace, making it hard to return after the leave) at 48.0 percent; and (2) financial insecurity (i.e., a 25 or even 40 percent salary guarantee is not enough of an economic incentive for either the mother or the father to take the leave) at 24.6 percent (Ministry of Health and Welfare 1999). In summary, any advance made by extending social care has been effectively canceled by the lack of progress in creating an equal and harassment-free working environment for women.

What, then, is the problem with the new family and child care policies in Japan, and what needs to be done? The main problem is that despite its critique of the corporate-centered welfare system, the state is not fully committed to changing the existing gender structure. Indeed, fundamentally, the Japanese state's perception of "the problem of gender inequality" is that it affects low fertility and thus the aging of society—not that gender inequality is a problem in itself. The extension of social care is therefore aimed at addressing the inordinate burden of family and child care placed on women under the existing system of gender relations, not necessarily at changing its basic structure. For working mothers, the huge burden of having to work as well as care for children can be relieved by greater access to child care. However, the current phase of welfare state restructuring is unlikely to change the policy expectation that women will continue to serve as the primary caregivers at home. It is therefore unlikely that expansion of the public child care and family support systems will lead to a fundamental restructuring of the corporate-centered welfare regime. Rather, given the corporate sector's unwillingness to provide child care and change employment practices, the new policies may even serve to encourage employers, since public child care will relieve them of their own responsibility for providing services without really changing the work environment.

The real problem, however, is that the state's motivation for expanding public child care is fundamentally misguided. Using child care as a pronatalist tool has a limited effect at a time when the main reason for a decline in the fertility rate is a lack of gender equality. Unfortunately, the current policy responses suggest that while the state recognizes the inherent problems related to existing gender relations, it is not yet ready to take on the issue of gender equality. However, the fact that the Japanese welfare state has had to seek some form of accommodation with regard to work and family reconciliation has brought to light the fact that current gender relations are seriously strained and in great need of correction.

Instead of making such changes single-handedly, what the state must do now is undertake a social dialogue—a serious negotiation—with the public (both men and women) on creating a new system of gender relations. As Japan's welfare state restructuring continues to pivot around the issues of the low birth rate and an aging society, the national fertility rate continues to drop. In 2000, policymakers were bracing themselves as the report of the further decline in fertility rate was announced. This should be seen as a sign that unless the state becomes more committed to restructuring gender relations and engages with the public in social dialogue to find solutions, the national birth rate is not likely to bounce back.

Notes

I would like to thank Pat Boling and Sonya Michel for comments on earlier drafts of this chapter.

1. This theoretical assumption has been variously explained. Jones (1995), for example, explains it in terms of the Confucian tradition shared by many of the East Asian countries, while others have sought to answer it in terms of the historical legacy of Japan's preindustrial political administration (Peng 1995). It is, however, important to point out that family centeredness is not entirely unique to Japan nor to East Asia. A notion of subsidiarity characterizes welfare regimes of the Netherlands and Mediterranean Catholic welfare states like Spain and Italy, which also share a similar idea about the role and responsibilities of the family in providing social welfare.

2. The proportion of people over the age of sixty-five receiving care services at home in Japan is also very low. Less than 1 percent of elderly people were in receipt of community care in Japan in 1996, as compared to 17 percent in Sweden and Denmark, 13 percent in the Netherlands, 8 percent in the United Kingdom, and about 8 percent in the United States.

3. Currently the parental contributions are divided into ten ranks, ranging from no cost for those with incomes equivalent to the public assistance level to full cost (i.e., no subsidy) for those in the highest income bracket. For these families the cost may come close to ¥100,000 per month (about U.S.$900 per month if calculated as 110 yen = 1 dollar) per child, depending on the age of the child. (It should be noted, however, that even for families in the highest income bracket there is a subsidy for the second child and subsequent children). Not surprisingly, this system is very important for families in the lower-income brackets, particularly single-mother families, whose average income is about 34 percent of that of two-parent families with dependent children (Ministry of Health and Welfare, 1996). However, as the total household income approaches the national average, the cost effective-

ness of certified child care becomes more dependent on the actual income of the second wage earner, who is, in most cases, the mother.

4. In Japan, public child care centers come in two forms: those run directly by the state and those that are contracted out by the state but run by private registered social welfare organizations (called *shakai fukushi hojin*). Both types must conform to the regulations set by the Ministry of Health and Welfare, which cover such items as the child-to-worker ratio, minimum space allocation per child, qualifications of the child care workers, etc. These centers—until 1998, when the reform was fully implemented—could only accept children who were sent there from the local government, and were paid by the local government according to the number of children in their care. In essence, both types of public child care centers function very much like state agencies, regardless of whether they are privately or publicly run.

5. There are different interpretations of family and child care policy developments. For example, Shimoebisu (1994) divides postwar child care policy into three developmental periods: (1) from 1947 to the end of the 1950s—the postwar economic recovery period; (2) from 1960 to the beginning of the 1970s—the rapid economic growth period; and (3) from the beginning of the 1970s to the end of the 1980s—the stable economic growth period. Sugimoto (1998) divides the trajectory of postwar family policy in Japan into (1) the high economic growth period (the 1960s to the beginning of the 1970s); (2) the emergence of the Japanese-style welfare society period (from the mid-1970s to the mid-1980s); (3) the emergence of the new Japanese-style welfare society period (mid-1980s to the mid-1990s); and (4) the women's independent living period (from the mid-1990s to the present). Finally, Shobi (1986) considers the postwar Japanese family and child care policies in terms of (1) the policy review period (mid-1970s to 1980); (2) the Japanese-style welfare society period (1980 to 1988); and (3) the new policy development period (from 1989 onward).

6. However, in retrospect, the inclusion of child care legislation within the Child Welfare Law has often resulted in very strict bureaucratic interpretations of child care. For more on this, see Peng (2000a).

7. As Garon (1997) points out, most of the women's groups established during this time were in fact remakes of earlier interwar era women's groups which had actively collaborated with the military government in the war effort.

8. Nonprofit social welfare organizations in Japan, the *shakai fukushi hojin*, are largely publicly certified private and often family-owned businesses—not to be equated with nonprofit organizations in the Western sense. These are nonprofit largely for tax reasons rather than because of their philanthropic orientation.

9. This group was renamed the National Council of Widows and Lone Mothers (Zenkoku Boshi Kafu Kyogikai) in the 1970s.

10. In the meantime, the Democratic Child Care Federation was forced to disband in 1952, partly as a result of the government crackdown on radical labor union activities, and partly due to sectarian divisions among its memberships (Minshu Hoiku Renmei News 1952). Two years after the dissolution of the federation, however, a new group called the Working Mothers' Committee (Hataraku Haha no Kai), organized by female professors and staff at the University of Tokyo, took on the mission of campaigning for public child care

(Hataraku Haha no Kai 1954). What is interesting about this committee is that it not only lobbied for public child care but also organized parents' cooperative child care and functioned as a support group for working mothers. Throughout the 1950s and '60s the Working Mothers' Committee lobbied for the rights of mothers to work by demanding reforms in child care and employment policies. The committee gradually broadened its membership by calling on all working mothers to unite in the common cause. After the 1960s the combination of the Working Mothers' Committee, the NCWWO, and the NOWCAV became an important political force behind the public child care movement in Japan.

11. According to the national survey, the total number of lone-mother families rose from 694,700 in 1952 to 1,029,000 in 1961, mainly as the result of death of husbands due to industrial and traffic accidents. In addition, the divorce rate was also beginning to rise; for example, the proportion of divorced, lone-mother families rose from 7.5 percent in 1952 to 16.8 percent in 1961, and finally to 26.4 percent in 1970 (Peng 1995).

12. Between 1985 and 1990, the proportion of lone-mother families receiving general welfare was cut by nearly a half, from 21.7 percent to 13.2 percent.

13. It should be pointed out here that, while the state (local governments) has been functioning as the gatekeeper for certified child care, the mismatch in the actual child care spaces and the number of children registered is not evenly spread across the country. In reality, in the large cities there are huge waiting lists, while in some rural areas certified child care centers are not able to get enough children because of the decline in the proportion of young families. For example, in 1998, the enrollment rate for child care centers across the country was about 88 percent, but there were about 40,000 children on the waiting list across the country. The breakdown of the waiting lists shows that unmet need is greatest for children under one, of whom approximately 11 percent were unable to get into certified child care. The figure varies from as low as 0 percent in rural areas such as Niigata, Kanazawa, Miyazaki, and Fukuyama cities to over 50 percent in Okinawa, Tokyo's Adachi ward, Musashino and Kohira cities, and Sakai city in Osaka (Hoikujoho 1998; 1999).

14. This year was notorious as the year of the fire-breathing horse (*hinoe uma*); it is believed that girls born in such a year will shorten the lives of their husbands. Such a year occurs only rarely; in the twentieth century it came only once—in 1966. Needless to say, the birthrate dropped from 2.14 to 1.58 in that one year.

References

Atoh, Makoto, Shigesato Takahashi, Eiko Nakano, Yoshikazu Watanabe, Hiroshi Kojima, Ryuichi Kaneko, and Fusami Mita. 1994. "Dokushin Seinenso no Kekkonkan to Kodomokan" (Attitudes toward Marriage and Fertility among Unmarried Japanese Youth). *Jinko Mondai Kenkyu* (Journal of Population Problems) 50, no. 1: 29–49.

Central Council of Social Welfare. 1971. *Community Keisei to Shakaifukushi* (Community Development and Social Welfare). Tokyo: CCSW.

Economic Council. 1960. *Kokumin Shotoku Baizo Keikaku* (National Income Doubling Plan). Tokyo: Economic Council.

_____. 1963. *Keizai Hatten ni Okeru Jinteki Noryokuhatten no Kadai to Taio* (Issues and Measures on Human Resource Development in Relation to Economic Development). Tokyo: Economic Council.

Economic Planning Agency. 1970. *Shin-Keizai Shakai Hatten Keikaku* (New Economic and Social Development Plan). Tokyo: EPC.

Esping-Andersen, Gøsta. 1997. "Hybrid or Unique? The Distinctiveness of the Japanese Welfare State." *Journal of European Social Policy* 7, no. 3: 179–89.

Garon, Sheldon. 1997. *Molding Japanese Minds: The State in Everyday Life*. Princeton, N.J.: Princeton University Press.

Goodman, Roger, and Ito Peng. 1996. "East Asian Social Welfare States." In *Welfare States in Transition,* ed. Gøsta Esping-Andersen. London: Sage.

Hataraku Haha no Kai. 1954. *Hataraku Haha no Kai no Kai Shuisho Heikaisoku* (Prospectus and Regulations of the Working Mothers' Committee). In *Nihon Fujin Mondai Shiryo Shusetu* (Collected Sources on Japanese Women's Issues) vol. 6, ed. Yasuko Ichibangase. Tokyo: Domesu.

Hoikujoho. 1998. "1998-nen 4-gatsu 1-nichi Genzai no Taikijisu Akiraka ni" (The Children on the Child Care Waiting List as of April 1, 1998). *Hoikujoho* 261, November: 20–22.

_____. 1999. "Joho Fairu" (Information File). *Hoikujoho* (Child Care Information) 265, March.

Hoshino, Shinya. 1995. "Fukushikokka Churyu Kaisoka ni Torinokosareta Shakaifukushi: Zenkoku Shohi Jittai Chosa no Deta Bunseki (I)" (The Forgotten Social Welfare in a Middle-Class Centered Welfare State: An Analysis of the National Household Consumption Survey I). *Jinbungaku Ho* 261.

Institute of Population Problems. 1993. *Nihonjin no Kekkon to Shussan* (Marriage and Fertility in Contemporary Japan), Survey Series no.7.

_____. 1996. *Latest Demographic Statistics*. Tokyo: Institute of Population Problems, Ministry of Health and Welfare, 1996.

Jenson, Jane. 1986. "Gender and Reproduction, or, Babies and the State." *Studies in Political Economy* 20: 9–46.

Jidofukushiho Kenkyukai. 1978. *Jidofukushiho Setsuritsu Shiryoshusetu* (Compiled Resources on Development of the Child Welfare Law), vols. 1 and 2. Tokyo: Domesu.

Jones, Catherine Finer. 1995. Personal communication with author.

Kaneko, Ryuichi. 1994. "Mikon Jinko ni okeru Kekkon no Jukyuyoin no Doko" (Trends in Demand and Supply Factors Regarding Marriage in the Never-Married Japanese Population). *Jinko Mondai Kenkyu* (The Journal of Population Problems) 50, no. 2: 1–24.

Kashiwame, Reihou. 1997. *Jido Fukushi Kaikaku to Jicchitaisei* (Child Welfare Reform and Its System of Implementation). Tokyo: Minerva.

Kimoto, Kimiko. 1997. "Shakai Fukushi to Gender" (Social Welfare and Gender). Paper presented at Gender Kenkyukai, Hokkaido University, February.

Korekara. 1990. "Korekara no Kazoku to Kosodate ni Kansuru Kondaikai Hokokusho" (Report of the Discussion Group on the Future of the Family and Childrearing). In *Heisei Gan'nen Kosei Hakusho: Chomyo Shakai ni Okeru Kodomo, Katei, Chiiki* (The White Paper on

Health and Welfare for the 1989 Budget Year: Child, Family, and Community within the Context of the Aging Society), ed. Ministry of Health and Welfare. Tokyo: MHW.

Liberal Democratic Party. 1979. *Kateikiban no Jujitsu ni Kansuru Taisaku Yoko* (Policy Outline to Establish the Foundation of the Family). Liberal Democratic Party, Management Research Committee, Subcommittee to Establish the Foundation of the Family.

Ministry of Finance. 1997. *Kokumin Seikatsu Hakusho* (White Paper on National Life). Tokyo: MOF.

Ministry of Health and Welfare. 1963. *Jidofukushi Hakusho* (White Paper on Child Welfare). Tokyo: MHW.

_____. 1978 *Kosei Hakusho* (White Paper on Health and Welfare). Tokyo: MHW.

_____. 1994. *21 seiki Fukushi Bijon* (21st-Century Welfare Vision). Tokyo: MHW.

_____. 1996. *Boshi Katei Chosa* (Survey of Lone-Mother Families). Tokyo: MHW.

_____. 1998. *Heisei 9-nendo Kosei Hakusho* (1997 White Paper on Health and Welfare). Tokyo: MHW.

_____. 1999. *Heisei 10-nendo Kosei Hakusho* (1998 White Paper on Health and Welfare). Tokyo: MHW.

_____. 2000. *Heisei 11-nendo Kosei Hakusho* (1999 White Paper on Health and Welfare). Tokyo: MHW.

Ministry of Labor. 1998. *Hataraku Josei no Jitsujo* (The Condition of Working Women). Tokyo: 21-seiki Shokugyo Zaidan.

Minshu Hoiku Renmei. 1946. "Minshu Hoiku Renmei no Shuisho, Kiyaku, Koryo" (Prospectus, Rules and Charter of Minshu Hoiku Renmei). In *Nihon Fujin Mondai Shiryo Shusetu* (Collected Sources on Women's Issues in Japan), ed. Yasuko Ichibangase. Tokyo: Domesu.

Minshu Hoiku Renmei News. 1947–1952. "Atarashii Hoikushisetsu no Ugoki" (Development of New Child Care Centers) . . . "Hataraku Hahaoya ni Nyuji Hoikusho wo" (Day Care Centers for the Small Infants of Working Mothers), nos. 4–21. In *Nihon Fujin*, ed. Yasuko Ichibangase. Tokyo: Domesu.

Miyamoto, Taro. 1997. "Hikaku Fukushikokka no Riron to Genjitsu" (Theory and Reality of Comparative Welfare States). In *Hikaku Fukushikokka Ron* (Theory of Comparative Welfare States), ed. Norio Okazawa and Taro Miyamoto. Tokyo: Hoken Bunka Sha.

Nakano, Eiko, and Yoshikazu Watanabe. 1994. "Mikon Danjo no Kekkonkan" (The Views of Marriage among Unmarried Youths in Contemporary Japan). *Jinko Mondai Kenkyu* (Journal of Population Problems) 50, no. 3: 18–32.

National Institute of Population and Social Security Research. 1997. *Nihon no Shorai Suikei Jinko, 1997, 1-gatsu suikei* (Estimated Future Population of Japan: The January 1997 Estimate.) Tokyo: NIPSSR.

Peng, Ito. 1995. "A Theoretical and Case Analysis of Japanese Lone Mothers and Their Relationship with the State, the Labor Market and the Family, with Reference to Britain and Canada." Ph.D. diss., London School of Economics, Department of Social Policy and Administration.

_____. 2000a. "A Recent Child Care Reform in Japan." In *Family Policy and Child Care,* ed. Thomas Boje and Arnlaug Leira. London: Routledge.

_____. 2000b. "A Fresh Look at the Japanese Welfare State." *Social Policy and Administration* 34, no. 1: 87–114.

Shakai, Hosho Kenkyujo, ed. 1975. *Nihon Shakai Hosho Shiryo* (Sources on Japanese Social Security), vol. 1. Tokyo: Shiseido.

Shimoebisu, Miyuki. 1994. "Kazokuseisaku no Rekishiteki Tenkai" (The Historical Development of the Family Policy). In *Gendai Kazoku to Shakai Hosho* (The Modern Family and Social Security), ed. Shakai Hosho Kenkyujo. Tokyo: University of Tokyo Press.

Shiota, Sakiko. 1992. "Gendai Feminizumu to Nihon no Shakaiseisaku: 1970–1990" (Modern Feminism and Japan's Social Policy). In *Joseigaku to Seiji Jissen* (Women's Studies and Political Practice), ed. Joseigaku Kenkyukai. Tokyo: Keiso Shobo.

Shobi, Yoko. 1986. "Wagakuni no 'Toshin' / 'Hakusho' ni miru Kazoku" (The Family as Perceived by the Government's Reports and White Papers). *Shakai Fukushi Kenkyu* 35: 44–50.

Sugimoto, Kiyoe. 1998. "Gender no Shiten kara mita Kazokuseisaku to Josei no Kenri" (Family Policies and Women's Rights from a Gender Perspective). *Shakai Fukushi Kenkyu* 70: 110–17.

Sukoyakani Kodomo wo Umisodateru Renraku Kaigi. 1992. *Sukoyakani Kodomo wo Umisodateru Kankyo Zukuri ni Kansuru Kankei Shocho Renraku Kaigi Hokokusho* (Report of the Interdepartmental Discussion Group to Develop a Supportive Environment for Childbirth and Childrearing). Tokyo: Ministry of Health and Welfare.

Yamataka, Shigeri. 1978. *Boshi Fukushi 40-nen* (Forty Years of Maternal and Child Welfare). Tokyo: Shobunsha.

CHAPTER 2

The Value of an Educational Emphasis:
Child Care and Restructuring in Spain since 1975

Celia Valiente

In many advanced industrial societies, child care provisions have fallen victim to the trend toward welfare state retrenchment that has occurred in the wake of recent global economic restructuring. This is not, however, true in Spain, where child care, in contradistinction to other forms of welfare, has increased steadily since the fall of the regime of Francisco Franco in 1975. How can this be explained? Rationales for child care policy usually fall into one of several categories: economic or labor market, poverty reduction, gender equality, or education. In post-authoritarian Spain, the educational rationale has prevailed, generally meeting with great success.

Conditions for deploying the other likely rationales have been less than favorable. For example, child care provisions have often been expanded during periods of labor shortage in order to facilitate the employment of married women with children, the most important available reserve of labor.[1] In Spain, however, there have been no such labor-force shortages for the past three decades. Indeed, since 1982, the unemployment rate has hovered above 15 percent, and it is unlikely that labor shortages will develop in the foreseeable future. At the same time, the political and social actors who after 1975 might have defined child care measures as programs that benefit working mothers—namely, the feminist movement, state feminists,[2] and the women's departments of trade unions—have in practice not consistently advanced this definition.

Instead, policymakers have relied primarily on the educational rationale, focusing on measures explicitly intended to benefit children. In this mode, they have chiefly extended programs that were in place before 1975—that is, educational services. As a corollary to the educational rationale, they have also deployed an antipoverty argument, claiming that preschool programs have the potential to diminish cultural differences among children from varying socioeconomic backgrounds. While these combined rationales have succeeded in expanding the supply of places in free public preschools, the very definition of these institutions as schools rather than child care centers has limited their utility for working parents. Nevertheless, in an era when most advanced industrial societies—including Spain—have witnessed dramatic cutbacks in all types of social services, Spanish preschool programs have not only held on but even grown.

This chapter seeks to explain this seemingly paradoxical set of developments, first by presenting the analytical framework used in my research; second, by describing child care policies in post-authoritarian Spain; and third, by examining the role of the main social and political actors in the area of child care policy.

Analytical Framework

In the recent debate on the potential crisis of the welfare state in postindustrial countries, some authors have argued that demands for retrenchment have been elaborated due to economic globalization, the slowdown in the increase of productivity and economic growth produced by the transition to a service economy, the rise of conservative parties, aging populations, and increasing costs of mature welfare states. Nevertheless, they have found that in many societies retrenchment has been difficult to carry out, in part because cuts in social policy are politically unpopular and therefore risky undertakings. Certain welfare state recipients (for instance, beneficiaries of old-age pensions and welfare-state employees) have organized to preserve social policy (Garrett 1998; Pierson 1996, 1998). In keeping with such findings, these scholars tend to identify patterns of resilience in social policy rather than of retrenchment.

Other analysts, in contrast, have argued that retrenchment has indeed occurred since the oil crisis of the 1970s in countries of the Organization for Economic Cooperation and Development (OECD), within a context of rising socioeconomic inequality (Clayton and Pontusson 1998). Generally speaking, moderate rollbacks in entitlements have been advanced, especially in the 1980s and 1990s, by left-wing and conservative parties. Nevertheless, in most (but not all) cases, the main institutional configuration of the different types of welfare states has remained in place (Stephens, Huber, and Ray 1999).

Feminist scholarship (Langan and Ostner 1991; Lewis 1992; O'Connor, Orloff and Shaver 1999; Orloff 1993, 1996; and Sainsbury 1996, among others) has argued that in all countries, women and men are differently affected by the welfare state. Historically, for instance, adult men have had access to the welfare state mainly via labor market participation, while adult women have also acquired rights to benefits through marriage, or more broadly speaking, family ties (Lewis 1992, 161; Orloff 1993, 308). Feminist scholars have emphasized the importance of some social programs for women's autonomy and their capacity to participate in equal terms in the labor market and in the community in general. In all societies, women are those who overwhelmingly provide care for people who, for any reason, need the care of others, such as the frail elderly, the disabled, the ill, or small children (Orloff 1993, 313). Therefore, some programs, such as child care, are especially important for women. These programs thus merit close attention, even if expenditure on care measures is smaller than on other types of policies, such as old-age pensions.

Child care policies provide a useful case for studying the impact and rationales for welfare state retrenchment. According to Gøsta Esping-Andersen's typology of welfare states in industrial capitalist countries,[3] that of Spain (and Italy, France, and the former West Germany, among others) is of a continental type.[4] Although benefit provision is mainly public, the welfare state aims at reinforcing the traditionally crucial role of the family as welfare provider. Thus, the state tends to intervene only when the capacity of the family to act as social provider is exhausted (Esping-Andersen 1990, 27–28, 48).[5]

In Spain, as in any other continental welfare state, participation in the labor market is the main route of access to welfare state benefits, since, generally speaking, most of these have been historically given to workers (and their dependents) who have made the required contributions to the system (Guillén 1992, 12; 1996). The two main exceptions to this general rule are health care and compulsory education (for children six to sixteen years old), which are programs of universal coverage.

By the same token, because the Spanish welfare state (like others of the continental type) is heavily transfer-oriented and offers very few social services,[6] it does little to facilitate female labor-force participation. In the early 1990s, approximately one-tenth of the expenditures of continental welfare states was dedicated to social services (health care excluded), while for social democratic welfare states, the figure was one-third.[7] Nevertheless, the continental welfare state is more resistant to cuts, because it is "the most consensual of all modern welfare states" (Esping-Andersen 1995, 1–2). Since most of its programs are contributory, these generate a sense of entitlement in many citizens/voters. Moreover, welfare programs have been advanced as part of breadwinners' salaries in the labor markets of these countries, on the assumption that these would support whole families, not only individual recipients.

Central State Child Care Policies in Spain

Since 1975, the main form of central state child care (for children under six, when mandatory schooling starts) has been the supply of free educational preschool programs for children aged three or over, administered chiefly by the Ministry of Education and Culture (Ministerio de Educación y Cultura, or MEC).[8] In the academic year 1996–1997, the proportions of children attending public preschool programs were 70 percent for those aged four and five, and 43 percent for three-year-olds. Since the private sector also provides preschool places, school attendance rates for three-, four-, and five-year-olds are comparatively high in Spain, at 67, 99, and 100 percent respectively. In contrast, the proportion of Spanish children aged two or under cared for in public centers is one of the lowest in the European Union (EU): only 2.5 percent. The proportion of children aged two or under cared for in private centers is also very small: 3.5 percent (Ministerio de Educación y Cultura 1999, 79, 132–34; my calculations).[9]

The absolute number and proportion of children who attend preschool programs in public centers has been on the increase since 1975. While such programs enrolled 347,026 children under six in the academic year 1975–1976, by 1996–1997 this figure had more than doubled, to 754,196 children. Seen from another perspective, in 1975–1976, more than one-third (38 percent) of children enrolled in preschool education attended public centers, and by 1996–1997, this proportion exceeed two-thirds (68 percent) (Instituto Nacional de Estadística 1977, 101; 1981, 12; and Ministerio de Educación y Cultura 1999, 53; my calculations). As the number of places in public child care centers has increased, that in private centers has fallen. In 1975–1976, 573,310 children were enrolled in private centers, while in 1996–1997, this figure had fallen to 361,948 (Instituto Nacional de Estadística 1977, 101–03; 1981, 12; and Ministerio de Educación y Cultura 1999, 53; my calculations).

Public preschool programs cannot be used by parents (or mothers) as perfect substitutes for child care, since preschool hours are shorter than working hours (and sometimes much shorter and interrupted by a break). Preschool holidays are also much longer than working holidays. For instance, preschool summer holidays last approximately three months, while paid summer holidays for workers last only one month. It is important to note that even if the percentage of women in employment is lower in Spain than in most EU member states, most Spanish women who work for wages have full-time jobs. In 1998, the Spanish female employment rate (35 percent) was the lowest in the EU, and much lower than the EU average (51 percent), but 83 percent of Spanish women workers were employed full-time. This figure (together with those of Portugal and Finland) was the third highest in the EU, after those of Greece (89 percent) and Italy (86 percent), and sixteen points above the EU average of 67 percent (Franco 1999, 8–9).

Other child care policies (state regulation of public centers, tax exemptions for child care expenses, and state scholarships for pupils in private centers) are much less important than the supply of preschool places in public centers. Regarding the regulation of private centers, in 1990, the state decreed that the minimum conditions required of public preschool centers (for instance, in terms of space per child or the number of children per care provider) would also apply to the private sector.[10] Nevertheless, private centers opened before 1990 were given until 2002 to conform to this regulation. In contrast to other countries, paid care provided for children under six in private homes (by baby-sitters, child minders, etc.) is not regulated by the Spanish state; there are no regulations regarding, for instance, the qualifications of care providers, the maximum number of children who can be cared for by one adult, or the characteristics of the home where care is provided.

With respect to tax relief, between 1991 and 1998, those who paid personal income tax could benefit from a deduction for child care expenses (for those under three) of a maximum of 25,000 pesetas per year (around U.S. $150) or the equivalent of 15 percent of child care expenses. There was a ceiling on the taxpayer's income, and both parents had to work outside the home. In fiscal year 1997 (corresponding to income generated in 1996), 116,371 taxpayers took advantage of this benefit, with an average deduction of 12,073 pesetas (approximately U.S. $70)

(Ministerio de Economía y Hacienda 1997, 119; data from the whole of Spain except the Basque country and Navarre). This form of tax relief was increased in 1998 but disappeared in 1999, as the result of a comprehensive reform of the personal income tax code.

Finally, with regard to state scholarships to attend private centers, the MEC has given grants to some families whose three- to six-year-old children attend private preschool programs. In academic year 1997–1998, 42,479 children received these scholarships, at an average amount of 54,729 pesetas (approximately U.S.$300; Consejo Escolar del Estado 1999, 34; my calculations).

Besides the pronounced expansion of the supply of public preschool programs, the other most important change in the area of child care policy has been territorial decentralization. Under Franco, the state was highly centralized, but during the transition to democracy, a broad process of devolution of powers from the central state to the regions (not so much to localities) was set in motion. Since the early 1980s, some regional governments have been acquiring responsibilities previously assigned to the central state (for instance, education). The process of devolution of full responsibilities on education to all regions was completed in the year 2000.[11]

Finally, it should be noted, the expansion of public preschools in Spain has occurred within a context of continuously declining fertility rates: the synthetic index of fertility decreased steadily from 2.79 in 1975 to 1.15 in 1998 (the 1998 data are provisional; European Commission 1999, 102). The decrease in fertility rates has meant that it was easier to provide a public preschool place for a higher proportion of children younger than six, but these school services were not used as pronatalist devices. As I have argued elsewhere (Valiente 1995), there have been no (explicit or implicit) pronatalist policies in postauthoritarian Spain. This can be explained in terms of the determined rejection of the type of family measures established during Franco's dictatorship. Population increase was one of the chief aims of this regime, and long after 1975, political and social actors have remembered the family programs that were so salient in Francoist official discourses and propaganda. Since then, any pronatalist policy has been associated with Francoist symbols and measures, and has thus been avoided.

Social and Political Actors in the Policy Area of Child Care

Since 1975, then, the pattern in Spain with regard to child care has been one of neither retrenchment nor resilience but of substantial expansion of the supply of public preschool programs—the main child care policy. This trend runs contrary to the predictions of the literature on welfare state restructuring, which foresees either retrenchment or resilience (but not at all a pronounced expansion) of social policy, including child care, in the last three decades. Why, then, is Spain an exception in this area? In order to answer this question, it is useful to study the role played by social and political actors with regard to child care.

As the foregoing description suggests, within the central state, child care falls under the rubric of education policy. This assignment has been confirmed by policy-makers from all the political parties that have come to power in postauthoritarian Spain. The main unit of the central state overseeing educational policy is the MEC. As such, the MEC has been chiefly responsible for defining the "problem" of child care for those under six years of age in Spain as one of a shortage of educational pro-grams. This MEC definition has, in turn, influenced the proposed "solution": expanding the number of preschool places for children over three in public cen-ters—that is, extending the type of services introduced before 1975.

In general, since 1975 there has been a continuous expansion of expenditures within the area of education, affecting all levels; the increase of public expenditure on education has been particularly marked (Bonal 1998; Calero and Bonal 1999; Uriel et al. 1997). In 1975, public expenditure on education amounted to 3.4 per-cent of the gross domestic product (Ministerio de Educación y Ciencia 1995, 124), while in 1997 the figure was 4.7 percent (OECD 2000, 15, 43). The increase in ex-penditure has been reflected in the growing number of children and youngsters of all ages enrolled in education. For instance, the proportion of children aged four-teen attending school rose from 72 percent in 1975 to 100 percent in 1996. The proportion of eighteen-year-olds who were enrolled grew from 31 percent in 1975 to 44 percent in 1996 (Instituto Nacional de Estadística 1977, 44; 1981, 12; and Ministerio de Educación y Cultura 1999, 64; my calculations).

In Spain, child care is not a part of the set of policies that welfare state re-searchers usually study—namely, pensions, health care, and social assistance. Re-strictive reforms (but also expansionary measures) have primarily affected income maintenance programs (pensions and unemployment benefits). Nevertheless, ac-cording to Guillén and Matsaganis (2000), "on balance, though the evolution of the Spanish welfare state underwent trends of expansion as well as of retrenchment during the last twenty years, the former were much more pronounced than the lat-ter." In contrast to some of the main welfare programs, expansionary measures have almost exclusively been undertaken in the area of child care policy.

While child care has been firmly lodged under the rubric of educational policy, it has not formed part of discussions of gender equality. Since 1975, gender equality policies have mainly been of three types. First, the 1978 constitution declares that female and male workers are equal before the law, a principle that has required cer-tain revisions in labor legislation. Second, measures to help parents combine their family and professional duties (principally paid maternity leave and nonpaid parental leave) have been expanded. Third, a few affirmative action schemes favor-ing women (chiefly, special training and preferential hiring) have been passed (Va-liente 1997, 147–53). In other countries some social and political actors (mainly feminists, state feminists, and feminist trade unionists) have advanced the demand for more extensive child care policies to help mothers reconcile professional and family obligations. In Spain, however, these actors have scarcely advanced this demand.

With regard to child care, Spain's major political parties have also remained relatively silent. The center-right Unión de Centro Democrático (UCD) governed Spain between 1977 and 1982. Absolutely nothing about child care was said in the UCD electoral program of 1977 (Unión de Centro Democrático 1977), but the 1979 program affirmed, in the section on education, that free preschool programs should cover all four- and five-year-old children (Unión de Centro Democrático 1979, 35). Although this objective was not fully achieved under UCD mandate, it is clear that already in 1979 child care programs were being defined as an extension of existing educational preschool activities.

The social democratic Partido Socialista Obrero Español (PSOE) held government positions from 1982 until 1996, was the main opposition party from 1977 until 1982, and has been again since 1996. The PSOE electoral programs and resolutions of federal congresses also contained a commitment to develop programs for those under six, again conceptualized as educational policies. Preschool programs are understood as tools to achieve a higher degree of class equality. According to this view, children from underprivileged social classes should be enrolled in public preschool programs, which would provide them with the educational skills necessary to succeed in elementary school. Preschool attendance would also diminish cultural differences among children from varying socioeconomic backgrounds. All these ideas reflect the PSOE leaders' opinion that the educational system should function as an efficient mechanism to reduce social inequalities (Partido Socialista Obrero Español 1979a: política sectorial 90, política municipal 8; 1981, 91, 277–79; 1982, 23–24; 1984, 66; 1986, 61, 63; 1988, 44; 1989, 29–30; 1990, 109; 1993, 29; 1996, 51–53). PSOE documents also contained some references to child care in the sections related to "gender equality," though these are far fewer than in the sections on "education" (Partido Socialista Obrero Español 1976, 19; 1979a: política sectorial 19–20; 1979b, 22; 1981, 233; 1982, 29; 1989, 66; 1990, 61, 109; 1993, 59; 1996, 66–67; 2000, 17).

The conservative party (under the names of Alianza Popular, Coalición Democrática, Coalición Popular, and Partido Popular [PP]), has been in power since 1996, and was the main opposition party from 1982 to 1996. The PP has also proposed extending the preschool programs already in place, understanding them as chiefly educational (Alianza Popular, 1977, 31; 1982, 104–5; Coalición Democrática 1979, 45; Coalición Popular 1986, 9; Partido Popular 1989,10; 1993, 56–58; 1996, 98–99; 2000, 29), and to a much lesser extent as gender equality measures and/or family policies (Coalición Democrática 1979, 37; Alianza Popular 1982, 135; Partido Popular 1989, 29; 1993, 81; 1996, 181–82, 187–89; 2000, 18, 58).

Policymakers in the Ministry of Education and Culture[12]

Policymakers from the MEC have conceptualized preschool experiences mainly as measures beneficial to children because, among other reasons, they promote sociability and develop learning abilities. In addition, MEC officials have maintained that such programs provide life-enhancing experiences to children from economically, socially, and culturally underprivileged families, partly compensating for the differences between these children and those who come from families from more privileged backgrounds (Boyd-Barrett 1995, 10; Ministerio de Educación y Ciencia 1989,104).

In order to reverse the past trend of unequal access to preschool educational services, MEC policymakers have been increasing the number of available places in public centers. In the 1970s and 1980s, educational services for those under six were mainly provided by the private sector. As a result, preschool education was restricted chiefly to families who could afford to pay the fees charged by private centers, and proportionally fewer families from more modest socioeconomic strata enrolled their children in these centers (Puelles 1986, 448–49; González-Anleo 1985,74; Medina 1976, 123; Muñoz-Repiso et al. 1992, 21–22).

The emphasis on the educational nature of services offered by public centers has led MEC officials (in cooperation with experts, teachers, and directors of centers) to devote considerable energy and resources to the development of the pedagogical techniques and materials used in centers (Puelles 1986, 315; Ministerio de Educación y Ciencia 1989, 41). In this respect, MEC policymakers have tried to distance themselves from the past, when (in their own view) public centers were either just places for children who could not be cared for by their working mothers during working hours (in Spanish derogatorily called "places for parking children"—*aparcamientos de niños*) or pseudo-elementary schools, with pedagogical techniques and materials appropriate for children aged six or older but not for younger children (Ministerio de Educación y Ciencia 1989, 89).

If preschool programs are defined as a service for pupils, one might ask: At what age should children start to attend education centers? In the past this was presumed to be around age six (Puelles 1986, 447–48), but three decades ago, it was lowered to four or five (Instituto de la Mujer 1990; Medina 1976, 115). At present, however, there is no consensus on the answer to this question, although numerous MEC officials have agreed that it should be at approximately age three. Significant sectors of the population concur with the views about the advantages of the preschool experiences described above and the age at which children should start attending preschool activities (Instituto de la Mujer 1990, 50–54; McNair 1984, 41–42). In practice, this consensus has important implications for child care provision, since it has resulted in the creation of numerous places in public centers for children aged three or older, but hardly any for those under three.

Finally, MEC officials have repeatedly emphasized that public centers are intended to provide children under six with educational services but not with care (Ministerio de Educación y Ciencia 1989, 103). MEC policymakers have implied that education and care are two completely different types of service. According to this discourse, those who work in public centers are teachers, an occupation requiring professional training. The staff of public centers is not composed of caregivers, a position for which professional skills are not required.

Feminist Advocates

I have argued elsewhere (Valiente 1995, 254–56) that, in contrast with those of other countries, Spanish feminist advocates (the feminist movement, state feminists, and the women's departments of the main trade unions) have advanced few rhetorical demands in the policy area of child care, primarily for two reasons. First, the right-wing authoritarian regime headed by Franco that governed Spain from the mid-1930s to 1975 actively opposed the advancement of women's rights and status. After 1975, the feminist movement had to pursue numerous objectives, including equality before the law and reproductive rights. In this situation, it was reasonable for feminists to concentrate on some demands and leave others—including child care—aside. Second, in paying considerably less attention to motherhood and child care than to other issues, Spanish feminists were rejecting, moreso than in other countries, a problematic past. After almost forty years of being literally bombarded by authoritarian policymaker's messages that mothering and caring are the most important tasks in women's lives, the last thing Spanish feminists wanted to do after 1975 was to pay much attention to those issues. At that point women's liberation was understood as an effort to broaden the definition of women's lives to include such concerns as waged work and control of the body. This definition carefully excluded motherhood and child care from the life of newly liberated female Spaniards.

Conclusion

This chapter has shown that the principal child care policy in Spain since 1975 has been a relatively ample supply of preschool services in public centers for children aged three to six. The extension of public child care programs has been reflected in a marked increase of the number of children who attend public preschool programs, paralleled by a continuous reduction of the number of children enrolled in private preschool programs. This trend represents a significant expansion of the existing programs in the of child care policy, rather than the cutbacks or the maintenance of the status quo predicted by the comparative literature on the welfare state retrenchment and resilience.

Spanish policymakers have framed preschool programs primarily as educational measures that benefit children, especially those coming from lower classes, not as measures to allow parents (especially mothers) to participate in the labor market. By contrast, demands for the establishment of child care alternatives which help women combine their professional and family responsibilities have not been advanced successfully by any social or policy actor, including feminists. To the extent that that last group has done so, it has been as part of an attempt to distance itself from the authoritarian past, where the official discourse continuously affirmed that motherhood was the principal duty of women toward the state and society.

In countries like Spain, where child care is part of the educational system, it is regarded as a special social policy rather than as one of the schemes to be included in the set of policies that welfare-state specialists usually study, such as income maintenance programs (pensions, unemployment benefits, etc.), the health system, or social assistance; for this reason it has been largely overlooked by these scholars. But it is also the case that the dynamics of child care policy have been different from those of other parts of the welfare state in Spain over the past three decades, and thus may require a different mode of explanation.

Notes

1. For Denmark, see Borchorst (2000, 9); for a qualification of this argument regarding Sweden, see Bergqvist and Nyberg (2000, 6–7).

2. Since the 1960s, institutions with the explicit purpose of promoting gender equality have been set up, developed, and sometimes even dismantled in most industrial countries. In social science literature such institutions have been called "state feminist" institutions or bureaucracies. The people who work in them are described as "femocrats" or "state feminists" (Stetson and Mazur 1995).

3. Esping-Andersen (1990, 3–4) analyzes the variation across welfare states along three dimensions: the type of social rights; the type of stratification that the welfare state produces; and the interrelation of the state, the market, and the family in the provision of welfare.

4. For a discussion on whether the Spanish welfare state is a continental welfare state or a Mediterranean welfare state see Esping-Andersen (1999, 74, 90); Ferrera (1996); Leibfried (1992); and Lessenich (1995).

5. Two other types of welfare states exist in the classification made by Esping-Andersen (1990, 27–28): the social democratic and the liberal welfare states. In the social democratic welfare state, which exists in Scandinavia, universal benefits are numerous. Decommodification is high. Social programs are directed to all social classes. The purpose of social policy is to attain equality. The state provides generous care services for children, the elderly, and other people in need of care.

In the liberal welfare state, which exists in the United States, Canada, and Australia, among others, "means-tested assistance, modest universal transfers, or modest social-insurance plans predominate. Benefits cater mainly to a clientele of low-income, usually working-class, state dependents." Decommodification is very low; the state encourages market provision of welfare.

6. For an analysis of the Spanish welfare state made with an analytical focus on gender, see Cousins (1995) and Guillén (1997).

7. If health care is excluded, social services include, among other things, "day care and youth services, care of the aged and disabled, home help services, and the like, but also employment-related services such as rehabilitation schemes and employment exchanges" (Esping-Andersen 1995, 2).

8. Before 1996 it was called the Ministry of Education and Science (Ministerio de Educación y Ciencia).

9. For preschool attendance rates in Spain and other EU and OECD member states see

Borchorst (2000, 2); European Commission (1998, 76); and Organization for Economic Cooperation and Development (2000, 135).

10. These minimum conditions were established in the Royal Decree 1,004 of June 14, 1991, and subsequent legislation.

11. As a result of the process of devolution, programs formulated by the MEC have affected a decreasing number of regions. Then, the data provided in this chapter on the 1990s (for example, the percentage of children younger than six who attended public preschool programs) are the result of public policies elaborated by the central state and regional governments with responsibility on education.

12. In order to analyze the role of policymakers of the Ministry of Education and Culture (MEC), I have used the following sources: the Act 1 of October 3 ,1990 (one of the main education acts of postauthoritarian Spain) and other pieces of legislation, published MEC documents (for instance, Ministerio de Educación y Ciencia 1989); the writings of MEC policymakers (for example, Marchesi 1990, 34–35 [Marchesi was a vice minister of education]); and in-depth interviews with three MEC senior civil servants.

References

Alianza Popular. 1977. ¿Qué es Alianza Popular? (What is the Alianza Popular?). Madrid: Alianza Popular.

_____. 1982. General Elections: electoral program.

Bergqvist, Christina, and Anita Nyberg. 2000. "Childcare and Welfare Restructuring in Sweden: From Universalism, Generosity and Egalitarianism to a Mean, Lean and Stratifying Welfare State?" Paper presented at the European Social Science History Conference, Amsterdam, April 12–15.

Bonal, Xavier. 1998. "La Política Educativa: Dimensiones de un Proceso de Transformación (1976–1996)" (Education Policy: Dimensions of a Process of Transformation 1976–1996). In Políticas Públicas en España: Contenidos, Redes de Actores y Niveles de Gobierno (Public Policies in Spain: Contents, Networks of Actors, and Territorial Levels of Government), ed. Ricard Gomà and Joan Subirats. Barcelona: Ariel.

Borchorst, Anette. 2000. "Danish Childcare Policy and Gender Equality." Paper presented at the European Social Science History Conference, Amsterdam, April 12–15.

Boyd-Barrett, Olivier. 1995. "Structural Change and Curriculum Reform in Democratic Spain." In Education Reform in Democratic Spain, ed. Olivier Boyd-Barrett and Pamela O'Malley. London: Routledge.

Calero, Jorge, and Xavier Bonal. 1999. Política Educativa y Gasto Público en Educación: Aspectos Teóricos y Una Aplicación al Caso Español (Education Policy and Public Expenditure on Education: Theoretical Aspects and Application to the Spanish Case). Barcelona: Pomares-Corredor.

Clayton, Richard, and Jonas Pontusson. 1998. "Welfare-State Retrenchment Revisited: Entitlement Cuts, Public Sector Restructuring and Inegalitarian Trends in Advanced Capitalist Societies." World Politics 51: 67–98.

Coalición Democrática. 1979. General Elections: electoral program.

Coalición Popular. 1986. General Elections: electoral program.

Consejo Escolar del Estado. 1999. *Informe sobre el Estado y Situación del Sistema Educativo, Curso 1997–98* (Report on the Situation of the Education System, Academic Year 1997–98). Madrid: Consejo Escolar del Estado.

Cousins, Christine. 1995. "Women and Social Policy in Spain: the Development of a Gendered Welfare Regime." *Journal of European Social Policy* 5, no. 3: 175–97.

Esping-Andersen, Gøsta. 1990. *The Three Worlds of Welfare Capitalism.* Princeton, N.J.: Princeton University.

_____. 1995. *Welfare States without Work: the Impasse of Labor Shedding and Familialism in Continental European Social Policy.* Centro de Estudios Avanzados en Ciencias Sociales, Instituto Juan March de Estudios e Investigaciones Estudio, Working Paper 71.

_____. 1999. Social Foundations of Postindustrial Economies. Oxford: Oxford University Press.

European Commission. 1998. *Social Portrait of Europe.* Luxembourg: Office for Official Publications of the European Communities.

_____. 1999. *Statistiques Démographiques: Données* (Demographic Statistics: Data) 1960–1999. Luxembourg: Office for Official Publications of the European Communities.

Ferrera, Maurizio. 1996. "The 'Southern Model' of Welfare in Social Europe." *Journal of European Social Policy* 6, no. 1: 17–37.

Franco, Ana. 1999. "Enquête sur les Forces de Travail: Principaux Résultats 1998" (Study of the Work Force: Principal Results 1998). *Statistiques en Bref: Population et Conditions Sociales* (Statistics in Brief: Population and Social Conditions) 11.

Garrett, Geoffrey. 1998. *Partisan Politics in the Global Economy.* New York: Cambridge University Press.

González-Anleo, Juan. 1985. *El Sistema Educativo Español* (The Spanish Education System). Madrid: Instituto de Estudios Económicos.

Guillén, Ana M. 1992. "Social Policy in Spain: From Dictatorship to Democracy (1939–1982)." In *Social Policy in a Changing Europe,* ed. Zsuzsa Ferge and Jan E. Kolberg. Frankfurt am Main and Boulder, Colo.: Campus Verlag and Westview Press.

_____. 1996. "Citizenship and Social Policy in Democratic Spain: The Reformulation of the Francoist Welfare State." *South European Society and Politics* 1, no. 2: 253–71.

_____. 1997. "Regímenes de Bienestar y Roles Familiares: Un Análisis del Caso Español" (Welfare Regimes and Family Roles: An Analysis of the Spanish Case). *Papers: Revista de Sociología* 53, 45–63.

Guillén, Ana M., and Manos Matsaganis. 2000. "Testing the 'Social Dumping' Hypothesis in Southern Europe: Welfare Policies in Spain and Greece during the Last Twenty Years." *Journal of European Social Policy* 10, no. 2: 120–45.

Instituto de la Mujer (Women's Institute) 1988. *Primer Plan para la Igualdad de Oportunidades para las Mujeres, 1988–1990* (First Equal Opportunities for Women Plan of Action 1988–1990). Madrid: Instituto de la Mujer.

_____. 1990. *El Reparto de Responsabilidades Familiares: Análisis de la Demanda Femenina y sus Expectativas sobre Las Redes de Cuidados de Hijos* (The Division of Family Responsibilities:

Analysis of the Female Demand for and Expectations of Child Care). Madrid: Instituto de la Mujer.

_____. 1993. *Segundo Plan para la Igualdad de Oportunidades para las Mujeres, 1993–1995* (Second Equal Opportunities for Women Plan of Action 1993–1995). Madrid: Instituto de la Mujer.

_____. 1997. *Tercer Plan para la Igualdad de Oportunidades para las Mujeres, 1997–2000* (Third Equal Opportunities for Women Plan of Action 1997–2000). Madrid: Instituto de la Mujer.

Instituto Nacional de Estadística (National Institute of Statistics) 1977. *Estadística de la Enseñanza en España: Curso 1975–76* (Statistics of Education in Spain: Academic Year 1975–76). Madrid: Instituto Nacional de Estadística.

_____. 1981. *Censo de Población,* tomo I, volumen I, *Resultados Nacionales, Características de la Población* (Population Census, ser. 1, vol. 1, National Results, Characteristics of the Population). Madrid: Instituto Nacional de Estadística.

Langan, Mary, and Ilona Ostner. 1991. "Gender and Welfare: Towards a Comparative Framework." In *Towards a European Welfare State?* ed. Graham Room. Bristol: School for Advanced Urban Studies, University of Bristol.

Leibfried, Stephan 1992. "Towards a European Welfare State? On Integrating Poverty Regimes into the European Community." In *Social Policy in a Changing Europe,* ed. Zsuzsa Ferge and Jan E. Kolberg. Frankfurt am Main and Boulder, Colo.: Campus Verlag and Westview Press.

Lessenich, Stephan 1995. *España y "Los Tres Mundos del Estado de Bienestar": Elementos para una Clasificación* (Spain and "The Three Worlds of Welfare Capitalism": Elements for a Classification). Universitat Pompeu Fabra Working Paper 95/9.

Lewis, Jane. 1992. "Gender and the Development of Welfare Regimes." *Journal of European Social Policy* 2, no. 3: 159–73.

Marchesi, Álvaro 1990. "La educación infantile" (Preschool Education). *Infancia y Sociedad* (Childhood and Society) 1: 33–40.

McNair, John M. 1984. *Education for a Changing Spain.* Manchester: Manchester University Press.

Medina, Aurora. 1976. "Problemática de la Educación Preescolar en España" (Problems of Preschool Education in Spain). *Revista de Educación* 247: 111–34.

Ministerio de Economia y Hacienda (Ministry of Economy and Treasury). 1997. *Memoria de la Administración Tributaria 1997* (Report on Tax Management 1997). Available online as of April 21, 2000 at http://www.meh.es/INSPGRAL/MT97/cap2.pdf.

Ministerio de Educación y Ciencia (Ministry of Education and Science). 1989. *Libro Blanco para la Reforma del Sistema Educativo* (White Paper on the Reform of the Education System). Madrid: Ministerio de Educación y Ciencia.

_____. 1995. *Estadística del Gasto Público en Educación: Presupuesto Inicial, Años 1985–1993* (Statistics on Public Expenditure on Education: Initial Budget, Years 1985–1993). Madrid: Ministerio de Educación y Ciencia.

Ministerio de Educación y Cultura (Ministry of Education and Culture). 1999. Estadística de la Enseñanza en España 1996/97: Resultados Detallados, Series e Indicadores (Statistics on Education in Spain 1996/97: Detailed Results, Series and Indicators). Madrid: Ministerio de Educación y Cultura.

Muñoz-Repiso, Mercedes, et al. 1992. *Las Desigualdades en la Educación en España* (Education Inequalities in Spain). Madrid: Ministerio de Educación y Ciencia.

O'Connor, Julia, Ann Shola Orloff, and Sheila Shaver. 1999. *States, Markets, Families: Gender, Liberalism and Social Policy in Australia, Canada, Great Britain and the United States.* Cambridge: Cambridge University Press.

Organization for Economic Cooperation and Development. 2000. *Education at a Glance: OECD Indicators, 2000 Edition.* Paris: Organization for Economic Cooperation and Development.

Orloff, Ann S. 1993. "Gender and the Social Rights of Citizenship: the Comparative Analysis of Gender and Welfare States." *American Sociological Review* 58, no. 3: 303–28.

_____. 1996. "Gender in the Welfare State." *Annual Review of Sociology* 22: 51–78.

Partido Popular (People's Party) 1989; 1993; 1996; 2000. General Elections: electoral programs.

Partido Socialista Obrero Español (Spanish Socialist Workers' Party) 1976; 1979a; 1981; 1984; 1988; 1990; 1994. Federal congresses 27–33, resolutions.

_____. 1977; 1979b; 1982; 1986; 1989; 1993; 1996; 2000. General Elections: electoral programs.

Pierson, Paul. 1996. "The New Politics of the Welfare State." *World Politics* 48:143–79.

_____. 1998. "Irresistible Forces, Immovable Objects: Post-industrial Welfare States Confront Permanent Austerity." *Journal of European Public Policy* 5, no. 4: 539–60.

Puelles, Manuel de. 1986. *Educación e Ideología en la España Contemporánea* (Education and Ideology in Contemporary Spain). Barcelona: Labor.

Sainsbury, Diane 1996. *Gender, Equality and Welfare States.* Cambridge: Cambridge University Press.

Stephens, John D., Evelyne Huber, and Leonard Ray. 1999. "The Welfare State in Hard Times." In *Continuity and Change in Contemporary Capitalism,* ed. Herbert Kitschelt, Peter Lange, Gary Marks, and John D. Stephens. New York: Cambridge University Press.

Stetson, Dorothy, and Amy Mazur, eds. 1995. *Comparative State Feminism.* Thousand Oaks, Calif.: Sage.

Unión de Centro Democrático 1977; 1979. General Elections: electoral programs.

Uriel, Ezequiel, María L Moltó, Francisco Pérez, Joaquín Aldás, and Vicent Cucarella. 1997. *Las Cuentas de la Educación en España y sus Comunidades Autónomas: 1980–1992* (Education Accounts in Spain and Its Regions: 1980–1992). Madrid: Fundación Argentaria and Visor.

Valiente, Celia. 1995. "Children First: Central Government Child Care Policies in Post-Authoritarian Spain (1975–1994)." In *Childhood and Parenthood: Proceedings of ISA Committee for Family Research Conference on Children and Families, 1994,* ed. Julia Brannen and Margaret O'Brien. London: Institute of Education, University of London.

_____. 1997. *Políticas Públicas de Género en Perspectiva Comparada: La Mujer Trabajadora en Italia y España (1900–1996)* (Gender Policies in Comparative Perspective: Working Women in Italy and Spain 1900–1996). Madrid: Universidad Autónoma de Madrid.

CHAPTER 3

Ideology, Economics, and the Politics of Child Care in Poland before and after the Transition

Jacqueline Heinen
Translated by Elizabeth Blount

Introduction

Because of the revival that has characterized the Polish economy since 1996—a revival described as a "virtuous" (as opposed to a "vicious") circle—Western economists often present Poland as an example of a successful "transition."[1] Among central and eastern European countries, all of which are confronted with the difficulties of postcommunist economic and social changes, it is indeed the only one that has managed to spread economic growth quickly while decreasing unemployment—at least up to a certain point.[2] On the whole, living conditions have improved, especially since 1996 (Blaszczak-Przybycinska et al. 1998). In spite of great resistance to the process of privatization, conflicting social relations, and the weak foundations of the administrations that have come to power since 1989, this country has emerged as the "star student," making it one of the first-wave candidates for admission to the European Union.

Yet Poland has been less successful in addressing its profound social problems. Indeed, in Poland, as in other Eastern European countries, the "social question" has remained the "poor cousin" on the political agenda driving the ten-year process of transforming the economy and society. As such, family politics, especially the politics of the collective care of young children, serve as a prime example of the scant attention paid by authorities to the existing needs in this area.

Since the early 1990s, a number of experts have been sounding the alarm about these issues, and their observations remain pertinent.[3] Deterioration, as much qualitative as quantitative, of public benefits and services (particularly in the area of child care and early childhood education) is leading to a marked increase in social polarization. In contrast to a successful minority embodied by the new affluent class, the bulk of the population is confronted with extreme economic difficulties. Large or one-parent families are the most vulnerable, and among them, women are of course primarily affected, since now, as before, they take on the principal domestic duties, including child care and childrearing.

In many cases, deterioration implies a perceived decline in living conditions compared with the mediocre but relatively egalitarian standard of living that characterized Poland before 1989. Indeed, under communism, though civil and political rights were largely formal, universal social rights ensured a minimum guarantee against the risks of misfortune. Job protection, with its related social coverage— mostly free services and state-controlled subsidies in domains like housing, health, transportation, and basic food supplies—conferred certain welfare-like traits on the "socialist" state even when the dysfunction and general economic waste were reflected in the ineffectiveness of many social services.[4] Their quality, by Western standards, left much to be desired, and child care services in particular were distinctly less well-endowed in Poland than in a number of neighboring countries.

The transformations of the last few years have fallen far short of meeting the needs of the population. In the beginning of the so-called transition phase, illusions about the anticipated benefits of the market economy were such that the majority of people believed that social rights would be extended and that the quality of services would improve. The rejection of the notion of egalitarianism, which was still associated with communism, would help to downplay the risk of growing social inequality. But these hopes were not realized.

It is now apparent that, despite egalitarian declarations, Soviet-type societies (with Poland in the lead) were distinguished by profound disparities of treatment between the sexes. Consequently, it is important to assess the extent to which the transformations under way over the past ten years have served to modify this pattern and to understand, in concrete terms, how family policies partake of present inequalities—between various social groups as well as between the sexes. This chapter will begin by reviewing the fluctuations and contradictions of the policies implemented during the communist regime and then examine the period of economic transformation linked to the market economy.

Women's Labor and Contradictory Politics under Communism

Analysis of the social measures toward women implemented in Poland since World War II reveals that there was not one but several different sets of policies, depending upon the phase of economic development and the political orientation of the dominant faction of the regime in place. As in most other Eastern European countries, the Polish constitution, adopted a few years after the Communist regime was instituted, proclaimed equality between the sexes in every context, whether it be work, family, or participation in social and political life.

Right after the war, the official position—responding essentially to the economic exigencies of the moment and the need to reconstruct a devastated country—declared that women should enter the paid labor force en masse. Because of the great number of men who had disappeared on the front or become invalids, implementation of the first five-year plans required mobilization of the entire remaining able-bodied population into the labor force; thus, a woman's economic role became all the more important. The rationale for women's participation in rebuilding the economy in the late 1940s was laid out in a propaganda campaign that presented the roles of both sexes as similar and maintained that paid work constituted a way of liberating women from male domination.[5] Moreover, the campaign stressed the need for essential improvements in a series of social domains in order to alleviate the difficulties of everyday life—particularly with regard to public child care facilities.

But a gap soon opened between efforts to meet production and social objectives. While the goals of the five-year plan for female employment had been exceeded, the same could not be said for increasing the number of available places in child care centers. There were also blatant inconsistencies in the application of the laws. Incidents of underemployment that led to genuine unemployment in predominantly female production sectors in the mid-1950s brought about a sudden and rather brutal reversal by the Polish authorities.[6] The declarations of the first period regarding the need for women's work to build socialism were displaced by a discourse that emphasized the importance of close relationships between mothers and children. A more general retreat from the social plan ensued within a climate of deterioration of the standard of living, which eventually provoked the Poznan workers' eruption of 1956.[7]

The change of regime in 1956 gave rise to great hopes, but they were short-lived. From the moment of his rise to power, Wladyslaw Gomulka declared his intention to reorganize the economy by sharply limiting social costs and renouncing extensive utilization of the labor force.[8] In this spirit, the issue of professional activity for women was called into question, and a law was passed by the Polish Parliament in 1961 calling for an increase in women's jobs only in fields where men would be lacking. The leaders did not hide their determination to "put women back in their place." This law had a direct impact on companies' overtly sexist hiring policies.[9] Although the rate of women's labor-force participation continued to rise, it was much slower than it had been in the first decade, and even though women's level of education advanced considerably during this period (by 1968, it was already higher than men's), they saw themselves being treated as reserve labor.

For its part, the 1957 Congress of the League of Women (a "transmission belt" for the Communist Party) advocated fighting for "the development of all part-time employment possibilities" and encouraging domestic work "for a very great number of women, taking into account the fact that it is not possible to hire all who are looking for work." (There was, of course, no question of part-time or domestic work for men.) At the same time, nothing was said of the need to expand the network of child care institutions. On the contrary, the state emphasized voluntary mutual aid to be given by families in both cities and the countryside. Women were asked to be "realistic" and to try hard to solve their "own" problems themselves. This discourse was accompanied by valorization of the role of nonworking women and severe self-criticism on the part of the government for having asked for "too much equality" in the past.

However, the disregard exhibited by the government for social demands and the concomitant deterioration of daily living conditions led to a new workers' eruption in 1970 as well as dismissal of the Gomulka administration, which was replaced by that of Edward Gierek. The new government quickly committed itself to a policy of borrowing from any source through Western bankers, a move that immediately and visibly improved living conditions and the network of social services, particularly for young children. But instead of reversing the discourse on women's place in society that had prevailed for years, there was a shift in the policies concerning women's work, with the authorities emphasizing factors that favored the flexibility of work. The government advocated a series of measures specifically aimed at women: temporary leave from work for those at the stage of "active" motherhood; for others, development of the types of jobs that allowed women "to better reconcile their working role and their family role," such as part-time work and paid work done at home.[10]

These measures were tightly linked to Gierek's goal of pushing pronatalist policies in an effort to offset the sinking birthrate. There was an obvious distance separating these from previous directives that had insisted on professional equality in fact. In spite of the "guarantees" given by the constitution, it was evident that women were far from being men's equals. Moreover, certain experts of the time did not hesitate to declare that female labor was to be considered more as a reserve than as a resource for national economic development.

With the exception of the first period of the Communist regime, it is clear that Polish women were incessantly treated as second-class citizens. This fact plainly stands out when one examines official positions in two areas that have contributed to shaping women's destiny and their mobility on the professional plane, namely, public child care and "parental" child care leave. These policies weighed heavily in the definition of women's status on the social and familial plane—a status tightly linked to the roles assigned to them in the household—by reinforcing the traditional private (feminine)/public (masculine) division.[11] This trend, which has sustained itself over time, is reflected today in the gendered nature of the citizenship.[12]

The Mirage of Child Care Centers and Nursery Schools

During the immediate postwar period, it was believed that the socialization of young children would become a nodal point of public policy toward women, in step with the then prevailing discourse that saw public child care facilities as one of the key factors in permitting women to initiate vocational activity. This discourse took concrete shape in statistics: from almost none in 1939, the number of available places in child care centers rose to nearly 50,000 by 1954, while the number of places in nursery schools almost quintupled, from fewer than 80,000 to nearly 400,000.[13] However inadequate the actual supply,[14] these statistics speak volumes about the efforts undergone during the first phase of "real socialism." As we have seen, however, this trend turned out to be quite vulnerable once the first symptoms of economic difficulty appeared. The invocation of state imperatives served momentarily to mask an ideological change that marginalized women's role in the economy—a point of view that the new leaders fully embraced. And it was accompanied by a reversal in child care policy. In fifteen years under Gomulka, despite evident needs,[15] only about one-third as many child care centers were constructed than during the preceding phase. The situation of the nursery schools was not as catastrophic, but still, the 500,000 places offered in 1970 covered fewer than 30 percent of children between three and six years of age, and this number was well below the results attained in other Eastern European countries during the same period.

The situation improved under the Gierek administration, as is illustrated in table 3.1, which indicates a marked increase in the number of places created in child care centers.[16] But given the increase in both the proportion of working women and the overall population, this did not constitute a true improvement of the situation. In 1978, only 4.9 percent of children under age three were accommodated in child care centers—almost the same proportion as in 1970—and the quality of conditions had hardly improved. Overcrowding was particularly severe; after 1960, the number of children in child care centers was almost always twice the number of recommended places.[17]

The proportion of children placed in nursery school rose from 29.5 percent in 1970 to 48.8 percent in 1980, but this statistical progress also masked deteriorating conditions resulting from overcrowding.[18] Consequently, the "institution" of the grandmother remained useful as a form of child care provision, even though the number of women still working at a "grandmotherly" age had increased. In response, the state took various measures—most notably the law of 1975 authorizing women to take early retirement—designed to encourage elderly women to keep the caretaking role they had previously played by giving up their paid occupations.

Compared with conditions in other Eastern European countries, the collective child care situation in Poland was one of the worst. Looking at the most favorable case—that of the German Democratic Republic—a real gap can be seen between the countries, since after 1970 East German child care centers admitted nearly one-third of children under three, while two-thirds of those between three and six were

	1960	1970	1975	1980	1984
TABLE 3.1: NUMBER AND PROPORTION OF CHILDREN ACCOMMODATED IN CHILD CARE CENTERS, 1960–1984					
Number of places in child care centers (in thousands)	51.5	64.9	82.1	103.5	102.2
Number of children accommodated (in thousands)	92.5	126.6	166.0	194.2	188.8
Percentage of children under three accommodated in child care centers	2.6	4.7	4.9	5.2	4.7

SOURCE: Uscinska 1986, 47.

placed in nursery schools.[19] These data notwithstanding, it should not be assumed that the East German authorities, more than their Polish counterparts, challenged the almost exclusive assignment of reproductive tasks to women, or that they directly attacked the foundations of the sexual division of work on the professional plane. Nevertheless, the existence of a large network of accommodation structures for young children led, in the two countries, to markedly different attitudes toward women's relationship to family, jobs, and the state. Women's tendency to withdraw into the family sphere, renewed in Poland in the late 1970s, was almost entirely absent in East Germany. As a result, when communism collapsed, East German women were better able to present themselves as autonomous individuals, particularly in forming egalitarian demands.[20] In this respect, the measures taken in the area of child care directly contributed to forging women's general social position, at the same time that they specifically affected gender roles.

The Influence of the Catholic Church and the Key Role of Child Care Leave

One of the factors that explains Poland's tardiness in socializing child care when compared to its neighbors is of course the weight of the religious establishment, which elsewhere had only limited if not negligible influence. From the early 1970s on, the stature of the Catholic Church was at a new high, thanks to the compromise reached by the Catholic hierarchy and the Gierek administration, whose rise to power the Church had indirectly supported.[21] According to the terms of this compromise, the state could intervene only marginally in domains the Church considered its own responsibility, starting with the family and a woman's place within it. From then on, in their Sunday homilies inspired by the circulars of the Polish episcopates, priests systematically stressed the Church's opposition not only to abortion but also to mothers' employment. At worst, women could work part-time; better, though, that they stay home and take care of the children. This perspective explains much about the evolution of attitudes toward paid work for women.

It was no accident that, particularly under the Gierek regime, a series of "preferential" measures were adopted with regard to women. The 1972 decision to extend child care leave from one to three years, unpaid, at first instituted in 1968 under the Gomulka administration, was adopted under the pressure of the events of 1971; one of the demands of the women workers of Lodz was to set up paid child care leave. Rather than granting compensation, the government extended the length of the leave and had it follow maternity leave, thus allowing women to stop working for a considerable length of time after giving birth. Another leave, for care of sick children, was introduced exclusively for women—a significant measure since it meant sixty paid days a year at 100 percent of one's salary. For its part, maternity leave was put at sixteen, eighteen, or twenty-six weeks, depending on the order of the birth. Other decisions of lesser importance completed this arsenal. Even though the various measures were officially presented as a way of addressing women's desire "to fully take on their roles as mothers," one of the undeclared objectives was to make up for the deficiencies of state politics concerning child care institutions; another (completely illusory) one was to arrest the fall of the birthrate. In any case, the policies had the effect of once again placing the responsibility of family-oriented tasks squarely on the shoulders of women, and they had the advantage of being much less costly than the construction of more child care centers.[22]

Given the difficulties of living with endemic shortages (with the exception of a few years of plenty, during which Gierek's Poland was up to its ears in debt) and an underdeveloped child care infrastructure, most of these measures met with immense success among those affected, who in most cases worked full-time. By 1978, two-thirds of eligible women had made use of the unpaid child care leave established ten years earlier. This shift can be explained by the continuing difficulties of daily life, of which women bore the brunt. Every day, for example, they were obliged to wait in lines to shop, and then had to compensate for the poor quality and scarcity of food products with tedious hours in the kitchen. As a consequence, however, the subject of *paid* child care leave reappeared during the strikes that gave rise to the Solidarność movement in 1980. In the twenty-one points of the Gdansk agreements, the principal demands that particularly affected women concerned that issue; thus, in 1981, child care leave was transformed into parental leave applicable to the father (but only in certain cases) and paid according to family income per person.[23]

Polish women's insistence on these demands masked a conspicuous shift in their attitudes. On the one hand, various surveys from the 1960s had shown that most women—especially those who were more highly qualified and had professional or political responsibilities—articulated aspirations to move to another social niche. Some even expressed critical opinions of the authorities. On the other hand, surveys done twenty years later uncovered attitudes that were infinitely more ambiguous and contradictory, revealing both men's and women's growing skepticism toward the validity of women's work.[24] It must be remembered that measures favoring the role of women as mothers were adopted during a period (the 1970s) marked by a greater and greater distancing from the discourses of the POUP (the Communist Party) and its satellite organizations—including the League of Women, which had been advocating equality of the sexes for decades without success.

In such a context, it is not surprising that child care leave was seen as a positive measure—with almost no one bringing up the problem of discrimination that it could later create—and that the subject of child care centers was made contingent. The family acquired heightened importance as a place of refuge allowing resistance to the powers that be and, in the midst of the acute economic crisis, it took on an even more central role. The difficulty of making ends meet with officially earned wages and the need to resort to all kinds of barters and schemes to face up to multiple shortages made the family all the more essential in assuring the reproduction of individuals—and therefore enhanced the significance of a woman's role within the home.

As the foregoing discussion shows, because of their social and family situations, women found themselves at the heart of the contradictory economic principles of the Soviet-type system, which was characterized by a worsening of daily living conditions. But beyond the cultural and religious factors, the very nature of public policy deployed since 1945 has played a determining role in maintaining (indeed, accentuating) the gendered division of labor that currently prevails in Poland. One cannot overestimate the potentially perverse effects of protective legislation like parental leave as it was defined before 1989, with an extremely small allowance and restrictive conditions concerning its use by fathers. It is not surprising, therefore, that it was seen almost exclusively as a measure for women.[25] Nearly 90 percent of the Polish women who were eligible took advantage of the leave as soon as it carried an allowance, in spite of its negative impact on their career development.[26] Leave for the care of sick children had similar effects. Both measures hindered the sharing of family chores and led to a reinforcement of the horizontal and vertical segregation of the labor market. One should not confuse the type of protective legislation mentioned here with the more preferential measures—also involving positive discrimination—encouraged by the European Union, which aim at reversing the processes of segregation by granting women access to areas of work or certain jobs from which they had previously been excluded. In this case, Polish laws reinforced the assignment of women to domestic work, to the detriment of plans for collective care of small children.

It must be noted, however, that far from criticizing the often discriminatory character of these politics, most women workers accepted their implications, even though today many fear that it serves as a pretext for employers to give preference to men. Relatively few women think about trying to find ways to induce fathers to take part in the responsibilities of raising young children. This type of attitude has in turn been heavily determined by the social and economic choices made by the new governments for a decade.

A Difficult Transition

With regard to social security, the first years of "transition" focused more on destruction of the old system than construction of a new one. After 1990, a series of choices of principle were made very quickly, in accordance with the logic of "shock therapy" adopted by the first administration. Their particular objective was to satisfy the demands of the International Monetary Fund (IMF), which predicates offers of aid on the adoption of measures limiting the budgetary deficit, such as suppression of state subsidies for consumption, disengagement of the state from the administration of social security on behalf of independent firms, decentralization of administration to the local or regional level, and funding through a system of dues from employers and employees.

Public services—especially in the areas of health and education—suffered the inevitable consequences of budgetary difficulties, which meant a marked deterioration of eligibility criteria just at the moment when social services previously linked to companies (health centers, facilities for children, canteens, convalescent homes, etc.) were also disappearing. The evolution of a certain number of general social measures adopted since 1989 shows that, whatever the stated intentions with respect to family policies, housing, health, or social assistance might have been, economic constraints almost always ended up prevailing over the official solutions.[27] Two trends accompanied this pattern: one was the effort to protect against risks, the priorities being unemployment and poverty; the other was the tendency to restrain spending by reducing the total amount of allowances and progressively narrowing categories of eligibility. The number of these "target people" was reduced more and more to include only the most impoverished individuals—those who fell into destitution.

The measures taken with regard to family allowances are a good example of this pattern. At the time of the Round Table of 1989, it was agreed that this benefit would be set at 8 percent of the average salary, but ultimately it was brought down to 3 percent in 1995 after the total amount was modified several times. To be sure, the right to receive this allowance, reserved for those who had been salaried workers in the past, was extended to students and the unemployed.[28] But at the same time, the age limit for a child pursuing her studies, previously fixed at twenty-five, was lowered to twenty. Today this previously universal allowance is awarded only under certain financial conditions: the level of family income per person must not exceed 50 percent of the average salary. Eligibility is therefore limited to poor families with only the social minimum as their income.[29]

It was apparent that many representatives sought to develop a profamily orientation (in reality, pronatalism), as is reflected in the fact that the total family allowance, unvarying in the past, now increases upon the birth of the third child. Most of the adopted measures, however, fall far short of their announced intentions. A 1998 proposal to reduce taxes for households with children was not adopted, nor was a measure to extend maternity leave to six months, nor one that suggested granting a special allowance (based on the calculation of the retirement pension) to mothers who renounced paid work to care for their children. In the end, all were judged to be too costly (Wiktorow 1999, 2–4).

Child Care Centers and Nursery Schools: A Collapse

In the area of social services, health and education among them, economic transformation and the process of privatization have had certain positive consequences, but also many negative ones (Heinen 1995, 1999a). Diversification and improvement of the quality of services can be seen as much in regard to caring work as on the educational and cultural levels. This progress, however, almost always rests on a commercial basis consisting of private companies whose objective is to profit from certain public services (increasingly abundant) that offer benefits for a fee. The result is a reinforcement of class divisions, since income determines who has access to quality services. In addition, these developments go hand in hand with the elimination of

many services traditionally linked to companies and the closing of other local services that municipalities cannot continue to maintain for financial reasons. The decentralization of social services also has contradictory aspects. On one hand, it
ideally allows a better response to those in need and provides a more rational management of services, but on the other, it generates inequalities between rich and
poor regions, even though basic needs are greater in the most impoverished places.
Opportunities for physical, intellectual, and cultural development tend to be increasingly different at the outset, particularly in the area of child care services.[30]
Taken as a whole, these conditions lead one to conclude that for most of the population, negative consequences prevail.[31]

In Poland, as we saw earlier, child care centers were never able to accommodate
more than 5 percent of those under three, while nursery schools accommodated at
best 40 to 50 percent of three- to six-year-olds. The situation was thus anything but
good, especially in comparison to what was happening in most other Eastern European countries.[32] But in the 1980s it became even worse as a consequence of the
economic and budgetary crisis. Legislative reform that involved transferring responsibility for subsidizing child care facilities from the central to local governments
led—in the same way as for elementary schools but in a more pronounced manner—to growing deterioration in the network of care facilities as a whole, reflecting the budgetary difficulties of the communes. Many local child care centers and
nursery schools had to close; from 1989 to 1996, the number of centers declined by
nearly two-thirds, while the number of nursery schools fell by nearly one-third
(IPSS 1997, 60). The decrease in the number of places was slightly less sharp, many
centers having decided to accept more children than before—but often to the detriment of the quality of services (see table 3.2).

For its part, the process of rationalization and privatization of the economy,
which encourages elimination of social spending judged to be superfluous, has led
to the closing of almost all child care centers and two-thirds of company-owned
nursery schools. In areas where the economic situation is at its worst, this evolution
often puts unemployed women who are mothers of small children in a no-win situation: lack of money forces them to take care of their children themselves, but then
they lose the freedom of movement that would allow them to actively seek a job or
undergo training that would improve their chances of finding one. Although the
child care system has always left something to be desired in Poland, the closing of
most public child care centers and company-owned nursery schools has largely
made things worse.[33]

It is important, however, to stress that the decrease in the number of children
cared for in collective facilities (see table 3.3) was not uniquely caused by the limita-
tion of potential capacity alone. On the one hand, the decline in the birthrate helped
curb the demand. On the other hand—and this is a determining factor—the rise in
the cost of services in public institutions has played a major role in reducing attendance; the monthly cost of a child care center for one child can be up to a third
(sometimes even half) of an average salary.

Ironically, Polish experts are increasingly recognizing the compensatory value of child care centers for poor children. As one has put it, "We have seen that removing children from the least comfortable and most impoverished environments for a stay in a child care center can help put the conditions of their development on an equal footing" (Balcerzak-Paradowska 1997, 59). For many families, however, the prohibitive cost discourages any vague desire of turning to outside child care, all the more so since they must allow for various supplementary expenses such as food and special activities. The cost of meals (food had before been practically free) becomes an insurmountable obstacle for households with the lowest incomes. In this way the current system very clearly favors the middle levels of society, to the detriment of the most impoverished ones. Several surveys show numerous cases of children who go all day without eating because the parents cannot meet these expenses, and care institutions rarely exempt low-income families from paying this type of cost (Baran 1998, 165). This is why, today, the care of young children is provided more frequently either by the mother herself in more than one-third of the cases (generally an unemployed mother who does not benefit from parental leave), or by another member of the family, in another third of cases (IPSS 1997, 60). At the same time, the proportion of children without any supervision at least two hours per day is increasing, especially among children of single mothers and in working-class families.

Private child care centers and nursery schools aiming to make up for the lack of places or offering high-quality services are simply inaccessible to those with the

TABLE 3.2: DECLINE IN CAPACITY OF CHILD CARE CENTERS AND NURSERY SCHOOLS
FROM 1989 TO 1997

NUMBER OF CHILDREN A – % of children B – % of age group served		1989	1990	1991	1992	1993	1994	1995	1996	1997
Child Care Centers	A	100	91.3	73.8	57.8	49.9	46.6	46.0	43.9	43.0
	B	100	95.4	70.4	59.1	53.5	52.2	52.2	54.5	56.8
Nursery Schools	A	100	93.0	81.4	85.7	83.4	84.7	83.9	82.8	81.8
	B	100	96.5	87.9	97.6	98.2	102.3	104.7	106.8	108.8

SOURCES: GUS Statistical Yearbook (1995, 1996, 1997).

TABLE 3.3: CHANGES IN ATTENDANCE AT CHILD CARE CENTERS AND NURSERY SCHOOLS
FROM 1989 TO 1997

NUMBER OF CHILDREN A – in thousands B – % of age group served		1989	1990	1991	1992	1993	1994	1995	1996	1997
Child Care Centers	A	150.6	137.5	111.2	87.0	73.8	70.2	69.3	66.1	64.9
	B	4.4	4.2	3.1	2.6	2.3	2.3	2.3	2.4	2.5
Nursery Schools	A	921.0	856.6	750.2	789.0	768.0	780.0	773.0	763.1	754.0
	B	34.0	32.8	29.9	33.2	33.4	34.8	35.6	36.3	37.0

SOURCES: GUS Statistical Yearbook (1995, 1996, 1997).

smallest budgets—particularly single mothers and mothers of large families, who need such services the most. Although the developments described here satisfy supporters of family policies in keeping with Catholic doctrine—which holds that the duties of supervision and financial responsibility for child rearing belong, above all, to the families—it is apparent that they have particularly negative effects for the population most in need of material aid. According to one expert, "The absence of family policies that seek to alleviate the consequences of the changes in effect (particularly by creating the necessary conditions for reinforcing the social character of child care institutions) . . . returns us to limiting access to care services and places children on unequal footing at the very beginning of their schooling" (Balcerzak-Paradowska 1994, 13).

Women Discriminated Against in Law and Practice

Analysis of state policies is useful for discovering what tendencies are at work in regard to social relations between the sexes. As many recent studies stress, the movement of social polarization pitting rich against poor is not only accompanied (in most countries of Eastern Europe but particularly in Poland) by a decrease in women's labor. It also includes marked effects in politics, especially in the decline in the number of women participating in state decision making.[34] The institution of a Western democratic system is thus being carried out in an almost exclusively masculine setting, even at a moment when parliaments are starting to mold social relations in a lasting way.

This situation found concrete expression in the challenge to abortion rights embodied in the legislation passed in 1993 that almost totally prohibited it, even though polls and surveys done at the time as part of a project supported by the Catholic hierarchy had shown repeatedly that the majority of the public was hostile toward legislation depriving a woman of the right to decide if she wanted to continue her pregnancy (Heinen and Matuchniak-Krasuska 1992; Heinen 1999b). Since that time, voluntary termination of pregnancy (VTP) has been illegal except in case of rape, deformation of the fetus, or when the life of the mother is in danger. This dispensation covers barely 5 percent of VTPs documented previously. A doctor who breaks this law faces two years' imprisonment. At the same time, parliament members on the far right, who made a pretense of instituting an allowance for pregnant women in order to encourage couples to have more children, have been manipulating its terms. With its initial six-month duration decreased to four months, this allowance (which can equal a quarter of the average salary) is now available only to the extremely impoverished, and the total subsidy given upon the birth of each child has been reduced by half.

Despite such blatant prejudice against them and the need to address their specific needs, one rarely sees examples of overt rebellions by women, as the weight of the Catholic Church acts as a brake upon expressions of discontent. Faced with these backward politics, and taking into account the difficulty and high cost of obtaining contraception, women have increasingly responded (according to accounts given by women militants working in the scarce family planning centers) by carrying out what nineteenth-century feminists called a "womb strike"—drastically limiting sexual relations with their partners. Indeed, one can see a severe drop in fertility in Poland, which was, until recently, one of the few countries of the region that surpassed the fateful 2.1 fertility rate necessary for assuring the reproduction of the population (Heinen 1999b).[35]

Marked differences between Polish women themselves evidently exist. It was true before in the areas of training and employment; it is true today within the context of the social polarization described throughout these pages, according to level of education, age, place of residence, and especially degree of material wealth. The press takes every opportunity to spotlight so-called success stories, which implicitly testify that women are men's equals. Space does not permit discussion here of the fantastic elements of these stories and how they simply ignore very real disparities in living conditions (see Heinen 1999a). More typical are the conditions described in what follows.

Discrimination toward women shows itself at many other levels: in law, practice, and representation. In the area of law, drastic reductions in state budgets have driven legislators to reform a whole series of legal clauses and structures judged too costly or contrary to the logic of the market economy. This is especially true for older protective laws that confer privileges on mothers or parents of young children (such as parental leave and leave for care of sick children) and on single mothers or fathers (priority of access to child care centers and nursery schools, doubling of family or care allowances,[36] privileged tax status, etc.).

Certainly efforts were made, under pressure of requirements for possible entry into the European Union, to modify the law in an egalitarian direction; parental leave and leave for care of sick children, for example, have been made available to fathers without restriction (this was not the case until 1996). Again, a close examination of the legislation shows that this concession has been completely formal; the role of women is emphasized throughout the argumentation, and the father only appears incidentally, at the very end of the text.

But above all and decisively, child care leave—for three years, accompanied by a small allowance (about one-fourth of the average salary)—was cut off, though it was one of the principal social policy attractions under communism. The right to return to a job after a work interruption has effectively been abolished in cases of mass layoffs or company closings, and financial compensation, pathetic as it was, has declined drastically, with the right to an allowance granted only to families with a per capita income below one-fourth of the average salary.[37] Such a plan proves to be a weak incentive for the mothers—and even less for the fathers—concerned. Consequently, the proportion of women making use of it decreased by two-thirds between 1990 and 1996 (Balcerzak-Paradowska 1997, 58).[38] As for leave for care of sick children (sixty days per year), also applicable to men since 1995 but with a total compensation reduced from 100 to 80 percent of the salary of the person concerned, very few women (to say nothing of men) use it today for fear of losing their jobs. One boss bluntly declares, "If someone goes too far with their absences, we fire them. . . . For women, we expect them to limit the absences they take to care for a sick child" (Zylicz 1999, no. 2, 5).

From a practical perspective, it is significant that economic recovery goes hand in hand with a deterioration of the situation of women in the workforce compared with that of men. Since 1996, when they made up "only" 53 to 54 percent of the unemployed,[39] women today constitute more than 60 percent of the jobless and have an unemployment rate more than double that of their male counterparts—in 1997, 16 and 8.7 percent, respectively. In regions that are most affected by the economic crisis, the proportion of women among the unemployed can reach 70 percent, and the vast majority judge their chances of finding a job to be practically nil. Moreover, the gap between long-term unemployed men and women is growing, especially beyond a span of two years; from 10 percentage points during the first half of the 1990s, it has now increased to nearly 14 points. Women represent more than three-fourths of this population and thus are the very solid majority of those who no longer receive unemployment compensation. This situation is the result of blatant discriminatory practices on the part of employers, in particular the suspicion shown toward the youngest women, who are treated as "at-risk" labor.

At the same time, growing wage differentials may be seen in many fields, reinforcing women's status as an economic minority. Although the wage gap has remained more or less stable since 1989—Polish women earn on average 20 to 30 percent less than Polish men with the same level of education and experience, according to the field—it has become much worse among blue-collar workers and the most highly educated workers (Heinen1999a).[40] There is little chance that these income gaps will decrease in the short term, as the assignment of women to domestic work limits their mobility.[41] They also have fewer opportunities to supplement their income with other sources of revenue (whether from secondary jobs or undeclared activities). The significance of the "informal" economy in a country like Poland is well known. Moreover, the proportion of women working in the rapidly expanding private sector, where wages are generally higher than in the public sector, is clearly less than that of men. And women are especially much less numerous among company executives, who are likely to become wealthy.

Consequently, the process of pauperization affects a large majority of women; indeed, one can speak of a genuine "feminization of poverty" (Kotowska 1995). As we have seen, this particularly concerns unemployed women, but it also includes single mothers and retired women. Single mothers indeed make up a disproportionate percentage of those who live on the threshold of poverty, since the laws assuring them a certain protection from the state were abolished in the first wave of reform. Moreover, they are part of a growing category, since the proportion of households with a woman at the head increased from 27 to 30 percent between 1995 and 1996 alone. For their part, retired women receive pensions that are on average quite inferior to those of men, given the facts that they are calculated according to past income and that women's mandatory retirement age is lower than men's (sixty for women, sixty-five for men). Women's pensions, on average, are 40 percent lower than men's.[42]

Among the extremely worrying symptoms of the deterioration of women's financial situation are the increase in domestic violence as well as the extent of prostitution and sexual commerce. So many of the elements that translate into a loss of autonomy undermine women's personal integrity (Bystydzienski 1999).

The Weight of Traditional Roles

The existence of all these discriminatory practices reflects the fact that, above all, Polish women continue to be perceived (and perceive themselves) as potential mothers. Their supposed availability to their families—and, more generally, to all dependents—restricts their freedom of movement. This stands out clearly in a recent survey administered to women workers and company directors (Zylicz 1999). Employers openly admit to preferentially hiring men, and for the most part, reiterate common stereotypes about "masculine" and "feminine" qualities: "Young women are less available and less efficient because of their children"; "Responsible positions suit men the best." Women, quite conscious of sexual inequality, describe all sorts of discriminatory practices: wage gaps, age barriers that are much more restrictive for women, personal and indeed intimate questions asked during interviews, obligations to sign agreements not to have a child for five years or not to resort to leave for care of sick children, and so on. They seem, however, resigned to the idea that they do not have the same opportunities as their male colleagues: "It's tradition." And they rarely express career aspirations.[43] Other surveys show that husbands are decidedly in favor of having their spouses devote themselves, first and foremost, to caring for children, and they are pleased that the idea of women's investing themselves in their maternal roles has lately gained ground (Firlit-Fesnak 1998, 25–27). One could say that the "maternal ideal" has had a tendency to reinforce itself (at least among the most disadvantaged social categories), which only serves to increase the feeling and the situation of dependence of the wife upon the husband.

In earlier work (Heinen 1993 and 1995), I have discussed how persistence of the sexual division of labor (professionally as well as in the family), combined with the burden of living conditions, has helped produce a strong desire to return to the family-oriented environment that characterized the lives of Polish women workers in the 1970s and 1980s. More generally, I have shown how much these conditions influenced the skepticism expressed by the majority of the population toward ideals such as the emancipation of women and equality between the sexes. Certainly the economic context has changed radically since then, along with a dramatic increase in unemployment. And the necessity—now as before—of having two incomes to maintain a decent standard of living for the family pushes most women to keep a job, regardless of the obstacles.

Indeed, contrary to numerous forecasts dating from the beginning of the 1990s, the rate of labor activity for women, though weakened, has not diminished significantly more than men's (Kotowska 1999). Young women in particular express career aspirations and display a much more assertive attitude toward work than their elders did ten years ago (a trend that partially contradicts the image emerging from the surveys mentioned above). One should take into account here the generation factor and not exclude the possibility of future changes in behavior. The drastic fall in the birthrate constitutes a phenomenon that can be interpreted as a sign of resistance by young women faced with financial difficulties and also as a response to employers who treat them as "unreliable labor" because they are liable to have children.

It cannot be said, however, that this has produced major modifications affecting the place of women in society. The ultra-Catholic offensive on reproductive politics, along with systematic propaganda in favor of the *matka-Polka* (Polish mother), has influenced employer practices and roles of women themselves (Bystydzienski 1999). It is therefore not surprising that the elders are pessimistic and that women workers in particular express both criticism toward the outcome of the "transition" and mistrust toward the private sector, as well as nostalgia for the past. Back then, they say, they felt more respected: "We felt more at ease. We could have children and go back to work afterward" (Zylicz 1999, 3).

The macroeconomic success and relative political stability of post-1989 Poland are undeniable, but with regard to social protection, Poland falls short of setting a good example for the other countries of Central and Eastern Europe. At the same time, its overall environment is far better than those of neighboring countries of the former USSR and bears little resemblance to the state of decay prevailing in Russia, where growing pockets of poverty, the decrease in real wages, and the wholesale breakup of social and family policies present a far more catastrophic image. Everything is relative.

But in the early 1990s, many Poles dreamed of creating a society based on the model of the Nordic countries—a task that now seems immense. This is particularly true for women, whose status in society has strongly deteriorated and who are often generally thought of as second-class citizens. The crumbling of child care provisions is but one aspect of women's overall marginalization on the economic and political plane—a position that bodes ill for the prospect of building a society of individuals equal in law and in practice.

Notes

1. On the ambiguity of the notion of transition, see Chavance 1998.

2. Having passed from more than 16 percent in 1994, the darkest period, to a little more than 10 percent in 1997, it then went back up to 13.6 percent in January 2000.

3. Debates between sociologists and economists of the East and West testify to this, in particular on the theme of the future of social politics. See especially Deacon and Szalai 1990; Deacon 1992; Ringen and Wallace 1993; OECD 1994; UNICEF 1994.

4. In spite of the existence of a certain number of social measures analogous to those that characterize welfare, regimes of the Soviet type and the welfare state in its normal form should not be placed on the same plane. One of the distinctive traits of welfare in the West—the "growth state," in the words of Castel (1995)—is that the institution of social compensation systems following World War II has been accompanied by a marked increase in salaries and improvement of consumption, which was not the case under "real socialism."

5. Without waiting for the adoption of the constitution of 1952, a series of decrees of an egalitarian bent were adopted, starting with the principle of equal pay for equal work. Various measures were taken in the vocational sphere to protect the health of female workers and mothers, including a twelve-week maternity leave with a fixed allowance of 100 percent of the average salary and transfer of pregnant women working in unpleasant conditions to an easier work assignment upon their sixth month of pregnancy.

6. The unemployment rate for women would rise to more than 16 percent in 1964.

7. Supply shortages went hand in hand with stagnation (even reduction) in real wages, as well as an extremely tight housing situation.

8. The proclaimed goal was to compel companies to adopt an intensive system of development that would assure optimal productivity with limited manpower, thus reducing social expenditures.

9. The politics of the authorities would shift a few years later, when it appeared that companies still "consumed" the same amount of labor and that attempts to change to a system of intensive economy had failed in most sectors.

10. The countless speeches and resolutions on this subject throughout this period had few results. Working women figured that for hourly wages equal to those of a full-time job, part-time work was not profitable, taking into account the loss of time due to commuting and difficulties regarding child care. As for the heads of companies, they proved incapable of reorganizing production in order to offer part-time positions. Work done at home was hardly more successful.

11. In the 1970s, services that were supposed to liberate women from domestic tasks remained quite underdeveloped, even though Polish women were handling between 80 and 95 percent of common household chores (cooking, cleaning, laundry, ironing, etc.). Only 10 to 12 percent of women turned to canteens for cooked food, while nearly 90 percent of them did their laundry at home.

12. One does not speak of "citizenship" with regard to the communist period, since the regime was clearly characterized by the negation of most of the rights that are fundamental to the definition of citizenship—whether they be civil (e.g., the negation of freedom of expression, organization, and movement) or political (e.g., the purely formal nature of "elected" authorities). What remained were social rights that assured a certain equality of mediocrity, which constituted one of the essential factors of submission to the all-powerful party-state.

13. Most of the data mentioned here concerning the communist period are taken from works and articles in Polish, references to which may be found in Heinen 1989.

14. In 1955, at the national level, only 2 percent of those under three could be accommodated in a child care center (and 5 percent in cities).

15. During the 1960s, the proportion of married women among female workers increased sharply. From less than one-third in 1956, it grew to more than half in 1960 and was near 70 percent in 1970. Three-fourths of these married women had children.

16. In the beginning of Gierek's "reign," from 1970 to 1975, nearly five times more places in the child care centers and six times more in the nursery schools were created, compared with the five preceding years under Gomulka.

17. This number is calculated according to space, personnel, and certain criteria concerning the quality of the accommodations.

18. From nearly one-third in 1970, the proportion of children exceeding the number of theoretical places in the nursery schools grew to two-thirds in 1980, even though budgets covered less than half of the stated needs. For data concerning child care centers and nursery schools at this time, see Kurzynowski 1979, 82–84.

19. On the eve of the fall of the Berlin Wall, the proportions were 65 and 95 percent, respectively—statistics, if the truth be told, superior to those of any European country, western or eastern.

20. Note, however, that after reunification, former East German women no more resisted the discriminatory measures of which they were the objects on the professional plane than Polish women did. Precisely because the sexual division of labor in both the private and public spheres had remained unchanged, even when the forms it took had been modified, East German women proved to be quite vulnerable to the sexist assaults of employers and the state.

21. Note especially the young people's marches at the Virgin of Czestochowa and other mass demonstrations that brought together the regime's supporters and opponents; events like these greatly increased in scale from this period on. The situation was very different from that of the mid-1960s, when relations between the Gomulka regime and the Church were extremely strained. Churches then were far from full; elderly women were the most likely to be found there.

22. Calculations made by Polish authorities in the 1970s and 1980s show that child care leave, even accompanied by benefits, turned out to be a third as expensive as child care centers, provided that the benefits given did not exceed a quarter of the average salary.

23. However, allowances that had been fixed in zlotys, and not by percentage of salary, quickly lost their value, given the rate of inflation and the absence of any indexing system.

24. With the passing years, trends in the relation of women to work have reversed noticeably, with more and more young women demonstrating their desire to stop working and devote themselves exclusively to take care of their children.

25. Less than 1 percent of fathers took the opportunity of going on parental leave in 1989.

26. As feminist economists have shown, stopping work for several years limits possibilities for advancement.

27. See IPSS 1997; GUS 1998a.

28. Since 1995, family allowances are no longer paid by social insurance funds (linked to salary benefits) but by the central state budget. They are thus given to those who do not pay any dues to social insurance offices, and constitute one of the elements of the social aid plan.

29. For more on the various changes with regard to social security benefits, see especially GUS/IPSS/UNICEF 1994 and Balcerzak-Paradowska 1999.

30. In the past, overall opportunities for children of the *nomenklatura* (the party elite) and those of ordinary workers differed greatly, but social polarization was still less, since the pockets of extreme poverty seen today did not exist.

31. According to estimates made by various organizations, the proportion of the Polish population qualified as poor, living beneath the absolute minimum threshold, grew from 30 to 40 percent until the mid-1990s (nearly twice as many as in 1989), but would fall, to 25 to 30 percent, by the end of the decade. At least some of this group lived in extreme poverty— which UNICEF situates at 60 percent of the poverty line: about 10 percent of households and 15 percent of the entire Polish population fell into this category in 1993 (UNICEF 1994). It must be emphasized, however, that pauperization is very uneven, not only according to social groups but also to region. The incidence of poverty is concentrated in certain towns or regions affected directly by economic restructuring (especially monoindustrial regions or towns and certain agricultural regions).

32. In 1990, the proportion of three- to six-year-olds accommodated in nursery schools was 95 percent in East Germany, 87 percent in Czechoslovakia, and 76 percent in Bulgaria (Balcerzak-Paradowska 1999, 249).

33. Note that in the area of child care services, the situation in other former communist countries is very similar to that of Poland. In certain cases, the decline is even worse, taking into account the slightly better Polish results in 1989. This is especially true for child care centers, whose capacities have decreased by half or even two-thirds, as is the case in the Baltic countries. For more, see UNICEF (1999, 54–55).

34. From the 25 to 30 percent that it was during the communist regime, the participation of women in the parliaments rarely surpasses 12 to 13 percent nowadays, to say nothing of women's near-absence from positions in the government. Even at the local level, their involvement is much weaker than before (Heinen 1998).

35. The fertility rate was 2.3 in 1980 and even went up to 2.43 in 1982 under the state of war. Then it decreased for reasons largely attributed to economic difficulties and reached 2.13 in 1988. By 1998, it had fallen to 1.5 (Kotowska 1999).

36. Total allowances remain higher for parents raising a child alone (women in more than 90 percent of cases): for this group, allowances total about one-third instead of one-fourth of the average salary.

37. This trend is seen in most of the other countries of the region, which have either reduced the range of those eligible for an allowance (as in Bulgaria and Russia) or completely done away with the right to parental leave, as in several ex-Soviet republics (UNICEF 1999, 55)

38. In the 1980s, 90 percent of women eligible for the leave took all or part of it, while fathers made up barely 1 percent of those concerned.

39. Their unemployment rate, it must be emphasized, was nevertheless higher (by 3 to 4 points) than men's for ten years, taking into account the lower rate of female labor-force activity.

40. Among blue-collar workers, twice as many women as men earn less than half of the national salary, while in the highest salary categories, they earn one-third less than men. In 1996, women with a university education only received, on average, 72.5 percent of the male salary in the same category, as opposed to 82.5 percent in 1989 (GUS 1998b).

41. In 1984, the average daily time spent on domestic work was six hours and twenty-nine minutes for women, and two hours and twenty minutes for men. Ten years later, thanks to improvement of living conditions and especially the disappearance of queues, the overall time devoted to these chores had declined, but the men's part of it even more: in 1994, women spent four hours and thirty minutes on chores, while men only spent fifty-three minutes.

42. This is to say nothing of the fact that years of military service are figured in with pension, while those spent on parental leave are not.

43. On the other hand, women who are heads of companies judge that they pull through as well as men from a professional point of view (which facts and statistics tend to confirm), but they also admit to paying a price as far as their personal and family lives are concerned (IPSS 1997, 100).

References

Balcerzak-Paradowska, Bozena. 1994. "Zlobki i przedszkola w okresie transformacji" (Child Care Centers and Nursery Schools in the Process of Transformation). *Polityka spoleczna* 10: 10–13.

_____. 1997. "Publiczne instytucje spolecznych a rodzina" (Public Social Institutions and the Family). In IPSS, ed., *Partnerstwo*.

_____. 1998. "State Policy Towards the Family." In *Social Policy in the 1990s. Legal Regulations and Their Prospected Results,* ed. Stanislawa Golinowska. Warsaw: IPSS.

_____, ed. 1999. *Sytuacja dzieci w Polsce w okresie przemian* (The Situation of Children during the Transformation Phase). Warsaw: IPSS.

Baran, Alina. 1998. "Education." In GUS, 1998a.

Blaszczak-Przybycinska, Ilona, Irena E. Kotowska, Tomàsz Panek, Jaroslaw Podgorski, Grazydn Rytelewska, and Adam Szulc. 1998. "Monitoring Household Living Conditions in Poland, 1995–1996." Report Summary. Warsaw: Institute of Public Affairs.

Bystydzienski, Jill M. 1999. "The Effects of the Economic and Political Transition on Women and Families in Poland." In *Women and Political Change: Perspectives from East-Central Europe*, ed. Sue Bridger. London: Macmillan.

Castel, Robert. 1995. *La métamorphose de la question sociale: Une chronique du salariat* (The Metamorphosis of the Social Question: A Chronicle of the Salaried Class). Paris: Fayard.

Chavance, Bernard. 1998. "Grand-route et chemins de traverse de la transformation postsocialiste" (Main Routes and Shortcuts through the Postsocialist Transformation). *Economies et sociétés* 36 : 141–49.

Deacon, Bob, ed. 1992. *The New Eastern Europe: Social Policy, Past, Present and Future*. London: Sage.

Deacon, Bob, and Julia Szalai, eds. 1990. *Social Policy in the New Eastern Europe*. Aldershot: Avebury.

Firlit-Fesnak, Grazyna. 1998. "Auswirkungen von Systemtransformationen und die soziale Situation der Frauen in Polen" (Effects of the Transformation System and the Social Situation of Women in Poland). *Osteuropa* 48, no. 1: 45–56.

GUS (Glowny Urzad Statystyczny [Central Statistical Office]). 1998a. *Diversification of the Polish Population in 1997*. Warsaw: GUS.

_____. 1998b. *Earnings Distribution in the National Economy as of September 1997*. Warsaw: GUS.

GUS /IPSS/UNICEF. 1994. *Social Policy and Social Conditions in Poland, 1989–1993*. Warsaw: GUS.

Heinen, Jacqueline. 1989. *Femmes en réserve. Les travailleuses polonaises entre la famille et l'emploi* (Women in Reserve: Polish Women Workers between Family and Work). Ph.D. diss. Paris: IRESCO-CNRS.

_____. 1993. "Le poids du passé sur un présent incertain. L'exemple de la Pologne et de l'ex-RDA" (The Weight of the Past on an Uncertain Present: The Example of Poland and the Ex-GDR). In *Le sexe des politiques sociales*, ed. Arlette Gautier and Jacqueline Heinen. Paris: Côté-femmes.

_____. 1995. *Chômage et devenir de la main-d'oeuvre féminine en Pologne. Le coût de la transition* (Unemployment and the Future of Women's Labor in Poland: The Cost of Transition). Paris: L'Harmattan.

_____. 1998. "Women in Local and National Politics in Central and Eastern Europe." In *Women in the Local and Regional Authorities*. Paris: CEMR.

_____. 1999a. "East European Transition, Labour Markets and Gender. In the Light of Three Cases: Poland, Hungary and Bulgaria," *Polish Population Review* 15: 106–27.

_____. 1999b. "La pénalisation de l'avortement en Pologne ou l'intrication entre le politique et le religieux" (Penalizing Abortion in Poland, or, The Imbrication of the Political and the Religious). In *Crimes et Cultures*, ed. Jean-Michel Bessette. Paris: L'Harmattan.

Heinen, Jacqueline, and Anna Matuchniak-Krasuska. 1992. *L'avortement en Pologne. La croix et la bannière* (Abortion in Poland: The Cross and the Banner). Paris: L'Harmattan.

IPSS (Instytut Pracy Spraw Socjalnych [Institute of Labor and Social Studies]), ed. 1997. *Partnerstwo w rodzinie i na rzecz rodziny* (Partnership in the Family and with Regard to Family Issues). Warsaw: IPSS.

Kotowska, Irena. 1995. "Discrimination against Women in the Labour Market." *Social Politics* 2, no. 1: 76–90.

_____. 1999. "Demographic Processes and Labour Market Developments in Poland in the 1990s." In *Demographic Changes in Poland in the 1990s from the Perspective of the Second Demographic Transition*, ed. Irena Kotowska. Warsaw: Warsaw School of Economics.

Kurzynowski, Adam. 1979. *Aktywizacja zawodowa kobiet zameznych w Polsce ludowej* (Married Women's Professional Activity in the Polish Population). Warsaw: KiW.

OECD. 1994. Organization for Economic Cooperation and Development, *Unemployment in Transition Countries: Transient or Persistent?* Paris: OECD.

Ringen, Stein, and Claire Wallace, eds. 1993. *Societies in Transition, East-Central Europe Today.* Prague: Central European University.

UNICEF. 1994. United Nations International Children's Emergency Fund, *Crisis in Mortality, Health and Nutrition.* Regional monitoring report no. 2. Florence: UNICEF.

_____. 1999. *Women in Transition.* Regional monitoring report no. 6. Florence: UNICEF.

Uscinska, Gertruda. 1986. *"Ewolucja swiadczen pienieznych z ubezpieczenia spolecznego z tytulu macierzynstwa"* (The Evolution of Social Benefits Linked to Motherhood). Ph.D. diss. Warsaw. IPSS.

Wiktorow, Aleksandra. 1999. "Polityka spoleczna panstwa wobec kobiet" (State Social Politics toward Women). Report of the Conference on the Consequences of Privatization for Women's Situation in Poland, April 22, 1999.

Zylicz, Barbara. 1999. "Spoleczne efekyy prywatyzacji: (1) Grupowe wywiadiy poglebione; (2) Wywiady z dyrektorami przedsiebiorstw" (The Social Effects of Privatization: [1] Detailed Discussions of Groups; [2] Discussions with the Heads of Companies). Report of the Conference on the Consequences of Privatization for Women's Situation in Poland, April 22, 1999.

the power of "choice"

CHAPTER 4

Australia: Child Care and State-Centered Feminism in a Liberal Welfare Regime

Deborah Brennan

Gender issues have been at the core of welfare-state restructuring in Australia for several decades. At the same time, the institutions, policies, and practices of welfare have been sites of considerable feminist scholarship and activism. Historically, many elements of Australian social policy assumed the presence of a male breadwinner: women's economic dependence was built into key aspects of the social security system as well as institutions such as the "family wage" paid to male workers. Since the early 1970s, however, the assumption of women's dependence has been weakened and the basis of many policies has shifted from "difference equality" (Cass 1995; Shaver 1995). The labor-force participation of women, especially mothers of young children, has risen dramatically, although it is still well below the levels of similar countries (O'Connor, Orloff, and Shaver 1999). Australian women continue to be responsible for the bulk of domestic and caring work, and are likely to have part-time rather than full-time employment. The increase in women's workforce participation and the associated growth of feminist activism nevertheless contributed to a political climate that was receptive to women's demands for recognition of their changing status and aspirations. Under the Labour governments that held power at the national level from 1972 to 1975 and 1983 to 1996, numerous "feminist-influenced, women-friendly reforms" were initiated and consolidated (Hancock 1999, 3). During this period Australia developed a world-class child care system more in keeping with the generous, public provision of social democracies such as Denmark, Sweden, and France than with the virtual absence of national support exemplified by other liberal regimes such as the United States, Canada, and the United Kingdom. The system was built around the principles of quality, affordability, and accessibility. At its core was a network of nonprofit, community-based child care centers and high quality family child care schemes. Services were open to children from all income groups, with fees determined by family income and commonwealth subsidies reducing the fees payable by low- and middle-income families.

A distinctive feature of the Australian case is that—although the challenge to the male breadwinner model has been less decisive than in other liberal regimes—publicly funded child care is far better developed. Australia's child care system is characterized by extensive coverage, high-quality care, and relatively generous subsidies, even though aspects of the policy have been weakened in the last decade. This chapter begins by outlining the main features of Australia's current system of child care, thus setting the scene for subsequent analysis. It then explores the politics that allowed Australian feminists and their allies to fashion an unusually progressive national child care system in the 1970s and '80s. In particular, it explains how Australia came to adopt not-for-profit, community-based care as the dominant form of provision, and outlines some of the strengths and weaknesses of this approach in contributing to broader goals of gender and class equity.

The next section examines the shift toward neoliberal economic and public policy approaches that occurred under Labour from the late 1980s onward. It considers the impact that these ideas had upon child care policy and looks at the tension that arose between the government's social justice and economic objectives as it attempted to open the Australian economy to international competition and deal with a radically changing labor market. The final section looks at child care and related policies under the conservative coalition government elected in 1996. Under the coalition there has been a deliberate attempt to reshape social policy in ways that are supportive of the male-breadwinner family form.

Australia's National Child Care Program

The assumption of women's dependence was built into the very foundations of the Australian welfare state. Most pensions and benefits assumed the presence of a male breadwinner and a female caregiver. Even the industrial relations system was based on this assumption, with its notion of a male "family wage." In a very real sense, Australia had a "men's welfare state" and a "women's welfare state" (Bryson 1992). Over the past three decades, changes in the nature of the labor force, the organization of work, and demographic and family patterns, combined with vigorous advocacy on the part of feminists and labor activists, have led to considerable institutional adaptation.

The growth in women's employment has been a central factor here. Although not high by northern European or North American standards, mothers' workforce participation grew rapidly in the 1980s and remains at an all time high, although the upward trajectory has stalled. Both parents are employed in just under half of all couple families with a child under five. Not surprisingly, the age of the youngest child has a marked impact upon mothers' labor-force participation. Thus, while only 32 percent of mothers with a child under one year of age are in the labor force, the figure rises to 52 percent when the youngest child is two years of age and 66 percent when the youngest child is six years old (ABS 1998). (Most Australian children start school around their fifth birthday—only a few are still at home by the time they turn six.) The increase in the number and proportion of sole parent families since the early 1970s has been another major factor shaping the Australian welfare state. Sole parents now constitute 21 percent of all families with dependent children. Most lone parents were previously in a relationship (only 3 percent are teenagers), and unemployment is frequently a contributing factor in relationship breakdown.

Since the 1970s there have been substantial changes in the Australian labor market. These include a dramatic increase in part-time and casual work (almost one-fourth of the Australian workforce are now employed part-time, compared with only 10 percent twenty-five years ago); far greater reliance on "nonstandard" forms of employment such as contract, seasonal, and "on call" work; increases in overtime; more jobs requiring employees to do split shifts, twelve-hour shifts, and weekend work; and a reduction in the proportion of jobs with fixed starting and finishing times. Only one-third of Australian workers are now engaged for the "standard" working week of thirty-eight hours worked on a predictable schedule (Lansbury 1997, 2).

Declining fertility and the aging of the population are also important. Australian women are having fewer children (the current fertility rate is around 1.74) and, in general, are having them later in life. The absolute number of children from birth to four years of age has been declining for several years; between 1995 and 1998 the number of children in this group fell by 15,900, or 1.2 percent. Projections indicate that the aging of the population, already evident, is set to continue. The proportion of the population aged sixty-five or over is expected to increase from 12 percent in 1998 to around 25 percent in 2051 (ABS 1998).

As mentioned briefly above, the level of child care provision in Australia has more in common with France and the Scandinavian countries than with other liberal regimes. In 1999, 40 percent of Australian children from birth to four years of age had some kind of formal care—long child care, preschool, family child care, occasional care, or a combination of these. This marked a substantial increase from 1987, when only 29 percent of this age group used formal services. "Long child care" (full-day) is the most commonly used formal service (used by 33 percent of this age group),[1] while 32 percent use preschool. Informal care (either exclusively or in combination with formal care) was used by 48 percent of children in this age group and remains the most common arrangement used by working parents. Such care is mainly provided by grandparents, siblings, and other relatives.

Care is provided through a mixture of public and private (both profit and non-profit) organizations. Most long child care places are provided by the private sector, while the majority of other services are the responsibility of state and local governments and the nonprofit sector. Family child care is of a high standard in Australia when compared to many other countries. It should not to be confused with the mere licensing of private individuals (which also occurs in Australia, but on an insignificant scale). Each Australian family child care scheme employs a small number of professionals who match selected and trained caregivers with appropriate families. Caregivers are supported in various ways by the coordination unit and may receive visits from child development specialists, regular playgroups, and subsidized access to equipment such as child car safety restraints and age-appropriate toys.

Publicly funded child care services are open to children from all income groups, and fees are determined according to family income. The commonwealth government provides a subsidy called Child Care Benefit (CCB), which substantially reduces the fees of low and middle-income families—although, as will be discussed later, there is growing concern about the ability of such families to afford child care. CCB is available to children using approved private centers, nonprofit centers, and family child care homes. As in similar countries, usage of formal care is more common as family income increases—reflecting the fact that having two parents employed raises family income and increases the need for child care. Less than half (46 percent) of children in families with weekly incomes below Aus. $400 attend child care, compared with 61 percent in families with weekly income of more than Aus. $2000. Still, the idea that children should be excluded because their parents' income is too high has no place in the Australian system. All families using child care for work-related reasons are eligible for some assistance. Supplementary funding is available for children with additional needs, including Aboriginal and islander children, children from diverse cultural and linguistic backgrounds, and children with disabilities.

The commonwealth requires all funded services to comply with state and territory regulations concerning quality, staffing, space, and facilities. Long child care centers must also participate in the Quality Improvement and Accreditation System which the Labour Party government introduced in 1991. Virtually all centers participate in this system; if they do not, the families who use them are ineligible for child care benefit. Child care remains an overwhelmingly female-dominated industry; of those employed in child care in 1998, 94 percent were women. About 40 percent of these worked part-time, compared with about 25 percent of the workforce as a whole. Child care workers are comparatively highly qualified—36 percent have a diploma or degree, compared with 27 percent of all workers. Child care is still poorly paid, however: women working full-time in child care earn 26 percent below the average for all women in full-time employment, while male child care workers earn just over half the average for men in all industries combined (Saunders 1999, 63).

From Philanthropy to Feminism

What are the origins of Australia's child care system? Child care emerged on the national political agenda in 1972 with the introduction of the Child Care Act by a conservative federal government. Although the Women's Electoral Lobby was formed that same year, feminists were not a driving force behind this initiative. Rather, the major catalyst for the legislation was the demand of employers for female labor. The government made it clear that its goal in extending support to child care services was to address a somewhat unfortunate social necessity—not to promote gender equity. In the words of one of the ministers who introduced the legislation into the Australian Parliament, "everybody would agree that the best place for a very young child is with its mother" (quoted in Brennan 1998, 68). Since the late nineteenth century, philanthropic organizations had provided a small number of kindergartens and day nurseries in the inner suburbs of the major cities. These services were funded and staffed largely through the efforts of women who lived in prosperous areas; they were modeled on the kind of institutional care provided in orphanages and hospitals. The conservative government's early attempts to expand government provision of child care were built upon the philosophies and practices developed by the traditional philanthropic organizations.

At around this time, newly formed child care advocacy organizations and women's liberation groups were beginning to formulate their own vision of publicly funded child care—a vision that drew explicitly on feminist analysis of the unequal gender relations within families and the wider society. While no single blueprint emerged, the broad feminist consensus was that child care should be freely available to all parents regardless of their workforce status. Child care should not be provided simply to free women to work outside the home, they argued, since "To only want child care on the ground that it will give us a chance to prove we are as good as men in a man's world is to entirely miss the point of the new feminism" (quoted in Brennan 1998, 67). Rather, child care should be seen as an essential element of the struggle toward less rigid sex role and generational stereotypes. Members of the Melbourne-based group Community Child Care went one step further, arguing that intense and exclusive mother-child relationships could be oppressive to both women and children. They argued that men should share in the joys and labors of caring for children both in the home and in public settings such as preschools and child care centers.

The election of a Labour government at the national level in 1972 coincided with the resurgence of feminist activity in Australia, and this was to have a major impact on the shape of Australia's child care program. Prime Minister Gough Whitlam was keen to attract and retain women's votes and, to this end, he appointed an adviser on women's affairs, Elizabeth Reid. Together with Labour Party activists and women from a range of community organizations, Reid worked tirelessly to ensure that the national child care program was brought more in line with democratic and feminist ideals. This meant, among other things, ensuring that established, conservative organizations (such as those that had pioneered children's services in the previous century) did not become the sole or dominant providers of government-funded child care. Community advocates wanted neighborhood groups and small nonprofit organizations to receive government financial assistance to operate services. This approach would enable parents to participate in the management and running of the service if they chose to do so. To use an expression of the times, professionals should be "on tap, not on top."

In late 1974 Labour announced its intention to establish a national network of flexible, community-based services that would cater to *all* children regardless of

their parents' workforce status. Under this policy there was to be no distinction between educating children and caring for them. Trained teachers were to be employed in all services caring for young children, not just preschools. In line with the
advocacy of women's lobby groups, nonprofit, community-based services were at
the core of the proposed system. The community child care approach was very
much in line with Arlie Hochschild's "warm modern" approach to care. Hochschild
has described this approach as warm because "[families] do not relinquish all care to
[professionals], and because men and women share in what we do not relinquish"
and as modern because "public institutions have a part in the solution" (1995, 341).
Importantly, the staff in Australian community-based child care services were to be
paid award wages—indeed, under the Child Care Act, commonwealth subsidies
were specifically linked to award wages.

Although government policymakers and child care activists had progressive intentions, some aspects of the Whitlam government's child care strategy scored very
poorly in terms of enhancing social and political equality. In keeping with its rather
naive focus on the power of "communities," the government relied upon submissions as the basis for deciding the location of new services. This approach severely
disadvantaged working-class localities whose members lacked the skills to write
submissions and who simply needed child care so that they could work. Well-organized groups from middle-class suburbs attracted most of the funds available
through the "community submission" approach while poorer neighborhoods and
rural and remote communities missed out.

Despite these significant limitations—and the government's untimely dismissal
from office—the initiatives of the Whitlam Labour government were of immense
significance for child care policy. They established a principle that would guide policy in this area for the next two decades—namely, that the central mechanism for
delivering services would be nonprofit community groups and local government
authorities. This principle was even extended to the work-based services developed
in subsequent years. These were, effectively, community-based care in a different location. Work-based child care services that received funding from the government
were run on a nonprofit basis; they had to be controlled by parents and staff; and
they had to be open to residents of the local neighborhood as well as employees.
While the conservative government of Malcom Fraser (1975–1983) retreated from
the relatively generous levels of funding provided under Labour and attempted to
restrict access to the "needy," the fundamental characteristics of the community-
based child care system devised under Whitlam were nevertheless retained.

Child Care and the Trade Union Movement

Following the election of Robert Hawke's Labour Party government in 1983, child
care moved to a central position on the policy agenda. Under previous administrations, child care had been a marginal issue, of interest mainly to women's organiza-

tions, child care lobby groups, and a small number of public servants. The attention given to child care by the Hawke government can be explained by two features of the new political environment: the emergence of corporatist political structures involving the trade union movement, employers, and government, and the new priority given to women and "women's issues" within the Labour Party and the union movement.

Under the accord, or agreement, between the Labour Party and the Australian Council of Trade Unions (ACTU), trade unions undertook to moderate their wage demands in return for policies which would lead to the growth of jobs and an extension of the "social wage"—broadly understood to mean publicly provided (or at least supported) benefits and services such as Medicare, child care, and superannuation. Throughout the 1980s, women continued to move into the labor force in increasing numbers. In 1980, 46 percent of married women with dependent children were at work; by 1992 this figure had reached 61 percent. Female lone parents also increased their labor force attachment, from 43 percent at the beginning of this period to 52 percent at the end (Cass 1995, 51). At the same time, male (especially blue-collar) employment was declining as a result of industry and economic restructuring. These developments changed the way in which "women's issues" were pursued *within* the labor movement as well as outside it. In 1983, Jennie George, a representative of the Australian Teachers Federation, became the first woman to be elected to the executive of the ACTU.

Following a campaign by trade union women, the ACTU in 1984 developed an Action Program for Women Workers. This located issues of prime concern to women, such as child care, equal pay, and antidiscrimination legislation, within the broader framework of the labor movement's agenda. The alliance formed among feminist trade unionists, child care lobbyists, and the labor movement proved crucial in the ensuing years. Child care was one of the policy areas singled out for mention in the original agreement between Labour and the unions and it consistently featured in the social wage claims put forward by the union movement in subsequent years. The ACTU lobbied vigorously around several aspects of child care—not simply an expansion in the number of places. It pressed the government to increase both community-based and work-based services, urged it to ensure that fees were kept at levels that could reasonably be afforded by low- and middle-income families, and campaigned for improvements in the pay and conditions of child care workers.

Within the government, women members of Parliament (MPs), supported by sympathetic men, also worked hard to promote the importance of child care on the government's agenda. Shortly after coming to office, Labour established child care planning committees in all states and territories. The purpose of these committees was to give advice on funding priorities and to ensure that new services were located in areas of greatest need. Although by no means a perfect system, the planning approach put an end to the enormous waste of time that had gone into submission writing and reduced the geographic and class inequities that had been rife under the old system. The Labour Party maintained its commitment to nonprofit, community-based care and expanded the number of such places at an unprecedented rate (see table 4.1).

In 1985 Labour instituted cuts to child care that it claimed were needed to put the program on a financially viable basis. The minister responsible for child care, Don Grimes, argued that he would be unable to secure cabinet agreement for continued growth in the program unless costs were contained and a higher proportion of children benefited from child care expenditure. In the mid-1980s, fewer than 10 percent of children below school age had access to government subsidized care (Brennan 1998, 182). Grimes asserted that he could not allow a situation "where some children have perhaps the highest quality of care in the western world while others have no chance of access." He added, "The Cabinet felt that we were at a watershed. There were major inequities in the program, and yet we were poised to launch into another major expansion. It would have been irresponsible not to take stock of the situation. . . . In essence what we [were] doing [was] finding a way to use the available funds more effectively so that our goals of expanding the program [could] be more equitably and more rationally achieved" (Grimes 1985). The cuts involved ending the payment of a fixed percentage of the award wages of qualified staff, and moving instead to a flat-rate per capita operational subsidy in respect of each funded place. To the dismay of those who cared about class as well as gender equity issues, this demonstrated that the government's primary concern was the ex-

TABLE 4.1: CHILD CARE IN AUSTRALIA, 1982–1999

YEAR	COMMUNITY-BASED CENTERS	FAMILY DAY CARE	OUTSIDE SCHOOL HOURS CARE	PRIVATE CENTERS	TOTAL
1982	18,600	15,100	7,900		41,600
1983	20,000	20,100	9,900		50,000
1984	23,000	24,300	11,600		50,000
1985	31,400	32,200	14,800		78,400
1986	34,600	34,000	15,900		84,500
1987	40,800	38,400	29,600		108,800
1988	44,200	39,500	30,200		122,400
1989	44,100	39,600	30,600		122,300
1990	44,400	41,000	37,200		122,600
1991	39,600	43,000	36,416	36,700	155,700
1992	40,300	45,700	44,500	53,200	183,700
1993	42,800	48,200	48,300	61,400	200,700
1994	43,400	51,700	50,300	80,400	225,800
1995	44,600	54,000	59,800	99,900	258,300
1996	45,600	60,100	64,100	122,500	292,300
1997	46,300	62,700	71,800	136,600	317,400
1998	51,700	63,700	134,400	142,900	392,700
1999	50,600	64,000	161,000	127,100	422,000

SOURCE: Department of Family and Community Services (1999b).

pansion of places—the quality of care received by children and the related issue of staff wages and conditions were relegated to secondary status. The ACTU condemned the new funding system, parents held protest rallies and demonstrations, child care workers went on strike (an extraordinary action for such an industrially weak group), but to no avail. In keeping with neoliberal ideas about the importance of avoiding "rent-seeking" behavior, the new system undermined the longstanding unity between parents and staff that had previously been the basis of joint parent/worker campaigns for improved staff pay and conditions.

Despite these measures, Labour continued to be divided over the merits of the child care program. Finance Minister Peter Walsh openly derided child care as middle-class welfare and expressed a preference for the introduction of vouchers which could be used in either public or commercial centers. Women within the parliamentary Labour Party were furious at Walsh's remarks and established an official working party to examine the government's role in child care. The report of the working party strongly endorsed the continuation of publicly funded services and argued that child care had been "a critical part of the Government's policy of economic recovery and increased productivity." It pointed out that child care services were a vital structural support that enabled women to enter the workforce, and that this in turn provided their families with a significant buffer against the reduced wages that were a consequence of the accord for many male workers. The report also discussed the political importance of child care provision, noting that polls conducted for the Labour Party in marginal electorates had shown that women in working-class suburbs rated child care as their most pressing need (ALP 1988, 7).

One of the most significant developments in the debate about the merits of child care occurred in 1987 when the minister for community services, Neil Blewett, commissioned a study from the Center for Economic Policy Research at the Australian National University on the economic benefits of child care. The center's report argued that there were net financial *gains* to government from the provision of high-quality, work-related child care. Such care, they argued, not only led to welfare savings but also helped to avoid the depreciation of "human capital" associated with the withdrawal of well-educated women from the labor force (Anstie et al. 1988, 12). The report received extensive publicity and proved to be crucial in countering the arguments of the finance minister and his department. Labour moved increasingly toward a workforce-oriented child care strategy. In 1988 it announced a National Child Care Strategy that would meet all demand for work-related child care by 1990. Despite this initial gain, the shift toward economic arguments for child care had profound long-term consequences.

The discursive construction of child care changed significantly during this period. Child care was said to be about "facilitating labor force participation," "enhancing productivity," and "assisting the welfare to work transition." While feminists were initially gratified to hear the prime minister describe child care as "an integral component of the Government's economic and social justice policies" and praise the expansion of the program as "one of the greatest social and economic reforms undertaken by the . . . Government," it soon became clear that allying child care so closely with economic benefits came at a price. By the early 1990s, the goals of the early feminist movement that promoted child care as enhancing women's autonomy, providing alternatives to the nuclear family, and encouraging independence and so-ciability among young children had all but disappeared. More significantly, children in families *without* work—that is, children in the poorest and most vulnerable fami-lies—were increasingly marginalized.

The Shift to Commercial Providers

Commercial child care had grown throughout the 1980s and for several years pri-vate providers had exerted pressure on the Labour Party to extend government as-sistance to families who used such services. This was an extremely difficult issue for Labour. On the one hand, it had decided after considerable internal debate and con-flict to give a firm commitment to the expansion of nonprofit, community-based services. On the other hand, its members (particularly those MPs whose seats were vulnerable) were sensitive to representations from constituents whose incomes would qualify them for assistance in a community-based center but who could not get help to use a private service. This was a particularly sharp issue if the only avail-able service was a private one. While advocacy groups such as the National Associa-tion of Community Based Children's Services and Community Child Care remained adamant in their opposition of the extension of subsidies to users of commercial care, the ACTU—once a staunch opponent of such subsidies—changed its mind in the run-up to the 1990 federal election and became a strong supporter of the move. This seems to have been crucial for the government. During the 1990 campaign it announced that it would extend subsidies to users of commercial centers.

   While equity between families in similar circumstances was the public rationale given by Labour for its change in policy, in fact there was another motive. Ever-vigilant finance and treasury officials had convinced their ministers that boosting private providers would take the pressure off the commonwealth to expend capital funds on the construction of new services. In fact, the government miscalculated disastrously on this issue. It based its costs on the assumption that 28,000 commer-cial child care places would become available in the first four years of the policy. In fact, this target was exceeded in the first year (see table 4.1). The scale of growth was so great that the commonwealth found itself footing a bill for child care assis-tance that exceeded the treasury's worst fears. Child care assistance outlays doubled between 1991 and 1996. Moreover, the "unpredictability and scale" of this growth meant the program continually required additional funds to cover shortfalls in esti-mates (DHFS 1996, 5). Numerous reports expressed concern about the inflation in the cost of child care assistance for the newly established private places (Australian National Audit Office 1994; EPAC 1996).

   As a direct result of the generous support provided by the commonwealth, the for-profit sector quickly became the major provider of center-based long child care in Australia, and the commonwealth increasingly defined its role in children's services as supporting other players—notably, employers, commercial providers, and state and local governments. Apparently unwilling to risk accusations of intervening in commercial decision making, the Labour Party government placed no limits or constraints on the growth of private, for-profit care. It subsidized new services in any location chosen by private businesses. To qualify for child care assistance, a service merely had to be open for a certain number of hours per day and weeks per year, be licensed by the relevant state or territory authority, and be registered with the Quality Improvement and Accreditation System. This was in direct contrast to the strict limitations that had governed the expansion of community-based child care throughout the 1980s.

The Hawke and Paul Keating Labour governments oversaw huge growth in the provision of publicly subsidized care—from 50,000 places in 1983 to 292,300 in 1996. The expansion of child care under Labour Party government was achieved, however, at a considerable price. In the rush to expand the sheer number of child care places, government policies brought an end to the goal of a national system of nonprofit, community-based child care. Labour presided over a shift away from community-based child care toward for-profit providers, and paved the way for further changes under the conservative government elected in 1996.

Choice—The New Conservative Rhetoric

"Family policy" is central to the agenda of the conservative government elected in 1996. Throughout his public life, Prime Minister John Howard has been committed to assisting families in which the mother cares for children at home. For years he promoted the idea of splitting income between spouses for taxation purposes—a policy measure designed to benefit single-income families and discourage secondary earners. Howard has always been uneasy with feminism and feminists; he actively opposed the establishment of a feminist network within the New South Wales branch of the Liberal Party (Puplick 1994, 133–34). He generally prefers to employ the rhetoric of "choice" rather than level any kind of direct attack upon child care provision. In one address he commented, "We are in the business of maximising . . . choice. We are not in the business of saying: you should do this or you should do that. And we are also not going to be intimidated against making these changes by the noise of some who see the tiniest acknowledgment of the rights and the interests of single income families as some kind of attempt to turn back a 30 year social revolution" (Howard 1998). The year before his election as prime minister, Howard released a document outlining the "values, directions and policy priorities" of a coalition government. This contained no specific references to women or child care policy, but in a section entitled "Greater Choice and Security for Families," it stated: "A Coalition Government will move immediately to reduce the economic pressures on families (especially those with dependent children), to increase the opportunities open to them and to give them more genuine choices about how they live" (Howard 1995, 36). Specific priorities included giving families "greater freedom to choose whether one parent cares full-time for their children at home or whether both are in the paid workforce" and "address[ing] Labour's current discrimination against parents who choose to remain at home to care for their children" (1995, 36). Howard also put forward a vision of his party as one that would govern "for all Australians" rather than respond to the demands of well-organized special interests. Although feminists were never identified as a "special interest group," Howard's previous record made it plain that they were in his sights. As one apprehensive woman commented, "anyone [outside] a family unit is seen as a special interest group" (quoted in Johnson 2000, 19).

The Howard government has a higher proportion of women parliamentarians than any previous federal government, yet its policies are anything but feminist. When the Labour Party was in government, Labour parliamentarians formed a women's caucus and monitored ministers to ensure that they implemented Labour policy on issues of concern to women; they were prepared to publicly challenge ministers on their government's performance in this policy area—especially any who were hostile to child care. Coalition members of parliament are not similarly disposed. A few have made private or semiprivate comments about particular policies, but it is rare for them to speak out publicly.

From the early months of the current government, it became apparent that a significant force within the party on social policy was the Lyons Forum, a group of about fifty coalition MPs committed to the view that "the family is the fundamental unit of society, the prime agency for the development and socialization of children and that marriage provides the optimum environment for the nurturing of children." The Forum aimed to "initiate and monitor legislation with respect to its influence and effect on the family unit" and to bring pressure to bear upon government if legislative proposals discriminated against traditional families (Savva 1997). Although there is little public information about the Lyons Forum, its members are believed to include more than a dozen ministers, among them Jocelyn Newman, the minister for social security and minister assisting the prime minister for the status of women. Prime Minister Howard claims not to be a member, but the views of the Lyons Forum accord closely with his long-held views on the family. The coalition's first budget contained measures that addressed both these concerns: it combined substantial cuts to child care (especially for families using community-based, long child care services) with new measures to assist families with one parent at home. The Lyons Forum may not have designed these policies, but its members are likely to have been pleased with them.

In its first budget, the Howard government introduced a series of taxation measures (known as the Family Tax Initiative, or FTI) directed at families with young children. The first part of the FTI increased the tax-free threshold by a modest $1,000 for one member of a couple (or a sole parent) where family taxable income is less than $70,000 (only about 10 percent of families would be excluded by this means test). The second part—said to have been insisted upon by Howard—specifically rewarded full-time parental care of preschool children. It provided an additional tax-free area of Aus.$2,500 with at least one child under the age of five, *but only for single-income families*. A family in which the same or a lower level of total income is earned by the efforts of two working parents is not eligible for this benefit. In this part of the FTI, the income test for the second earner (usually, of course, the woman) was set so low that even those with a few hours work each week would be ineligible. In a startling indication of the deeply ideological wellspring of this policy initiative, women who earned up to $20,000 investment income from trusts and shares (but who did not transgress gender norms by "going out to work") were to be eligible for the concession. This part of the policy was later modified (Wallace 1997, 168).

Also in its first budget, the coalition removed the operational subsidy from non-profit child care centers—despite an explicit election commitment that it would be retained. The removal of the subsidy was in line with sustained lobbying from the commercial sector. Although greeted with dismay by community based centers, it was not unexpected; operational subsidies for long child care centers would almost certainly have been removed by the Labour Party government had it remained in power. In confirmation of this view, a subsequent inquiry into the Howard government's child care policies that was dominated by Labour senators did not recommend reinstatement of the operational subsidy (SCARC 1998). The coalition's first budget also froze the fee ceiling used by the Department of Family and Community Services to calculate families' entitlement to fees subsidies. In order to contain costs, subsidies are based not on the actual fee charged by individual services, but on an "average" fee determined by the department. This change in policy substantially increased the cost of formal child care for low- and middle-income families and decreased the viability of community-based long child care. Despite some changes to child care subsidies in 2000 that went some ways toward alleviating the high cost of care, affordability is now a major concern in Australia.

Other policy and funding measures designed to promote gender equality or provide structural support for women's participation in the labor force have also been reduced or downgraded. The budget of the Office of the Status of Women was cut by 40 percent in 1996; the following year the government abolished the Women's Bureau in the Department of Employment, Education, Training and Youth Affairs—the oldest women's unit in the federal bureaucracy—and disbanded the Women's Statistics Unit in the Australian Bureau of Statistics. Of equal, if not greater significance, numerous nongovernment organizations representing women have lost not only their funding but also their access to ministers and bureaucratic decision makers (Sawer 1999, 44).

The impact of the changes to child care under the Howard government has been the subject of bitter exchanges between the government and community advocates. Government ministers contend that expenditure on children's services has increased, supply has grown and women's workforce participation remains steady

(Newman 1999). Such statements are technically true, but they gloss over the re-shaping of policy that has taken place within the program. Child care groups correctly point out that government statements deal only with aggregates and mask the complex reality of class- and neighborhood-based difference. This dispute illustrates the importance of understanding changes to the *structure* of programs and of not relying upon expenditure figures to tell their own story.

Research conducted by a range of nonprofit organizations suggests that many middle and low-income Australian families can no longer afford child care. Some parents have been compelled to reduce the number of hours their children spend in child care or withdraw them from formal care altogether (at the same time reducing their own commitment to paid work); children are increasingly subjected to "patch-work" arrangements involving family care, informal care, and limited formal provision; and some parents, as a last resort, have withdrawn from paid employment. These trends have been demonstrated by the Brotherhood of St. Laurence in conjunction with Community Child Care (Tasker and Siemon 1998), the Council of Social Service of New South Wales (1997), the National Association of Community Based Children's Services (1997), the Queensland Child Care Coalition (1998), Tasmanian Association of Children's Services (1998), and the private research agency Families at Work (Warrilow 1997). The government has rejected such research as "anecdotal" and insufficiently rigorous, but the consistency of results makes them difficult to dismiss. Collectively they suggest that the changes have driven many parents away from formal services, compelled others to reduce their hours of work and usage of formal care, and caused still others to move their children to informal care and/or "patchwork" arrangements. Services that previously had lengthy waiting lists are now experiencing vacancies for the first time. These studies also indicate that services are closing and that communities have been deeply affected by these measures. The choice of combining parenting with paid work appears to be rapidly disappearing for many families.

Although child care workers have increased their level of political and industrial awareness over the past two decades, child care continues to be characterized by low levels of understanding of existing award conditions; small, isolated workplaces; and poor bargaining skills (on the part of both employers and employees). Child care workers are low paid, some work extremely long hours; and award breaches persist (ACIRRT 1996, 12).

Conclusion

The classification of a country as belonging to a particular type of welfare regime is of limited use in predicting the nature of particular policies, especially those related to gender equity. Cross-national differences *within* regime types arise as a result of women's political and industrial mobilization, the strength of antifeminist groups, the nature of incumbent political parties, and the political opportunity structure

(O'Connor, Orloff, and Shaver 1999, 202–3). Australia's public child care system—the most comprehensive provided by any liberal welfare regime—can be understood only in the context of the tactics adopted by the Australian women's movement and the strategic alliances formed between feminists, the trade union leaders, and Labour governments. The cuts to funding and the reshaping of the program that have occurred since the mid-1990s reflect the growing influence of neo-liberal policy prescriptions, the election of a government keen to promote traditional family structures, and the marginalization of groups whose agenda includes gender and class equality.

Importantly, while the Australian child care system has been restructured and refocused it has not been subject to wholesale retrenchment. There has been an explicit effort to enhance the role of commercial providers and reduce the significance of community-based providers. The shift to private provision raises broader issues. With community-based child care now providing only a minority of available places, pressures to reduce licensing standards and to move away from the current system of accreditation toward industry self-regulation are likely to grow. The nonprofit sector has traditionally been the guardian of child care standards and, in the past, was able to link campaigns for improved pay and conditions to the quest for higher quality care. The private sector has different interests and it would be naive to expect it to promote quality care (beyond what is required by regulation and accreditation) or improved industrial conditions. Despite such changes, Australia still has a national child care system, aimed in principle at supporting the participation of parents in the workforce and in other forms of social and economic participation.

Note

1. "Long child care" is the term used in Australia for centers that meet the needs of working parents. In order for the families using them to qualify for commonwealth assistance, long child care centers must be open at least eight hours per day, forty-eight weeks of the year. They may provide both full- and part-time care and must offer developmental programs within their care programs. Some long child care centers provide care for limited numbers of primary school children before and after school and during school holidays.

References

Anstie, Robert, Robert Gregory, Steve Dowrick, and Jonathan J. Pincus. 1988. *Government Spending on Work-Related Child Care: Some Economic Issues.* Canberra: Centre for Economic Policy Research, Australian National University.

ABS (Australian Bureau of Statistics). 1997. *Family Characteristics, Australia,* April. Cat. No. 4442.0, Canberra: ABS.

_____. 1998. *Population by Age and Sex, Australian States and Territories*, June 1997 to 1998. Cat. No. 320. Canberra: ABS.

ACIRRT (Australian Center for Industrial Relations Research and Training). 1996. "Child Care in a Changing Industrial Relations Environment." In EPAC Child Care Task Force, *Interim Report: Commissioned Studies*. Canberra: AGPS.

Australian Institute of Health and Welfare (AIHW). 1999. *Australia's Welfare 1999*. Canberra: AIHW.

ALP (Australian Labour Party). 1988. "Report of the Working Party on Child Care to the Caucus Committee on Welfare and Community Services (internal party document)," November.

Australian National Audit Office. 1994. *Mind the Children: The Management of Children's Services*. Canberra: Australian Government Publication Service.

Baldock, Cora and Bettina Cass. 1988. *Women, Social Welfare and the State in Australia*, 2d ed. North Sydney: Allen and Unwin.

Brennan, Deborah. 1998. *The Politics of Australian Child Care: Philanthropy to Feminism and Beyond*, 2d ed. Cambridge: Cambridge University Press.

Bryson, Lois. 1992. *Welfare and the State*. London: Macmillan.

Cass, Bettina. 1992. "Caring Work and Welfare Regimes: Policies for Sole Parents in Four Countries." In *Comparative Perspectives on Sole Parents Policy: Work and Welfare*, ed. S. Shaver. Social Policy Research Center, University of New South Wales, Reports and Proceedings no. 106.

_____. 1994. "Citizenship, Work and Welfare: The Dilemma for Australian Women." *Social Politics* 1, no. 1: 106–24.

_____. 1995. "Gender in Australia's Restructuring Labor Market and Welfare State." In *Women in a Restructuring Australia*, ed. A. Edwards and S. Magarey. St. Leonards: Allen and Unwin.

_____. 1999. "The Social Policy Context." In *Contesting the Australian Way*, ed. P. Smyth and B. Cass. Cambridge: Cambridge University Press.

Castles, Frank, ed. 1993. *Families of Nations: Patterns of Public Policies in Western Democracies*. Hants, Aldershot, Eng.: Dartmouth.

_____. 1996. "Needs-Based Strategies of Social Protection in Australia and New Zealand." In *Welfare States in Transition: National Adaptations in Global Economies*, ed. G. Esping-Andersen. London: Sage.

[Australian] Department of Family and Community Service (FACS). 1999a. *Annual Report 1998–99*. Canberra: FACS.

_____. 1999b. *Child Care in Australia*. Canberra: FACS.

[Australian] Department of Health and Family Services (DHFS). 1996. "The Development of a National Planning Framework for Child Care." Canberra: DHFS.

Economic Planning Advisory Commission (EPAC). 1996. "Future Child Care Provision in Australia Interim Report." Canberra: EPAC.

Esping-Andersen, Gøsta. 1990. *Three Worlds of Welfare Capitalism*. Cambridge: Polity Press.

_____. 1999. *Social Foundations of Postindustrial Economies*. Oxford: Oxford University Press.

Grimes, Don (Minister for Community Services). 1985. "Child Care." Press release, November 6.

Hancock, Linda. 1999. "Women's Policy Interests in the Market State." In *Women, Public Policy and the State*, ed. L. Hancock. South Yarra: Macmillan.

Hochschild, Arlie. 1995. "The Culture of Politics: Traditional, Post-Modern, Cold-Modern and Warm-Modern Ideals of Care." *Social Politics* 2, no. 3: 331–46.

Howard, John. 1995. "The Australia I Believe In: The Values, Directions and Policy Priorities of a Coalition Government." Sydney: Liberal Party of Australia.

_____. 1998. Address to Family Forum, Clayfield Girls College, Brisbane. Transcript available online at http://www.pm.gov.au/news/speeches/1998/family1808.htm.

Johnson, Carol. 2000. "John Howard and the Mainstream." In *Howard's Agenda: The 1998 Election,* ed. Marian Simms and John Warhurst. St. Lucia, Australia: University of Queensland Press.

Landsbury, Russell. 1997. "Rethinking Work: Employment and Incomes Policies." In *Divided Work, Divided Society,* ed. Bettina Cass and Rowanne Couch. Sydney: Research Institute for Humanities and Social Sciences, University of Sydney.

National Association of Community Based Children's Services (NACBCS). 1977. *Cost versus Quality.* Canberra: NACBCS.

_____. 2000. *Vision 2000: An Early Childhood System for Australia.* Melbourne: NACBCS.

Newman, Jocelyn. 1999. Women's Management Network Luncheon 1999–2000. Budget Speech, Adelaide, May 19.

O'Connor, Julia, Ann Shola Orloff, and Sheila Shaver. 1999. *States, Markets, Families: Gender, Liberalism and Social Policy in Australia, Canada, Great Britain and the United States*. Cambridge: Cambridge University Press.

Orloff, Ann. "Gender and the Social Rights of Citizenship: State Policies and Gender Relations in Comparative Research." *American Sociological Review* 58: 303–28.

Parliament of the Commonwealth of Australia. 1999. Senate Select Committee on A New Tax System, Main Report, April.

Powlay, John. 1999. "Child Care Affordability." Paper presented at the seventh Australian Institute of Family Studies Conference, Sydney, July 24–26. Available online at www.aifs.org.au/institute/afrc7/powlay.html.

Puplick, Christopher. 1994. *Is the Party Over? The Future of the Liberals.* East Melbourne: Text Publishing.

Sainsbury, Diane, ed. 1994. *Gendering Welfare States*. London: Sage.

Saunders, Peter. 1999. "Changing Work Patterns and the Community Services Workforce." In *Australia's Welfare 1999,* ed. Australia Institute of Health and Welfare. Canberra: AIHW.

Savva, Niki. 1997. "The God Squad." *The Age,* April 2.

Sawer, Marian. 1999. "The Watchers Within: Women and the Australian State." In *Women, Public Policy and the State,* ed. L. Hancock. South Yarra: Macmillan.

SCARC (Senate Community Affairs References Committee). 1998. *Report on Child Care Funding*. Canberra: Commonwealth of Australia.

Shaver, S. 1995. "Women, Employment and Social Security." In *Women in a Restructuring Australia*, ed. A. Edwards and S. Magarey. North Sydney: Allen and Unwin.

Tasker, Gillian and Don Siemon. 1998. *Is Child Care Affordable? Pressures on Families and Their Use of Formal Long-Day Child Care*. Melbourne: Brotherhood of St. Laurence.

Tasmanian Association of Children's Services (TACS). 1998. *Report on Community Based Long Day Care in Tasmania*. Hobart, Australia: TACS.

Wallace, Christine. 1997. *The Victory*. St. Leonards: Allen and Unwin.

Warrilow, Prue. 1997. *Report on the Impact of Changes in Commonwealth Child Care and Funding on Families in New South Wales*. Sydney: Families at Work.

CHAPTER 5

The Illusion of Free Choice: Ideals of Care and Child Care Policy in the Flemish and Dutch Welfare States

Monique Kremer

In 1996, a telling headline appeared in a Dutch newspaper: "Belgian Child Only Comes Home to Sleep" (Utrechts Nieuwsblad 1996). The piece that followed was written by a Dutch correspondent who had recently been sent to Belgium. The newly arrived man wanted his young daughters to become quickly and smoothly integrated into Belgian society. He described how the Belgian state cares for young children: when they are babies they go to child care, and at the age of two and a half they go to school, where they stay from 8:30 A.M. until late in the day. They have lunch there, and when classes are over, they can go to clubs until 6:30 P.M. The Dutch journalist was shocked. "How does this full-time care affect the welfare of children?" he queried. He decided not to let his daughters assimilate any further into their new home country. Instead, they came home for lunch to eat their bread with peanut butter, "just as if we are still in the Netherlands."

This chapter focuses on differences in child care policy in two welfare states that are always clustered together: Flanders and the Netherlands. They are part of the same cultural family—the national language is Dutch (Castles 1993)—and they are both considered conservative-corporatist regimes, though with a touch of social democracy (Esping-Andersen 1990; Kersbergen 1995; Knijn and Kremer 1997; Cantillon 1999). Christian democracy has been the dominant political ideology, particularly with regard to welfare policies. Yet when it comes to child care, the differences between the two countries are striking and illuminating. While Flanders has a well-developed, state-financed child care system, in the Netherlands—an otherwise well developed welfare state—child care services are still in their infancy.

In the Netherlands in 1988, only 2 percent of all young children (from birth to three years of age) used state-financed child care. This figure has risen to around 10 percent to date, indicating the rapid expansion of child care in the 1990s (ECNC 1996; Tweede Kamer 1998–1999). However, this state intervention was based on a welfare mix that stresses the responsibility of employers and employees, with the result that Dutch child care is one of the most expensive provisions in Europe (Bradshaw et al. 1996). Moreover, the market supply of child care does not function as some economists would have us believe: that is, there is a tremendous supply problem, and demand continues to grow. Many working parents try to find a child min-der/housekeeper on the "gray market," but they are not always lucky. For older children (four to twelve), child care is even more problematic. After-school services are hardly developed. Some schools, like those to which the journalist refers, still have a long lunch break in the middle of the day, during which children are supposed to go home to eat bread and peanut butter with their mothers. This pattern reflects an ideology of full-time motherhood, which is still predominant in the Netherlands.

Flanders has a much longer history of state intervention into child care. The Flemish child care level of the 1980s was higher than today's Dutch provision. In 1988 the state subsidized 18 percent of all places for children under age three. After-school care is also well-organized. In addition, as the journalist noted, children from age two and a half and above have the right to attend school. By the late 1990s, one-third of children from birth to three years of age use state-subsidized child care—the same level as in Sweden (ECNC 1996; VWS 1997; Kind en Gezin 1997). Child care is almost completely state controlled and state subsidized. The Flemish welfare state includes both a highly varied system of home-based day care mothers and child care centers, and child care is comparatively inexpensive (Bradshaw et al. 1996). In general, Flemish child care policy is based on the notion that mothers should have a "free choice"—not only between working and caring, but also concerning which type of care facility they want to use if they decide to work.

How can two welfare states that are so similar be so different? How can a welfare state like that of the Netherlands contain such poorly developed child care? How can a conservative welfare state like that of Flanders contain state child care on the level of Sweden's? How is it possible to develop child care during a period that so often is labeled one of welfare-state crisis? And finally, how does the development of child care relate to women's labor-market participation?

It is impossible to answer all these complex questions fully in one chapter. Instead, I will use a cultural-institutional approach, which is one way to explain the differences in recent state interventions. A welfare state has many faces. It can be seen as a merchant (helping to bring supply and demand together) or as a notary (adjudicating the social contract between people and between people and the state), but above all, a welfare state is a priest. It tries to prescribe norms and values, and, through financial incentives, limit people's choices. At the same time, the range of policy options is limited because it has to fit in with the dominant culture (some call it "ideology") in order to become accepted. The culture is, in turn, linked to institutional settings. This view of the state is my point of departure.

For this chapter I chose to discuss the case of Flanders rather than all of Belgium because child care policy is the full responsibility of the local community, not of the federal state. I selected Flanders rather than Walloon because it more closely resembles the Netherlands in terms of ideological and cultural background. Sometimes, however, reliable and comparable statistics are available only for the federal level, in which case I refer to Belgium, as I do when discussing the early development of child care policy before the communal split in 1980.

The Conservative-Corporatist Regime and Ideals of Care

In both the Netherlands and Flanders, Christian Democratic coalitions were vital for the development of the welfare state, and Christian Democrats have always held the cabinet seats for welfare, child care, or family policy. According to Gøsta Esping-Andersen (1990), in conservative-corporatist welfare state regimes the role of the church is pivotal. With churches continually warning against unbridled capitalism, the state has pleaded for intervention, but only to the extent that formulations of social rights would not ignore the "natural order" or turn it upside down. Therefore, this type of regime preserves status, class, and gender differentials. In practice this means that benefits and taxation encourage full-time motherhood, and social insurance is based on dependency relations within the family—that is, women are presumed to be financially dependent upon their partners. Consequently, women's labor-market activity is low. This is also a cause-and-effect of the lack of care facilities. The state, in conservative-corporatist regimes, intervenes only when the family's resources are exhausted. This ideology is based on the principle of "subsidiarity" (Catholic) or "sovereignty" in one's own circle (Protestant).

Although the conservative-corporatist regime type is useful for identifying certain common cultural and political factors, it is too broad to explain differences or analyze distinctions among continental European welfare states. The Netherlands, Germany, Austria, Italy, Switzerland, Belgium, and France—nearly all Western European countries are considered conservative-corporatist, although in certain respects they are very different from one another, with child care provisions and female labor-force participation in Flanders and the Netherlands being a case in point. In order to understand differences in this particular policy area, we must adapt the corporatist-conservative framework to take account of families as well as the state in shaping labor markets, and also consider the role of women's movements in mobilizing their power resources and political rights in order to establish social rights.

This adapted heuristic framework for the analysis of regimes directs us to many pressing questions about child care policy in Flanders and the Netherlands. When and in which institutional context did the state take (any) responsibility with respect to child care? What were the reasons for intervention? How flexible is the Catholic concept of subsidiarity? Does Christian democracy have the same meaning in Flanders as in the Netherlands? What is the role of social movements, such as the women's movement? How does the mix of child care relate to women's labor market participation and dependency relationships within the family?

In the sections that follow, I first analyze family, state, and the market mix of child care in relationship to mothers' labor-market participation; the focus is on child care for children from birth to three years of age in the 1980s and '90s. I then examine the history of child care provisions, showing that state intervention in Flanders came much earlier and proceeded incrementally. It was motivated by microeconomics: with state child care provisions, families would be able to support themselves financially. In the Netherlands, even moderate state intervention did not begin until the 1990s, and then it was motivated by macroeconomic argumentation. Intervention occurred within a more liberal institutional setting, which in practice meant that (individual) employers and (individual) employees were made responsible. In the next section I discuss the 1980s and '90s further, asking why child care policy in the Netherlands and Flanders is so different. This question will be answered by examining the ideological concept of "free choice," which nowadays is much more illuminating as a key word than the notion of subsidiarity. I will focus on liberal and Christian Democratic interpretations of free choice, as well as on different institutional settings.

To be able to understand the difference in child care policy between the two cases more fully, we need one more instrument in our tool kit. For the purpose of studying child care, I want to propose a cultural framework that helps explain the origins and outcomes of child care policy. For this cultural dimension of welfare states, I use the notion of "ideals of care." A care ideal, as Arlie Hochschild has put it, "implies a definition of care, an idea about who gives it, and how much of what kind of care is 'good enough'" (1995, 333). Care ideals define what is "appropriate care." More specifically, they imply something about where it should be given (home or institution) and in what way it contributes to the upbringing of children. Is it better than, worse than, or just different from mother care?

Ideals of care are an answer to the moral predicament of working and caring. Obviously, one can stick to the traditional ideal of full-time mother care and consider this the most appropriate way to care for young children. But if women want or need to enter the labor market, new care ideals must be developed. Since this is the case in all contemporary welfare states, cultural shifts have taken place and new ideals have arisen everywhere. Welfare-state analysts often use a bipolar approach that assumes there is only one alternative to the male-breadwinner model, namely the individual model, wherein each adult is regarded as a wage-earner in his or her own right. The male-breadwinner model can be found in the United Kingdom, the Netherlands, and Germany, whereas the individual model is an exclusive Scandinavian model (Sainsbury 1996; Lewis 1992 and 2001). I use a more differentiated approach that distinguishes between the full-time mother care ideal and parental sharing, intergenerational care, surrogate mother, and professional care, and I argue that cultural ideals are not hegemonic or mutually exclusive. The moral predicament of work versus care is likely to be solved through a strategy of "pick and mix," so hybrid ideals are possible. Care ideals are part of an adaptation process on the level of individual mothers (and sometimes fathers), but they are also embedded in organizational structures such as schools, enterprises, social service agencies, political parties, and social movements, and therefore also in welfare-state regulation. In different welfare states, different mixes will exist.

Ideals of care thus operate on two levels, and, consequently, contribute to the theoretical framework of Esping-Andersen in two ways. First, ideals of care can help to explain differences in policy in the last decades. Few welfare states, political parties, or social movements still embrace the ideal of full-time motherhood. To understand why and how various patterns of state intervention in child care developed as they did, we need a new, more subtle, analytical framework. In the case of Flanders, care ideals can help explain how state intervention in child care could be reconciled with a conservative-corporatist welfare regime, while in the case of the Netherlands, the same concept can help explain the *lack* of state intervention. Care ideals thus account for why some policy choices can be made and others cannot.

Second, ideals of care can help explain gender relations (outcomes). They can contribute to an understanding of the differences between categories of women (e.g., grandmothers, lower-class women, and professionals) in terms of citizenship and labor-market participation. Some ideals contest full-time mothering while others reproduce this practice.

Most welfare state analysis is based on a specific idea about human behavior: using a notion of *homo economicus*, it assumes that citizens make well-informed choices based on economic models of rationality. The study of social policy therefore focuses on "financial incentives." Such analysis views the relationship between child care and women's status as follows: if child care is cheap and available, women will be engaged in the labor market. If breadwinner arrangements are rewarded by tax policy and social security, women stay at home. Women thus enter the labor market when the state takes over the "cost of familyhood," but stay at home when financial incentives encourage them to do so (see, for instance, Esping-Andersen 1990 and, even more, 1999; Anttonen and Sipilä 1996; Sainsbury 1996; O'Connor, Orloff, and Shaver 1999).

The notion of ideals of care proposes a different understanding of how social policy affects people's behavior. Would mothers work en masse if tomorrow plenty of child care became available or if all male breadwinner advantages were eliminated? It is difficult to answer this question with an unqualified *yes*. Women would probably enter the labor market only if the financial incentives and the nature of child care provisions fit their ethos. Take the example of lone mothers. Rosalind Edwards and Simon Duncan (1996), who studied the British case, argue that many lone mothers appear to behave irrationally, at least when it comes to pursuing their own economic self-interest. Well-educated mothers in particular would be much more economically successful if they entered the labor market, but they do not do so en masse. Why not? According to Edwards and Duncan, "lone mothers' individual calculations need to be placed in the framework of gendered moral rationalities that are constructed, negotiated and sustained socially in particular contexts." Or, as James March and Johan P. Olsen (1989) put it, human behavior is circumscribed by a culturally specific sense of appropriate action. When the Dutch journalist criticized the Belgian child care system, he did not speak about the costs of child care, nor was he making a rational economic choice when he decided his kids should come home for lunch. Rather, his ideal of care—full-time motherhood—was different than the one considered "appropriate" in Belgium.

Financial incentives, such as affordable child care services, are therefore probably effective only when they fit smoothly into a broader cultural context and thus should be examined accordingly. Financial incentives, economic distribution, and the economic value attached to certain types of care are embedded in and part of "ideals of care." Inversely, social policy is more than a set of financial structures that limit and accommodate people's choices: social policy can also be read as a sermon, or a set of cultural messages, which can become clear when analyzing political debates and policy papers. Some measures and regulations at first sight have few (financial) consequences, but they can have enormous influence on the cultural level. As Philip Corrigan and Derek Sayer put it, "states . . . state" (1985, 3).

The final sections of this chapter will illustrate how different ideals of care can be studied, using as examples the surrogate mother in Flanders and parental sharing in the Netherlands. How do these ideals of care fit the conservative-corporatist regime? What do they mean for gender relations? This approach further illuminates the configuration of economic and cultural dimensions of welfare states.

The State of Care Today

Much more than in the Netherlands, the Flemish state has intervened to provide care for children when mothers are at work. In the Netherlands much less money has been allocated for child care, even though the country has three times as many children as Flanders. These financial differences are mirrored in the number of children who use state-financed child care. While the Netherlands still subsidizes few facilities for young children, Flemish rates are higher than those in France (by 23 percent), and they are even comparable with the Swedish (ECNC 1996). Moreover, in Flanders the state pays most of the costs of child care, while in the Netherlands parents and employers have to contribute substantially (see table 5.1). Therefore it is not a coincidence that child care services in the Netherlands are among the most costly for parents in Europe (Bradshaw et al.1996).

In the Netherlands in 1988, only 2 percent of all children used subsidized child care. This has risen from 13,000 children in 1989 to 60,000 in 1995 to almost 66,000 in 1997 (VWS 1997; Tweede Kamer 1998–1999). This was due to the Stimulative Measure on Child Care, which the government launched in 1990 and which was in place until 1996. With this measure the dominant ideology of child care became clear: the state contributes only when both employer and employee pay for child care. Employers are supposed to buy *bedrijfsplaatsen*—"company places"—for their employees in (public) child care institutions. Over the years, their contributions became increasingly important. In 1989 the state paid 55 percent, parents 35 percent, and employers 10 percent. In 1995 this ratio changed to 40:40:20. As parents' contribution increased substantially, that of the state decreased. However, new but partial measures have been taken. In 1996 the Dutch government proposed to spend more to subsidize child care for single parents, allocating a sum of money especially to this group. Much more is spent on after-school child care, which is also poorly developed in the Netherlands. More recently, due to growing economic prosperity, more public investments have been proposed. All told (including after-school as well as preschool services), the Dutch government wants to expand child care by 71,000 available places by 2002. This would mean a doubling of existing places. It is doubtful, however, whether this is a realistic target given the moderate amount of subsidy (Tweede Kamer 1998–1999).

In Flanders, by contrast, the development of child care was much more incremental. In the 1960s the state began subsidizing child care so that by 1983, 17 percent of children from birth to three years of age were already using state-subsidized child care. In the 1980s and 1990s this proportion grew steadily. In the late 1980s, subsidies were frozen, but when shortages arose, they increased once more, with the result that there has hardly ever been a real shortage of child care in Flanders. By 1988, 23 percent of children were cared for in state-funded child care; by 1993, this had risen to 31 percent (Kind en Gezin 1997). This level has remained steady up to the present.

State investment in child care has meant a complete reshaping of the Flemish child care landscape. To be more precise, it meant a formalization of child care. The increase of state financing has not, however, led to an increase in the proportion of children being cared for outside the nuclear family. From the mid-1980s to today, that number has held steady at 60 percent. Subsidies have meant that informal arrangements were formalized, and supervised child minders have displaced the caregiving of grandparents and unregulated child minders.

Of all Flemish children who are cared for outside the home, 30 percent now receive care from day care mothers, two-thirds of whom are subsidized by the state (see table 5.2). These women are linked to a *dienst voor opvanggezinnen* (a service for day care mothers), which controls the quality of care and sorts out the finances of day care mothers. Parents pay according to income. Since the 1980s, the bulk of state child care subsidies have gone to this type of child care. In 1987 the state funded 10,000 places with day care mothers and 10,000 in child care institutions; in 1996, 12,000 places were available in day care institutions while more than 20,000

TABLE 5.1: SUBSIDIZED CHILD CARE AROUND 1995

	THE NETHERLANDS	FLANDERS
State subsidies	234 billion guilders	2,820 billion frank (155 billion guilders)
Percentage of all children under the age of four who use subsidized child care	8 percent	30 percent
Costs to the account of:		
State	40 percent	75 percent
Parents	40 percent	25 percent
Employers	20 percent	0 percent

SOURCES: VWS (1997), Kind en Gezin (1997), ECNC (1996).

places were available with day care mothers (Kind en Gezin 1997). Nearly all day care families or child minders are registered and controlled by the quasi-state organization of Kind en Gezin (Child and Family; formerly the National Office of Childhood). This is a consequence of a tax measure that was introduced in 1987. Parents can deduct about Bfr345 per day (approximately 8.55 Euros), but only if their children are in registered and state-controlled child care. This fiscal measure unintentionally "whitened" the gray market of child care, so that informal paid child minding has become a rare phenomenon in Flanders (Kind en Gezin 1997).

Day care mothers, or child minders, are also known in the Netherlands, but those who are registered by the state are hardly used. In 1995 only 2 percent of working mothers with children under the age of four used these *gastgezinnen*, or "host families" (Groot and Brink 1998). Also, in contrast to Flanders, their labor is not subsidized. In the Netherlands there is a real shortage in child care. Existing institutions can not handle the demand; in 1998, there were about 32,000 children on their waiting lists (Schippers et al. 1998), and they are also more expensive than child minders. As a result, around a quarter of working mothers with children under four use privately paid child minders. Moreover, of all Dutch working women with children under the age of four, 40 percent use a *bedrijfsplaats,* company care partly subsidized by the employer (Groot and Brink 1998).

Women's Labor Market Participation and the Use of Child Care

The type and financial structure of child care is also related to the consumers of child care and how it is used. In both countries, the so-called Mattheus (Matthew) effect may be observed. As the Bible says, "those who already have will gain more, those who have little will lose." In other words, those who are well off are more likely to use welfare state services, while those who actually need subsidized services are less likely to have access to them. In Flanders as well as in the Netherlands, state-subsidized care is used mainly by more highly-educated mothers. This partly reflects the fact that such mothers are more likely to work, as can be seen in table 5.3. In Flanders, working mothers who are less educated, as well as lone mothers, are more likely to use informal arrangements (such as the help of grandparents) that are even cheaper than state-subsidized child care (Storms 1995; VWS 1997). Furthermore, particularly in the Netherlands, formal child care facilities are primarily

TABLE 5.2: CHILD CARE ARRANGEMENTS OUTSIDE PARENTAL CARE FOR CHILDREN FROM BIRTH TO THREE YEARS OF AGE, FLANDERS, 1996

	PERCENT OF CHILDREN
Grandparents	40
Day care mothers	30 (20 percent subsidized)
Day care institutions	20 (10+ percent subsidized)

SOURCE: Kind en Gezin (1997).

used by mothers with "big" part-time jobs (twenty-four hours or more per week). Thus, the higher the income the more mothers use child care institutions that are subsidized by either the state or an employer.

Another crucial difference between the two countries is that facilities are mostly used part-time in the Netherlands and full-time in Flanders. Hardly any Dutch mother will leave her child in care for the entire day. This reflects the composition of mothers' employment, as we can see below. In the Netherlands, only 10 percent of more highly educated mothers work full-time, whereas in Belgium this figure is 54 percent. Child care in the Netherlands is hardly ever used five days a week—two or three days is common practice—whereas in Flanders full-time, full-week care is common.

The use of state-subsidized child care seems to reflect the composition of women's labor but not the percentage of mothers who do participate. In the Netherlands mothers are more likely to work part-time, and child care services are thus used part-time. In Flanders and Belgium mothers are more likely to work full-time and use child care services full-time. The number of wage-earning mothers in Belgium is higher than in the Netherlands.

Yet if child care is cheap, available, and heavily state-subsidized and controlled, why is the difference between the Netherlands and Belgium not more significant? Belgian rates are even lower than in the United Kingdom, which is known for its lack of child care. Sweden has the same level of state-subsidized child care, but the labor-market participation rates of mothers are much higher than in Belgium. Why is this so? Later, I will return to these questions. First, however, I will discuss the origin of state intervention in child care.

The Origin of State Intervention: The Labor Market Paradigm

Flanders

In Belgium, the National Office of Childhood was already established in 1919. This organization controlled and subsidized kindergartens, particularly in the cities.

TABLE 5.3: LABOR MARKET PARTICIPATION OF MOTHERS (AGED TWENTY TO FORTY-NINE) WITH A DEPENDENT CHILD (FROM BIRTH TO FIFTEEN YEARS) ACCORDING TO LEVEL OF EDUCATION, 1996

COUNTRY	LEVEL OF EDUCATION		
	LOW (FT/PT)	MEDIUM	HIGH
United Kingdom	50 (15/35)	64 (22/42)	79 (38/41)
Belgium	43 (25/19)	64 (37/27)	83 (54/29)
Denmark	56 (37/19)	75 (50/25)	90 (58/32)
Netherlands	38 (4/34)	59 (6/53)	76 (10/66)

SOURCE: Rubery, Smith and Fagan (1996).

Because of industrialization and the concentration of people in cities, working mothers were merely considered an urban phenomenon—one that was, however, seen as a social problem. In that context child care was regarded as a necessary evil, something which could solve the financial problems of the family. The National Office wrote in 1940, "The crèche is just a pressing necessity. Many housewives work outside the home, but we may hope that this situation will improve, and we look forward to a future in which they do not have to leave their homely hearth" (quoted in Lambrechts and Dewispelaere 1980, 38).

But the situation did not change; mothers' labor-market participation continuously increased. The Belgian government, however, could not excuse itself from a responsibility already taken. In this case, *path dependency,* or Paul Pierson's (1994) term *policy feedback,* is applicable. Families began to become dependent on this state intervention and adapted their working and caring life accordingly. Since 1960, subsidized child care has increased continuously. In 1965 kindergartens came under a legal framework; in order to be recognized and subsidized, they had to fulfill certain criteria. At that time, however, public child care was still considered bad for children. But for parents with low income, it was legitimate. By the late 1960s all crèches—seventy-eight in total—were at least implicitly reserved for children of parents with low incomes (Deven 1998).

This pattern reveals that "subsidiarity," an important Catholic concept, did not mean that the state should not intervene, as it is often interpreted. Theo Salemink (1991) points out that many Catholic politicians and thinkers have argued that upon careful reading, *Quadragesimo anno* (1932; the Pope's encyclical) means that the state has a duty to support families. "Help" is the original Latin meaning of *subsidy*; in the context of child care, it meant that the state has a duty to support low-income families with child care facilities in order to protect families from falling into poverty.

During the late 1960s and the 1970s, women's labor-market participation became an issue of emancipation as well as economic necessity. Employed women as well as feminists defined work as such: working was a way to express oneself, meet other people, and have power in the public arena. Notions of economic independence seemed less important, and financial necessity became less crucial as a motive for working, although this was truer for more highly educated women, since less-educated women were less likely to have well-paid work (Pauwels 1978). The women's movement in Flanders was broad and certainly not exclusively socialist; the Catholic Working Women was a large and influential organization with strong links to the Christian Democratic Party.

At the same time, however, the ideal of full-time motherhood was still embedded in society. In 1976, when mothers' labor market participation was already substantial, the Belgian Parliament (thus the Socialist and Christian Democratic Parties) agreed on a "Social-Pedagogical Premium"—a bonus for mothers who stayed at home. Because of the pressure of the women's movement—which lobbied strongly against it—and the financial costs of such payments, this law was never implemented, though it did pass parliament (Lambrechts 1979). This development reveals that in Flanders, as in many countries, there was a continuous debate between the protagonists of the ideal of full-time mothering and those who supported working mothers.

Subsidized child care grew steadily in Flanders. Apart from a short period between 1983 and 1987 when subsidies were frozen, the state increased its subsidy to child care every year. Child care policy remained firmly rooted in a labor market paradigm. For example, the law on child care stipulates that "priority should be given to children whose parents are not able to bring up their children themselves because of work, or to children who because of social and/or pedagogical motives are dependent on guidance and care outside the home, and children whose parents have the lowest income" (*Welzijnszakboekje* 1993, par 5, BS December 30, 1983). Thus child care is by no means a universal right. Although it is primarily aimed at "needy" children and those whose (low-waged) parents are at work, in practice, all parents can use subsidized care—there is hardly any control over whether parents meet the conditions. The law, however, still reveals its origins: child care was subsidized because women had to work to keep the family from poverty; for this reason, the state subsidized the necessary evil of child care, and to a certain extent the stigma remains.

The Netherlands

The labor market rationale also became the basis of Dutch state intervention, but from a different (macro- rather than micro-) economic perspective and during a very different period, from the end of the 1980s through the early 1990s. Unlike their Flemish counterparts, Dutch women never had to work because of economic necessity. According to Janneke Plantenga (1996), the economic factor explains why women's labor-market participation was always significantly lower than elsewhere in Europe. Many European countries, including Flanders, cherished the idea that women's destiny was to bring up children at home and not to be employed, but it was only in the Netherlands that economic conditions allowed these ideals to become reality. Compared to Germany as well as Belgium, the average income level was much higher, making it possible to maintain this ideal of care for a long time. In other words, the Dutch could afford to allow mothers to remain at home and put into practice the ideal of full-time mothering, which was dominant all over Europe.

Thus, at a time when the Flemish state was already supporting kindergartens, there was hardly any need to develop child care in the Netherlands. In the 1950s and '60s, child care was regarded as something that would be immoral in a well-developed welfare state such as the Netherlands (Bussemaker 1998). For this reason public child care services were established only sporadically in cities where there was a "demonstrated need" and for cases where the family situation was "abnormal." But since economic conditions were better than in Flanders, comparatively few crèches were set up.

In the 1970s child care did became a political issue: women from social democratic and communist backgrounds (not Christian democrats, as in Belgium) became strong advocates for public child care. Dutch women differed from their Belgian counterparts in several ways; first, the Dutch women's movement itself lacked consensus on the question of whether child care was important for women; moreover, the movement was not strong enough and had not built a viable, recognized constituency in the political arena (Bussemaker 1998); therefore it could not break the dominant rationale in the political discourse—the rationale of children's interests, through which child care was seen as a dangerous expression of mothers' self-interests. This rationale predominated well into the 1980s. The Christian Democratic minister then in office, Eelco Brinkman, rejected government-subsidized child care; pointing to what in the Netherlands were pejoratively labeled "American situations," he argued that "many families no longer exist as such because both man and woman have to work or want to work, and that value is considered more worthy than raising a child" (quoted in Bussemaker 1998, 85).

It was not until the late 1980s and early 1990s that child care became a serious political issue in the Netherlands. At that time child care was still considered a response to a critical situation, something that would enable women to enter the labor market but would not enhance children's welfare. The difference between the Dutch and Flemish situations, however, was that the Dutch rationale was not related to microeconomics (the need for families to have dual earners) but to macroeconomics (the crisis of the Dutch welfare state).

The welfare state was criticized in two ways. First, it was argued that the welfare state contributes to an immoral ethos: people would become dependent on the state, and this causes selfishness. To turn back this culture of dependency, the state should decentralize responsibilities and make the family responsible again for the welfare of society. In the Netherlands this became a Christian Democratic critique of the perverse consequences of the state, but one framed in a neoliberal language. Dutch Christian Democrats became strong advocates of the market and the community.

Second, it was argued that the welfare state was too expensive. When the Dutch prime minister Ruud Lubbers stated in 1984 that the Netherlands were "ill," he was referring to high unemployment, the largest state deficit in Europe, and a large number of people dependent on (sickness) benefits—a situation that was dubbed "the Dutch disease." A report by the Scientific Council for Government Policy entitled "A Working Perspective" (WRR 1990) summarized the problem and in so doing marked a turning point, particularly for women. The report said that in the Netherlands a large amount of human capital was wasted because women were largely inactive. And for a sustainable welfare state, particularly in the light of the graying of society, we need to invest in female labor-market participation and therefore in child care. Notably, at first, women in general were encouraged to take up paid employment, but since the mid-1990s, single mothers have been specifically mandated to do so. Since they are dependent on public assistance, the government has the policy levers to enforce this work mandate.

In the 1990s, all parties agreed that child care was necessary to raise women's productivity. The Dutch government understood that the substantial number of inactive women contributed to the crisis of the welfare state. Using a macroeconomic rather than the Flemish microeconomic rationale, the state therefore introduced the Stimulative Measure and reserved 300 million guilders for investment. It is telling that this money was derived from the extra tax incomes of dual-earner couples.

Child care in the Netherlands thus "boomed" in a very different time frame from that in Flanders. Flemish child care had a much longer history and was characterized by incremental change, whereas Dutch provisions developed rapidly in the early 1990s, when the Dutch welfare state entered a period of restructuring. The Dutch pattern has had crucial consequences for the distribution of responsibility among the market, families, and the state.

Free Choice and Restructuring of the Welfare State

Explicit child care policy in the Netherlands started only in the beginning of the 1990s, when the welfare state was undergoing restructuring. In Flanders the so-called crisis of the welfare state went hand in hand with an increase in state subsidies. Why in the Netherlands did the market become so important for child care? Why is the mixture of family, state, and market different in the Netherlands? More than the notion of subsidiarity, the ideological notion of "free choice," which is so dominant in the political discourse of the 1990s, is important for analyzing recent welfare-state restructuring. It should be used to conceptualize the relationship between the individual, the market, and the state in both cases.

Flanders

In Flanders, the notion of free choice has been crucial for child care policies on two levels: first, people (read: mothers) must have a free choice between paid employment and caring. Second, if mothers do decide to work, they must have a free choice as to which type of care they use for their children. On the first level, the most influential—Christian Democratic—view on working and caring holds that it is not up to the state to decide whether women should work or should care, though the state does have to facilitate this free choice. Therefore incentives both to work and to care are embedded in social policies. Financial structures should be in place to ensure that mothers *can* stay at home if they wish. The Belgian tax system, for instance, includes the so-called marriage quotient (passed in 1987), a form of financial compensation which, according to the Christian Democratic minister then in office, Wivina de Meester, should be seen as "a direct compensation for the employment of the wife who works at home" (Vanistendael 1989). Indeed, the marriage quotient is popularly known as "a wage for child rearing" (*opvoedersloon*). At the same time, child care facilities should be available and affordable for all families.

Guaranteeing free choice is the way the quasi-state organization Kind en Gezin defines its responsibility and task. Their 1988 white paper, "Child Care: A Growing Choice for Parents," emphasized that it was not their aim to influence the decision of families, though it was the duty of the state to enable families to make the choice.

When parents on a large scale opt for child care, Kind en Gezin has to acknowledge that choice and supply the necessary services. The increase in child care thus reflects parental preferences since, according to Kind en Gezin, the state is obliged to follow the demands of the parents.

But the principle of free choice not only concerns the dilemma of choosing between working and caring. If they opt for work, parents should also have a free choice about how their children are cared for. This is also embedded in the practice of social policy and, again, it is visible in the tax system. As noted above, workers may deduct some of the costs of child care, whether it is provided by centers or by a mother or grandmother. The Christian Democratic party and the traditional mothers' organization (Thuiswerkende Ouder, Gezin, Samenleving, or Homeworking Parent and Family Society) insisted that parents who use unpaid informal care (such as grandparents) or who stayed at home should not be at a fiscal disadvantage.

In the supply of child care services, free choice between different types of care is also crucial. Kind en Gezin asserts that parents should be able to choose between day care mothers, institutions, or care by grandparents, and that the government should not show its preference or make judgments about parents' choices. According to Kind en Gezin, "To be able to chose freely means that care in the familial environment (the day care mother) and in an institution are both possible. Both formulas must be available for parents in all of Flanders" (Kind en Gezin 1988, 11–12). Parents are responsible for choosing, and the state has to guarantee that the options of choice are available. In Flanders the state is at the service of the parents.

The Netherlands

In the Netherlands in the 1980s and 1990s the notion of free choice also became crucial, but it embraced a different meaning and entailed different consequences. In the Netherlands free choice also meant that parents should be able to chose freely between work and care, but then they should also bear the consequences of their choices. *Free choice* referred primarily to the responsibilities of the parents, not of the state. In contrast to Flanders, the Dutch state used free choice against—not for—the expansion of child care. As the state expressed its position regarding child care in 1984, "The Government puts value on the freedom of choice and the parents' own responsibility. Therefore the Cabinet prefers to introduce the possibility of a tax deduction, rather than increasing the budget for child care" (Bussemaker 1993, 226). When in the 1990s the state did intervene with the Stimulative Measure, it still stressed that parents should remain primarily responsible.

With this policy in place, however, the state tried to help parents by making a partnership with employers. Since child care was a way to attract the human capital of women, it was felt that employers should take some responsibility. But the government was disappointed. According to a recent policy paper (Ministry of Social Affairs and Employment 1996), 40 percent of the collective agreements between employers and employees contained no regulations regarding child care. Therefore, it asserted, "The Government will address the social partners on their responsibility." Nevertheless, the financial structure will be kept in place: employers are still held responsible for a large proportion of child care financing.

The language of the market became predominant in Dutch social policy, spoken by Social Democrats, liberals, and Christian Democrats alike. According to this rhetoric, the state should facilitate and not obstruct the natural processes of the market, as it used to do. The language of the market, according to Trudie Knijn, has meant that "transforming public goods into private goods sold for profit in a free market can reshape clients into consumers who have freedom to select the care they need" (1998, 89). Parents thus became consumers rather than clients, but in a very poorly stocked marketplace.

Understanding the Difference: The End of Pillarization

State intervention into child care in the Netherlands began in the early to mid-1990s, when liberal ideology was at a high. This context has meant a completely different structure of the supply of care and a different notion of free choice than in Flanders. Why do these different interpretations of free choice exist? Why, for instance, is the language of the market not spoken in Flanders?

The notion of free choice today is readily associated with liberalism, but the notion of free choice has also played a crucial role in confessional and particularly pillarized societies. Until the postwar period, Belgium and the Netherlands shared a typical corporatist setting of pillarization. This refers to "consociational democracy," a harmonious way to create consensus and stability in a system where no single political party holds a numerical advantage over the others (Lijphart 1968). In practice this meant rule by a coalition government made up of subcultural organizations of different religious (denominational) and quasi-religious (liberal and socialist) groups, all of which had their own organizations (Bussemaker 1998). These organizations structured society in all dimensions, including the media, education, welfare, and sports. One reason for this system was to achieve pacification and enhance domestic consensus. According to Peter Katzenstein (1985), this is a characteristic of all small, open nations. Yet, pillarization as a system of pacification was also necessary because of differences in society. Unlike the Scandinavian countries, the Netherlands and Belgium are not homogeneous. In Dutch society, religious differences (Protestant and Catholic) were crucial, while in Belgium there was opposition between religious (Catholic) and anticlerical (socialist) movements. An important consequence of pillarization was that dominant ideals were firmly rooted in all segments of society, ensuring that they remained stable (see Plantenga 1993).

In such an institutional setting, "free choice" becomes a vital concept. Because of the ideological and religious heterogeneity of the society, it is believed that citizens should have free choice to decide, for instance, which schools their children will attend. Parents can choose between a Catholic or secular school in Belgium and among different religious schools in the Netherlands. This principle of choice also applies to hospitals, sports clubs, home care organizations, and the like. *Freedom of choice* would be an empty concept if the state did not guarantee choice. Pillarized societies are, therefore, characterized by "subsidized freedom"; the state must have respect for people's choices and enforce pluralism and diversity (Groof 1983). This resembles Isaiah Berlin's ([1958] 1969) notion of positive freedom. Freedom is *negative* when individuals or groups can and should do what they want without interference from other citizens or the state. Freedom is *positive* when the individual has the possibility to develop or choose the direction she wants and the state is responsible for widening a citizen's range of options. Free choice in the pillarized societies of Belgium and the Netherlands can be translated into the objective of "state pluralism": the state enforces a pluralist society.

In the Netherlands, the heyday of the pillarized system occurred before World War II, when the political elite of the pillarized organization was in power. From the 1950s onward, however, this situation turned around. Because of the processes of secularization and democratization, the pillars became more and more dependent on the goodwill of the state. Civil society reorganized, professionalized, and became highly dependent on state subsidies in a process that has been called the "etatism of civil society" (Zijderveld 1983). The pillars became "trapped" by the state. By accepting state subsidies, the pillars themselves became less important (Van Doorn 1978). In Belgium, by contrast, the political elite of the pillars—and thus the heads of child care services, trade unions, elderly care, education, and the like—have always been more powerful. The pillars "overruled" the state—not the other way around, as in the Netherlands (Hellemans and Schepers 1992).

In the Netherlands, however, secularization and democratization led to the erosion of civil society and the old pillarized system. In the 1980s most of the pillarized organizations merged, as it was the only way to survive. The end of the pillarization marked a new era—that of neoliberalism. This gave way to a new language for describing what society should be: a market of individuals. Faith in God became faith in the market and in the importance of individuals who are not tied to "pillars" but can act freely in the market (Duyvendak 1997).

The language of the market was hardly spoken in Belgium. In contrast to the Netherlands, in the 1980s and 1990s the system of pillarization, with a strong focus on institutionalizing free choice, was still in place. Throughout Europe the restructuring of welfare states was going forward, but in Belgium the welfare state remained relatively untouched. Free choice kept its "traditional" meaning and legitimized substantial state intervention in child care policy.

Ideals of Care

The Flemish Christian Democratic notion of free choice sounds very attractive, but it is an illusion to believe that social policy can really facilitate free choice. Free choice gives the impression that the state does not regulate or institutionalize choices, but the state always limits the available options and produces new ones. When Berlin ([1958] 1969) pleaded that the state should strengthen people's positive freedom, he also meant that the state could never be neutral. It has to make decisions and be directive. Just as in the Netherlands, in Flanders the notion of free choice is not neutral; institutionalizing pluralism is always a restricted matter. There is always a certain "palette" of pluralism and of policy options. There is always implicitly or explicitly a message about what can be considered "the good life" and how citizens should behave.

Thus, in Flanders as well as in the Netherlands, child care policy expresses different notions about what is appropriate care. In order to study child care policy (or other kinds of social policy involving care, such as policy toward the elderly), it is useful to distinguish five ideals of care that seem to be dominant in Europe at present.

The first and most obvious is the ideal of *full-time mother care*, which considers continuous mother care performed at home the best way to bring up children. In the wake of World War II, this ideal became hegemonic in nearly every welfare state outside of Scandinavia and was strongly reinforced by psychologists, pediatricians, and other children's professionals who stressed the importance of a strong mother-child bond as a necessary condition for children's development. The ideal of full-time mother care may still be seen in all welfare states. A 1993 Eurobarometer survey (Malpas and Lambert 1993), for instance, posed the question: is it better for a young child if the mother stays at home to look after the child, or if the mother continues to work outside the home? In all countries of Europe, the majority of people, both male and female felt that it is best when the mother stays at home. The majority was smallest in Denmark (60 percent) and Belgium (66.4 percent) and much higher in the Netherlands (71.3 percent) and the United Kingdom (72.8 percent). Full-time motherhood seems to be a persistent ideal, and it is only because of the increase in women's labor-market participation that new ideals have developed in contrast to it.

The second ideal is *parental sharing*. This model is based on the assumption that men can care for children just as well as women; indeed, advocates for this model sometimes even go so far to argue that an increase in fathers' care would be *better* for children. For example, in 1998, the Dutch government tried to enforce parental sharing by running a campaign entitled "Who is that man who comes to our home to cut the meat?" Similarly, the Norwegians and Swedes have "daddy leave," a law on parental leave with special rules for fathers. In this model, caring is just as important as working. Accordingly, men should exchange time at work for time at home, whereas mothers should do the opposite. The ideal of parental sharing is subversive because it degenders caregiving. Nevertheless, in this model, good child care is still presented as home-based.

This is also the case in the third ideal, that of *intergenerational care,* in which the first generation (grandmothers) cares for the third generation (children). In return, the second generation (daughters/mothers) will care for the grandparents when they become frail. This is not just a calculated system of family exchange; it guarantees good child care, because who could better care than the mother's mother? The ideal of intergenerational care is not gendered in theory, but it still is in practice; grandmothers, daughters, and granddaughters are the ones most likely to provide care. The ties that bind are matrilineal and familial, and the family is regarded as a haven that protects its members from having to seek care in the outside world, from the market or the state.

The fourth ideal, that of *professional care,* strongly contests the ideal of full-time motherhood because it maintains that professionals provide a different type of care than mother care but offer something that should still be part of the upbringing of every child. Often, professional care takes place in child care institutions or is part of the education system, and its purpose is defined as improving children's welfare, enhancing their development, socializing them, and preparing them for school and for society. In fact, all welfare states implement the ideal of professional care for children aged five, six, seven, or older through schools, many of which begin with kindergarten. The ideal of professional care for younger children (from birth to four years) is mainly manifest in a country such as Denmark, which has the best-trained child care workers in Europe. The Danes believe that child care improves children's welfare, and that the "social-pedagogical" aspects of care are crucial for this purpose (see Borchorst, in this volume). In other societies, such as Britain, education rather than welfare seems to be the most important rationale for professional care at the moment.[1]

The fifth ideal is that of the *surrogate mother.* According to this model, good care is still best given by *a* mother, even if it is not *the* mother of the children. Care is done by a child minder, baby-sitter, or family provider, usually for little pay, and because it is offered in the provider's home, it most closely resembles home-based care. "It may not help, but it can't do any harm either" is the rationale for this kind of care; its purpose is to "look after" or "keep an eye" on the child when the mother is at work. Surrogate mothers are not supposed to change or influence the upbringing of children; they do not give something "extra" to the child. Professionals, in contrast, have different qualities and qualifications from parents; surrogate mothers, however, are considered to have the same kind of qualities as mothers have—motherly warmth, attention, patience—yet they remain surrogate, because it is still better if motherly warmth and attention is given by the real mother.

The ideals of the surrogate mother and of intergenerational care may not contest full-time motherhood ideology as much as professional care or parental sharing. The last two challenge the notion that child care by persons other than the mother is only a necessary evil because women want to work. Professional care or parental sharing are positive alternatives to full-time mother care and are believed to improve children's upbringing. As a consequence, women's labor is positively regarded, and care the potential to become degendered. In the other two models, surrogate and intergenerational care mothers remain at the heart of care and, in the end, may reinforce rather than contest the ideology of full-time motherhood since they implicitly seek to reproduce the type of care that that ideal offers.

In all welfare states, mixes of ideals coexist. Nowadays most European welfare states promote the ideal of parental sharing alongside other models. But in the Netherlands this ideal has a firm tradition and is the dominant ideal. In Flanders, parental sharing has also become a topic, but the emphasis is much more on the ideal of the surrogate mother, which is almost absent in the Netherlands. Both ideals do, in some way, fit Christian Democratic ideology, which cherishes self-care (as opposed to institutional provisions) and home-based caring. Yet the effects on child care subsidies and gender relations are quite different in the two countries.

The Surrogate Mother in Flemish Child Care Policy

Until the 1970s, institutions, mostly urban, were the dominant type of state-subsidized day care in Belgium. As a counterpart to these, organizations of day care mothers developed; they were seen as the answer to collective, "cold and formal" institutions as well as to the increased employment of rural women. The Catholic agrarian women's movement, KVLV (Katholieke Vrouwenbeweging van de Landelijke Vereniging), was the first to call for an organization for child minding. When they launched their plan in the early 1970s, they had to convince day care mothers to join, mothers to use the service, and last but not least, the government to fund the initiative. Child care at that time was often seen as a necessary evil; therefore the agrarian women argued that "bringing up children in a 'second' home is not necessarily worse if the quality is guaranteed." Organized day care mothers, with the help of the state, could guarantee this quality: "in the countryside many women and families are prepared, with some guidance and information, to provide care successfully." In addition, it was suggested that organized day care mothers would activate family and neighborhood life, which was said to be eroding (KVLV 1977).

It was surely an attractive bargain. The state had only to interfere a little, just to make sure that people would support each other. In addition, organizing and subsidizing day care mothers was very cheap compared to day care institutions, while the quality of child care was guaranteed and social cohesion could be revived. The initiative was "crowned" in 1975: day care families would be subsidized. From then on, day care mothers were embraced by the Christian Democratic Party and the ministers in charge of child care. The increase of child care subsidies from the end of the 1980s onward were to a large extent used for the development of the Diensten voor Opvanggezinnen, or Bureau for Day Care Families. Today more children are cared for by subsidized day care mothers than in day care institutions.

Subsidizing day care mothers has offered a way out of a deadlocked situation. In many welfare states, "warm care," represented by a dedicated mother who continuously cares for children, was counterposed to "cold" institutional care, in which indifferent professionals care for children for long hours. In the first case mothers have to sacrifice for their children, while in the second, children suffer because of mothers' selfishness. Such a contradiction was certainly characteristic of the Flemish debate, as we have seen in the discussion of the mother's bonus. Caring at home was weighed against day care institutions, the interests of children against the interests of mothers (Somers and Peeters 1991; Kind en Gezin 1988). In no way did the existing (urban) day care institutions resemble home-based care. Historically, they were part of a medico-hygienic regime. The institutions were large, the staff were nurses, the available places even labeled "beds" (Hermans 1984). Day care mothers provided an alternative that was much more in keeping with the wishes and values of Flemish parents as well as Christian Democratic ideology: children would be cared for in homelike surroundings. (Again, this is the surrogate mother ideal in which the children are cared for by a mother, even though it is not their own mother.)

A system of child care built largely on the services of day care mothers fits well the conservative-corporatist welfare-state model, for, to some extent, it reinforces class differentials. Such a system depends on the existence of a great number of married mothers who themselves want to remain at home—in other words, a large reserve army of mothers who prefer to stay at home to care. Julia O'Connor, Ann Orloff, and Sheila Shaver note the "liberal" phenomenon of "off-loading" carework for the middle class onto other women of less-advantaged social status (for example, immigrants and poor women; 1999, 35). While there are class differences between mothers and providers in Flanders, the contrast is not as stark as in liberal regimes. It is true that the women who use the services of day care mothers are generally highly educated, but the providers themselves are not only women with little education; many have had an average level (Werkgroep Vlaamse Diensten voor Opvanggezinnen 1992).

Indeed, the Flemish system of day care mothers appears to reinforce class differentials to a lesser extent than it does gender asymmetries. The system of subsidizing day care mothers rests entirely on married mothers' dependency on male breadwinners. Day care mothers pay hardly any tax or insurance contributions; what they receive is more an allowance than a wage. In return, they must depend on male breadwinners for social rights such as pensions. Also when they are ill or need a holiday, a "real" earner in the family is a necessity. Moreover, their remuneration is not high enough to achieve financial independence. In a welfare state where married women's dependency on their partners is taken for granted and strong breadwinner regulations are still in place, subsidizing day care mothers has been a perfect and cheap solution. While the system serves to legitimize paid work for one group of mothers, it simultaneously depends on another group who prefer to stay at home and care for their own children. This fits well with Christian Democratic ideology, preserving existing gender differentials as in a conservative-corporatist regime.

It is also believed that this type of care does not harm the children because it is like home, and safety and a minimum level of quality are guaranteed. Unlike professional providers, day care mothers are not expected to fulfill children's special needs or offer something extra—something they might not receive at home. Day care mothers' care is the same as a mother's, though they remain surrogates. In this form, child care has no independent legitimization; children receive care because their mothers want to work, not because it may be good for them. Such a system rests on shaky grounds, for it depends, in the end, on women's activity in the labor market. When women are no longer economically necessary, state subsidies may be in danger.

For this reason, Kind en Gezin is slowly seeking to weaken the hold of the ideal of the surrogate mother by enhancing the reputation of professional care and trying to show that child care outside the home can be good for the welfare of children, and they have been working hard to improve its quality. The medico-hygienic regime, for instance, has been transformed into a child welfare regime, with concomitant education, training, and regulation of child care workers. Nurses have been replaced by pedagogues and psychologists, and large centers by smaller ones, with Kind en Gezin regularly supervising the pedagogical aspects of the program. The needs of children receive more attention, and while parents' wishes are still important, they are considered alongside children's welfare. The most recent state policy paper even argues that child care should become a *basisvoorziening*—a basic service for all children. This can mean a break with the labor market paradigm, as it may lead to universal child care (MWEHO 2000). It may thus well be that in the future the ideal of the surrogate mother will slowly be replaced by professional care. Perhaps the ideal of the surrogate mother was a necessary stage in the development of child care in a conservative-corporatist regime like that of Flanders; it certainly enabled a Christian Democratic government to legitimize a level of state intervention in child care as high as Sweden's.

However, the increase in state subsidies to child care did not go hand in hand with a rise in the use of formal child care and a substantial increase of mothers' labor market participation as it did in Sweden. This is because the ideal of the surrogate mother, which was so well entrenched in Flemish culture, discourages mothers' labor-market participation since it implies that children are best cared for by their own mothers. (Conversely, professionalizing Flemish child care encourages mothers' labor-force participation and concomitant absence from the home by advancing the claim that it is better, or at least just as good, for children to be cared for by professionals.) Flemish child care policy and financial arrangements reinforce the ideal of the surrogate mother—and its conservative implications—by offering women the option of remaining at home by either becoming day care mothers themselves or relying on state financial incentives such as the marriage quotient and social security (Cantillon 1999). This option has proven most attractive to mothers with little or average education who have young children (see table 5.1). Although in theory Flemish mothers have free choice, this particular group tends to follow the ideal of full-time mothering.

Parental Sharing in the Netherlands

In the Netherlands, the dominant ideal for resolving the moral predicament of working and caring is parental sharing. Because it is based on the idea that both parents work and care part-time, this ideal makes the development of child care less urgent. One of the most crucial policy papers of the 1990s in the Netherlands is a report called "Unpaid Care Equally Shared," published by the Commission for Future Scenarios for Unpaid Care (Commissie Toekomstscenario's Herverdeling Onbetaalde Arbeid 1995). The Dutch minister of employment asked the commission to develop scenarios for the future of paid work and unpaid care, and this body concluded that the most desirable scenario was based on "combination." This meant that all people, men as well as women, should work thirty-two hours per week. Not only should all the available paid work be shared, but unpaid carework should also be shared equally between men and women. In addition, some of the caregiving work should be done by professionals. The commission also agreed that the state should take responsibility for care, but to a much lesser degree than, say, in Sweden or Denmark. The commission concurred with the anti-Scandinavian sentiment clearly evident in the Netherlands: it was felt that parents should do the bulk of the parenting themselves. The Dutch government endorsed the findings of the commission, stating that the combination scenario, with its emphasis on parental sharing, should be the basic model on which modern welfare states would be built.

Parental sharing has two central features: part-time rather than full-time employment is the norm, and while men should become more involved in caring, women should not eliminate all of their caring activities. Attracting men to care is considered primarily an issue of socialization. In 1993, a course on caring (*Verzorging*) became part of the national curriculum; children (but it was implicitly meant for boys) up to age fifteen were supposed to learn to care. The objective was to degender caring while emphasizing its importance and difficulty (Grünnel 1997). More recently, men were addressed more directly through the aforementioned television campaign with the slogan "Who's that man who comes to our home to cut the meat every evening?" Fathers who are not recognized by their children, the ad implies, are not very modern. It tries to appeal to a feeling fathers supposedly have: missing the upbringing of their children. In the early 1990s, the trade unions ran a similar campaign with billboard ads picturing a man whose message was, "Hi, I'm your dad."

The importance of part-time work is the second leg of government policy toward parental sharing. The Netherlands is regarded as "the first part-time economy in the world." Part-time work, particularly for women, has become the "normal" job. The majority of women (60 percent) and a small but sizable proportion of men (16 percent) are working part-time. The growth of women's labor-market participation can be attributed almost entirely to the increase in part-time work. Mothers, more than women in general, work part-time; only 5 percent of mothers with children under three work full-time. Thus, the full-time working mother who needs full-time care for her children (the Scandinavian anti-ideal) hardly exists in the Netherlands. In Belgium, by contrast, full-time work is much more common among mothers as well as women in general (see table 5.3; Plantenga 1996; Visser 1999).

Whether a part-time economy really leads to parental sharing is not clear. Optimists will point out that more Dutch fathers also work part-time than in any other country (7 percent, as compared to the European Union [EU] average of 1 percent). Among couples with children, in 4.2 percent of the cases, both parents work part-time, while the EU average is 0.6 percent (Visser 1999). Of the 22 percent of male workers who say they want to work less, one-fourth explicitly express a desire to have more time with their children, but many fear that their desire for part-time work will not be accepted (NYFER 1999). Pessimists will point out that men are only forced to share the work at home equally if women work just as much as they do. Particularly when women work less than twenty hours a week, much of the caregiving falls on their shoulders. Women who work more than thirty-two hours a week are more likely to have a partner who contributes to household tasks (NYFER 1999). Pessimists would therefore argue that parental sharing institutionalizes the second shift rather than equal sharing.

In the Netherlands, the optimists are dominant. Part-time work is now embraced by individuals, the state, and trade unions (Visser 1999). As early as the 1970s, women who wanted to marry and become mothers asked their employers for permission to work part-time, and this became common practice, particularly in areas of labor shortage such as education and nursing. By the late 1970s, more than one-third of all jobs in these service sectors were part-time. In the 1980s and '90s, this became further institutionalized as part-time work appeared to be the most viable option given the lack of child care facilities. Moreover, part-time work offered a solution to the dilemma of working full-time or staying at home, and fit the Christian Democratic principle that children should be mainly cared for at home.

In the 1980s, the Dutch state began to promote part-time work, presenting it as an emancipation measure as well as a way to redistribute available labor. In the beginning, both the trade unions and the women's movement were opposed to this type of work; they were worried about the marginalization of part-time workers and their lack of social rights. Instead, they preferred shorter working weeks for everyone. But from the time of the Akkoord of Wassenaar (1982)—a national agreement between employers and employees—onward, part-time employment became a more feasible option. The National Federation of Employers asked their members to accept part-time work as a solution to the economic downturn (related to the crises of the welfare state in the late 1970s and 1980s, discussed above) to avoid firing employees. They also found out that it was not expensive to reorganize and reschedule labor in such a way that part-time employment was possible.

Trade unions also became more favorable to part-time work. In 1990 one of the large federations of Dutch trade unions, the FNV (Federatie Nederlandse Vakbeweging), called for part-time employment—the first union in Europe to do so (Visser 1999). This position can be explained by the fact that women really wanted to work part-time and that they had gained more power in the trade unions (Grünnel 1997). In 1996, part-time workers gained the same (social) rights as full-time workers. Employers were no longer allowed to make any distinction when it concerned working conditions. In addition, a law soon to be implemented will grant all citizens the right to part-time work. It stipulates that if it will not affect the interests of the company, employees have the right to work more hours, but also to work fewer.

To understand the effects of this part-time economy for women's position in the labor market, it is necessary to make a distinction between "small" part-time jobs (less than twenty hours per week) and "big" ones (thirty to thirty-two hours). Small jobs are predominant; one-third of all women have small part-time jobs (NYFER 1999), but often they require low skills, and are less well-paid, offering little prospect for career advancement. As a result, the financial independence of Dutch women is still among the lowest in Europe (Bianchi, Casper, and Peltola 1996), and 18 percent of the women in small jobs say they would prefer big ones (NYFER 1999). Even though they are still part-time, big jobs do provide more financial independence and career possibilities, and with legal protection and social security firmly in place, they offer the same security as full-time positions. For many women, mainly the more highly educated, part-time work allows them to combine work and caring and is therefore a feasible emancipation strategy. If fathers become more engaged in caregiving, this may even lead to a further degendering of part-time work (Plantenga 1996).

Still, part-time work and the ideal of parental sharing have ambivalent consequences for women's positions in the labor market. Moreover, the ideal of parental sharing relieves the state of responsibility for developing substantial child care services. If parental sharing of child care responsibilities—home based, and performed by both men and women—is considered the best way to bring up children, child care services will always remain additional or marginal. It is therefore no coincidence that in the Netherlands most children are placed in child care for only a few days a week, and that it is primarily more highly-educated women who use such facilities. The question is whether it will ever become economically feasible for less well-educated women to hold part-time jobs and use these expensive (because barely subsidized) services. With the professional ideal still quite weak in the Netherlands, the predominant approach is to degender the act of caring and involve fathers in child care. This places a great deal of hope in the prospect of changing men's behavior, and whether this can be achieved remains to be seen. In the meantime, the ideal of parental sharing legitimizes the lack of substantial state intervention in child care.

Conclusion

Expansion of child care in the Netherlands began only in the 1990s and developed in a chaotic mixture of employer, employee, and state responsibility. Until then, all political parties embraced the ideal of full-time motherhood. In contrast to many other European welfare states, in the Netherlands it was economically possible to uphold this ideal. By the late 1980s, however, macroeconomic exigencies and demographic worries led to a new labor market paradigm: women should work. This new ideal of working mothers was, however, limited to part-time work, allowing parental sharing to take hold as the ideal solution for child care needs. This not only accorded with Christian Democratic ideology, but also fit in with the neoliberal politics that became hegemonic when the Dutch welfare state became secularized and the system of pillarization eroded in the 1980s. The liberal interpretation of free choice gave direction to the new policy area of child care. As a consequence, employers and employees in particular have been made responsible for child care. This has lead to shortages in the market and some of the most expensive child care in Europe, which only more highly educated women can afford to use.

In Flanders, due to financial necessity, mothers did participate in the labor force much earlier than in the Netherlands. The notion of subsidiarity legitimized state intervention rather than the withdrawal of the state, since it holds that when families need help, the state has to support them. To avoid poverty in the family, the Flemish state had already taken responsibility for child care before World War II. In addition, the notion of free choice was interpreted differently than in the Netherlands. In Flanders, free choice meant that it was the responsibility of the state to enable people to choose freely between working and caring. Consequently, the state has to subsidize staying at home as well as providing sufficient child care. This interpretation was related to Christian Democratic ideology as it played out in the typical institutional setting of pillarization. Although this so-called state-pluralism was also a concept in the Netherlands, by the time child care policy developed there, the pillarized system had already been replaced by the market.

Last year Belgian politics (like the Dutch in 1994) took a historic turn. The Christian Democrats are no longer in government; instead, a "purple and green" coalition of socialists, liberals, and the ecology minded has come to power. The question is, Will this government reorganize the welfare state? Corporatist structures, as the Dutch example shows (see Visser and Hemerijck 1997), can change. However, it is doubtful whether the still-pillarized system in Belgium will allow radicalism. Belgium, in contrast to the Netherlands, seems to be more fragile as a nation-state; as such the traditional Christian Democratic notion of free choice will probably remain powerful.

At the same time, however, Flemish citizens cannot really choose freely, since state-subsidized child care points parents in the direction of day care mothers rather than child care institutions. In the 1990s, the number of subsidized day care mothers almost doubled, while the number of available places in institutions remained level. Day care mothers fit the Flemish cultural preference for home-based, "mother-like" care without actually displacing mothers as the preferred caregivers. The strength of this ideal helps explain why—though the level of state-subsidized child care in Flanders is as high as Sweden's—the female employment rate falls short. It also explains how it is that a Christian Democratic regime came to invest so heavily in child care.

While the prevalence of surrogate mother care reinforced the ideal that children are best cared for by their mothers (it was also embraced by the Christian Democratic women's movement and the Christian Democratic Party), it also provided a rationale for the Christian Democratic regime's well-developed child care policy.

Part-time work and its related preference for parental sharing is very different from the surrogate mother as a way to resolve the moral predicament between working and caring. Both, however, fit into a Christian Democratic ideology that places high value on caring within the family in the environment of the home. In social-democratic countries such as Sweden and Denmark, the ideal of professional care legitimizes state intervention. Conservative-corporatist regimes, however, are more likely to pick and choose from among the ideals of parental sharing, the surrogate mother, and intergenerational care.

However, the outcomes of different ideals for gender relations in conservative-corporatist regimes may be quite different. "Parental sharing" will always mean that professional child care is additional, supplementary, and thus marginal. Both men and women are supposed to do the bulk of the caring at home and work part-time. If men would really change their behavior, this could indeed lead to equal gender relations—at least in theory. So far, however, women in the Netherlands continue to perform most of the caring tasks. Their part-time jobs have fewer career prospects, except when they are "big" and performed by more highly-educated women. The ideal of the surrogate mother, which is predominant in Flanders, goes along with full-time employment and financial independence for one group of mothers, but it reinforces dependency on a male breadwinner for the day care mothers themselves. In addition, the fact that the surrogate mother ideal reinforces a preference for mother care may have a depressing effect on mothers' activity rates, particularly if financial arrangements make it possible for mothers with lower or average education to stay at home.

Ideals of care thus help explain how similar types of welfare states can have different child care policies—how, for instance, a corporatist-conservative regime can subsidize child care on a large scale. Furthermore, the focus on ideals of care reveals the role of the welfare state as a kind of priest. Every welfare state displays notions about what type of child care is appropriate: it stresses certain financial arrangements, subsidizes certain types of care, expresses its views in policy papers and campaigns. People receive many cultural messages about how children should be cared for. The notion that people should have a free choice, so often preached and interpreted differently, is really an illusion.

Note

1. This is a relatively recent development. Previously, professional care was available primarily only for "problem families."

References

Alber, Jens. 1995. "A Framework for the Comparative Study of Social Services." *Journal of European Social Policy* 5, no. 2: 131–149.

Anttonen, A. and J. Sipilä. 1996. "European Social Care Services: Is It Possible to Identify Models? *Journal of European Social Policy* 6, no. 2: 87–100.

Berlin, Isaiah. [1958] 1969. "Two Concepts of Liberty." In *Four Essays on Liberty.* London: Oxford University Press.

Bianchi, Suzanne M., Lynne M.Casper, and Pia K. Peltola. 1996. "A Cross-National Look at Married Women's Economic Dependency." *Luxemburg Income Study,Working Paper Series* no. 143. Luxemburg: Ceps/Instead.

Bradshaw, Jonathan, Steven Kennedy, Majella Kilkey, Sandra Hutton, Anne Corden, Tony Eardley, Hilary Holmes and Joanna Neale. 1996. *The Employment of Lone Parents: A Comparison of Policy in Twenty Countries.* London: Family Policy Studies Centre.

Bussemaker, Jet. 1993. *Betwiste zelfstandigheid. Individualisering, sekse en verzorgingsstaat* (Contested Independence: Individualization, Gender and the Welfare State). Amsterdam: SUA.

_____. 1998. "Rationales of Care in Contemporary Welfare States: The Case of Childcare in the Netherlands." *Social Politics* 5, no. 1: 70–96.

Cantillon, Bea, ed. 1999. *De welvaartsstaat in de kering* (The Changing Welfare State). Kapellen: Pelckmans.

Castles, Francis G., ed. 1993. *Families of Nations: Patterns of Public Policy in Western Democracies.* Aldershot: Dartmouth.

Commissie Toekomstscenario's Herverdeling Onbetaalde Arbeid. 1995. *Onbetaalde zorg gelijk verdeeld* (Commission for Future Scenarios for Unpaid Care: Unpaid Care Equally Shared). Den Haag: Vuga.

Corrigan, Philip, and Derek Sayer. 1985. *The Great Arch: English State Formation as Cultural Revolution.* Oxford: Basil Blackwell.

Deven, Fred. 1997. "Belgium as a Cross-roads for Child Care in Europe." In *Child Care*, ed. Schippers et al.

Doorn, van, Jacobus Andrianus Antonius. 1978. "De verzorgingsstaat in praktijk" (The Welfare State in Practice). In *De stagnerende verzorgingsstaat* (The Stagnating Welfare State), ed. J.A.A. van Doorn and C. J. M. Schuyt. Meppel: Boom.

Duyvendak, Jan Willem. 1997. *Waar blijft de politiek? Essays over paarse politiek, maatschappelijk middenveld en sociale cohesie.* (What's Keeping Politics? Essays on Purple Politics, Civil Society and Social Cohesion). Amsterdam: Boom.

ECNC (European Commission Network on Child Care). 1996. *A Review of Services for Young Children in the European Union 1990–1995.* Brussels: European Commission.

Edwards, Rosalind, and Simon Duncan. 1996. "Rational Economic Man or Lone Mothers in Context? The Uptake of Paid Work." In *Good Enough Mothering? Feminist Perspectives on Lone Motherhood*, ed. Silva E. Bortolaia. London and New York: Routledge.

Esping-Andersen, Gøsta. 1990. *The Three Worlds of Welfare Capitalism.* Cambridge: Polity Press.
_____. 1999. *The Social Foundations of Postindustrial Economies.* Oxford: Oxford University Press.

European Commission. 1997. *Employment in Europe.* Directorate-General for Employment, Industrial Relations and Social Affairs. Brussels: European Union.

Groof, Jan de. 1983. *Pluralisme: kind van de democratie?* (Pluralism: A Child of Democracy?) Leuven: Davidsfonds.

Groot, Wim, and Henriëtte Maassen van den Brink. 1998. "Return to Child Care: Trends in Child-Care Use, Labor Force Participation and Earnings of Women with Young Children 1991–1995." In *Child Care,* ed. Schippers et al.

Grünnel, Marianne. 1997. *Mannen die zorgen, zijn de kerels van morgen. Hoe jongens, dertigers en vijftig-plussers zich laten aanspreken op onbetaald werk.* (Men Who Care Are Tomorrow's Heroes: Boys, Men, and Unpaid Labor). Utrecht: Ivan van Arkel.

Hellemans, Staf, and Ria Schepers. 1992. "De ontwikkeling van corporatieve verzorgingsstaten in België en Nederland" (The Development of Corporative Welfare States in Belgium and the Netherlands). *Sociologische Gids* (Sociological Guide) 5–6: 346–64.

Hermans, An. 1984. "Wie zal er ons kindeke douwen? Uit de geschiedenis van de kinderdagverblijven" (Who Will Care for Our Children? From the History of Child Care Institutions). *Het Kind* (The Child) 1: 13–24.

Hochschild, Arlie. 1995. "The Culture of Politics: Traditional, Postmodern, Cold-Modern, and Warm-Modern Ideals of Care." *Social Politics* 2, no. 3: 331–46.

Katzenstein, Peter J. 1985. *Small States and World Markets: Industrial Policy in Europe.* Ithaca, N.Y.: Cornell University Press.

Kersbergen, Kees van. 1995. *Social Capitalism: A Study of Christian Democracy and the Welfare State.* London: Routledge.

Kind en Gezin. 1988. *Kinderopvang: een groeiende keuze van ouders. Studie van en voorstellen voor kinderopvang in Vlaanderen* (Child Care: A Growing Choice of Parents. Study and Plans for Child Care in Flanders). Brussels: Kind en Gezin.
_____. 1997. *Jaarverslag 1996. 10 jaar Kind en Gezin.* (Annual Report 1996: Ten Years of Child and Family). Brussels: Kind en Gezin.

Knijn, Trudie. 1998. "Social Care in the Netherlands." In *Gender, Social Care and Welfare State Restructuring in Europe,* ed. Jane Lewis. Aldershot, Hants, Eng.: Ashgate.

Knijn, Trudie, and Monique Kremer. 1997. "Gender and the Caring Dimension of Welfare States: Towards Inclusive Citizenship." *Social Politics* 4, no. 3: 328–61.

KVLV (Katholieke Vrouwenbeweging van de Landelilijke Verenignig). 1977. *Een dienst onthaalgezinnen in het kader van de v.z.w. Gezinszorg van de Landelijke Beweging* (A Service for Family Day Care in the Context of the Rural Movement). Leuven: KVLV.

Lambrechts, E. 1979. *Vrouwenarbeid in België: Het tewerkstelling sheleid inzake vrouwelijke arbeidskranchten* (Women's Work in Belgium: Employment Policy toward Women Workers), 1930–1972. Brussels: CBGS (Center for Population and Family Studies).

Lambrechts, E., and L. Dewispelaere. 1980. *Het nationaal werk voor kinderwelzijn. Een overzicht van de ontwikkeling sinds 1957* (The National Organization for Child Welfare. A Survey of Developments since 1957). Brussels: CBGS.

Lewis, Jane. 1992. "Gender and the Development of Welfare Regimes." *Journal of European Social Policy* 2, no. 3: 37–55.

_____. 2001. "The Decline of the Male-Breadwinner Model: Implications for Work and Care." *Social Politics* 8, no. 2: 152–69.

Lijphart, Arend. 1968. *The Politics of Accommodation: Pluralism and Democracy in the Netherlands.* Berkeley and Los Angeles: University of California Press.

March James G., and Johan P. Olsen. 1989. *Rediscovering Institutions: The Organizational Basis of Politics.* New York: Free Press.

Malpas, Nicole, and Pierre-Yves Lambert. 1993. *Europeans and The Family.* Results of an Opinion Survey. Commission of the European Communities, Directorate-General for Employment. Industrial Relations and Social Affairs. Brussels: EC.

MSEA (Ministry of Social Affairs and Employment [Netherlands]). 1996. *Kansen op combineren.* (Opportunities to Combine). The Hague: MSAE.

MWHEO (Ministry of Welfare, Health and Equal Opportunities [Belgium]). 2000. *Blauwdruk voor een toekomstgerichte uitbouw van het kinderopvanglandschap in Vlaanderen* (Blueprint for the Future Expansion of the Child Care Landscape in Flanders). Brussels: MWHEO.

NYFER (Nijenrode Forum for Economic Research). 1999. *Meer werken, minder zorgen. Arbeid en zorg in wetgeving en CAO's* (More Work, Less Worry: Labor and Care in Law and Collective Labor Market Agreements) Breukelen: NYFER.

O'Connor, Julia S., Ann Shola Orloff, and Sheila Shaver. 1999. *States, Markets, Families: Gender, Liberalism and Social Policy in Australia, Canada, Great Britain and the United States.* Cambridge: Cambridge University Press.

Pauwels, Koenraad. 1978. *De arbeidsparticipatie van de gehuwde vrouw. Onderzoeksresultaten Nego* (Labor Market Participation of Married Women). Brussels: Centrum voor Bevolkings-en Gezinsstudiën.

Pierson, Paul. 1994. *Dismantling the Welfare State? Reagan, Thatcher, and the Politics of Retrenchment.* Cambridge: Cambridge University Press.

Plantenga, Janneke. 1993. *Een afwijkend patroon. Honderd jaar vrouwenarbeid in Nederland en (West-) Duitsland* (A Deviating Pattern: A Century of Women's Labor in the Netherlands and [West] Germany). Amsterdam: SUA.

_____. 1996. "For Women Only? The Rise of Part-Time Work in the Netherlands." *Social Politics* 3: 57–71.

Quadrogesimo anno. 1932. "Overhet herstel der sociale order" (On the Recovery of the Social Order). Utrecht: Urbietorbi, rpt. 1993.

Rubery, Jill, Mark Smith, and Colette Fagan. 1996. *Trends and Prospects for Women's Employment in the 1990s.* European Network of Experts on the Situation of Women in the Labor Market. Report for the Equal Opportunities Unit, DGV of the European Commission. Manchester: Manchester School of Management.

Sainsbury, Diane. 1996. *Gender, Equality and Welfare States.* Cambridge: Cambridge University Press.

Salemink, Theo. 1991. *Katholieke kritiek op het kapitalisme. 1891–1991. Honderd jaar debat over vrije markt en verzorgingsstaat.* (Catholic Criticism on Capitalism 1891–1991: A Century of Debate on the Free Market and the Welfare State). Amsterdam: Acco.

Schippers, Johannes J., Jacques J. Siegers, and Jenny deJong-Geirveld, eds. 1998. *Child Care and Female Labour Supply in the Netherlands: Facts, Analyses, Policies*. Amsterdam: Thesis Publishers.

Skocpol, Theda. 1992. *Protecting Soldiers and Mothers: The Political Origins of Social Policy in the United States*. Cambridge, Mass.: Harvard University Press.

Somers, Ann, and Jan Peeters. 1991. "Over slechte moeders, goede kinderopvang en vice versa. Grasduinen in de geschiedenis van de visie op moederschap en kinderopvang" (On Bad Mothers, Good Child Care and Vice Versa: Browsing through the History of Views on Motherhood and Child Care). Utrecht: GS (Shtichting Gestructureede Samenwerking Interdisciplinair Onderzoek Gebouwde Omgeving) Jaarboek.

Storms, Berenice. 1995. *Het matteüs-effect in de kinderopvang* (The Matthew Effect in Child Care). CSB berichten. Antwerpen: Centrum voor Sociaal Beleid/UFSIA.

Trommel, Willem, and Romke Van der Veen, eds. 1999. *De herverdeelde samenleving. Ontwikkeling en herziening van de Nederlandse verzorgingsstaat* (The Redistributing Society: Development and Restructuring of the Dutch Welfare State). Amsterdam: Amsterdam University Press.

Tweede Kamer. 1998–1999. *Beleidsnota Kinderopvang* (Parliament Policy Paper on Child Care), 26587, no. 2. The Hague: Tweede Kamer.

Utrechts Nieuwsblad. 1996. "Belgisch kind komt alleen thuis om te slapen." (Belgian Child Only Comes Home to Sleep). April 24.

Vandemeulebroecke, L. 1993. "Kinderopvang in Vlaanderen" (Child Care in Flanders). *Pedagogisch Tijdschrift* 18, nos. 5–6: 309–23.

Vanistendael, F. 1989. "Gezinsfiscaliteit" (Family Finances). *Algemeen Fiscaal Tijdschrift* (General Fiscal Journal). De hervorming van 1988 (The Reform of 1988). January: 12–20.

Visser, Jelle. 1999. *De sociologie van het halve werk* (The Sociology of Half-Time Work). Amsterdam: Vossiuspers AUP.

Visser, Jelle, and Anton Hemerijck. 1997. *"A Dutch Miracle": Job Growth, Welfare Reform and Corporatism in the Netherlands*. Amsterdam: Amsterdam University Press.

VWS (Ministerie van Volksgezondheid, Welzijn, Sport [Ministry of Health, Welfare and Sport]). 1997. *Zes jaar Stimuleringsmaatregel Kinderopvang 1990–1995* (Six Years of Stimulative Measure Child Care 1990–1995). Rijswijk: VWS.

Welzijnszakboekje 1992–1993 (Welfare Handbook). 1993. Zaventum: Kluwer.

Werkgroep Vlaamse Dienster voor Opuanggezinnen (Organization for Flemish Services for Family Day Care). 1992. "Who Are the Family Day Carers?" St. Niklaas: Werkgroep.

WRR (Wetenschappelijke Raad voor het Regeringsbeleid [Scientific Council for Governmental Policy]). 1990. *Een werkend perspectief. Arbeidsparticipatie in de jaren negentig*. (A Working Perspective: Labor Market Participation in the Nineties). The Hague: WRR.

Zijderveld, Anton C. 1983. "Transformatie van de verzorgingsstaat" (The Transformation of the Welfare State). In *De nadagen van de verzorgingsstaat. Kansen en perspectieven voor morgen* (The Twilight of the Welfare State), ed. Philip A. Idenburg. Amsterdam: Meulenhoff.

CHAPTER 6

Does Anyone Have a "Libre Choix"?
Subversive Liberalism and the Politics of French Child Care Policy

Kimberly Morgan

Some students of social policy dismiss claims of welfare-state retrenchment because there have been few clear instances of major cutbacks, and aggregate data reveal considerable continuity in spending on social security (Pierson 1996; Fligstein 1998). Yet, when viewed from a gender perspective, the effects of economic restructuring and budgetary austerity on the welfare state become more apparent. The evolution of French child care policy offers a useful window onto these processes. France has one of the strongest child care systems among the Organization for Economic Cooperation and Development (OECD) member states, yet a closer look reveals that welfare state and economic restructuring have taken their toll. Currently only 9 percent of children under the age of three have a place in one of the famed crèches, while 50 percent are cared for by a parent, usually their mother (see table 6.1). The rest are looked after by nannies or are in family child care (CNAF 1997a). State spending on collective child care has been surpassed by the amount now spent on individualized forms of care, such as nannies or family child care, revealing a weakening commitment to the traditional crèche.[1] After promoting women's insertion in the labor market in the 1970s, both socialist and conservative governments have subsequently favored policies that encourage mothers' exit from the labor force. New forms of service provision reflect the search for greater flexibility in service delivery to match the proliferation of atypical employment, such as part-time work or evening shifts. These trends have had important qualitative and quantitative effects on child care provision that aggregate spending data fail to capture.

TABLE 6.1: PERCENTAGE OF FRENCH CHILDREN UNDER 3 IN CHILD CARE	
Crèches	9%
Licensed family child care	13%
Subsidized nannies	2%
Home	50%
Unknown	26%

SOURCE: CNAF (1997a).

Three dimensions of the welfare state crisis have had important implications for child care policy in France, as in other states. First, there has been a very real *financial* crisis, as France has struggled to maintain budget balance in the face of growing social security costs. The time for massive new spending initiatives has passed, as governments now concentrate resources on meeting existing commitments. In fact, it is precisely the political strength of well-established programs that makes it difficult to embark on new, expansive policies (Rieger and Leibfried 1998). This has hurt child care policy in France, where the development of collective child care services was just beginning to get off the ground in the 1970s when economic crisis set in. The real secret of France's position as an international leader in child care provision—its universal system of full-day preschools—was already well in place by the mid-1970s. With their broad-based constituency and place within a powerful, centralized education ministry, these programs have been immune to budget austerity, and have taken up much of the responsibility for child care.

Second, there is an *employment* crisis that has had important ramifications for the course of child care policy over the past two decades. In addition to its budget-busting effects, chronic unemployment has diminished the commitment of the French state to encouraging women's labor force participation. Pragmatic French political elites, who had promoted women's employment in the 1970s with seemingly few qualms, quickly abandoned these goals when unemployment began to climb. The vaunted state goal of ensuring women's *libre choix* (free choice) was reinterpreted from enabling women's workforce participation to promoting their role as caregivers in the home. French governments have also redeployed child care policy as a way to encourage job creation by subsidizing parents who hire their own child care workers. This is part of a larger strategy of promoting new, flexible forms of employment, including part-time work. Women are the ones who disproportionately take up these new forms of employment. This has put strains on the child care system and has encouraged the move away from traditional public services toward individualized modes of care, more adaptable to atypical employment schedules.

Finally, there is a crisis of welfare state *legitimacy*, in which critics on both the left and the right have questioned traditional modes of social service provision. The decentralization of central government functions to the local level was one response to these critics, and it has been accompanied by efforts to shift greater responsibility for child care provision to the voluntary sector. There also has been a diversification of the kinds of services available to families, with the creation of part-time care programs, play centers, and parent-child centers. These new kinds of services address a broader range of family needs. At the same time, the resources available for child care must be divided among more services in order to accommodate a larger range of interests. While such an approach may be more responsive to the demands of many parents, this has come at the price of redistributive fairness.

This chapter will first describe France's child care system in the context of the French welfare state. The remainder will then evaluate how the three forms of welfare state crisis outlined above have influenced child care policy over the past two decades, and how the economic and political environment have shaped the politics of parental "choice" in matters of child care.

Child Care and the French Welfare Regime

The French welfare state fits imperfectly in the category to which it is most often assigned in typologies of welfare regimes—the conservative-corporatist or Christian Democratic cluster that includes the Netherlands, Germany, Austria, Italy, and possibly Spain and Portugal (Esping-Andersen 1990; 1999; Kersbergen 1995; Levy 1999). Various authors describe social policy in these countries as having been "forged in the crucible of conservative clericalism" (Levy 1999, 245), as a product of corporatist guild traditions, and/or as reflecting the machinations of bureaucrats or dictators. In this view, it was nineteenth-century authoritarians and/or Christian democratic parties that crafted social policies in these countries. As both were minimally concerned with either market efficiency or leveling social divisions, continental welfare states offer generous resources to alleviate human suffering, yet they do so in a way that reproduces existing hierarchies and social stratification. This includes gender stratification, as Catholic social thought endorsed the traditional division of labor in workplace and home. Social benefits for workers are generous, but there are few public services that could offer women a source of employment and socialize care work. According to the Catholic principle of subsidiarity, the lowest possible level of society—the family, churches, or the voluntary sector—holds responsibility for tending to human welfare needs.

Many aspects of the French welfare state are consonant with this description. French social spending is quite high and, as in other "conservative" welfare states, this produces only a moderate-level of "decommodification." Social benefits are differentiated by status-reproducing occupational schemes, and France has huge public employee pension programs (Esping-Andersen 1990). In addition, as will be detailed below, the French response to unemployment in recent decades has been to promote "labor shedding" rather than active labor market policies and public employment that could sop up excess labor (Esping-Andersen 1996).

When gender-related measures are taken into consideration, however, France diverges from the conservative model. One important difference lies in women's labor-force participation. Since the nineteenth century, French women have been in the labor force in far higher numbers than women in other European countries.

Historians have linked the high rates of women's labor force participation in the nineteenth and first half of the twentieth century to late industrialization, the continued importance of the family farm, and low birthrates that shrank the pool of labor and drew women into the workforce (Tilly and Scott 1978). The percentages of women in the labor force dipped in the 1950s and 1960s, a time referred to by some as the "golden age of familialism," in which the traditional male-breadwinner/female caregiver model was upheld in both societal discourse and public policy

(Prost 1984). Even then, 46.6 percent of women were working outside the home, compared to 49.2 percent in Germany, but only 26.2 percent in the Netherlands and 38.7 percent in Italy (OECD 1997).[2] Since the late 1960s, the percentage of women in the labor force steadily increased in France as in nearly all OECD states. It is the very high rate of maternal employment that distinguishes France from other European states. In 1997, 82.4 percent of mothers with two children were in the labor force in France, compared to 61.5 percent in Germany, 59.8 percent in the Netherlands, and 57.6 percent in Italy (Fagnani 2000).[3]

This reflects, in part, the fact that working mothers have access to greater supports and services in France than in the other conservative welfare states. An index of policies that support mothers' employment puts France as one of the high achievers among OECD states, far above the other "conservative" welfare states (Gornick, Meyers, and Ross 1997). In 1997, there were spaces in publicly supported child care for 24 percent of children under the age of three, and places in preschools for at least 35 percent of two-year-olds (see tables 6.1 and 6.2). While only 9 percent of children under three are in an actual public child care center, the commitment of substantial state resources to subsidizing family and in-home child care reveals a willingness on the part of state officials to endorse and support mothers in the labor force. In addition to state payments covering part of the operating costs of child care centers, the French state offers subsidies for parents using family child care, subsidies and a special tax break for parents who employ nannies, and another tax break to reduce child care costs for parents (David 1999).[4] In addition, nearly 100 percent of children aged three to six attend free, full-day preschools. These programs follow the school schedule (8:30 A.M. to 4:30 P.M.), and around 12 percent of children under six have a place in an afterschool program that rounds out the rest of the day (CNAF 1997a). These supports and services have enabled French women to work at high percentages while maintaining one of the higher fertility rates in the European Union (EU). While French fertility rates are lower than they were during the baby boom years, the current rate of 1.75 is well above the EU average of 1.45 (Fagnani 2000).

The historic evolution of the French welfare state departs from the story outlined above, and this helps to account for why French policy toward working mothers differs from that found in much of continental Europe. The welfare state in France arose not in the context of authoritarianism and clericalism, but in a republic

TABLE 6.2: PRESCHOOL ENROLLMENT

AGE	PERCENTAGE ENROLLED
2	35%
3	99%
4	100%
5	100%

SOURCE: Ministère de l'Education Nationale (1997).

shaped by nationalism and anticlericalism. In the late nineteenth century, republicans cemented state control over the education system to wrest the socialization of the nation's children away from the Catholic Church and forge a loyal republican citizenry. This process began with the *école maternelle*, or preschool, which was incorporated into the national education system in the 1880s (Dajez 1994; Luc 1997). After World War II, the number of preschools expanded rapidly. By the 1970s, these schools were universally available, making France one of the leading providers in the world of early childhood education programs.[5] As many students of the welfare state neglect the education system, they miss the important role these programs play in France in providing young children with educational opportunities while offering support to many working parents.

The administration of the écoles maternelles is separate from that of the *crèches* and other forms of child care that are part of social welfare and family policy. Still, the development of the crèches also departs from the conventional "Christian Democratic" or "conservative corporatist" story of welfare state development. In contrast to Germany or the Netherlands, where the principle of subsidiarity in the social services has been paramount, child care in France was incorporated into the realm of state policymaking and regulation in 1945. This was due in part to pronatalist objectives; given the demographic imperative of protecting the health of young babies, government officials believed that the crèches were too important to be left to private charities (Norvez 1990). As a result, the government in 1945 created the *Protection maternelle et infantile* to regulate all establishments involved in the health and care of infants, toddlers, and preschool-age children. It has continued to do so ever since, imposing high standards of hygiene and personnel training on the crèches.

Governmental intervention in the realm of child care also results from the role of a distinctive set of family policy-making institutions.[6] The Caisse Nationale des Allocations Familales (CNAF), or national family-benefits fund, oversees the management of the family benefits funds into which workers and employers pay contributions. The national level fund sets overall priorities, and its 125 local equivalents, the Caisses d'Allocations Familiales (CAFs), are responsible for distributing these benefits to families. This family-benefits system is fairly unique in continental Europe, both for the generosity of the benefits and the structure of its administration. Ironically, the most "familialist" welfare regimes tend to have the most passive family policies, offering low levels of family benefits and other forms of assistance (Esping-Andersen 1999). France was one of the first countries to develop an extensive and generous system of family allowances. Since its inception, a portion of the resources collected in these funds has been diverted to support family-related social services. Starting in the 1970s, these funds became the main source of financial support for child care.

These features of French social provision reflect the ideologies and ambitions of those political forces with power in the postwar period. France differs from other continental European countries in the relative weakness of Christian democratic political movements. The Mouvement républicain populaire (MRP) was a major political party during the Fourth Republic (1946–1958), and its traditional views of women's roles and the family marked the more traditionalist elements of the post-war family benefits system. However, with the MRP's declining influence in the 1950s and its eclipse in the Fifth Republic (1958–) came a diminishing commitment to the traditional family model (Prost 1984; Laroque 1985). Gaullist parties have been the dominant force on the right in the Fifth Republic, and they have diverged from many of the tenets of Christian democracy. The period of greatest welfare state expansion in the 1960s and 1970s occurred under secular, Gaullist elites who had as their objective economic development and modernization rather than the preservation of traditional status categories and the defense of the Church (Morgan 2000).

It was also in this period that the issue of child care came on the national agenda, and many Gaullist political elites responded with a pragmatic view of the family and mothers' employment that waved aside anxieties over family breakdown and maternal deprivation. Elite pragmatism in these matters was evident already in the 1950s, when political leaders with modernizing ambitions called for married women to join the labor force as a remedy against labor shortages (Commissariat Général du Plan 1958). An influx of immigrants temporarily solved labor supply problems. The issue of child care did not seriously resurface until the late 1960s and early 1970s, when there was much discussion of the new values and aspirations of many women, who were no longer leaving the labor force after the birth of their children. Women's groups and other May '68 movements called for universal child care. In

FIGURE 6.1: NUMBER OF AVAILABLE PLACES IN CRÈCHES, 1970–1995

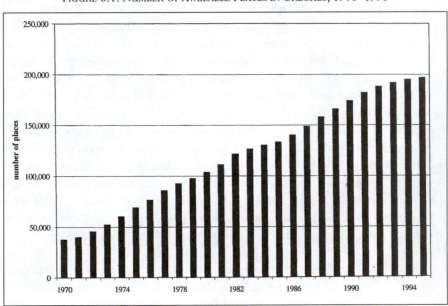

SOURCES: SESI (1998, 1985, 1982, 1980); *Annuaire statistique sanitaire et sociale* (1995, 1996).

response, two different center-right governments diverted 100 million francs from the family benefits funds to jump start the creation of public crèches. The administrative council of the CNAF created a new financing system to cover some of the operating costs of social services such as child care (Ancelin 1997). The number of places in public crèches began rapidly increasing (see fig. 6.1).

By the mid-1970s, then, the French state had made a clear commitment to furthering the creation of public child care, and a new financing system was in place using the resources of the family benefit funds. An extensive system of public preschools was universally available to all children at no charge to their parents. How would this system of early childhood care and education hold up with the onset of economic recession in the late 1970s?

Diverging Fates: Education and Social Services Policy in an Era of Economic Crisis

While the fiscal crisis of the welfare state has not prompted large-scale retrenchment in France, it has influenced the evolution of child care policy. Conservative and socialist governments alike did not cut existing child care programs and, by and large, official policy has continued to support the development of child care services. At the same time, however, the rate of growth of public child care services slowed considerably in the 1990s. Places in public crèches remain scarce, and parents joke that they have to register with a crèche within weeks of conception if they hope to get a place for their child. France has maintained its position as an international leader in child care in large measure because its preschool system was already in place by the 1970s and covers many of the needs of working parents.

Starting in the mid-1970s, France began to experience the strains on its social welfare system that affected most OECD countries at that time: demographic change, fiscal imbalance, rising unemployment, and sluggish economic growth. People were having fewer babies and living longer, which was reducing the ratio between contributors and beneficiaries to social programs. This began producing deficits in the social security system, which were exacerbated by rising health care costs (Ross 1988). At the same time, the phenomenal economic growth of the postwar period, known as the *trente glorieuses*, came to an end. Whereas annual economic growth between 1960 and 1973 averaged 5.4 percent, in the 1973–79 period the rate of annual growth slowed to 2.4 percent, dropping to 2.1 percent for 1979–89. Accompanying this economic slowdown was stubborn unemployment. France went from having an unemployment rate of less than 2 percent to a persistent 10 percent in the 1980s. Unemployment hovered around 12 percent for much of the 1990s and has only recently begun to decline (OECD 1997; 1999).

Accompanying these new economic realities was a set of international constraints that came into bold relief in the early 1980s. When the Socialists came to power in 1981, they attempted a program of Keynesian demand stimulus at odds with the economic tightening being pursued by its neighbors. In a world of growing economic interdependence, these policies provoked capital flight that threatened the domestic economy and France's commitment to the Exchange Rate Mechanism of the European community. The lesson was clear: international economic factors put new constraints on the autonomy of economic policymaking. By 1983, the socialists had converted to budget austerity and tight monetary policy (Loriaux 1991; Hall 1986). In the 1990s, the move toward a European monetary union and its strict fiscal requirements only accentuated these external constraints. With diminished autonomy in budgetary and monetary policy, massive new spending commitments are untenable.

The combined pressures of internationalization and domestic structural change have produced a "subversive liberalism" in which there is less a full-blown retrenchment of the welfare state than a steady erosion of state commitments because of the imperative of cost containment (Rhodes 1995). This is evident in France where, as a whole, the state has continued to grow. Government spending as a percentage of gross domestic product hovers around 55 percent today, compared to 39 percent in 1974 (OECD 1997). At the same time, French governments have made budget balancing one of their main priorities. They have managed to maintain existing commitments to areas such as pensions and health care by raising taxes and selling off national companies (Parker 1998). Governments also have trimmed social policies around the edges through cuts in benefits, higher eligibility criteria, and fees for services (Ross 1988; Falkner and Talos 1994).

The new context of budget austerity has had different consequences for the crèche and the école maternelle. By the time the economic crisis set in, the preschool system already was well-established. While children of the working classes were traditionally the main pupils in the école maternelle, after the Second World War middle-class parents began demanding places for their children in these schools. The phenomenal expansion in public demand in the 1950s and 1960s came as a great surprise to education ministry officials and government planners, and they hastily moved to try and satisfy the demand. Often, they did so by relying on very high teacher-student ratios; it was not uncommon to have one teacher for a class of fifty-five or sixty children. This did not diminish parents' enthusiasm for the programs. By 1975, 80 percent of three-year-olds, 97 percent of four-year-olds, and 100 percent of five-year-old children were attending these noncompulsory schools (Ministère de l'Education Nationale 1997). Particularly after 1968, with the growing interest in early childhood education as a remedy for inequality, the place was secured for the French école maternelle as one of the most popular elements of the education system.

These programs clearly benefit from being linked in the public mind and discourse with educational questions rather than with caregiving and gender roles. The massive increase in preschool attendance in the 1950s and 1960s was unrelated to rates of women's labor-force participation, which generally decreased in this period (Plaisance 1986). Instead, parents sought out the schools for their educational value.

While today many parents rely upon these programs as a form of child care, their official mission is one of education, not child care. This is repeatedly underlined by officials in the Ministry of Education, union leaders, and teachers, all of whom are eager to distance themselves from mere *garderies*, or child care centers (Norvez 1990; Merlen and Baehr 1999; Lamy 1999). The école maternelle has a very broad base of support, as both two-earner families and more traditional households rely on the programs for their educational merits. As the *première éducation* of the nation's children, the schools also benefit from being part of the large and powerful education bureaucracy (Plaisance 1986).

It comes as no surprise then that the école maternelle has been fairly immune to retrenchment pressures. As governments became increasingly reluctant to devote resources to the crèches, much responsibility for child care shifted unofficially to these programs. While the decision to build a school lies with the city government, which covers building and maintenance costs, the national education ministry pays teacher salaries, which is often the most expensive part of public services. Investing in preschools is therefore a cheaper way for city governments to show their responsiveness to parents' demands. The preschools follow the regular school schedule, which means they traditionally have been closed at lunch-time and on Wednesdays. In recent years, many municipalities have created afterschool services that extend the programs to cover a full day. Even where such programs are lacking, the école maternelle has already covered much of the day, at no cost to parents.

The one way in which the development of public preschool places stagnated in the 1980s was in the provision for children under three. By law, the youngest age at which children can attend a preschool is two and a half. During the 1960s and 1970s, the percentages of two-year-olds in the preschool system increased rapidly: from 9.9 percent in 1960, the figure reached 18 percent in 1970, and 36 percent in 1980. Since then, the percentage of two-year-olds has remained at around 35 percent. For many years, teachers' unions opposed admitting such young children, fearing that it was a step toward degrading the école maternelle into a mere caregiving service. With declining school enrollments, however, unions became more favorable to expanding the pool of possible students. Throughout the 1980s and 1990s, they called for measures to adapt preschools so that they can accommodate the needs of these younger children. Thus far, governments have made few efforts to meet these demands. Whether or not this is a reflection of budget austerity in the 1980s, it is related to reticence on the part of public officials about the merits of placing children under three in the school system (Conseil Économique et Social 1981; Baudelot 1999). Many teachers also remain uncomfortable about the idea of having these younger children in the classroom (Baudelot 1999).

The crèches have fared less well in the context of welfare state crisis and economic restructuring. While by the 1970s, the preschools were available to nearly all children, the crèches never developed into a similarly universal service. After an initially strong commitment to the public child care centers in the 1970s and part of the 1980s, there has been a marked decline in the pace of development. Between

1970 and 1980, the cumulative growth in child care spaces amounted to a 176 percent increase. In the 1980s, overall growth slowed to 68 percent, and between 1987 and 1997, the increase was only 26 percent. In the 1990s, the annual increase in the number of places available amounted often to only 1 or 2 percent growth. This is not due to shrinking demands on the part of parents. Public crèches report long waiting lists for a space and high demand among parents. One estimate in 1990 determined that for children under five, nearly half of those needing child care were not receiving it. A survey at the same time showed that 80 percent of parents believed the supply of child care was inadequate (David 1999).

The Socialists came to power in 1981 promising 300,000 new places in public crèches and a paid parental leave that would be generous enough so that men would also take advantage of it. The new government created a Secrétariat d'Etat à la Famille, which immediately commissioned a report on child care that advocated a major increase in public child care (Bouyala and Roussille 1982). The number of public child care places climbed between 1981 and 1983. After that year, with the implementation of the first of several decentralization measures, the development of new child care places stagnated until the late 1980s, when it began to climb again (see fig. 6.2). In the 1990s, the pace of development slowed dramatically. As will be discussed below, this was the time when governments began devoting more resources to paid care leaves and individualized forms of child care.

In short, the fiscal crisis of the welfare state had the greatest impact on the social services sector. While the sector did not suffer actual cuts, the pace of child care development slowed. The crèches were only beginning to gain acceptability and wider

FIGURE 6.2: ANNUAL INCREASE IN NUMBER OF AVAILABLE CRÈCHE PLACES, 1971–1995

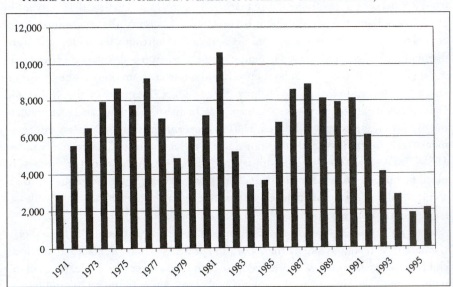

SOURCES: SESI (1998, 1985, 1982, 1980); *Annuaire statistique sanitaire et sociale* (1995, 1996).

use in the 1970s, when new strains on state budgets diminished the enthusiasm of many state leaders for these costly programs. By contrast, the preschools already were institutionalized, benefiting from the legitimacy of their association with public education, the strength of teachers' unions, the widespread popular support they enjoyed, and their mission of promoting educational equality and healthy child development.

Reinventing Child Care Policy As Employment Policy

The second way in which pressures on the welfare state and structural economic changes have affected child care policy in France is through a growing tendency in the 1980s and 1990s to deploy child care policy to combat unemployment. This has taken two forms: (1) encouraging more individualized solutions to child care, such as subsidizing parents who hire child care workers in the home, as a way to create employment; and (2) offering subsidies to parents who leave the labor force to care for their own children. Both have been pursued under the rubric of promoting libre choix, or parental choice—particularly mothers'—in child care matters. Such a policy also has, at times, dovetailed with pronatalist objectives. Throughout the 1980s and 1990s, the child care policies adopted by different governments have embodied a shifting constellation of pronatalist, employment, and redistributive objectives.

Since the late 1970s, both socialist and conservative governments began looking for less expensive ways to address the demands of working parents for child care. Since the early 1970s, the French government had been experimenting with *crèches familiales*, or child care centers, in private homes. These differ from "family child care" in many other countries because they are publicly financed, substantially more regulated, and are managed by personnel that have the same qualifications as the directors of the traditional crèches. At the same time, these services cost much less than a traditional crèche, and watered down regulations in the 1970s aimed to reduce their costliness even further (Norvez 1990). An even cheaper form of child care for the state is that which resembles American family child care—private individuals called *assistantes maternelles* who care for several children in their own home, often while looking after their own children. This has long been, and continues to be, the most widely used form of child care in France. In 1977, the government awarded these workers official status and some benefits, provided they were licensed by the state. In return for a health exam and inspection of their home, they receive the right to a basic salary (although the exact pay they would receive was left to the negotiations between parents and the caregiver), social security, paid sickness and maternity leave, four weeks of vacation, and the right to sixty hours of training, the details of which were left to the discretion of local administrations (Desigaux and Thévenet 1982).

As it became apparent in the 1980s that the promised 300,000 new places in crèches were not going to materialize any time soon, there were renewed efforts to encourage the use of assistantes maternelles by offering subsidies to parents. The Prestation Spéciale Assistante Maternelle was created in 1980, covering part of the social charges that parents pay on behalf of their child care worker. In 1990, a socialist government replaced the benefit with the Aide à la Famille pour l'Emploi d'une Assistante Maternelle Agréée (AFEAMA). This benefit, open to all parents regardless of income, pays the social charges for an assistante maternelle employed by parents for a child under the age of six. Since 1989, the government has supported *relais assistantes maternelles* (family child care networks), which are places where parents and child care workers can meet, gain information about child care issues, and assistantes maternelles can sometimes benefit from some training (CNAF 1996b).

While efforts to license and train assistantes maternelles preserved some form of state supervision over the health and safety of children in these private arrangements, the use of public funds to subsidize parents who hire nannies departed entirely from the practice of regulating child services (Math and Renaudat 1997). In 1986, a conservative government created the Allocation de Garde d'Enfant à Domicile (AGED), a payment to cover a portion of the costs of the social charges parents must pay on nannies they hire to care for children under the age of three. The benefit is awarded to parents without requiring licensing of the caregiver. There is also a tax break to help parents with the cost of this form of care. Both policies subsidize the use of private options that alleviate the demand for public crèches places and promote employment in the private market. With these aims in mind, a conservative government in 1995 substantially increased the tax break, doubled AGED's reimbursement ceiling, and extended its use to cover children aged three to six. The number of families benefiting from the AGED increased by 170 percent in two years (Fagnani 1997). A number of measures also were taken in the 1990s to simplify the process of creating family employment and of calculating and paying social charges.

The move toward more individualized forms of child care provision signifies an important qualitative shift in child care services that is particularly evident when juxtaposed with the preschool system. The école maternelle was generalized in the late 1950s and 1960s, a time when there was a strong commitment on the part of the state to developing public services. Currently over 85 percent of French preschoolers are in state-run programs, the remainder being typically in parochial schools (largely Catholic) that receive extensive state support (Ministère de l'Education Nationale 1997). Teachers' unions fought to expand the public preschool system, both out of an interest to protect their jobs and because of their long-standing antipathy to religious education. Many argued that if the state did not act to create more public preschools, a private system would spring up in response to parental demands for these services, and that in the long run this would sap support and resources from the public schools (Morgan 2000).

The failure to develop an equivalent set of public crèches, coupled with active state support for private alternatives, threatens to produce the sort of evolution feared by the teachers' unions. The generous subsidies awarded to parents using these individual alternatives hurt the public crèches in the mid-1990s, as competition from nannies and family child care lured middle and upper class parents away from the traditional crèche (David 1999). Higher-income parents are often essential to the financial well-being of child care centers, as they pay higher fees than the lower-income clientele. Allowing private opt-outs also furthers the growth of a "divided constituency," in which different parents have diverging interests in the kind of child care system they prefer, thereby fragmenting support for a unified child care policy (Michel 1999). The failure to unionize most child care workers prevents them from playing the same role teachers' unions have played as advocates of the public system. With the move toward more individualized services, such as nannies and family child care, the possibilities for such unionization become even more remote as these workers are extremely difficult to organize (Farrache 1998).

Recourse to individualized services has been furthered by structural economic trends that also have been encouraged by state policy. Since the early 1980s, French governments implemented a number of measures to encourage greater flexibility in employment conditions and work schedules. The percentage of part-time employment doubled from 6 percent in 1981 to 12 percent in 1997 (Audric and Forgeot 1999). While women in France still work part-time at far lower percentages than in most OECD countries, the percentage of women in part-time employment grew from 20 to 30 in this period (Sandoval 1999). Similarly, the prevalence of atypical work schedules has increased as well. Sixty-five percent of workers had a fixed schedule in 1969, compared to less than half today (Bloch-London and Boisard 1999). The recent law reducing weekly work hours to thirty-five has furthered this evolution. In negotiations over the implementation of the new law, many employers have secured more flexible work arrangements in return for the reduced work week. All of this has made it more difficult for parents to arrange child care, particularly as the crèche usually follows traditional working hours. As a result, parents often prefer nannies and family child care workers as more accommodating for their own difficult work schedules (Fagnani 2000). The latter, nonunionized and in an individual employment relationship that is often a black-market one, are not always in a position to protest parents' demands for these atypical work schedules.

The second way in which child care policy has blurred into employment policy is in efforts to encourage women to leave the labor force and care for their young children themselves. Since the onset of economic crisis, this approach has combined fiscal, demographic, and labor market objectives in various permutations. Already in the late 1970s, with the onset of economic crisis, the government began turning toward a strategy of encouraging women's exit from labor markets. After a spate of progressive family and gender-related policy measures under President Valéry Giscard d'Estaing, the government began adopting a more traditional approach. In 1977, the government created the Congé Parental d'Éducation (CPE), which allowed a working parent of a child under three to suspend work for two years without pay (Jenson and Sineau 1998). In the two decades that followed, the CPE was progressively reformed to make it compatible with part-time work, and expanded to make it available to more parents.

In 1985, a socialist government made a renewed effort to lure women out of the labor force by creating the Allocation Parentale d'Éducation (APE), a form of paid parental leave for those parents with three or more children. The leave was available for two years, but the parent needed to have worked for two years in the thirty months prior to taking the leave. The strict work requirement is revealing of the APE's underlying motive as an antiunemployment mechanism. As the benefit was only for families with three or more children, it also had clear pronatalist aims. When few parents took advantage of the new law, the conservative government that came to power in 1986 passed a new law that diminished the work requirement to two years out of the last ten, and offered the paid leave for three years (Jenson and Sineau 1998).

An even greater liberalization of the APE occurred in 1994 under another conservative government. The 1994 *loi de famille* (family law) made the APE open to families with only two children, and required that the parent taking the leave had been in the workforce for two years during the last five. The value of the benefit also was increased substantially, and parents could now combine it with part-time work. The expansion of the benefit had immediate effects on the number of mothers of young children in the labor force. Between March 1994 and 1997, the percentage of mothers of two children (the youngest being under age three) in the labor force dropped from 69 to 53 as the number of beneficiaries of the APE tripled. One estimate holds that 60 percent of women having their second child and withdrawing from the labor

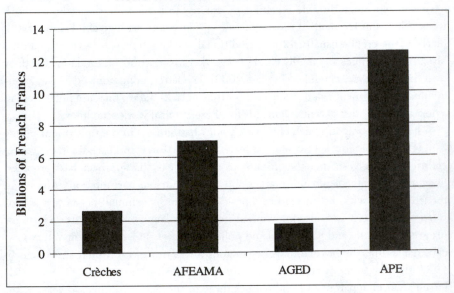

FIGURE 6.3: PUBLIC SPENDING ON CHILD CARE

SOURCE: CNAF (1997a).

AFEAMA = subsidy for licensed family child care workers
AGED = subsidy for in-home care
APE = paid parental leave, up to three years

force would not have done so had the APE not existed (Afsa 1998). APE's effects fall mostly almost entirely upon women; even though the benefit is technically open to men, 99 percent of beneficiaries are women. The same is true for the CPE.

In sum, French child care policy over the past two decades shows how economic forces have shaped state policy toward women's employment. Persistent unemployment in the last two decades redirected state efforts from prioritizing the traditional crèche toward supporting parental or individual modes of care (see fig. 6.3). However, the move toward more flexible social service provision in recent decades also reflects a third, wider trend in the welfare state.

The Welfare State's Crisis of Legitimacy

The third dimension of welfare-state restructuring that has affected French child care policy is a shift in the delivery of social services. Since the early 1980s, devolution of government functions from the central to the regional or local level decentralized responsibility for social services planning. At the same time, voluntary associations have begun to play a significant role in providing these services, an important departure from the previous state monopoly over social service delivery. While these trends have been facilitated by the desire of state officials to shed responsibility for public services to other levels of government and society, they are not simply the product of neoliberal ideas and financial pressures. There is a larger crisis in the legitimacy of the welfare state, spurred by New Left critiques of bureaucracy and by social movements favoring increased citizen participation in the management of local services. The result for child care policy has been an enhanced role of local governments and associations in policymaking, which has favored a diversification of the kinds of child care services available.

As noted earlier, the most rapid growth in public crèches came in the 1970s when the central government made several direct investments in public child care. The slowdown in the rate of increase in these services corresponds with the Decentralization Law of 1982, which fundamentally restructured center-periphery relations in France. The law gave full responsibility to local governments for deciding whether or not to build child care centers. At the same time, the government also decentralized financing for these projects, as the national family benefits fund transferred many of its resources down to its local equivalent, the CAF. There is no national requirement that localities support child care, nor is there an effort at the national level to develop a unified, coordinated plan for the development of these services across the country. The most that the CNAF can do to promote child care programs is to try to incite local CAFs to prioritize certain services over others and to offer incentives to local governments.

Had it not been for the CNAF and its subsidiaries, it is doubtful that child care services would have advanced much at all after the decentralization law. The CNAF has been the motor behind the continued development of new child care centers. In a 1981 *circulaire* laying out its social services objectives for the next five years, the CNAF affirmed that its first priority would be to support crèches, kindergartens, play centers, and other services for families with children (CNAF 1981). In 1983, the CNAF created a system of contracts to be negotiated between local funds and local governments, in which the local government agreed to develop a plan for creating public child care. In 1988, the CNAF developed a new form of contract that applied to a much broader range of social services for children. CNAF spending on child care in this period increased by 33 percent (in constant francs) over five years (Ancelin 1997). Throughout the 1990s, the CNAF has continued to make child care for children under six one of the highest priorities of its spending on family services (CNAF 1997b).

Without the ability to impose upon local governments the requirement that they build and support public child care, the CNAF can only have so much influence. There is no requirement that any level of government build child care centers, and for many local governments the costs remain prohibitive. A local government also may decide to solicit funds to support other forms of family-related services instead of investing in crèches geared to working parents. As a result, even though the CNAF continually holds up collective child care as the main priority among family services, the actual development of these programs usually falls short of the hopes of national officials.

Economic slowdown and budget pressures certainly encouraged the move to decentralize government functions. Political sentiment favoring decentralization had been building since the 1960s, however, and the reforms were in many ways a response to declining public confidence in the welfare state (Tymen and Nogues 1988; Jallade 1992). In a number of OECD countries, movements to promote citizen participation in local government and in the management of social services began sprouting up in the late 1960s. New social movements were a reaction against bureaucracy, neo-corporatist bargaining, and the welfare state, and they came not only from a neoliberal or New Right perspective, but were leftist movements to improve the responsiveness of political elites to people's needs (Alber 1988). Their demands came at a time of growing complexity in the tasks of the state, with the appearance of new forms of poverty, increasingly heterogeneous populations, and changes in the nature of risk owing to family breakdown and irregular forms of employment.

Similar movements arose in France out of the May '68 revolts. One was the movement for *autogestion,* or self-management of the workplace, a concept that came to encompass calls for a wider devolution of power in French society. Of particular importance was the idea of increasing citizen participation in local government, particularly in their position as clients of government programs. Some advocated the creation of *groupements d'action municipale*—community action groups that would be active on local issues such as housing, schools, and transportation (Schmidt 1990; Ullman 1998). A number of state officials held similar views, believing that decentralization of government functions would restore effectiveness to a bloated, overly-centralized, and inefficient state apparatus (Ullman 1998). Gradually, these ideas influenced socialist party and, to a lesser degree, communist party doctrine. By 1980, the socialist platform promised a substantial decentralization program, many of the features of which were implemented through the 1980s.

The decentralization of state power was matched by a flowering of associational life and an increasing role for these nonprofit organizations in the management of public services (Mizrahi-Tchernonog 1992; Ullman 1998). The effects are evident in the child care sector where, initially, most centers were run by the state. In 1979, 11 percent of all child care centers were run by voluntary associations; by 1993 that figure had risen to 30 percent (SESI 1982; CNAF 1996a). These associations have benefited from a partnership with the local family benefits funds (CAFs), which devote considerable resources to financing association-based services (Ancelin 1985). This includes nearly all of a more recently developed form of child care—the crèche parentale. These crèches originated in the ambitions of some May '68 activists to transform the practices of child socialization through collective forms of care. This was a reaction against the sterile, hospital-like crèches run by the state, as well as a plea for child care to liberate mothers from the burdens of child rearing (Mozère 1992). Initially, these crèches sauvages were run independently of the state, to the great irritation of many government health officials who were anxious to maintain their control over these services. Today, these child care centers receive state funding, but are entirely managed by parents. Parents are responsible for staffing the centers as well, which means that the crèche parentale requires a greater degree of parental involvement than other forms of child care. One recent study showed that parents using a crèche parentale spend on average nearly fourteen hours a month either at the center or involved in work for the association (Feretti, Jade, and Passaris 1994).

These new forms of child care add diversity to a system that has grown increasingly complex in recent years. In addition to the traditional crèche, crèche familiale, crèche parentale, and assistante maternelle, other forms of support to families include part-time child care centers (halte-garderies), play centers (ludothèques), after-school programs, and parent-child centers. The CNAF and CAFs promoted the diversification of child care services in the late 1980s when they replaced an earlier form of child care financing that targeted entirely the crèches with a system of financial supports for a much broader range of services. One area of particular growth has been in part-time child care centers, the need for which has grown alongside the increasing prevalence of atypical or part-time employment. Between 1985 and 1995, the overall increase in the number of part-time center places was 67 percent, compared to a 47 percent increase in the number of full-time crèches places (SESI 1982; CNAF 1996a). How have these trends affected the qualitative and quantitative development of child care services? Many advocates of the nonprofit sector argue that associational involvement in service provision has improved the responsiveness of the state to parents' needs and preferences. Diversity may come at the cost of the overall level of services available, however, as the pie must now be divided among a greater range of programs than in the past. Even if it wanted to, the French state could no longer embark upon a massive program of public construction today as it did with the development of the education system. The incorporation of associations in the policy-making process, with their demands for a diversified set of public services, precludes one-size-fits-all kinds of approaches to child care. In addition, government decentralization has produced great regional variations in availability. As the next section will reveal, the decentralization and diversification of social services policy caters to a wider set of interests, but at the cost of distributional fairness (Jallade 1992).

The Politics of Parental "Choice"

Since the 1970s, then, and particularly with the advent of welfare state crisis and economic restructuring, French child care policy has evolved from support for the traditional crèche toward a diverse array of services and subsidies. This trend has been accompanied by rhetoric about the importance of offering "choice" to parents in matters of child care. In the 1970s, the promotion of free choice was about promoting the full labor force participation of mothers. By the 1980s, however, the term was used to justify policies for both mothers working outside and in the home and full-time caregivers. Support for individualized forms of care also comes under the rubric of improving parental choice. Instead of moving toward a Scandinavian-style system of extensive public child care services, French public policy settled into a compromise position that supports full-time work and full-time caregiving, as well as a range of services outside of the traditional child care center.

This is a reflection of the policymaking process in the family policy sector. Family benefits and services are largely a product of decision-making in the para-public CNAF and CAFs. Representatives of business, labor, and family associations sit on the administrative council of the CNAF, as well as the equivalent councils running the CAFs, and hammer out compromises over the kinds of services deserving of public support. The more conservative family associations generally do not oppose the public crèches, but they prefer individualized forms of care, as well as services that address the needs of housewives with young children at home. The communist union, the Confédération Générale de Travail, lies on the opposite end of the spectrum in its unyielding advocacy of a vast system of public services. Other groups on the councils hold views somewhere in between these two perspectives (Ancelin 1998). While there has been no overt ideological backlash against women's employment, there has also been no consensus large enough to support engaging state resources in a major public child care initiative. Instead, the position that emerges in the CNAF, the local CAFs, and government ministries is one of subsidizing women who care for their own children as well as those who use child care in one or several of its myriad forms. Stretching resources to try to satisfy all camps tends to satisfy no one completely, although the recent increase in the home care allowance (APE) appears to have improved the option for women to stay home.

While governments on both the left and the right have maintained this compromise position in family policy, there are differences of emphasis. Conservative governments generally have tried to offer greater subsidies to individualized forms of child care, particularly for nannies. These forms of child care usually benefit middle- and upper-class families, who gain the most from tax breaks and who have the resources to pay for child care in the home (Fagnani 1997). The right also was behind the greatest expansion in paid care leaves in the 1990s, which spurred a substantial drop in maternal employment. On the left, there continues to be more support for the traditional crèche. The current socialist government has been sympathetic to claims that individualized forms of child care compete with and will ultimately undermine the public services. In response to these fears, the government of Lionel Jospin in 1997 reduced the tax break and the value of the AGED by half. Recently, the socialist government promised substantially to increase spending on crèches in order to create up to 40,000 new child care vacancies in the next few years. Notably, this comes at a time when the economy is growing again, the fiscal situation has improved, and unemployment has begun to decline. Still, this government has maintained the paid care leave (APE), although its most recent proposal would offer incentives to help draw women back into the labor force toward the end of this care leave.

How well do these policies accord with parental preferences? Public opinion studies show that many parents would rather reduce their work time than use a child care service, and many still believe that child care is the mothers' responsibility (Commaille, Strobel, and Villac 1994). In one recent study of parental preferences, 43 percent of women said they would like to quit work or reduce their work time after having children (Fagnani 2000). In addition, parental preferences for child care are quite diverse. Parents who are actually using crèches report the greatest satisfaction with their child care services of any group of parents using nonmaternal care. Still, only 22 percent of all parents say the crèche would be their preferred mode of care, with family child care as the most preferred form (32 percent), followed by grandparents (23 percent) (David 1999). Current policymaking seems to be consonant with the stated preferences of many French parents.

The price of greater responsiveness to parental preferences is distributional fairness. Those who have most benefited from the move toward individualized modes of care have been middle- and upper-income families. These forms of child care charge all parents the same, regardless of income, and families who have higher incomes benefit the most from tax credits to subsidize these services. Only the public crèches gradate the fees parents pay according to income and thus offer the most help to low-income families. Yet, this is the form of child care in shortest supply and to which poor parents often lack access. The shortages have been exacerbated in France by the decentralization law, which has produced great regional disparities in the availability of child care services. As a result, many parents lack a real choice in the matter of child care, and use whatever form of care is available to them. Lower-income parents usually end up relying upon black-market child care, which is the first choice of only 4 percent of parents, and receives the lowest satisfaction rating by parents of any form of child care (David 1999).

These policies also have implications for the gender division of labor and women's long-term well-being. Extensive care leaves hurt the long-term position of women in the labor market, and this is most detrimental for low-income women (Fagnani 1998; Math and Renaudat 1997). The APE tends to be taken by less skilled, lower-income mothers who are already earning fairly low salaries and thus have less to lose by leaving the labor force. Recent studies have shown that these marginalized female workers often have a difficult time being reinserted in the labor force, should they attempt to do so after the benefit expires (Fagnani 1996). Currently 27 percent of recipients of the APE are without employment at the end of the paid leave, contributing to the higher rates of unemployment among women than men—11.9 percent for women versus 8.4 percent for men as of March 2000 (Ministère de l'Emploi et de la Solidarité 2000). In the context of women's higher unemployment rates and greater risk of poverty, a policy that promotes women's exit from the labor market may only increase their potential for marginalization.

Conclusion

Economic crisis and welfare state reform have not produced massive cutbacks that would roll back fifty years of French social spending, yet they have had substantial effects on child care policy. Budget austerity, stubbornly high rates of unemployment, and a crisis in the legitimacy of the welfare state have changed the face of French child care policy. An extensive system of early childhood education already was well in place before the onset of the economic crisis, and it has been the secret to France's success in providing child care services to working parents. Yet growth in the nascent system of public crèches in the 1970s slowed with the strain on fiscal resources. Efforts to redress chronic unemployment led to a redefinition of the notion of facilitating women's free choice. By the 1980s, state efforts were dedicated less to promoting women's insertion into labor markets, as had been the case in the 1970s, than to encouraging women's exit from work when there were young children in the home. The imperative to bolster job growth also led to a diversification of the existing modes of child care, as state policy began subsidizing individual forms of care such as nannies or independent caregivers.

The growing complexity of the French child care system reflects a policymaking process that attempts to satisfy a wide range of groups with often diverging preferences. Yet, the resulting policy of libre choix has not produced a situation of real choice for most parents. In emphasizing individualized solutions and "choice" for parents, distributional fairness has been subordinated to employment and budgetary objectives. It remains to be seen if economic growth and declining unemployment will spark a renewed commitment to the crèche, or if the diversification of the existing system has created a constituency of parents calling for more individualized solutions to their child care needs.

Notes

1. In the French terminology, "collective" child care refers to crèches, or child care centers, nearly all of which receive substantial public subsidies or are run by local governments. "Individual" modes of child care include family child care (*assistantes maternelles*) and nannies.

2. Data are from 1960, calculated as a percentage of the female population aged fifteen to sixty-four.

3. These figures are for women with two children, the youngest being under the age of six. Note that the figure for Germany is only for the West German lander (states).

4. In 1999, the general tax break was for 25 percent of spending on child care, up to a FF15,000 ceiling per child; in addition, for parents employing a nanny in the home, there is a tax break worth 50 percent of spending, up to a limit of FF45,000 per child (David 1999).

5. A comparable evolution occurred only in Belgium and, to a lesser degree, Italy.

6. Belgium is one exception to this generalization.

References

Afsa, Cédric. 1998. "L'allocation parentale d'éducation: entre politique familiale et politique de l'emploi" (Paid Parental Leave: Between Family Policy and Work Policy). *Insee Première* 569: 37–40.

Alber, Jens. 1988. "Continuities and Changes in the Idea of the Welfare State." *Politics and Society* 16, no. 4: 451–68.

Ancelin, Jacqueline. 1985. "L'action sociale de la branche famille" (The Social Share of the Family Branch). *Droit social* 5: 438–47.

_____. 1997. *L'action sociale familiale et les caisses d'allocations familiales: Un siècle d'histoire* (The Social Family Share and Family Benefits Funds : A Century of History). Paris: Association pour l'étude de la sécurité sociale.

_____. 1998. Former CNAF official, personal interview with the author, March 9.

Annuaire statistique sanitaire et sociale (Social and Health Yearbook). 1995, 1996. Paris: Documentation Française.

Audric, Sophie, and Gérard Forgeot. 1999. "Le développement du travail à temps partiel" (The Growth of Part-Time Work). In *Données sociales*. Paris: INSEE.

Baudelot, Olga. 1999. Centre de Récherche de l'Education Spécialisée et de l'Adaption Scolaire, personal interview, January.

Bergmann, Barbara R. 1996. *Saving Our Children from Poverty: What the United States Can Learn from France*. New York: Russell Sage Foundation.

Bloch-London, Catherine, and Pierre Boisard. 1999. "L'aménagement et la reduction du temps de travail" (The Conversion and Reduction of the Work Week). In *Données sociales*. Paris: INSEE.

Bouyala, Nicole, and Bernadette Roussille. 1982. *L'enfant dans la vie. Une politique pour la pe-*

tite enfance (The Child in Life: A Policy for Young Children). Paris: Documentation Française.

CNAF. 1981. *L'Action sociale et familiale des caisses d'allocations familiales. Orientations générales 1981–1985* (The Social and Family Share in Family Benefits Funds: General Trends 1981–1985). Circulaire no. 1315, March 2, 1981. Paris: CNAF.

_____. 1996a. *Les crèches en 1993* (Child Care Centers in 1993). Paris: CNAF.

_____. 1996b. *Les relais assistantes maternelles* (Family Child Care Networks). Paris: CNAF.

_____. 1997a. *L'accueil des jeunes enfants. Chiffres-clés 1997* (Accommodation for Young Children: Key Statistics, 1997). Paris: CNAF.

_____. 1997b. *Les orientations de l'action sociale familiale des CAF 1997–2000* (Trends in Social Family Shares of CAFs, 1997–2000). Circulaire no. 17–97, June 17. Paris: CNAF.

Commaille, Jacques, Pierre Strobel, and Michel Villac. 1994. *Enjeux et Perspectives de la Politique Familiale Française* (Stakes in and Prospects for French Family Policy). Unpublished manuscript.

Commissariat général du plan de modernisation et d'équipement. 1958. *Troisième plan de developpement économique et social. Rapport général de la Commission de la main d'oeuvre* (Third Economic and Social Development Plan. General Report of the Commission of Labor). Paris: Documentation française.

Conseil économique et social. 1981. *Les modes de garde des jeunes enfants* (Forms of Care for Young Children). April 30.

Cooper, Candy J., with Michelle J. Heuman. 1999. *Ready to Learn: The French System of Early Education and Care Offers Lessons for the United States.* New York: French American Foundation.

Dajez, Frédéric. 1994. *Les origines de l'école maternelle* (Origins of the Preschool System). Paris: Presses Universitaires de France.

David, Olivier. 1999. *L'accueil de la petite enfance: Services et aménagement du territoire* (Accommodation of Young Children: Services and Space Development). Rennes: Presses Universitaires de Rennes.

Desigaux, Jacques and Amédée Thévenet. 1982. *La garde des jeunes enfants* (Care of Young Children). Paris: Presses Universitaires de France.

Esping-Andersen, Gøsta. 1990. *The Three Worlds of Welfare Capitalism.* Princeton, N.J.: Princeton University Press, 1990.

_____. 1996. "Welfare States without Work: the Impasse of Labour Shedding and Familialism in Continental European Social Policy." In *Welfare States in Transition: National Adaptations in Global Economies,* ed. Gøsta Esping-Andersen. London: Sage Publications.

_____. 1999. *Social Foundations of Postindustrial Economies.* Oxford: Oxford University Press.

Fagnani, Jeanne. 1996. "Retravailler après une longue interruption. Le cas des mères ayant bénéficié de l'allocation parentale d'éducation" (Going Back to Work after a Long Hiatus. The Case of Mothers Who Benefited from Paid Parental Leave). *Revue française des affaires sociales* 3: 129–52.

_____. 1997. "L'allocation de garde d'enfant à domicile: profil des bénéficiaires et effet d'aubaine" (The Home Child Care Benefit: Profiles of Beneficiaries and the Effects of Windfall). *Droit Social* 11: 944–48.

_____. 1998. "Lacunes, contradictions et incohérences des mesures de conciliation travail/famille. Bref bilan critique" (Gaps, Contradictions, and Inconsistencies of Work/Family Conciliatory Measures. Brief Critical Assessment). *Droit social* 6: 596–602.

_____. 2000. *Un travail et des enfants: Petits arbitrages et grands dilemmas* (Working, with Children: Small Arbitrations and Big Dilemmas). Paris: Éditions Bayard.

Falkner, Gerda, and Emmerich Talos. 1994. "The Role of the State within Social Policy." *West European Politics* 17, no. 3: 52–77.

Farrache, Jacqueline. 1998. Confédération Général du Travail, personal interview with the author, April 22.

Feretti, Alan, Evelyne Jade, and Solange Passaris. 1994. *Crèches parentales, crèches associatives à participation parentale en 1994. Resumé* (Parental Child Care Centers and Cooperative Child Care Centers with Parental Participation in 1994. Summary). Paris: Association des Collectifs Enfants Parents Professionnels.

Fligstein, Neil. 1998. "Is Globalization the Cause of the Crises of Welfare States?" EUI Working Paper SPS no. 98/5, September.

Gornick, Janet C., Marcia K. Meyers, and Katherin E. Ross. 1997. "Supporting the Employment of Mothers: Policy Variation Across Fourteen Welfare States." *Journal of European Social Policy* 7: 45–70.

Hall, Peter. 1986. *Governing the Economy.* New York: Oxford University Press.

INSEE (L'Institut National de la Statistique et des Études Économiques). 1998. *Annuaire Statistique de la France* (Statistical Yearbook of France). Paris: INSEE.

Jallade, Jean-Pierre. 1992. "Is the Crisis Behind Us? Issues Facing Social Security Systems in Western Europe." In *Social Policy in a Changing Europe*, ed. Zsuzsa Ferge and Jan Eivind Kolberg. Boulder, Colo.: Westview Press.

Jenson, Jane and Mariette Sineau. 1998. "La France: Quand 'liberté de choix' ne rime pas avec égalité républicaine" (France: When "Freedom of Choice" Doesn't Rhyme with Republican Equality). In *Qui doit garder le jeune enfant? Modes d'accueil et travail des mères dans l'Europe en crise* (Who Should Care for the Young Child? Mothers' Work and Child Care in a Europe in Crisis), ed. Jenson and Sineau. Paris: Librairie Générale de Droit et de Jurisprudence.

Kersbergen, Kees van. 1995. *Social Capitalism: A Study of Christian Democracy and the Welfare State.* London: Routledge.

Lamy, Marie-Madeleine. 1999. Preschool director, personal interview with the author, January 12.

Laroque, Pierre. 1985. *La politique familiale en France depuis 1945* (Family Policy in France since 1945). Paris: La Documentation Française.

Levy, Jonah. 1999. "Vice into Virtue? Progressive Politics and Welfare Reform in Continental Europe." *Politics and Society* 27, no. 2: 239–73.

Loriaux, Michael. 1991. *France After Hegemony, International Change and Financial Reform.* Ithaca, N.Y.: Cornell University Press.

Luc, Jean-Noël. 1997. *L'invention du jeune enfant au XIXe siècle. De la salle d'asile à l'école mater-*

nelle (The Invention of the Young Child in the Nineteenth Century: From Sanctuary Rooms to Preschools). Paris: Éditions Belin.

Math, Antoine, and Evelyne Renaudat. 1997. "Développer l'accueil des enfants ou créer l'emploi? Une lecture de l'évolution des politiques en matière de modes de garde" (Develop Child Accommodations or Create Jobs? A Reading on the Evolution of Policy on Forms of Child Care). *Recherches et Prévisions* 49: 5–17.

Merlen, Annick and Marie-Laure Baehr. 1999. Syndicat des Enseignants, personal interview with the author, January 15.

Michel, Sonya. 1999. *Children's Interests / Mothers' Rights: The Shaping of America's Child Care Policy.* New Haven, Conn.: Yale University Press.

Ministère de l'Education Nationale. 1997. *Repères et références statistiques* (Statistical Indicators and References). Paris: Ministère de l'Education Nationale.

Ministère de l'Emploi et de la Solidarité. 2000. *Conférence de la Famille: Dossier de Presse* (Conference on the Family: Press Document).

Mizrahi-Tchernonog, Viviane. 1992. "Building Welfare Systems through Local Associations in France." In *Government and the Third Sector: Emerging Relationships in Welfare States,* ed. Benjamin Gidron, Ralph M. Kramer, and Lester M. Salamon. San Francisco: Jossey-Bass Publishers.

Morgan, Kimberly. 2000. "Whose Hand Rocks the Cradle? The Politics of Child Care Policy in Advanced Industrialized States." Ph.D. diss., Princeton University.

Mozère, Liane. 1992. *Le printemps des crèches: Histoire et analyse d'un mouvement* (The Beginning of Child Care Centers: History and Analysis of a Movement). Paris: Editions L'Harmattan.

Norvez, Alain. 1990. *De la naissance à l'école. Santé, modes de garde et préscolarité dans la France contemporaine* (From Birth to School: Health, Forms of Child Care and Preschooling in Contemporary France). Paris: Presses Universitaires de France.

OECD. 1997. *Historical Statistics 1960–1995.* Paris: OECD.

_____. 1999. *Employment Outlook.* Paris: OECD.

Parker, David, ed. 1998. *Privatization in the European Union: Theory and Policy Perspectives.* London: Routledge.

Pierson, Paul. 1996. "The New Politics of the Welfare State." *World Politics* 48: 143–79.

Plaisance, Eric. 1986. *L'enfant, la maternelle, la société* (Children, Preschools, and Society). Paris: Presses Universitaires de France.

Prost, Antoine. 1984. "L'évolution de la politique familiale en France de 1938 à 1981" (The Evolution of Family Policy in France from 1938 to 1981). *Le Mouvement Sociale* 129: 7–28.

Rhodes, Martin. 1995. "'Subversive Liberalism': Market Integration, Globalization, and the European Welfare State." *Journal of European Public Policy* 2, no. 3: 384–406.

Rieger, Elmar, and Stephan Leibfried. 1998. "Welfare State Limits to Globalization." *Politics and Society* 26, no. 3: 363–91.

Ross, George. 1988. "The Mitterrand Experiment and the French Welfare State: An Interesting Uninteresting Story." In *Remaking the Welfare State: Retrenchment and Social Policy in America and Europe,* ed. Michael Brown. Philadelphia: Temple University Press.

Sandoval, Véronique. 1999. "Les transformations du marché du travail des jeunes et des femmes en France et dans trois autres pays européens" (Changes in the Job Market for Young People and Women in France and Three Other European Countries). In *Données sociales*. Paris: INSEE.

Schmidt, Vivien A. 1990. *Democratizing France: The Political and Administrative History of Decentralization*. Cambridge: Cambridge University Press.

SESI (Service des Statistiques des Études et des Systèmes d'Information). 1980. *Santé Securité Sociale* (National Health Insurance) 2, March-April.

_____. 1982. *Santé Securité Sociale* (National Health Insurance) 2, March-April.

_____. 1985. "Les Familles en France" (Families in France), *Solidarité Santé Cahiers Statistiques* 3.

_____. 1998. *Activité de la protection maternelle et infantile au cours des années 1994 et 1995* (Activity of Mother and Infant Welfare during 1994 and 1995), no. 308. Paris: Ministère de l'Emploi et de la Solidarité.

Simons, Marlise. 1997. "Child Care Sacred as France Cuts Back the Welfare State." *New York Times*, December 31: 1.

Tilly, Louise A., and Joan W. Scott. 1978. *Women, Work, and Family*. New York: Holt, Rinehart and Winston.

Tymen, Jacques, and Henry Nogues. 1988. *Action sociale et decentralisation. Tendances et prospectives* (Social Services and Decentralization: Trends and Future Prospects). Paris: L'Harmattan.

Ullman, Clare F. 1998. *The Welfare State's Other Crisis: Explaining the New Partnership between Nonprofit Organizations and the State in France*. Bloomington: Indiana University Press.

the impact of neoliberalism

"Modernization" and Welfare-State Restructuring in Italy: The Impact on Child Care

Vincent Della Sala

Italy presents an interesting case to help make sense of the debates concerning the nature, scope, and intensity of welfare-state restructuring in advanced industrialized societies. The attempt to understand the restructuring of the Italian welfare state is as fraught with paradoxes and tensions as was its evolution. On the one hand, it has all the marks of welfare-state retrenchment, with an emphasis on fiscal capacity rather than social rights and collective responsibility for important areas of life. On the other hand, many of the changes have been carried out using the discourse of "modernization," "flexibility," "equity," and "efficiency." This has been particularly the case with respect to policies that affect families and women's labor-market participation. Governments in the latter part of the 1990s presented their plans to radically change the Italian economy, and ultimately society, within a framework that spoke little of retrenchment. This created an opportunity for a significant change in the structures and processes that affect gender relations. However, as we will see shortly, "modernization" may not necessarily mean a move to expanded citizenship rights.

With regard to child care, Italian social policy does not present a single, clear trajectory. Although very few children under the age of three are in child care, there has not been an active national political campaign, led by women's groups or political parties, to reverse the trend. Since the number of available child care spaces is so small, child care policy has been marginal to the debate about welfare state restructuring; indeed, neither funding nor the number of publicly funded child care spaces have been cut. By contrast, over 90 percent of children between the ages of three and six are in preschools, with the majority in state-run schools.

An examination of this paradox—between limited child care for children under three and almost universal access for those between three and six—may shed some light on the politics of welfare state restructuring in Italy. In order to gain an insight into this process, we need to understand how and why reform was attempted and what structures and legacies constrained it. As this chapter will demonstrate, reform was carried out in the name of "modernization" of large parts of Italian economic, political, and social life; the reconciliation of work and family, especially for women, figured prominently in this project. Because modernization brought together a constellation of forces that sought change for different reasons, the process was complex. The example of child care will reveal that while the center-left governments of the 1990s tried to respond to new visions of citizenship, important obstacles to access to social rights remain.

Globalization, along with European monetary integration, has been an important catalyst for change in the Italian welfare state in the 1990s, with market forces gaining a more prominent place and the state retreating. This process did not, however, simply result in welfare state decline; instead, it produced complex, even contradictory, results. These become particularly evident when one focuses on gender, which was an important dimension of the modernization discourse that served as the channel for restructuring. On the one hand, globalization presented as modernization led the center-left governments to consider issues such the reconciliation of work and family. On the other hand, the financial constraints associated with globalization provided few new resources to address these issues, while the emphasis on individual choice and market mechanisms mitigated against the development of universalist policies. With regard to child care, policy and political legacies also shaped the process of restructuring, producing uneven results. While the discourse of reconciling work and family was used to pry open the old regime, the agents and aims of this modernization did not aspire to a renewed citizenship regime with extensive and universal social rights that would include women.

Creating the Italian Welfare State

The framing of the issue of welfare state restructuring in terms of modernization—with its attendant discourses of "flexibility," "equity," and "efficiency"—raises a number of challenges for the scholar attempting to understand the dynamics and consequences of change. Early attempts to categorize the Italian welfare state have produced very mixed results. Gøsta Esping-Andersen first identified it as a corporatist-conservative welfare state regime (1990, chaps. 1–2). According to his definition, which emphasizes the scale and intensity of decommodification, this seems reasonable: Italy's provisions for pensions, unemployment, and sick benefits made it comparable to France and Germany. Yet some analysts, such as Maurizio Ferrera and Franca Bimbi, argue that the reforms in the 1970s in areas such as health care introduced elements of universalism and social rights that pushed Italy in the direction of social democratic welfare regimes (Bimbi 1993; Ferrera 1995). The case of health care is particularly revealing, as the 1978 creation of a national health system not only provided a comprehensive public system but also tried to democratize the formulation and delivery of health policies. While such measures challenge efforts to categorize Italy as a form of residual welfare-state regime, they are not entirely convincing, since major areas of social policy—especially income maintenance and housing—have remained largely immune to a discourse of social rights and universalism (Ferrera 1997).

The ambiguity about the type of welfare-state regime in Italy muddles the already difficult task of trying to understand the nature and consequences of welfare-state restructuring in the period since the signing of the Treaty on European Union. As we will see shortly, a number of important reforms in the 1990s forced an examination of how the role of the state in securing social and economic rights—indeed the very definition of those rights—may have changed. On the one hand, they can be seen as part of a process that leads to a "hollowing out," not simply of the state but of the legitimacy of thinking about social rights. This is part of a process to create what Bob Jessop (1993) called "the Schumpeterian workfare state," with an emphasis on "competitiveness" and means-testing in the provision of social programs. The creation of the single market and single currency was simply an instrument to bring about market liberalization that made anything but a residual welfare state untenable. On the other hand, there is evidence to support Paul Pierson's contention that a close look at the politics of welfare state reform may identify sites of resistance and reveal that increased capital mobility and economic liberalization do not necessarily affect the fundamental nature of the welfare state regime. Pierson (1996) argues that groups and political forces that have staked a claim in the welfare state may be in a position to resist major changes.

While this debate between the "hollowing out" and the adaptability of the welfare state is an interesting one, it may not provide us with a basis for fully understanding changes of the last decade, especially in the Italian case. The welfare state decline approach tends to focus on changes to expenditures and the (re-)commodification of some social services. While expenditures may affect quality, create pressures for commodification, and possibly produce a different role for the state, they may not indicate that social and political relations have changed. Moreover, simply pointing out a displacement from the public to the private sphere may not tell us whether the nature of a social program or service has been transformed (O'Connor, Orloff, and Shaver 1999). Part of the argument for "positive welfare" made by "third-way" advocates is based on the claim that introducing market conditions does not necessarily weaken attempts to pursue a "politics of emancipation." However, attempts to provide empirical evidence tend to focus again on levels of expenditure, and on assessing their impact on the delivery of services (Clayton and Pontusson 1998). This is especially the case in Italy, where reform has focused less on the total amount of expenditures on social policy than on how the funds were spent and who benefited. The adaptability approach, while encouraging a closer look at the politics of welfare-state reform, also fails to address directly the extent to which changes may affect social relations. It also essentially evades the question of how much "adaptability" needs to take place before we have something qualitatively different from the welfare state as it emerged in the postwar period. One way to examine welfare state restructuring is to look closely at the politics of change—more precisely, examining how change is carried out, and its possible consequences for particular political and social groups. This is why a gender analysis of the welfare state may provide some useful insights into the complexities of restructuring (Pierson 2000).

The Emergence of the Social State

Italy's welfare state, often called *lo stato sociale* (the social state), was shaped by the dynamics of party competition. There were two important features here. First, the political and constitutional regime, now referred to as the First Republic, was based on the monopolization of most parts of the state by political parties. This involved parceling out ministries, state-held firms, and agencies to different parties and factions, including those of the opposition. Using the state to develop social capital and trust or redistribute wealth was secondary to deploying it to distribute rewards to mobilize support for the regime. Second, the party-state was also a consensual one, aimed primarily at creating a form of elite accommodation that ensured access to decision making for all the political parties (Ferrera 1997, 243). The welfare state expansion of the late 1960s was as much about accommodating a wide range of political interests as it was about redistributing wealth or dealing with market failure.

The second half of the 1960s and the 1970s saw the establishment of the main features of the Italian welfare state. Although many would lament the decline of the Keynesian welfare state in later decades, the Italian version lacked many essential Keynesian features. It was based on the social and economic demands of the industrial northeast, with its high rates of unionization, relatively low levels of unemployment, and strong consumer demand. In addition, many of its essential features, especially those related to income maintenance and support, were consistent with a male-breadwinner model of the family and work. Throughout the period, the welfare state was expanded with a series of measures that were not part of a comprehensive program but that radically transformed the way in which citizens perceived the state. It became one of the principal means of addressing social divisions that could not be mediated through political representation, partly because the largest opposition party, the Italian Communist Party (PCI), was condemned to permanent opposition (Maestri 1987). Moreover, widening citizenship rights, or responding to demands for such, was often incidental to developing a welfare state that could maintain a balance between political parties.

The welfare state did direct benefits to very particular groups. For instance, some pensions—known as "seniority" pensions—were extended so that benefits could be collected after thirty-five years of contribution, regardless of age. Moreover, a fragmented pension system was created piecemeal with at least seventeen different funds for specific groups, ranging from shopkeepers to journalists. A much more generous interpretation of disability insurance was implemented, allowing officials to grant compensation with few medical controls in parts of the country that had high unemployment. At the same time, however, Italy, with few positive labor market strategies, ranked among the Organization for Economic Cooperation and Development (OECD) countries that spent the least on training and skills development for workers (Negrelli 1997). Little was done to help families or the growing number of women entering the labor market, beginning in the 1970s (Saraceno 1998).

Child Care: Moving Away from the Familial Model?

It is not easy to provide a simple description of Italy's policies for the care of children. As noted above, it has minimal child care provisions but nearly universal attendance at preschools. Progressive maternity leave policies were implemented as early as the 1950s but, unlike other countries, Italy had no widespread debate about the care of children and how it reflected and affected women's participation in labor markets or their relative autonomy with respect to choices about the family. Moreover, change would come only very slowly to the dominant "familial" model that emphasized that families—more specifically, mothers—were responsible for the care of children (Bimbi and Della Sala, 2001).

Discussions about policies to address issues such as women's participation in paid work outside the home were largely absent in the first two decades of the postwar period. The 1968 debate over a proposal to create public preschools (for children from three to six) was an important turning point, for the law would establish the principle that the state had a role to play in children's lives. The measure would make preprimary schools part of the public education system, under the control of the central Ministry of Education. The central government would fund the teachers and provide subsidies for the school, which would be run primarily by local authorities or, in some cases, private organizations. Regional and local authorities would also contribute to the funding of state-run preschools. Although the proposal challenged some of the basic principles of the familial model, especially its responsiveness to Catholic influence, it did not alter its foundations.

One important issue that emerged in the parliamentary debate was whether or not to make the preschools compulsory. The fact that the schools would not be obligatory reflected, perhaps, a compromise. On the one hand, there were those that held the idea that the function of the preschools was to complement the family, not substitute for it. On the other were those who looked to the schools as an opportunity to lighten, however marginally, the load of responsibilities placed on the family. This group, which comprised mostly women on the left, but also some from the Christian Democratic Party, hoped that making preschools free would establish a social service that could begin to shift the care of children into the public realm.

The number of children who were in some form of preprimary schools at the time of the debate was not insignificant. According to the Education Commission of the Chamber of Deputies, 48.5 percent of children between the ages of three and five already attended such schools in 1962–63; by 1968–69, the figure reached 50.8 percent (Pinelli 1983). They were, however, overwhelmingly in private schools; only 4.8 percent of children in this age category were in an institution funded and controlled by the central government. Fully 70 percent were in private schools, while the rest attended schools run by local authorities or some other public body (Pedrazzi 1966). It also was clear that the "private" schools were largely under the control or influence of religious orders. This meant that any overt attempt to set up a rival "public" system could face serious challenges from Catholic forces. Article 1 of the bill makes it quite clear that the preschools were not meant to supplant the role of the family in childrearing, but to play an important role in children's intellectual and personal development.

Conventional factors such as pronatalism and the labor market did not play a significant role in the passage of this law. With regard to demographics, this was surprising because birth rates were declining during this period. Between 1946–50 and 1966–70, the birth rate dropped from 21.5 to 17.4 (Livi Bacci 1980). Following on the immediate postwar baby boom, large internal migration and significant differences in demographics across regions helped create the impression that Italian families remained prolific (Livi Bacci 1980). Thus, there was hardly any mention of a "crisis" of the family based on its size; rather, there was some concern of the effects of individualism and consumerism on conventional family structures.

With regard to the labor market, the legislation was equally surprising, since it was passed during a period when women's labor-market activity was actually declining. In 1959, women constituted 31.2 percent of the labor force; by 1966, the figure had dropped to 27.1 percent (OECD 1968). Perhaps this was due to the displacement of women workers from agriculture, without a corresponding increase in their employment in industry. In addition, women employed in industry tended to be found in weaker sectors such as textiles, while the range of benefits available to predominantly male workers in strong industrial sectors favored the male-breadwinner model. There was, then, little demand for preschools on the part of employed mothers.

Instead, the impetus for the reform had two principal sources. First, it was seen as an important step in modernizing Italy's education system and as a response to pedagogical research pointing out the importance of the preschool years for children's intellectual development. (This also included the provision of meals for children as part of their overall development.) Second, the dynamics of the center-left governing coalition were significant. The Socialist Party (PSI) had been brought into the governing coalition in 1963 for what was supposed to be the start of a modernizing era. By the late 1960s, however, the promised reforms, including a major change in education, had not materialized. The preschools were seen as less controversial than schools and universities, making agreement easier to reach.

There was, then, no vision of the preschools as an integral part of a child care system that would facilitate raising larger families—no explicit pronatalist motivation for the policy—nor was there a sense that preschools were needed to compensate for changes to family structures resulting from maternal employment. Overall, the policy had little effect on the Catholic view of the family as a natural unit with rights that extended beyond the limits of state intervention. Moreover, it entailed little recognition that postwar economic and social changes were beginning to have an impact even on those women who were not entering labor markets, as the general drop in birth rates indicated.

In 1971, two important legislative developments aimed at the care of children under three occurred, again in the absence of broad programmatic or policy responses to the changing needs and behavior of women. The first, Law 1204, of December 30, 1971, extended the maternity-leave provisions first introduced in the 1950s, granting women giving birth five months' leave at 80 percent of their salaries and the option of staying out for up to a year at 30 percent. The terms of the leave provisions were most favorable to women working in full-time, most likely industrial, employment, but they provided little for women in part-time work or on flexible, short-term contracts.

The second important piece of legislation, Law 1044, proposed a five-year plan to increase the number of day nurseries from less than 1,000 to 3,800 and to shift them from almost total private control to state administration and financing. It committed the central government to providing an amount equivalent to 0.1 percent of employer contributions to the Institute for Social Security fund, the largest state pension fund, to regional governments for the day nurseries (European Commission Network on Child Care 1996, 23). This grant was part of a complex funding arrangement for nurseries, by which only a small portion would come directly from the central government itself. The bulk of the funding, however, would be provided by the block grant from the central government to regions. These in turn would fund local governments, either with funds specifically allocated for nurseries or through general grants to local authorities.

This left decisions about funding the nurseries to the discretion of authorities at different levels of government, largely regional and local, with few national standards or conditions to guarantee more uniform provision. It was thus difficult to speak of a national child care plan; unlike the preschools, the nurseries had little national oversight (Camera dei Deputati 1971). Other levels of government would be responsible for administering child care to children under three. This gave the regions the power to decide on broad principles such as the private-public mix in the delivery of child care services, and local authorities the right to make decisions on service delivery, including user fees. Few measures were put in place to monitor national standards or, more importantly, to ensure that funds destined for child care would in fact be used for that purpose (Visco Comandini 1992).

The issue of regional disparities in the delivery of child care emerged almost immediately. That is, while the law seemed to implement a universal system of child care for children under the age of three, in practice, delivery was rather selective. Regional and local rules and regulations restricted the service to employed women, in particular to lone mothers, poor families, and children with disabilities. In many instances, parents were charged fees on the basis of their incomes.

Such limited access to services may be traced to a number of factors: the historical legacy; representation by social actors, many of whom wanted to protect women working outside the home; and the lack of financing and coordination on the part of the central government. The discretionary powers exercised at the regional and local levels reflected the support mobilized by social groups, variations in administrative capacity and significant differences in regional economic development. The result was that personnel-to-children ratios soon varied across regions, while many local authorities quickly abandoned the notion that day nurseries were a free social service. Families had to pay fees set according to income (CENSIS 1978).

The case of the day nurseries reflects many of the tensions and contradictions of the Italian welfare state. By 1976, some 1,080 day nurseries had been established; ten years later, the number had grown only to 1,964 day nurseries, even though the five-year plan implemented in 1971 had called for the creation of 3,800 day nurseries by 1976. The doubling of the number of day nurseries may seem impressive, but it was not unprecedented. In 1963, the Opera Nazionale Maternita ed Infanzia (OMNI) administered 562 nurseries; ten years later, they had 1,000. The fact remains that the state has never come close to achieving its original objective of 3,800 day nurseries; in the 1990s, the number stabilized at about 2,100 (ISTAT 1995).

It is not surprising, then, to find that the number of children in day nurseries has never reached any significant level. In 1963, 2.2 percent of children at or below the age of three attended one of the day nurseries administered by the OMNI; the figure dropped slightly to 2.1 percent in 1976 and rose to 5.2 percent in 1986. A number of factors may be seen as contributing to the limited presence of center-based care: the reluctance of many regions to actually build day nurseries; the high cost to local governments of delivering the service; and the high standards for personnel that drive up costs. The basic problem was, and has remained throughout the period since 1971, the lack of adequate funding from the central government to achieve the initial objectives set out in the legislation. More importantly, the central government has been incapable, and perhaps unwilling, to ensure that objectives set out in the law would be implemented by regional and local governments.

Policies for the care of children, then, embodied many of the contradictions of the Italian welfare state. Principles of universal access were in place, but fragmented policymaking structures and delivery meant that provision was uneven. Moreover, the care of children, whether through nurseries or preschools, never became firmly entrenched as a necessary element of reconciling work and family. The welfare state directed particular benefits to specific targets, consistent with a male-breadwinner model. It reflected a delicate political compromise between the Catholic Church and left-wing political parties and did not challenge the basic premise that the care of children was a family matter. It was only in the 1990s that the familial model began to face serious challenge, and then there emerged a full discussion about how to reconcile work and family.

The Politics of Welfare State "Modernization"

After decades of stagnation, Italian political life became very turbulent in the 1990s. The social, political, and economic bases of the postwar order were challenged and, possibly, irreversibly changed. The welfare state did not escape the turbulence, and a serious discussion about how to respond to social and economic pressures ensued.

As we will see shortly, the impetus for welfare-state change came from domestic sources, but the possibility of welfare-state reform was shaped by external events. There is no lack of evidence to show that globalization—especially in the form of European monetary integration—served as a catalyst for restructuring; it provided an external shock to a petrified political system with entrenched economic and political oligarchies.

The globalization discourse went largely uncontested in Italy in the 1990s, for it made very little reference to the loss of sovereignty or the displacement of political power that resulted from more prominent market forces. Rather, globalization was presented as an opportunity to open up large parts of economic and social life that had been closed to many parts of the population, including women. Paradoxically, while globalization has often been portrayed as offering a rather narrow basis for citizenship, the opposite occurred in the Italian case.

Although different attempts to restructure the welfare state had been made in the 1980s, these produced few significant changes. The decade was characterized by broad coalition governments that were held together by using public expenditure to maintain support. The signing of the Treaty on European Union brought spending into focus, and opened the debate about the social state. The center and left governments, led first by Romano Prodi after the 1996 elections and then by PDS (Partito Democratico di Sinistra, or Democratic Left Party) leader Massimo D'Alema after October 1998, made restructuring, or "modernization," of the welfare state one of its priorities. A committee of experts from a wide range of areas, known as the Commissione Onofri, was created almost immediately by Prodi to examine social programs. The committee's mandate was to examine the "compatibility" of social spending with macroeconomic objectives. Implicitly, its concern was ensuring that social spending could remain under control given the parameters of monetary integration, and that social programs would contribute to a more active labor market along the lines set out in the 1994 OECD jobs study. Social spending in Italy, at 25 percent of gross domestic product, was not out of line with other European Union (EU) countries, but it was the nature of that spending that set it apart. In 1994, over 60 percent was dedicated to pensions and survivors' benefits, against an average of 45 percent for these expenditures in the rest of Europe. By contrast, less than 1 percent was spent on employment services, and only 2.3 percent went to unemployment (Commissione Onofri 1997, 3–6). The committee concluded that active labor-market policies needed to be given a central place in social spending. This would ensure that the basis of the social state would be transformed from "passive" social programs to social spending that was "more active" and would increase "opportunity and promote change" (Commissione Onofri 1997, 18). The committee claimed that monetary integration provided an opportunity for Italy to become more "European," not simply by being part of the single currency and bringing its public finances under control, but also by creating an opportunity to dislodge the "protected" interests of the existing social state and to redirect resources toward areas that would produce more "positive" welfare measures (Commissione Onofri 1997, 29). The

Onofri committee produced few concrete results, but it did serve as the basis for a renewed discussion about reforming the welfare state in 1997 and 1998.

For the center-left governing coalition in the 1990s, meeting the convergence criteria was a sign of the modernization not just of the Italian economy but of its politics and society as well. It pursued a broad strategy tied to the image of a New Left that broke with the past, including the welfare state it had helped to create. It tried to project a new political agenda for the Left, one that sought to bring transparency, efficiency, and accountability to all areas of public life and to make this the basis of a more participatory democracy. Compared to the secret deals of the First Republic carried out not in boardrooms but in even more obscure settings, equity markets were presented as democratic arenas that were accessible and transparent, operating according to rules that were fair and equal for all. Privatization and pension funds, then, became a means of democratizing the economy and taking power away from the private interests and party factions that continued to occupy state holdings.[1] The same argument was made with regard to restructuring the welfare state. A more "efficient" welfare state was seen to be more transparent, outside the control of vested interests and accountable to representative institutions, not party elites.

An important part of the modernization agenda included a discourse that addressed what Esping-Andersen has described as the "less tangible needs for new modes of social integration, solidarity, and citizenship" (1996, 27). The welfare state as it emerged from the 1970s had been based on a model of citizenship that tied access to social rights largely to industrial employment. It excluded groups such as youth, the unemployed, and women, including those employed in the underground economy and those working part-time and on short-term contracts. Restructuring the welfare state was presented, then, not simply as a means of dealing with financial constraints but as an opportunity to use to social policy to reflect and affect changes in social relations and demands from a changing society. For instance, D'Alema, in a 1999 speech in Napoli, emphasized that future restructuring of the welfare state did not center on cuts to spending but on a reallocation of priorities (Luzi 1999). It was no mere coincidence that he chose to make his remarks in the largest city in southern Italy. Nor was it a coincidence that he made his remarks about the need to further reform the welfare state—especially pensions—in the same speech in which he spoke of investment and entrepreneurship in the south.

These themes appeared constantly throughout the discourse of the center and left governments' period in power. The passive, privileged position of particular interests that had benefited from the previous regime—mostly male unionized industrial workers from the baby boomer generation—were cast as obstacles to the adjustment of groups and regions to the new competitive environment of the EU. The debate about pensions broadened to address arguments about how pensions increased labor costs and, therefore, deterred Italian savings away from investment in industry and into financial instruments.[2] Pensions for baby boomers—mainly for male industrialized workers—were seen as a legacy of the old political regime that penalized the young unemployed and women seeking to enter labor markets.

Clearly, the debate had moved well beyond simply the question of financial sustainability of the pension regime.

This was especially apparent in the approach to women and work and to easing access to labor markets. Despite gradual increases in women's employment rates throughout the 1990s, from 34.1 percent in 1989 to 37 percent in 1998, the fact that Italy had one of the lowest participation rates in the EU (and in the OECD) attracted a great deal of attention from the center and left governments in the late 1990s (European Commission 1999). The gender dimension of broader long-standing problems, such as unemployment in the South and youth unemployment, came into focus. For instance, the D'Alema government repeatedly pointed out that not only did fewer than one-fourth of the women in southern Italy participate in labor markets, but the unemployment rate for southern women in 1998 rested at 31.8 percent, compared to 18.2 percent for men (while 43.4 percent of women in northern Italy were in the work force and only 9.8 percent were unemployed; European Commission 1999). The objective of increasing participation rates for women was driven not only by changing notions of citizenship but also by the demands of labor markets. Labor shortages in northern and central Italy became an issue of concern for policymakers in the late 1990s; one way to address them was to help integrate more women into the work force.

The debate about welfare restructuring also touched upon the question of Italy's low fertility rates and decreases in population. Fertility rates among women dropped from 2.4 births per 100 women in 1960 to 1.2 in 1993, while the population went from a net increase of 8.81 persons per 1,000 in 1960 to minus 0.51 in 1995 (although there was an overall net increase in the population of 1.12 per 1,000 in 1995, due largely to immigration) (European Observatory on National Family Policies 2000). The declining birthrates were seen as a problem for an aging population that already faced labor shortages in some parts of the country and would have great difficulties financing a pay-as-you-go pension scheme once the large baby boom generation retired. One solution was immigration, but a more immediate answer lay in policies making it easier to reconcile work and family, especially for women (Luzi 2000).

Given the financial constraints imposed by the convergence criteria for monetary integration, and global economic pressures in general, there was very little question that addressing work/family issues could imply new or increased expenditures. It would mean that existing resources would have to be reallocated or that the policy responses would have to be revenue-neutral. Proposed changes were presented as part of a broader process by which Italy's welfare state could be made to adapt to the new demands not only of "competitiveness" but also of groups largely excluded from existing social programs. They were contrasted to the "vested" interests of the welfare state—namely, industrial workers (mostly male) and public sector workers. The path to reconciling work and family, then, would run partly through welfare state restructuring that would redress priorities and the allocation of resources.

Child Care between Modernization and the Familial Model

The attempt to "modernize" the welfare state by helping to reconcile work and family would mean challenging the familial model. It would have to address the fragmented nature of Italian policymaking and the welfare state, which produced different outcomes in child care provisions for children, especially those under three. A recent study of regional models of day nurseries that looked at standards set in regional laws and regulations found that Emilia-Romagna maintained the highest quality standards, while the general quality was high in the central regions such as Tuscany and Umbria, mixed in the northwest regions, relatively low in the northeast, and low in the south (Becchi and Bondioli 1992). The result was that access to child care services for young children varied greatly across regions. In Emilia-Romagna, 18.9 percent of eligible children attended day nurseries, while in the northeastern Veneto region, sharing many similar economic characteristics, attendance was only 4.8 percent. The contrast with the south was even greater. While 9.6 percent of eligible children had places in the north in 1994, only 2.2 percent did in the south (Saraceno 1998).

The limited supply, mostly in the north, and demand, primarily in the south, for child care spaces contrasts with Italy's record on preschools for children between three and six. Public preschools have been one of the relatively unknown success stories of the Italian welfare state. In a short period of time, the percentage of children in preschool rose from 50.8 in 1968–69, to 76.8 in 1980, and to 93.8 in 1996–97 (Ministero della Pubblica Istruzione 1999, 3–14). More impressive was the extent to which a network of state preschools was established, with the first appearing in the late 1960s, and the total climbing to over 10,000 by 1976–1977. This corresponded to the steady rise in the number of children attending state-run schools. The percentage of children attending preschools run by the Ministry of Public Education increased from about 5 in 1969–70, to 40 in 1980–81, and to 58 in 1996–97 (Ministero della Pubblica Istruzione 1999, 11–14). As in the case of nurseries, regional differences can be found in the percentage of children attending preschool, but they are less marked. For instance, 96.7 percent of the age group attended preschool in the northeast, and 95.9 in the northwest, while the lowest figure could be found in the islands of Sicily and Sardinia, with 85.4 percent. Notably, the islands were the only part of the country below the national average.

The near-universal coverage for children between three and six, and the low participation rates for women in the workforce, suggest that almost all families used the preschools—not just dual-earner families. While the preschools did facilitate the entry of women into work, they were presented primarily as serving an educational, not a child care, function. This was recognized by the Ministry of Education in a ministerial decree in 1991 stating that, "the preschool has become the first stage of the education system" (Ministero della Pubblica Istruzione 1991). While most families seemed to make use of the preschools, families with working mothers were more likely to choose the nonstate schools. This did not necessarily mean placing children in preschools run by religious organizations. Working mothers predominated in central and northern Italy, where nonstate preschools were more often run by local or provincial authorities than religious organizations. The preference for nonstate preschools in these regions was probably not due to different hours of availability, as these are not decidedly different in the state sector. According to the 1968 law, state-run schools were to remain open at least seven hours per day, and local school officials could decide to lengthen the hours if they deemed it necessary. The more likely reason for the preference for nonstate schools is that local authorities and third sector providers, such as cooperatives, have a long history in northern and central Italy as providing high-quality social services.

The care of children in Italy, then, required a delicate balancing act between instituting elements of the modern welfare state and contending with significant political constraints. This meant that the care of children under three rested primarily with the family, and women, while the preschools assumed an almost universal presence. Families tended to rely on informal structures for the care of children under three, an indication that the welfare state would have difficulty breaking through the familial model (ISTAT 1999a). The preschools afforded a small opening, and while the number of women who entered the workforce remained low, their availability did make it easier for families with working parents. The dramatic increase in the number of state-run preschools and their attendance levels, at the same time as women began entering the labor force in greater numbers in the 1970s and 1980s, indicates that the schools did help families reconcile work and child care. The emphasis on the preschools as essential for children's intellectual and emotional development remained throughout the 1990s, but there was growing recognition that they also served an important child care function for many parents. The Ministry of Education, in its survey of preschools throughout the country, used as an indicator of the quality of preschools the hours they remained open, including Saturdays. The report did go on to say that the schools would have to provide meals and recreational facilities, for those that kept extended hours through the afternoon could have some children for up to ten hours (Ministero della Pubblica Istruzione 1999). Clearly, this is a sign that these "educational" structures were being used by some parents for the care of children while they worked.

Growing concern with the state of Italy's public finances meant that financial considerations created pressures to redefine the very nature of child care services for the very young. In the mid-1980s, for instance, the national government stated that the day nurseries were demand-driven services and indicated that it would likely weaken or abandon the commitment to universal provision of child care services. The central government was not very precise about what this meant in practice, but visible signs of a change included an increase in the percentage of costs that local governments must pass on to parents, from 25 percent in 1983 to 32 percent in 1987 (Moss 1990). This contrasted with the fact that the only charge to parents of children in the preschools was a small amount for meals. Governments have taken measures to counter the increasing fees that parents face for child care by providing greater tax breaks for parents with children. However, tax relief does not change the fact that the nurseries are a selective service based increasingly on financing by local governments and parents. As it was never adequately financed, child care never fully developed into a universal and extensive social service.

Two issues have emerged as important since the end of the 1980s: a concern with demographic decline, and the increasing costs for local governments for the care of children. In 1988 the central government moved away from conditional grants and toward a block grant that gave the regions the responsibility for making difficult decisions about how to distribute a smaller amount of funds. Thus day nurseries must compete for regional government funds that must be divided among a range of social services, all of which are under financial pressure. Preliminary evidence seems to indicate that those regions that had a weak commitment to child care in the past, such as Calabria and Sicily in the south, now dedicate even fewer resources to this service (ISTAT 1999a, 143–48).

The change in central government funding also had consequences for local authorities, for they now had to deliver services with even fewer resources coming from the regions. As a result, local governments have had to turn to different forms of delivering the service, including increasing reliance on nongovernmental organizations and attempts to combine day nurseries within preschools. Now, as already noted, they must also generate a greater percentage of their revenues from parental fees. Between 1990 and 1992, for example, the percentage of revenues for day nurseries across Italy that came from fees increased from 11.8 percent to 15 percent. While the—very minimal—central state funding remained the same, the percentage of regional funds decreased from 14.6 percent to 12.7 percent of costs, while the local government contribution also dropped from 71.4 percent to 69.8 percent (ISTAT 1999a, 143–48). One clear consequence of such changes is that the decentralization of discretionary decision making has further fragmented a citizenship regime already lacking coordination and coherence. In this rather confused context, it has been easier for authorities to make changes to the nature of child care, and indirectly to the rights of women as workers, without any visible political debate. There does, however, seem to be a connection between the higher labor force participation rates for women in northern and central Italy and greater access to child care.

The center-left governments elected since 1996 have addressed the question of child care. In March 1999, the government introduced a bill that would reform the child care system (Camera dei Deputati 1999b). It does little to address the wide regional differences in the delivery of services, nor does it promise a large number of new spaces. But it states quite clearly that child care is both an important part of the education and socialization of children and a service that facilitates women's access to labor markets. This marks a shift in the view of child care as a residual service for mothers and families unable to find their own form of child care. In an attempt to introduce elements of flexibility into the system, the bill proposed to regulate care provided in homes as well as in day nurseries. It complements this by proposing standards for the qualifications of caregivers and directors of services and for professional and educational requirements. Finally, the bill sets a limit of 30 percent of operating costs as the maximum amount that parents are to pay for spaces in public day care centers.

The preschools have not escaped the reform agenda. The major change in the state sector was the introduction of "comprehensive institutes" in the early 1990s; that is, preschool classrooms may now be contained within larger structures that include elementary and middle schools. The "comprehensives" were intended originally for mountain and other isolated communities, where there were not sufficient numbers to justify having separate buildings for the different school levels. However, the comprehensives spread quickly to other areas, so that by 1998, there were 673 throughout the country, including some in large suburbs in major metropolitan centers (Ministero della Pubblica Istruzione 1998). The fact that the preschools were considered as the first stage of the educational system made it easier to justify placing three-year-olds in the same schools as older children. However, strong financial pressures may have play a role as well, as education spending in Italy declined steadily as a percentage of GDP and public spending throughout the 1990s.[3]

The comprehensives have further entrenched preschools as part of the educational system despite their apparent use by some parents as a form of child care. Preschools, then, have become part of the package of citizenship rights associated with education. This has affected women and the care of children in a number of important ways. First, with women constituting the vast majority of the more than 120,000 teachers, preschools have enabled many women to enter the labor force (Ministero della Pubblica Istruzione 1999, 27). Second, the educational rationale has removed the issue of preschools from the more contentious arena of political debate over the role of the family and the state in the care of children. The focus is not on a challenge to the familial model, but on the pedagogical and psychological needs of children in their intellectual development. Third, as part of the education system, preschools allow women and families to pursue strategies to reconcile work and family once ensured of access for their children above the age of three. This same level of assurance and access is not available to them for children under three.

The initiatives on nurseries in the 1990s, along with a parallel measure on maternity leave, do signal an attempt to break new ground designing policies for the care of young children; and, perhaps, charting a new course for changing gender relations. It is no coincidence that they have come from a government of the center-left that has tried to present itself as a catalyst of "modernization." As part of their effort, the government has moved away from conceiving the welfare state as one based on male industrial workers, toward recognizing changing patterns of work and the growing importance of women in labor markets. Modernization, in this sense, entails facilitating greater "flexibility" in labor markets—that is, greater ease in hiring and firing, and lower social costs for employers. This allows the government to neutralize some parts of the center-right of the political spectrum, which wants to see a retreat of the state from many areas of economic and social regulation. At the same time, it is presented as a way to break from the old man-as-bread-winner model of the welfare state, with its attendant emphasis on the familial care of children, and as an important part of women's participation in paid work. This divides or fragments parts of the left of the spectrum.

The forces splinter into those groups, largely the trade unions, who want to safeguard the status quo, with its emphasis on industrial employment. Then there are groups, which includes some parts of the PDS, who would like to move away from the male-breadwinner model but do not support the emphasis on reforms that are aimed primarily at making labor markets more "flexible." A third group includes those, such as parents and women's groups in central regions, that support the changes even though they are part of a broader "modernization" package that may restructure the fundamental basis of the welfare state.

The government coalition that introduced the changes contained many centrist elements with deep roots in the old Christian Democratic Party. They consistently blocked any attempt to address issues, such as the rights of common-law couples, same-sex benefits and reproductive technology, that would require changing the definition of the "traditional" family. More importantly, while the law on child care seems to promise a great deal, a close look reveals that it also entrenches a number of features that may not have such a positive effect on gender relations. First, rather than addressing the question of means-testing and user fees, the law merely establishes a maximum amount that may be generated by "coparticipation" (parental fees). Second, given that the law does not address the significant regional differences in child care provisions, it is easy to see how the bill may be aimed at easing labor market shortages in parts of central and northern Italy while ignoring other problems. That is, it does not seem to establish a right to child care for parents throughout the country; but simply accepts the regional variation in access to services.

The recent attempt to introduce changes that affect the care of children highlight many of the tensions inherent in the restructuring of the Italian welfare state. It has become less an issue of protecting the familial model, enshrined in the male-breadwinner model, so important to the center-right that governed the country for most of the postwar period. Weaving its way through the modernization project are discourses that touch regional, intergenerational and gender struggles that have provided some space for change. By playing upon some of those struggles, including establishing the principle of women's participation in labor markets, governments have introduced changes that slowly dismantle an old regime. A political space has been created for new claims but it is not entirely clear that what is emerging will or can respond to them.

Finally, there are few new resources provided to child care and no commitment to create new places. This is consistent with a broader approach to the welfare state that has much to say about the need to introduce restructuring and "flexibility," but whose real focus is easing labor markets rather than expanding social rights and collective responsibility. This approach targets particular groups in particular areas. So while there may be a discourse about "modernizing" gender relations, tax relief gives greater help to middle-income earners than to low-income families, and recent changes in child care help areas with labor shortages more than those with high unemployment. The modernization discourse creates a constellation of forces that can find some basis for popular support—especially if it is presented as dismantling the old regime. However, it does not address structural problems, such as the low rates of child care provision for these under three in certain parts of the country. This makes it harder to see how broader policy objectives, such as increasing labor force participation rates for women in the south, can be achieved. The modernization project is weak on changing social relations by emphasizing principles of social justice and equity. More particular to women, it does little to advance a citizenship regime based on the kinds of entrenched social rights that can provide a basis for autonomy in fundamental life choices.

Notes

1. It is not surprising, then, that the PDS/DS (Democratici de Sinistra, or Left Democrats) has been one of the strongest advocates of the creation of pension funds to ensure that privatized firms do not continue to fall under the control of the narrow group of large capital. See: Camera dei Deputati (1994, 468); and Cofferati (1999).

2. See the statement by the Governor of the Bank of Italy, Antonio Fazio, to the Budget Committee of the Chamber of Deputies: Camera dei Deputati (1999a, 588–93).

3. Education spending was 10.1 percent of public expenditures in 1986 and 5.1 percent of GDP; by 1996, the percentages were, respectively, 8.9 and 4.7 (ISTAT 1999b, 16).

References

Becchi, Elena, and Anna Bondioli. 1992. "Gli asili nidi in Italia: Censimenti e valutazioni della qualità" (Nurseries in Italy: Surveys and Quality Assessment). *Bambini* (Children), suppl. no. 2: 1–31.

Bimbi, Franca. 1993. "Gender, 'Gift Relationship' and Welfare State Cultures in Italy." In *Women and Social Policies in Europe*, ed. Jane Lewis. Aldershot: Elgar.

Bimbi, Franca, and Vincent Della Sala. 2001. "Italy: Policy without Representation." In *Who Cares? Women's Work, Child Care and Welfare State Redesign*, ed. Jane Jenson and Mariette Sineau. Toronto: University of Toronto Press.

Camera dei Deputati (Chamber of Deputies). 1971. Sixth Legislature, *Commissioni Riunite* (Joint Committees). November 18.

_____. 1994. Twelfth Legislature. *Atti Parlamentari: Discussioni* (Parliamentary Acts: Debates). Vol. 1, June 2.

_____. 1999a. Thirteenth Legislature, *Atti Parlamentari. Indagini Conoscitivi. V Commissione* (Parliamentary Acts: Inquiries—Fifth Committee). February 24.

_____. 1999b. Thirteenth Legislature. *Proposta di legge* (Proposed Legislation). No. 5838. March 23.

CENSIS (Center for the Study of Social Investments). 1978. *Rapporto sulla situazione sociale nel Paese* (Report on Social Conditions in Italy). Roma: CENSIS.

Clayton, Richard, and Jonas Pontusson. 1998. "Welfare-State Retrenchment Revisited." *World Politics* 51: 67–98.

Cofferati, Sergio. 1999. "Il capitalismo e i fondi pensioni" (Capitalism and Pension Funds). *La Repubblica*, February 28: 13.

Commissione Onofri. 1997. *Commissione per l'analisi delle compatibilita' macroeconomiche della spesa sociale—Relazione Finale* (Committee for the Study of the Macroeconomic Sustainability of Social Spending—Final Report). Roma: Presidenza del Consiglio dei Ministri.

Esping-Andersen, Gosta. 1990. *The Three Worlds of Welfare Capitalism*. Princeton, N.J.: Princeton University Press.

_____. 1996. "After the Golden Age? Welfare State Dilemmas in a Global Economy." In *Welfare States in Transition*, ed. Gøsta Esping-Andersen. London: Sage.

European Commission. 1999. *1999 National Action Plan for Employment—Italy*. Available at http://www.europa.eu.int/comm/employment_social/empl&esf/naps/napit_en.pdf.

European Commission Network on Child Care. 1996. *A Review of Services for Young Children in the European Union, 1990–1995*. Brussels: European Commission.

European Observatory on National Family Policies. 2000. *Statistics Italy*. Available at http://europa.eu.int/comm/employment_social/family/observatory/statisticsitaly.html

Ferrera, Maurizio. 1995. "The Rise and Fall of Democratic Universalism: Health Care Reform in Italy, 1978–1994." *Journal of Health Politics, Policy and Law* 22, no. 2: 275–302.

_____. 1997. "The Uncertain Future of the Italian Welfare State." In *Crisis and Transition in Italian Politics*, ed. Martin Bull and Martin Rhodes. London: Frank Cass.

ISTAT (Instituto Nazionale di Statistica [National Institute of Statistics]). 1995. *Rapporto sull'Italia* (Report on Italy). Roma: ISTAT.

_____. 1999a. *Rapporto Annuale, 1999* (Annual Report, 1999). Rome: ISTAT.

_____. 1999b. *Italia in Cifre, 1999* (Italy in Numbers, 1999). Rome: ISTAT.

Jessop, Bob. 1993. "Towards a Schumpeterian Workfare State? Preliminary Remarks on Post-Fordist Political Economy." *Studies in Political Economy* 40: 7–39.

Livi Bacci, Massimo. 1980. *Donna, fecondita e figli* (Women, Fertility and Children). Bologna: Il Mulino.

Luzi, Gianluca. 1999. "Cambiamo le pensioni" (Let's Change Pensions). *La Repubblica*, July 15, 4.

_____. 2000. "D'Alema: italiani, fate piu' figli—Sugli immigrati dice: Sono utili" (D'Alema to Italians: Have More Children; Immigrants Are Useful). *La Repubblica*, February 2: 17.

Maestri, Ezio. 1987. "La regolazione dei conflitti redistributivi in Italia: il caso della politica pensionistica (1948–1983)" (The Regulation of Redistributive Conflict in Italy: The Case of Pensions Policy"). *Stato e mercato* 20: 249–79.

Ministero della Pubblica Istruzione (Ministry of Education). 1991. Decreto Ministeriale (Ministerial Decree). March 6.

_____. 1998. *Annali della Pubblica Istruzione—Gli Istituti Comprensivi* (Educational Annuals—The Comprehensive Institutes) 53.

_____. 1999. *La scuola materna statale e non statale* (State and Nonstate Preschools). Rome.

Moss, Peter. 1990. *I servizi per l'infanzia nella Comunita' Europea* (Services for Children in the European Community). Brussels: European Commission.

Negrelli, Stefano. 1997. "Social Pacts and Flexibility: Towards a New Balance between Macro and Micro Industrial Relations—The Italian Experience." In *Social Pacts in Europe,* ed. Giuseppe Fajertag and Philippe Pochet. Brussels: ETUI.

O'Connor, Julia, Ann Shola Orloff, and Sheila Shaver. 1999. *States, Markets, Families.* Cambridge: Cambridge University Press.

OECD. 1968. *Statistiques de la population active 1956–1966* (Statistics on Labor Market Activity) Paris: OECD.

Pedrazzi, Luigi. 1966. *Libro bianco sulla scuola maternale: testi e documenti dagli atti parlamentari* (White Book on Preschools). Bologna: Il Mulino.

Pierson, Paul. 1996. "The New Politics of the Welfare State." *World Politics* 48: 143–79.

_____. 2000. "Three Worlds of Welfare State Research," *Comparative Political Studies* 33: 800–810.

Pinelli, Antonella. 1983. *La scuola materna negli anni '80* (Preschools in the 1980s). Roma: Universita' La Sapienza.

Saraceno, Chiara. 1998. *Mutamenti della famiglia e politiche sociali in* Italia (Changes in the Family and Social Policy in Italy). Bologna: Il Mulino.

Visco Comandini, Vincenzo. 1992. "Il coordinamento finanziario delle Regioni sugli enti locali: il caso degli asili nidi" ("The Coordination of Finances by the Regions over Local Government: The Case of Nurseries"). In *Regioni ed Enti Locali* (Regions and Local Authorities), ed. Istituo di Studi sulle Regioni (Institute for the Study of the Regions). Milano: Giuffre.

CHAPTER 8

Dual-Earner Families Caught in a Liberal Welfare Regime? The Politics of Child Care Policy in Canada

Rianne Mahon and Susan Phillips

In Canada, welfare-state restructuring is following the broader OECD pattern, which involves the erosion of forms of social citizenship established in the postwar era and the introduction of reforms often inspired by neoliberal views of the proper relationship of states, markets, and citizens. Such restructuring involves not only cuts in social expenditures but also changes in the very structure of programs. Thus, one important example of the neoliberal turn is the elimination of universal, flat-rate programs developed in the immediate postwar years, and their replacement by measures based on negative income tax/guaranteed annual income (NIT/GAI). Although there have been efforts to introduce such reforms in the United States, too, Canadian governments have been far more successful (Myles and Pierson 1997). Welfare state restructuring is also implicated in the broader reconfiguration of relations among the different layers of the state (federal, provincial, municipal). Inasmuch as these changes have been associated with funding cuts, they involve a destruction of the important set of supports constructed in the postwar era. In the process of welfare state restructuring, state-civil society relations are also being reconfigured. In spite of longstanding and growing responsibilities for service delivery, the role of civil society organizations as public policy advocates has been reshaped in significant ways by the state, thereby undermining the postwar system of representation (Bach and Phillips 1998).

All of these trends are visible in the field of Canadian child care policy, which occupies a special position in this process of welfare-state restructuring as a result of changing gender relations, notably the erosion of the man-as-breadwinner family form. The rise of dual-earner and lone-parent families poses new challenges for the welfare state. As elsewhere, the emergence of the time-pressed, dual-earner family has generated a need for support services like child care. Yet in Canada this transformation has received at best limited support from the state. For the most part, governments have assumed that middle- and upper-income families are able to look to the market to meet their needs, though limited relief has been available since 1971 in the form of the Child Care Expense Deduction. Between 1966 and 1996, subsidies were also available to those "in need or in danger of becoming in need" under the Canada Assistance Plan (CAP). As we shall see below, however, the CAP system left the initiative to the provinces, which allowed a very uneven development of child care across the country, in coverage as well as form.

Such limited support is not surprising because Canada's child care policy forms part of the broader "liberal" welfare regime within which it is embedded and liberal regimes tend to minimize the state's role relative to families and markets. Yet there are important differences among liberal welfare regimes that warrant investigation. This chapter sheds light on why the Canadian state was more open to action to correct for market and family "failure" in child care arrangements than the American— but less so than the Australian. Welfare regimes are not cast in stone, however. Rather, they are historical products and are themselves subject to change. Like other welfare regimes, Canada's is undergoing restructuring in response to contemporary challenges. Its liberal foundations may have left it more vulnerable to neoliberalism than some, but path dependency only goes so far: politics can matter. This chapter begins with a brief description of child care arrangements in Canada and the shaping thereof. The main focus, however, is on the politics of welfare state restructuring as these shape, and are being shaped, by the struggle for universal child care.

Child Care in Canada: Dimensions of a Challenge

Along with the United States and the social democratic regimes of Scandinavia, the shift from the man-as-breadwinner to the dual-earner family form is most advanced in Canada. As a recent study noted, "Dual-earner families are now the norm. In 1994 both spouses worked in seven out of 10 married or common-law couples (under the age of 65), up significantly from about one-third of couples 30 years ago. Only one in five couples relied on a single male earner in 1994. Even among couples with children under the age of seven, 70 percent were dual-earners" (CCSD 1999, 11). The shift began to occur in the 1960s and accelerated through the 1970s and 1980s. Another reflection of the decline of the male breadwinner family norm is the rise in the proportion of lone-parent families,[1] and here again, Canada ranks with the United States—and not far behind the Scandinavian countries—in the labor force participation rates of lone parents.[2]

As in the United States and Scandinavia, women's rising labor-force participation rates coincided with the shift to postindustrial employment.[3] Whereas in Sweden the pattern of service sector growth—with strong growth in publicly provided social services, including child care—has supported working parents, in Canada, as in the United States, the postindustrial shift has been associated with a polarized labor market, with a concentration of "good jobs, bad jobs."[4] It has thus "pushed" women into the labor market as two incomes have become increasingly necessary to make ends meet. Among countries in the Organization for Economic Cooperation and Development (OECD), in fact, Canada ranks second (after the United States) in the share of low paid full-time work (CCSD 1999, 8). In both countries, moreover, the majority of part-time jobs fall into the "bad jobs" category, with low skill requirements, low pay, limited hours, and poor working conditions (O'Connor, Orloff, and Shaver 1999, 73). Young families—and lone-parent families—have been especially hard hit.[5]

Canada's fertility rates have fallen from the baby boom highs of 4.0 (1959) to 2.5 in 1970 and 1.7 in 1992 (Baker 1995, 47). This trend is also visible among other OECD countries, but Canada's rate is now below that of both Sweden and the United States (both 2.1). There is also a concomitant aging of the population. As Jane Beach, Jane Bertrand, and Gordon Cleveland note, "in 1961, the 'aging' index, or the ratio of the population 65 or over to every 100 persons under 15 years of age, was 22.5. By 1993, the index had risen to 57.0, and by the year 2016, it is expected to be 108.3" (1998, 48). This demographic profile, which contributes to the travails of the postwar welfare state,[6] cannot be "blamed" on the shift from the male bread-winner family to the dual-earner family, as it is also visible in OECD countries where women's labor force participation rates remain relatively low. Taken with the changes in family form, however, it does suggest that Canada clearly faces the set of challenges and opportunities highlighted by Gøsta Esping-Andersen.

That is, the time-pressed, dual-earner (or lone-parent) family needs help. A strong set of child care arrangements, along the lines pioneered by Scandinavian social democracies,[7] could do so in a manner that would mitigate the tendency toward labor market polarization. In particular, a high quality, accessible, and affordable child care system would provide an important measure of support for both dual-earner and lone-parent families. This would make the decision to have children easier and thus could help improve the demographic profile. At the same time, a national program aimed at providing affordable, high quality child care, would create decent jobs, requiring postsecondary skills and commanding commensurate wages. This is not what Canada has at present.

According to a recent study, about one-half of children under twelve whose parents work or study are in some form of nonparental care, and the main form of child care is unregulated care, provided by unlicensed caregivers outside the home or by nannies (Beach, Bertrand, and Cleveland 1998, 17).[8] The rest have been fortunate enough to find places either in licensed family child care or in child care centers, but the latter are concentrated in large urban areas.[9] Moreover, child care centers still tend to focus on the preschool group, so spaces for infants and toddlers are scarce.[10]

The Canadian state supports, in a limited and uneven way, parental child care, through its parental leave policy. As of 1999, if they meet unemployment insurance eligibility standards parents of newborns can take paid leave for up to twenty-five weeks (ten weeks maternity leave and fifteen weeks parental leave). Although this was extended to one full year as of January 2001, changes introduced in the mid-1990s mean that many will not qualify. Although the new legislation covers part-time work, the number of hours required for qualification have been increased; nor are those involved in other forms of "nonstandard" work—temporary and self-employment—eligible.[11] For those who are eligible, the replacement rate has been cut to 55 percent, and there is a cap of $413 per week. In addition, those with annual *family* incomes above $48,750 get less than the official maximum, as benefits are clawed back (Jenson and Stroick 1999).

One of the key barriers to nonparental child care is cost. Child care is labor intensive. Without public financial support, parents and caregivers are caught in a dilemma. Decent wages for workers in child care centers or licensed family daycare come at the expense of affordability. The Canadian policy of subsidizing only those in need has thus meant that many middle- and upper-middle-income families have to look to various forms of unlicensed care, which tends to be less expensive than center-based care by professionals.[12] Of course, since 1971, parents have been able to deduct part of their child care expenses under the Child Care Expense Deduction provision, but this requires receipts and the majority of unlicensed caregivers do not provide receipts.[13] Nor has public support done much to improve the position of child care workers. As Beach and colleagues have noted, "center-based caregivers with a college diploma or certificate working full-time and for the full year received less than 75 percent of the annual income of the average full-time, full-year female worker with the same education. This amounted to less than 60 percent of the annual income earned by the average full-time, full-year worker, male or female, with the same education. Yet, center-based child care workers are better compensated than others in the child care workforce; regulated and unregulated family home caregivers and in-home caregivers are often less well paid than those in center care" (1998, 77–78).

While caregivers in child care centers are better paid than licensed and unlicensed home child care providers—with average wages of $19,000 in 1990—they still fell well below kindergarten or elementary teachers ($34,000—with education equivalent to the caregiver in a center; Beach, Bertrand, and Cleveland 1998, 9).

The Canadian system between does need to be placed in broader perspective. Thus, in keeping with the liberal orientation of the Canadian welfare state, Canadian support for the dual-earner or lone-parent family was not universal but rather focused on those less well off. Compared to the United States, the Canadian welfare regime was generally marked by a stronger element of "social liberalism," blended with growing recognition of the links between family and market status (O'Connor, Orloff, and Shaver 1999, 198); so too in this area it was prepared to do more to support dual-earner or lone-parent families than its U.S. counterpart. It did so, moreover, in a way that favored nonmarket solutions. As Jenson and Stroick note, "a positive side of this [CAP] funding philosophy was that it legitimized the political actions of community groups which sought to develop child care services in poor neighbourhoods and to use child care centers as focal points for community development. Extra funds were even made available for such initiatives through the federal government's Local Initiative Projects. At the same time, relatively high cutoff points for defining 'need' in some provinces meant that subsidies could reach upward toward the middle class. Further, all children in a daycare center, regardless of family income, could benefit from the center's operating grant" (1999, 64). The effects are still visible in the relatively high proportion of child care centers (approximately 60 percent) under nonprofit auspices.

Nevertheless, the system fell far short of the national child care provisions of the Scandinavian welfare regimes. While from the early 1970s CAP allowed a fairly generous definition of "need," the 1986 Cooke Task Force on Child Care found that *no* province or territory used an income or needs test as generous as that established in federal guidelines (Cooke 1986, 184). Moreover, while the financing route that secured federal contributions for operating costs as well as fee subsidies was restricted to nonprofit providers, the other "social assistance" route made funding available for spaces in commercial child care centers.[14] Richer provinces like Alberta could afford to forego federal funds and construct a child care system in which 80 percent of the places are in commercial centers. Finally, the CAP set no standards regulating the quality of care. Thus, provisions for licensing, training, and the rest vary widely across the country, depending on provincial preferences (Beach, Bertrand, and Cleveland 1998, 35–42).

The Making of Canadian Child Care Policy: Phase One

To argue that the Canadian child care system reflects the liberal character of the broader welfare regime within which it is embedded is not to suggest that this is the way it "had to be." In fact, the struggle around child care really developed when the push to transform the Canadian welfare regime was at its height in the 1960s and early 1970s. A breakthrough on child care, like the important victory on health care, might have helped to tip the balance in favor of a strong version of "social liberalism,"[15] just as happened in Australia. Moreover, at this juncture, the system of representation opened up, admitting new actors such as the women's movement. Those seeking to change the system proved strong enough to widen the definition of those "in need" so that it might have included a substantial number of middle-income families (Cooke 1986). They were not, however, strong enough to secure universal child care.

The decision to include child care among the services eligible for federal cost-sharing grants under the CAP (1966) coincided with the appearance of the first signs that the family form was changing.[16] Yet the connection between the two was tenuous, at least initially, because second-wave feminism, which sought to accelerate that change, had yet to claim its place in national politics. For the most part, neither policymakers nor the general public were conscious that mothers were working in ever larger numbers when the terms of CAP were being worked out. Rather, CAP needs to be located as part of the wave of liberal reforms that developed through and built upon the foundations of executive federalism laid down in the 1930s and 1940s.[17] Feminists subsequently played an important part in advancing the demand for universal child care. In this they, and child care advocates at the grassroots level, were aided by the state's acceptance that a vital democracy required public support for citizen groups (Jenson and Phillips 1996). Well before CAP was terminated in 1996, however, the tide had turned. Neoliberalism was on the ascendance, the federal system was in crisis, and the state had abandoned its commitment to public advocacy in favor of narrower "partnerships" and contracting arrangements.

The story of Canadian child care policy from 1966 to 1993 in many respects reflects these broader trends. At the same time, it testifies to the state's difficulty in carrying out these changes, due to the strong tensions they have generated. In particular, the state has found it harder to put the "advocacy" genie back in the bottle. Child care advocates and their feminist and labor allies may have had to alter their tactics, but they have not given up the battle for accessible, affordable, and high-quality child care.

The move away from the male breadwinner as the paradigm of Canadian social policy began when labor markets were tight, job growth was increasingly concentrated in the service sector, and women's labor-force participation had begun to rise. This was also a time of new political openings to forces favorable to a deepening of the "social liberal" dimensions of Canada's welfare edifice. With the formation of the Canadian Labor Congress (CLC) and its support for a renewed social democratic party (the New Democratic Party), the labor movement seemed poised to challenge the old-line parties. The wave of wildcat strikes and the struggle of public sector workers for collective bargaining rights gave class-based issues a new salience. The New Left in anglophone Canada helped to spawn a movement for an independent, socialist Canada and, in Quebec, the unions and the fledgling women's movement helped to shape the visions that blossomed during the Quiet Revolution.[18] In anglophone Canada, too, feminism was beginning to stir, but it was not strong enough yet to make child care an issue of gender equality. Rather, the growing need for child care was mainly articulated through the network of local social workers organized by the Canadian Welfare Council (CWC) (Finkel 1995; Mahon 2000). Their concerns, backed by the then lone representative of working women's concerns in the Canadian state, the director of the Women's Bureau of the Department of Labor, remained marginal to those involved in hammering out the details of CAP.

The main target of federal and provincial welfare officials was the low-income male breadwinner. Child care was but one of the "rehabilitative services" whose primary aim was "to enable the individual to attain or regain the fullest measure of self support and independence of which he is capable."[19] And the officials clearly saw that individual as a "he." As the deputy minister argued, one of the main causes of poverty was that male breadwinners had families too large in relation to their wages.[20] CAP's main innovation was thus the introduction of the needs test, which allowed officials to take the size and age of a man's family into account in determining whether and how much assistance to provide. The issue of getting mothers off social assistance and into the labor market, which played such an important part in the American debates at that time, was all but ignored in Canada. To be sure, under CAP, for the first time provincial mothers' pensions became eligible for cost sharing; yet the prevailing attitude toward lone mothers at the time, while hardly lacking moralistic paternalism, was one that supported their right to stay at home with their children like their more fortunate (i.e., married to a male breadwinner) counterparts (Little 1998). Thus, federal contributions to daycare subsidies were not seen as a part of a broader strategy to get single mothers off social assistance. They simply made it possible for mothers in low-income families to *choose* to work.[21]

While the ultimate target was the low-income male breadwinner family, CAP also aimed to add another layer to the intergovernmental arrangements designed to secure place-based equity and with it, pan-Canadian identity (Jenson and Phillips 1996). That is, the federal government sought to guarantee that all Canadians would have equivalent social rights, no matter where they lived. In this, it was building on the system of equalization payments to poorer provinces—like those in the Atlantic region and Quebec—that were inaugurated in the 1950s to compensate for their lower tax base and hence their inability to provide services equivalent to those offered by the richer provinces. Those who framed CAP were cognizant of recent provincial inquiries that were redefining the relationship between provincial governments and the municipalities in recognition of the latter's inability to meet the growing demand for support services.[22] CAP's provisions were designed to assist the provinces in assuming these new responsibilities. Thus, in the name of place-based equity, CAP helped to build a nationally based set of "nesting" arrangements.[23] In the words of one federal official, the measure would "assist and enable the provinces to develop and maximize the potential of Canada's human resources by facilitating, for those Canadians now unable to do so, their participation in, and contribution to, the social and economic growth of their home, community, province and nation."[24] As we shall see, this system would begin to unravel only a decade later and this has affected the shape of Canada's child care policy.

While CAP would become the main form of federal support for child care in the late 1960s and early 1970s, another important source of federal support came in the form of grants to community groups provided through programs like Opportunities for Youth (OFY) and the Local Initiatives Program (LIP).[25] The latter, in turn, should be seen as part of the federal government's attempt to forge a new relationship with civil society organizations, many of which were infused with the values of the new social movements. These organizations not only had roles to play as providers of community services, but also as policy advocates. State support was thus partly motivated by the aim of fostering more equitable access to political power (Jenson and Phillips 1996). And there are certainly important examples of this in local struggles for child care. Thus, for example, the Company of Young Canadians helped to finance the newsletter of a newly formed child care advocacy group in Vancouver (Griffen 1992, 28). In Ontario, the Toronto Day Care Organizing Committee, founded in 1970, was funded by an LIP grant.[26] As Donna Lero notes, the committee "represented the kind of demand for child care voiced by [local] feminist groups of the time. . . . The group produced a newsletter called Day Care for Everyone, operated a resource library and developed a slide show describing day care programs. . . . By 1974 it had built a community network of support for non-profit child care and helped launch the group for Day Care Reform" (1992, 371–72). In Montreal, too, LIP and OFY funds were being used by local activists to develop nonprofit day care programs (Desjardins 1992, 36). LIP funds also enabled an increase in the number of nonprofit day care centers, mainly in the Halifax-Dartmouth area, from seven in 1971 to thirty-four in 1975 (Canning and Irwin 1992).

In terms of the development of a demand for a *national* child care policy, however, one of the federal government's most important initiatives was the appointment of the Royal Commission on the Status of Women. The commission held hearings across the country, giving a new national visibility to what had hitherto largely remained a set of local, grassroots movements. Its final report, released in December of 1970, constituted the first attempt to codify a new understanding of gender relations. In it glimmered a vision of a future in which men and women would be able to participate equally in the worlds of paid work and parenting (Burt 1986, 117). Prominent among the reforms it proposed was the demand for a universal child care system, available to "all families who need and wish to use it" (RCSW 1970, 268, 270).

The commission's demand for a national child care policy was not met. Nevertheless, in 1971 the Child Care Expense Deduction was introduced and the Unemployment Insurance Act was revised to permit funded maternity leave. More importantly, the terms of CAP, applicable to child care, were changed to allow subsidies to a wider income group and direct operating grants to nonprofit centers were also made available under the welfare services route. Here the Interdepartmental Committee on the Status of Women, and the first Coordinator for the Status of Women, Freyda Paltiel, played an important role (Mahon 2000).

The absence of a strong child care advocacy network at the national level,[27] however, meant that the new "femocrats" were strong enough to secure modifications to CAP but not strong enough to win the battle for a new policy framework based on the principle of universality. As a result they needed to secure the support of the Department of Health and Welfare—the department in charge of CAP. The latter, in turn, was preparing to take the federal "nest-making" strategy one step further. Their representatives on an interdepartmental committee stressed the growing importance of community care services—"those functions or roles that have been culturally assigned to the family or that the individual, under normal circumstances, has been traditionally expected to perform for himself."[28] In the past, families that could not perform these services had been able to look to local voluntary agencies, but the rapidly growing need for such services was straining the latter's resources and those of the local communities on which they relied. The time had come for greater federal support than could then be offered under CAP; it was thus revised to provide stronger incentives for the provinces to support community care services.

The 1972 revisions to CAP that resulted from these intragovernmental rules opened up the "welfare services" route. As noted above, CAP not only offered subsidies to those who met the more broadly defined income (rather than means) test, it also made it possible for the federal government to contribute to the direct operating costs of child care centers, and *only* to those run by nonprofit groups. A Day Care Information Center was established to provide information and counsel to provinces, municipalities, and local groups wishing to set up child care operations. The first child care counselor appointed, Howard Clifford, would become an important force helping to give local and provincial groups a national voice. These reforms did not, however, change child care from an antipoverty measure into a social right available to all.

Universal day care in a sense remained on the federal government's agenda through the social policy review initiated by the minority Liberal government in the mid-1970s. The review opened up the possibility that CAP and other pieces of federal social policy legislation would be replaced by a comprehensive act. Although the main focus was on income security and income support measures, employment and "community care" services were included, and this would have created the possibility of federal support for all who want and need it. The reforms envisaged offering the provinces a range of different formulae from universality at no cost, to sliding fee scales that, unlike even the revised CAP, could encompass all (Haddow 1993, 154). As a letter to a representative of the National Action Committee on the Status of Women (NAC) from the then coordinator of the Royal Commission on the Status of Women indicates, child care was certainly one of the services that was intended to become universal in scope.[29]

The social security reform, and with it, the possibility of an affordable and accessible child care program, foundered, however, on the deepening crisis of the postwar order. That crisis has two factors. The first is the "nesting" arrangements, whereby the federal government used its spending powers to induce and to support provincial social policies (with the latter, in turn, supporting municipalities and nonprofit community care providers). The social services bill was withdrawn in the fall of 1977 to be replaced by a social service financing act that embraced the principle of block funding. The latter was seen as more in line with the provinces' demand for greater autonomy. This move marked the beginning of a serious challenge to the postwar system of intergovernmental relations in which two national projects—the pan-Canadian view, as developed by the Liberal supporters of Pierre Trudeau, and Quebec's newly minted sovereigntist claims, recently given real force by the election of a Parti Québécois government—increasingly clashed.

The second factor forms part of the broader crisis of the Keynesian welfare state which, in turn, opened the way for the ascendance of neoliberalism over social liberalism. In August 1978, then prime minister Trudeau returned from a meeting in Bonn, a convert to fiscal austerity. The Social Services Financing Act, which would have replaced CAP, was thus sacrificed in lieu of cuts to the Established Programs Financing Act, through which the federal government helped finance core areas like postsecondary education and health (Haddow 1993, 161). In addition, to soften the blow of cuts to the universal Family Allowance, a refundable tax credit designed on NIT/GAI principles was introduced, targeted at low-income families with children (Myles and Pierson 1997, 455). The idea behind the new tax credit came out of the debates on the GAI as a means for deepening of social liberalism—that is, as a *supplement to* existing universal programs. Subsequent reforms placed it clearly within a neoliberal framework, as a *substitute for* universal programs, whether family allowances or the yet-to-be-won right to child care.

The issue of a national child care program did not, however, disappear despite these signs that the heyday of social liberalism had come to an end. In fact, it gained new impetus with the emergence of an alliance of child care advocates at the national level. During the 1970s, local child care advocacy groups had started to come together at the provincial level,[30] but there was still no national advocacy group. The federal government's child care consultant, Howard Clifford, worked with the Canadian Council on Social Development (successor to the Canadian Welfare Council) to change that. In 1982 the second national conference on child care, funded by the Department of Health and Welfare (Clifford's office), was held in Winnipeg. The conference led to the creation of not one, but two national child care advocacy groups, each with funding from different federal agencies.[31] The first, the Canadian Day Care Advocacy Association, or CDCAA (now Child Care Advocacy Association of Canada, or CCAAC), backed the position articulated by Toronto-based Action Day Care at the conference, which called for universally accessible, comprehensive, high-quality day care to be provided under *public or nonprofit* auspices. The second, the Canadian Day Care Federation (now the Canadian Child Care Federation, or CCCF), whose members included operators of commercial child care centers, was not opposed to the extension of public funding to for-profit centers (Friendly 1994). This split in the child care advocacy community would become important when the federal government again took up the question of a national child care policy in 1986.

The issue of child care was placed squarely on the government's agenda by the Abella Commission on Employment Equality and the Cooke Task Force on Child Care.[32] Both strongly articulated the need for a national child care act in the name of equality of the sexes. The two reports were commissioned by a Liberal government that retained enough of a social liberal orientation to make such an option plausible. Yet it was a Conservative government that would be in a position to act and the latter took office in 1984 committed to pursing a markedly neoliberal agenda. Moreover, while there were feminists in the Tory Party, the New Right was also well represented, as was evident in the support within its caucus for REAL Women, an antifeminist group.

The Tories' proposed Canada Child Care Act sought to replace CAP as the vehicle for federal funding, as many child care advocates had long demanded. Under the proposed legislation, federal funds could be used not only to cover 50 percent of

operating costs but also to contribute 75 percent of capital costs as a means of encouraging the construction of new facilities. A top-up for poorer provinces, to allow
them to catch up, was proposed (to a maximum of 90 percent). The move was not,
however, greeted with acclaim by the CDCAA and its allies. The Tories' proposal
would have allowed the federal government to put a ceiling on federal transfers ($4
billion over the next seven years), something it could not then do under CAP.[33] Nor
did the Tories' bill specify any national standards of the sort that the Cooke Task
Force had clearly demonstrated were needed. The issue that really divided the child
care advocacy community, however, was that auspice. Whereas under CAP, the federal government did not contribute to the operating costs of commercial child care
centers, the proposed act would have made them eligible.[34] While the smaller Canadian Day Care Federation approved this move, it was flatly rejected by the much
larger CDCAA. The latter worked closely with the CLC, the NAC, and other popular groups to oppose the bill, which died on the government's order paper when the
1988 election was called and was not revived.

Two other elements of the Tories' child care policy did make it through the
House of Commons. The first, the Child Care Initiatives Fund, can almost be seen as
a continuation of such 1970s programs as LIP, which had helped fund some of the
earlier grassroots child care initiatives.[35] This time the focus was specifically on innovative child care projects, with a particular emphasis on services for Aboriginal
children, children with special needs, children of parents who do shift work or work
part-time, and children in rural areas (CCCF 1995). In this sense, it sustained the
spirit of those earlier initiatives. The second, however, harkened back to a very different move from the 1970s: the introduction of an NIT/GAI –based approach to
family policy. In this instance, however, neoliberal ideas blended with the preferences of the New Right. Thus, the Tories' refundable Child Tax Credit offered several billion dollars tax assistance to certain lower- and middle-income parents. It
provided some assistance to those who had to rely on unreceipted child care. And,
in line with REAL Women's demands, it provided tax relief for traditional man-as-
breadwinner families. In 1992, the Tories announced a new Child Tax Benefit that
would replace previous tax credits as well as the last vestige of the postwar family
policy, the once universal family allowance.

In its second term, the Conservative government announced a new initiative, a
focus on "children at risk" that was intended to demonstrate a continuing interest
and hold out future possibilities of a national strategy for child care. It was strong on
rhetoric, but unmatched by specific policy or funding commitments. In 1992, the
prime minister and his government walked away completely from their earlier commitments to child care by announcing that, due to economic conditions, the federal
government could not afford a national child care program. By this point, the Conservative government and the CDCAA (now officially the Child Care Advocacy Association of Canada, or CCAAC) and feminist groups were so at odds that there was
little point in further advocacy at the federal level.[36]

Different Government, Same Pattern: Phase Two

The Liberal government that assumed office in 1993 followed a remarkably similar pattern to the Conservatives: initial enthusiasm, introduction of a national strategy and retreat. Once again the politics of fiscal restraint and crisis of federalism would be the primary reasons for the demise of the new initiative. This time, however, the Liberals took important steps toward transforming the postwar state. They began to dismantle the old system of intergovernmental "nesting" arrangements, replacing the CAP with a new (and much reduced) funding mechanism. This was accompanied by quasi-constitutional changes in federal-provincial arrangements that augured poorly for the launching of new national initiatives, like a national child care program. The system of representation had also changed. Whereas earlier Liberal governments had been open to participation by new collective actors and had even helped to support the mobilization of national child care advocacy associations, the government of Jean Chrétien, like its Tory predecessors, tried to limit the politics of representation by its recognition and support of some advocacy groups over others. The discursive terrain had also been altered by an important strategic turn in the antipoverty community. Partly in response to the cold political climate, antipoverty activists had seized on "child poverty" as the potential chink in neoliberalism's armor. This created a space for child care advocates, but not one conducive to their arguments for a universal program.[37]

The Liberals had entered the 1993 electoral campaign armed with a policy book, known as the "Red Book" (after the Liberals' official color), which outlined in quite specific terms what it would do if it were elected. Child care formed a key element. In opposition, the Liberals had been strong critics of the Tories' strategy and their abandonment of child care. Chaviva Hosek, who had been a president of the NAC before turning to party politics, was given responsibility for formulating the Liberal Party's alternative. Hosek was thus well aware of child care advocacy community's critique of the Tory plan and the kind of national child care policy they sought in its stead. The Liberals' commitment to child care was, however, both limited and contingent. It promised $720 million for a federal-provincial cost-shared program that would expand existing child care by as much as 150,000 new spaces over three years *if* annual economic growth was at least 3 percent and provincial agreement was obtained. The original intent was that the program would be designed as a top-up within the CAP system, rather than a separate program. It would consist of a 40-40-20 cost-sharing arrangement involving the federal government, provincial governments, and parents, with the latter contributing according to their ability to pay. In its first budget, the Chrétien government began to attach dollars to its electoral promise, committing almost half the allocation over three years, although most of this would later be withdrawn. The Human Resource minister whose department would be responsible, Lloyd Axworthy, was a strong proponent of child care, yet he would face an uphill battle with the Ministry of Finance that has assumed an increasingly important role in social policy formation.[38]

In its first year, the Liberal government announced a comprehensive Social Security Review (SSR) that had two main objectives: to reduce child poverty and to encourage people to get and stay off social assistance by offering them support.[39] For many in the child care community, this appeared to be a good opportunity to reinforce the need for a national program. Yet when the 1994 budget established the savings targets for the SSR even before it had begun its work, it was clear that cost cutting was becoming the main objective (Doherty, Friendly, and Oloman 1998, 39). In total, the views of over 100,000 Canadians were heard as part of the review, although the minister and a parliamentary committee were criticized for unduly limiting who was permitted to speak. Many social policy advocates felt that those who wanted to reinforce the value of universality and existing programs were summarily dismissed.

The government's primary objectives in the SSR gave child care a particular cast. First, it was viewed as having a double benefit. It would support employment by turning "unproductive" individuals (mainly lone mothers on social assistance) into productive workers. Second, it had a role to play in fighting child poverty as quality care was presented as an important investment in early child development, one which could counteract the long-term negative effects of growing up in poverty.[40] Although both of these objectives fit awkwardly with the demand for universal child care, child care advocates took heart from the supplementary paper prepared for SSR, which talked of a national framework of principles to guide and consolidate investments in child care and reaffirmed the Red Book's commitment for substantial investment (Doherty, Friendly, and Oloman 1998, 40). Neither the national framework nor the financial investment was realized, however, because the twin agendas of fiscal restraint and national unity interceded.

In social policy terms, the February 1995 budget was one of the most significant of the postwar period. The Ministry of Finance had clearly won the battle over priorities, as extensive cuts to social programs were announced in the name of what was now the overriding goal of eliminating the deficit. The minister of finance had assumed control over the ministers of line departments not only for global budget allocations, but also for program design (Jenson with Thompson 1999, 38). The SSR, which had tried to align social policy with the labor market and to work within fiscal constraints, had clearly been derailed. The budget affected the national child care strategy in several ways. First, it eliminated the cost-shared CAP and rolled this money into the existing block fund arrangement covering the federal government's contributions to postsecondary education and health care. The fund was renamed the Canada Health and Social Transfer (CHST). Second, the federal government cut its contribution to the transfer by one-third over three years. Programs like the child care subsidy now had to fight for declining dollars with health care and other provincial priorities. As there are no conditions attached to the funding, other than the provisions of the Canada Health Act, the former CAP-supported programs have come up the consistent losers. Moreover, as block funding became the norm, it would be more difficult to launch a new national child care strategy through a conditional, cost-shared approach. Finally, the child care allocation that had already been committed in the previous budget also disappeared. Instead, child care was folded into a new investment fund explicitly tied to assisting employability (Doherty, Friendly, and Oloman 1998, 40). This gave the message that child care is a tool to foster employability only for those unemployed or underemployed, not a right for all children nor a means to advance gender equality.

The politics of national unity meant that the idea of establishing national principles to guide the development of child care policy that had been considered as part of the SSR also disappeared. The CHST had significantly exacerbated the tensions within federalism by giving weight to provincial arguments that the federal government could no longer claim a legitimate role in setting national standards in social policy since it was not putting up its share of the cash. The federal government was also prepared voluntarily to restrain itself, however. It did not want to provide any leverage for sovereigntists, in the lead up to the 1995 referendum on Quebec's sovereignty, by appearing to interlope on provincial jurisdiction. At the same time, the intergovernmental realm was becoming more organized and influential, placing the provinces on the offensive. The Provincial/Territorial Council on Social Policy Renewal, which involved all provinces except Quebec, was formed in 1995 to develop a provincial vision for national social programs. Its first report, released December 1995, was unequivocal in its view that the federal spending power should not be used to mount new social programs without prior provincial approval. It explicitly recommended that services for children and families be delivered exclusively by the provinces and territories.[41] Although this position did not necessarily preclude a federal role in shaping and funding a national child care strategy, most provinces had their own views about the best way to tackle child poverty while also getting mothers off social assistance. The council strongly favored the development of a national child tax benefit, rather than universal child and family programs like child care (Bach and Phillips 1998, 242). The displacement of the federal government by the council as the center of the social policy community also helped to marginalize child care advocates as well as the somewhat more radical coalition fighting child poverty. Whereas the federal department had long-standing links with nongovernmental actors, intergovernmental arenas like the council are the least prepared to hear from such actors, in part because all meetings are closed to the public.

Despite the enormous financial and political difficulties posed by the creation of the CHST and state of Canadian federalism, the federal child care plan was not immediately scuttled for two reasons. First, Axworthy, the minister in charge of the SSR, remained strongly committed; second, a number of provincial governments had signaled an interest in continuing in this direction. In spite of resistance from the Ministry of Finance and the central agency responsible for intergovernmental relations, the minister sent federal negotiators to consult with the provinces in the fall of 1995, with a proposal of $630 million over five years, plus funding for aboriginal communities and research that had already been committed. The federal proposal was purposely vague, mentioning neither national principles nor specific program details. Provincial response varied, ranging from enthusiastic to noncommittal, but even Quebec did not immediately reject the plan. Liberals, however, suddenly abandoned their proposal for child care, arguing that there was insufficient provincial interest, even though the negotiations had never been given a chance to succeed or fail.[42] The minister sympathetic to the child care initiative had been moved to another portfolio, to be replaced by a new minister whose primary commitment was to reform unemployment insurance. In the 1996 Speech from the Throne, the government appeared to preclude any future initiatives of this sort by unilaterally declaring that it would not use its spending power to create new programs in areas of exclusive provincial jurisdiction, without consent of a provincial majority.

The abandonment of the child care initiative promised in the Red Book may well have seemed a political risk the government could afford to take. Public opinion had become schooled to the need to eliminate the deficit and pay down the national debt. In addition, the government had continued the effort to reshape the nature of representation by advocacy groups begun by the Tories. Federal grants to citizen groups were subjected to deep and continuous cuts. The objective was not merely cost containment since many of these cuts were explicitly redirected to other program areas (Phillips 1991). Rather, the underlying intent was to reduce the influence of advocacy associations. One of the program areas hardest hit was the Women's Program, which funded a wide variety of women's organizations, including the CCAAC (Jenson and Phillips 1996). Although the CCCF was the group preferred by government, it too faced severe financial trouble. Indeed, by late 1995 the CCCF was ready to close its doors due to lack of funding and was only saved by a large grant from the federal child care research fund. Although it cannot be said that the CCCF was co-opted by this support, it and other child care advocacy groups became preoccupied with sheer survival. More time had to be spent seeking project money and providing research and other services, which limited the time and resources for advocacy.

Postdeficit Politics and Horizontal Governance: Phase Three

As part of the postdeficit era, a "children's agenda" has emerged as a top priority for federal and provincial governments. Yet, even though the dark days of deficit fighting have ended, changes established in that period have shaped the parameters of this agenda. Two trends are of particular relevance to child care. First, while the struggle against child poverty may have mitigated the politics of welfare state retrenchment, the National Child Benefit (NCB), which forms part of the children's agenda, has sanctioned an even narrower focus on the "needy" than in the days of the CAP.

Rather than viewing child rearing as a benefit to society as a whole, the value of which should be recognized and supported by the state, the focus is on the working poor, narrowly defined. Child care advocates, along with their allies in the women's movement, labor, and the more radical wing of the antipoverty community, have fought an uphill battle, with declining resources, to make the system more inclusive. Second, while CAP allowed for considerable differences among provincial delivery systems, the emergent system of federal-provincial arrangements substantially increases the room for diversity. Although the NCB creates a common platform of income support, provinces differ extensively in the variety and design of programs; levels of support; and preferred mix of market, nonprofit, and government providers for child care and related services. This reflects the broader trend toward the bifurcation of federal and provincial roles. The federal government narrowed its role to focus on transfers to individuals, primarily through the income tax system, putting aside any interest in direct support for program delivery.

More broadly, although the "children's agenda" promises new funding for children's programs, it does so in the context of a new social union in which intergovernmentalism replaces federal leadership. In other words, in the intergovernmental environment of the new social union, negotiation among governments is more important than leadership by any one government. Ministers of finance remain key institutional actors, but ministries of intergovernmental affairs have assumed a new prominence and are able to place their own stamp on issues. Thus they tend to care more about relationships and political image than policy content. The scope for learning from the expertise of voluntary organizations, which are so centrally involved in the delivery system and in advocacy work, has accordingly been limited. The "children's agenda" has also helped to foster an environment of horizontal governance. The emphasis is on a children's *agenda* as a policy framework that includes a wide variety of child and family services, of which child care is only one, submerged, aspect. The nature of representation has, in turn, changed in a manner reflecting these changes. Thus strong, slightly competitive advocacy associations, reinforced by networks of allies, have been replaced by true coalitions—to both the advantage and detriment of child care advocates.

These trends are closely tied to the construction of a new "social union" out of the ashes of the old system of federal-provincial negotiations. The formal expression of a new social union occurred in February 1999 with the signing of an agreement known as the Social Union Framework Agreement (SUFA), between the federal government and provincial/territorial governments, with the exception of Quebec. The new social union represents an explicit attempt to redefine relationships among Canadian governments, between states and markets and between governments and citizens (Boismenu and Jenson 1998). As noted above, with its emphasis on intergovernmentalism, SUFA actually marginalizes an already weakened advocacy community. Instead, it addresses the democratic deficit in a language of "results" and "accountability." That is, results are to be transparent to citizens through the development of accountability frameworks before new programs are initiated, and by assessment and public reporting of program outcomes. As we shall see, SUFA is also reshaping the relationship among states, markets, and *low-income* families to the extent that it provides new tools for inducing, forcibly or otherwise, social assistance recipients to (re)enter the labor market. That is, the NCB, hailed as the exemplar of collaborative federalism, reinforces the move to social policy in the form of the NIT/GAI *instead of* universal programs like the family allowance program eliminated by the Tories. It also reflects the neoliberal and "third way" liberal/social democratic emphasis on getting people off of social assistance and into the (low-wage) labor market. It does so, moreover, in a way that allows the provinces to decide which form—the coercive tack of neoliberalism or the "facilitative" approach of the third way.

As a solution to the crisis of federalism, SUFA ostensibly concentrates on "doing what works for Canadians" rather than jurisdictional authority.[43] It sets out certain principles, notably the avoidance of residency-base barriers to mobility and access to social services of reasonably comparable quality, regardless of where one lives in Canada. In this way, the old commitment to place-based equity is reaffirmed. At the same time, it establishes limits to federal funding of national social programs.[44] This may offer a workable formula for the federal government, the nine provinces, and the territories, but it has not resolved the Quebec question. For Quebec, this logic does not spell better social policy or better federal-provincial relations. Rather, it is seen as a derogation of the basic principles of federalism, which are built on respecting the constitutional division of powers (Noël 2000). Hence it has refused to sign the agreement.

SUFA's impact on child care will most likely be shaped by two agreements developed under its umbrella. The first is the creation of the new tax measure, the NCB, announced in 1997.[45] More specifically, the NCB is an agreement between the federal government and provinces by which Ottawa assists low-income families, regardless of whether they are receiving social assistance or working poor, through a new tax benefit called the Canada Child Tax Benefit (CCTB). In addition, a low-income supplement is paid to working families, the full amount of which goes to parents with incomes less than $20,921, thus providing an incentive to remain in the workforce. Beyond this level of income, the benefits are taxed back so that the low-income supplement disappears completely once family income exceeds $29,590.[46] A third component of the NCB substitutes federal benefits for provincial social assistance payments. The provinces can deduct the amount of the supplement from their payments made to social assistance recipients. Funds thus saved may be reinvested by the provinces in social services for children or paid as additional income supplements. The key is that the provinces maintain sole responsibility for deciding how these "savings" are to be used. On average, 31 percent have gone to child and earned income supplements; 39 percent to child care subsidies; 5 percent to early childhood services; 3 percent to supplementary health benefits; and 22 percent to other types of assistance (Federal/Provincial/Territorial Ministers 1999, 23).

Although hailed by the participating governments as a major step toward more collaborative federalism, the NCB has several drawbacks from the standpoint of child care. Like CAP, the NCB is part of the welfare system: it targets low-income families. This time, however, the target group is more narrowly cast. Whereas during the 1970s CAP's income ceilings were raised so that provinces could include a substantial number of middle-income families, the NCB focuses solely on social assistance recipients and families with very low annual incomes. Second, it is unlikely to lead to a significant expansion of the badly deficient supply of quality, regulated child care spaces, especially as again, unlike CAP, there are no limits on the type of child care eligible for funding. Thus, several provinces have reinvested their NCB funds to expand unlicensed, informal child care.[47] Moreover, whether the tax credit supplement is devoted to child care, other services, or additional income support—for the working poor or those on social assistance—is entirely up to the provinces.

The second major SUFA instrument is the National Children's Agenda (NCA) that emanated from the Federal/Provincial/Territorial Council on Social Policy Renewal and has been endorsed by both levels of government (with the exception of Quebec). It is a policy framework that is touted as providing a comprehensive strategy for improving the well-being of all Canadian children—not merely poor children. The federal government signaled its strong support for the NCA in the 1999 Speech from the Throne, which held up the possibility of a federal-provincial agreement on a national action plan on early childhood development by December 2000.[48]

In its underlying intent to enhance the well-being of all Canadian children regardless of family income, the NCA is somewhat at odds with the existing trends because it presupposes both targeted and more broadly accessible programs. It does not involve a standardized system of uniform programs and services in every province, but in accordance with SUFA, it does imply that Canadians have access to programs of reasonably comparable quality regardless of where they live, and that residency-based barriers to mobility are not erected. In this sense, the objectives of place-based equity and reinforcement of a national labor market are simultaneously served.

Under the rubric of the NCA, child care is subsumed under services for early childhood development. The notion of child care as a support for gender equality (or for employability, as in the NCB) disappears. This discursive shift reflects the impact of "population health" experts on official social policy discourse, but the advocacy community has participated in this shift.

Since the early 1990s, political mobilization around child care has changed significantly. While, in the late 1980s and early 1990s, advocacy for a national strategy was led by two relatively strong, somewhat competitive associations and surrounded by a network of allies, by the late 1990s these had been displaced by a form of "coalition" politics. The difference between associational and coalitional politics is one of relative autonomy. In alliances or networks of associations, members work together to develop advocacy strategies based on commonality of interests and positions. Coalitions tend to work by committee: a single position as well as advocacy strategies are developed by the collective and then assumed by the member associations. Given the trade-offs involved in establishing a consensual position, some issues may become secondary or differences are subsumed under a common banner.

Coalitions, formed as a way of strengthening the voice for children and families, have some important advantages for child care advocacy. In an era focused on "children at risk" and targeted funding, neither child care nor other universally accessible child and family services had much of a chance of succeeding on their own. The only way to keep alive the notion of universal access to child and family services was to increase the bandwidth of the message, that is, to establish a more collective and comprehensive position. Two broad coalitions, with some overlapping membership, formed. Campaign 2000, with over seventy national, provincial, and community partner organizations, was concerned primarily with reducing child poverty. The National Children's Alliance, created in 1996 by some thirty national organizations, has the express purpose of advancing a broadly based national children's agenda. The federal government has made the alliance its favored sounding board on children's issues and has engaged in a more reciprocal relationship with it than with the more critical Campaign 2000. The disadvantage for child care advocacy is that, while the alliance has been very effective in speaking as a consistent and coherent collective, advocates for child care constitute but one voice within it.[49]

It was widely anticipated that the 2000–2001 federal budget would be the "children's budget" that would begin to make serious financial commitments to the vague vision of the NCA. Although the value of the CTB was increased and the length of parental leave under the employment insurance system was extended, the focus on children was displaced in favor of health care and tax cuts.[50] Yet the issue is not dead. In the same week that the British Columbian government announced its intention to launch a major new child care program for school age children,[51] the federal minister for human resources announced that she was prepared to bring new money to the table to put flesh on the NCA.[52] It should be noted, however, that even if the governments (or the majority thereof) manage to come to an agreement, child care again will be but one of the possibilities.[53] This only serves to reproduce the politics of horizontal governance, and the coalitional forms this fosters, at the provincial level.

Conclusion

The idea of public support for the construction of a quality, affordable, regulated child care system on a national scale has been on the Canadian agenda for three decades but has not progressed very far. Although there have been several attempts to create a national child care system, all have failed. The preoccupation with fiscal restraint and the ascendance of neoliberal views in the 1980s and 1990s as to the appropriate relation between markets and states has been important, but it does not provide the whole explanation. An equally important part of the puzzle is the layered nature of the Canadian state. Here the legacy of the British North America Act, which made the provinces responsible for social services while leaving the federal government with superior fiscal resources, has been important. The Canada Assistance Plan provided a solution that worked for a while, although it institutionalized a liberal bias (targeted subsidies) that proved difficult to throw off. The deepening crisis of the postwar system of federal provincial arrangements have deterred the federal government from following through on any strategy that links funding mechanisms with national principles or standards.

At the moment, a truly national child care strategy seems as remote as ever. In the politics of the social union, intergovernmental process takes primacy over federal leadership. This not only ensures the protection of jurisdictional autonomy, with a reluctance to create anything national in scope; it also establishes a political process largely closed to the influence of nongovernmental actors. In addition, the emerging preference for horizontal governance embodied in broad policy frameworks and intergovernmental agreements has submerged child care in a wider array of child and family services. The shift from programs to agendas has also affected the nature of political representation, relocating child care advocacy from associational to coalitional politics. The National Children's Agenda is by no means a bad thing, if it is treated as a package and if it produces a system of coordinated services. Nevertheless, it potentially allows governments to pick selectively from the package, offering limited investment in a few high-profile programs or demonstration projects. With an agenda that puts the child alone, rather than the child and family or child and (gendered) citizen at the center of the discourse, we cannot be optimistic that serious discussion of accessible child care, regardless of income and place of residence, will be a serious part of the agenda.

In spite of the rhetoric of a comprehensive strategy to improve the well-being of all Canadian children, the emerging reality is a system of income support and subsidies targeted at very poor families. The result is not a retreat back to the man-as-breadwinner family form. Rather, the majority of dual earner families are left to buy the child care they can afford, with a little help from the Child Care Expense Deduction.[54] Even the "beneficiaries" of the National Child Benefit—lone mothers on social assistance or with low-income jobs— are finding that the terms of securing a limited degree of economic autonomy are changing. Remaining on social assistance is becoming an option few can afford. In some provinces, their (re)entry into the labor market will be cushioned by provision of quality child care as well as training in (temporary) income supplements. In others, however, they will be forced to make whatever care arrangements they can, with limited support from their provincial governments.

Notes

The authors thank Sonya Michel and Wendy Atkin for comments on an earlier draft of this chapter.

1. Lone-parent families rose from 11 percent to 20 percent of all families with children between 1961 and 1991 (Baker 1995, 63). Canada's divorce rate—2.8 per 1,000 population in 1992—was behind that of the United States (4.8) but above Sweden's (2.6) (Baker 1995, 59, table 2.8).

2. While in Sweden 88 percent of lone parents are in the labor force, in Canada and the United States the labor force participation rate is just under 60 percent. In the United Kingdom and Australia, where the man-as-breadwinner family form retains a stronger hold, only 43.7 and 35.3 percent, respectively, of single parents work (O'Connor, Orloff, and Shaver 1999, 71, table 3.2).

3. Between 1960 and 1990, the share of the labor force employed in services rose in Canada from 59.7 percent to 73.3 percent. Comparable figures for the United States are 59.4 percent to 73.3 percent, and for Sweden, 49.8 to 71.6 percent (O'Connor, Orloff, and Shaver 1999, 68, table 3.1).

4. The current debate on welfare states tends to blame labor market polarisation on the postindustrial turn. (See Iversen and Wren 1998; Pierson 1998; and Esping-Andersen 1999). Yet both the Economic Council's original study and the subsequent studies done for Statistics Canada have been careful not to assign responsibility for polarization to postindustrialism per se. The same pattern of polarization has appeared in the goods-producing sector, in part a reflection of the employers' ability to wring concessions from unions that disproportionately affect younger workers. It is the latter group, of course, that is also most likely to have young families.

5. The proportion of young families in the bottom decile increased from 17 percent in 1980 to 27 percent (CCSD 1999, 7). Lone mothers have it even worse, going from 24 percent of the bottom decile in 1970 to 40 percent in 1995 (Jenson and Stroick 1999, 11).

6. Demographics, along with the structure of the postindustrial labor market, are seen as important contributors to the current dilemmas faced by welfare states by authors Pierson (1998); Iversen and Wren (1998); and Esping-Andersen (1999).

7. The Scandinavian social democracies are not, of course, the only ones to have developed a fairly comprehensive child care system, as the chapters on France and Belgium in this volume show. Yet in these countries, child care forms part of a wider network of public services provided by unionized workers. Moreover, in France a number of recent reforms have favored the spread of cheap, in-home child care. See Jenson and Sineau (2001) as well as Morgan, in this volume.

8. According to Beach, Bertrand, and Cleveland, in 1994, 34 percent of those under twelve whose parents were working or studying were in unregulated care and about 14 percent were being cared for at home by a nanny (1998, 22, 23).

9. Among children six and under of working or studying parents and living in cities over 500,000, 24.8 percent had spaces in centers while in rural areas only 13.7 percent were able to find spots in child care centers.

10. Varga argues that this trend was established as day nurseries began to adopt the "early child development" philosophies of psychologists like Gesell and Hall in the 1920s and 1930s (1997, chap. 2).

11. A study by the Canadian Labor Congress (2000) shows that women were particularly affected by these changes.

12. In 1994, "31.1 percent of the children in families with incomes below $30,000, compared to 17.2 percent of the children in families with incomes over $30,000, were in center-based care" (Beach, Bertrand, and Cleveland 1998, 28). This is in marked contrast to Sweden, where middle- and upper-middle-income families are overrepresented in child care centers (LO 1996).

13. According to Beach and colleagues, only 35 percent of unlicensed caregivers provide receipts (1998, 31). See Vincent and Woolley (2000) for a discussion of the narrow range of beneficiaries of the income tax deduction.

14. After 1972, CAP offered two funding routes. The most generous was the "welfare services" route, which required an income test (administered through the tax system and thus less invasive) and provided federal funds for fee subsidies and a share of operating costs including salaries and fringe benefits, training, materials and supplies, but was only available to nonprofit providers. The second was the "social assistance" route based on a traditional means test. Under this provision, federal funds simply cover 50 percent of the subsidy for those in need but the subsidy can be used in commercial as well as nonprofit centers. See Cooke (1986), section on CAP financing, for more details.

15. As O'Connor and colleagues recognize, liberalism has various facets including social liberalism (1999, 49–52). The latter not only accepts a more active role for the state vis-à-vis the economy (liberal variants of Keynesianism) but also the recognition the social citizenship complemented, rather than undermining, civil and political citizen rights.

16. The studies commissioned by the Women's Bureau (1958, 1964) began to document the rise of women's (and mothers') labor-force participation rates. A new feminist movement had begun to form and, in Quebec, the new Fédération des Femmes du Québec included universal daycare in their demands. Until the Royal Commission on the Status of Women, however, second-wave feminism had little impact on the national agenda.

It should be noted that, as in the United States, the Canadian government did subsidize child care during World War II but canceled the program at the end of the war. Instead, the family allowance, spousal and dependent child tax allowances, and housing supports bolstered the reassertion of the man-as-breadwinner family form. See Prentice (1993) for a richly detailed analysis of wartime policy and the struggles to maintain day care in Ontario after the wartime grants were terminated. There were fewer protests in Montreal, in part because the few centers then operative served minority anglophone communities. The Catholic Church maintained an implacable opposition to daycare and French Canadian mothers who worked (and many did in industries like textiles) relied on extended families (Desjardins 1992, 33).

17. Executive federalism is the term coined by Smiley (1976) to refer to the channels of intergovernmental bargaining that mushroomed in the postwar years. The foundations were laid in the 1930s, however.

18. The "Quiet Revolution" refers to the period inaugurated in 1960, when the Liberals put an end to the regime of Maurice Duplessis, which had acted, among other things, as a brake on modern welfare state construction in Quebec and instituted a series of sweeping reforms to social services and economic life.

19. NAC, RG 29, Records of the Department of National Health and Welfare, vol. 1620, file "Canada Assistance Plan" (Development of Public Assistance Act)-1965/08–1966/03, 1.

20. NAC, RG 29, Records of the Department of National Health and Welfare, vol. 868, file 20-C-215, part 1.

21. NAC, RG 29, Records of the Department of National Health and Welfare, vol. 1620, file 122-1, Speaking Notes for the Minister on second reading of the bill.

22. Health and Welfare's files explicitly refer to the Boucher inquiry in Quebec, the Bryne inquiry in Newfoundland, and the Michener inquiry in Manitoba. RG 29 box 17, 3203–2 part 1. Report on the Meeting of Ministers of Welfare, May 1964 and Summary of Reports, DM of Welfare, July 12, 1964.

23. The reference to "nesting" is to Soja's metaphor for the relationship among different sites—"a mutable hierarchy of nested locales" (1989, chap. 6). One of the aspects of the crisis of the Keynesian welfare state is the disruption of the system of connections establishing that hierarchy.

24. NAC, RG 29, Box 17 3203–2, pt. 1. From the Director of Unemployment Assistance to the Deputy Minister of Health and Welfare, January 1, 1965.

25. OFY was designed to address youth unemployment while LIP more generally aimed to provide employment opportunities in poorer communities. Both programs funded local community development projects.

26. The Statistics Canada study from which these examples are drawn provides a tantalizing glimpse of the role played by grassroots organizations, often inspired by New Left and feminist ideas, which seized the initiative from the older networks constituted by the local welfare councils. The detailed stories have yet to be told. See Atkin (1998), however, for the one detailed scholarly account of one such initiative currently available.

27. In this regard, it is interesting to compare the results of the first national conference on day care, held in Ottawa in 1971, with that of 1982. The latter not only drew back from demanding a new national child care act. It also left the child care advocacy community pretty much as it was—unevenly developed across provincial and even intercity lines and with no national voice. The second national conference resulted in the creation of two strong child care advocacy groups. See below.

28. NAC, RG 106, Record of the Coordinator, Office of the Status of Women, vol. 3, file Working Party IV, *Background Paper on Revision of the Canada Assistance Plan—Community Care Services (Daycare and Homemaker Services)*, April 24, 1971.

29. NAC, RG 106, Records of the Coordinator of the Status of Women, vol. 68, file 1320, Julie Loranger, Coordinator, Status of Women, to Ruth Shaw, National Action Committee on the Status of Women, November 11, 1976.

30. The best-known story is perhaps Ontario's, in which the Toronto-based Action Day Care (founded in 1978) and the Ontario Coalition for Better Day Care (1981) play a key role (Prentice 1988; Lero 1992; and Friendly 1994). Similar groups were emerging in a number of other provinces, however. In British Columbia, the Vancouver-centered Child Care Federation (1973–76) and the Coalition for Improved Daycare Services (1976–78) were followed by the formation of the BC Daycare Action Coalition in 1981 (Griffen 1992). By 1974 a child care advocacy association had been formed in Manitoba, bringing together child care workers, members of the boards of nonprofit child care centers, parents, and others. In 1981 the association gained core funding from the Winnipeg Foundation (Humphrey

1992). In Saskatchewan, Action Child Care developed out of the Saskatoon Community Development Program (Nykyforuk 1992), while the Day Care Committee of the Halifax-Dartmouth Welfare Council laid the basis for the Citizens Day Care Action Committee and the Nova Scotia Child Care Council in Halifax (Canning and Irwin 1992). The 1973 Citizens Rights and Freedoms conference in St. John's, Newfoundland, resulted in the formation of the Day Care Action Committee (Glassman 1992). Most of these coalitions followed the same pattern, bringing parents, child care workers, early childhood educators, and social agencies together with women's groups and unions. On the role of unions in the struggle for daycare in Canada, see Rothman and Kass (1997).

31. The CDCAA received funding from an important site of feminist activity within the federal bureaucracy, the Women's Branch of Secretary of State. See Findlay (1987) for more on the Women's Branch. Health and Welfare provided funds to support the Canadian Day Care Federation.

32. When they returned to office in 1980, Liberals visibly positioned themselves to appeal to the women's movement. Among various initiatives they appointed the Abella Commission on Employment Equity, which reported in 1984, and set up the Cooke Task Force to follow up on the Abella report's recommendations with regard to the need for new child care arrangements.

33. In 1990 the Tories did put a cap on CAP for the three richest provinces, Ontario, Alberta, and British Columbia.

34. The Cooke Task Force had also recommended this as an interim measure. While Cooke recommended that "good faith" and direct child care funding subsequently be limited to licensed centers operated under public or nonprofit auspices (recommendation 6), it recommended that the government lift restrictions on contributions to operating grants for commercial centers under CAP (recommendation 15; Cooke 1986, 373–74).

35. See the various provincial stories in the Pence (1992) collection for some interesting examples.

36. For a discussion of the relationship between women's groups and the federal government during this period, see Bashevkin (1998) and Dobrowolsky (2000).

37. For more on this, see McKeen (1998). One of the advocacy coalitions, Campaign 2000, tried to assert the importance of universality, but the very antipoverty focus played into the shift to targeting associated with neoliberalism.

38. As the ministry responsible for the budget, Finance has always had considerable influence in social policy decisions. Yet the turn to reliance on tax deductions and credits as the preferred social policy tool has added to Finance's strength at a time when the fixation of deficit reduction enhances its classic powers. Thus, as Michael Prince and James J. Rice note, "Finance officials have essentially determined the development, deadlock, and decline of social policy making in Canada over the last two decades" (2000, 144).

39. Both neoliberals and "third-way" liberals and social democrats favor the reduction of social assistance rolls but the former place more emphasis on coercion while the latter talk about inducements. The reforms Minister Axworthy envisioned belong more to the "third-way" camp.

40. The research by Fraser Mustard, which has demonstrated that a child's brain devel-

opment in the first six years of life sets a lifelong foundation for learning and behavior, has been highly influential in linking the issue of child care to that of early childhood development. Mustard's study of the early childhood years commissioned for the Ontario government encouraged it to establish parenting centers to help teach better parenting skills that would stimulate their children's brain development (McCain and Mustard 1999).

41. In addition to the ten provinces, Canada has three territorial governments, all in the northern half of the country (see Provincial/Territorial Council on Social Policy Renewal 1995, 14). The council initially included only provincial/territorial ministers responsible for social policy but in 1996 the federal government was invited to join, making it the Federal/Provincial/Territorial Council. Quebec does not officially participate.

42. In fact, Wendy Atkin, who had been involved in this process as a representative of the CCAAC, notes that the federal government deliberately suppressed indications of provincial support (Atkin 1998).

43. Government of Canada, Treasury Board Secretariat, "Analysis of the Social Union Initiatives: Staff Working Paper," available online at http://www.tbs-sct.gc.ca.

44. Interestingly, the limits on federal spending power are less stringent than those the federal government imposed on itself in the 1996 Speech from the Throne.

45. Although the NCB was actually implemented before SUFA was signed, it is entirely compatible with the SUFA principles and objectives, and thus is regarded as one of the exemplars of cooperative social policy and attendant accountability frameworks that SUFA is intended to produce.

46. The February 2000 budget improved the level of NCB benefits up to a maximum of $2,056 for the first child and $1,805 for the second child by July 2000. These levels will rise to $2,400 and $2,200 respectively by 2004. In addition, the 2000 budget reindexed them to inflation. Yet these changes do not go far enough, leaving many working poor without any supports whatsoever.

47. These include Ontario, one of Canada's richest provinces, as well as New Brunswick.

48. From commitments announced in the 1999 Speech from the Throne, the federal government has undertaken a number of specific initiatives with regard to children and families. These include the extension of parental leave to twelve months—for those able to qualify. For more detail see the HRDC website at http://www.hrdc-dhrc.gc.ca.

49. The National Children's Alliance incorporates a diverse set of organizations, including large, quite traditional groups such as the Canadian Public Health Association.

50. In the months immediately before the budget was due, a report by the auditor general critical of the main department responsible for social policy—Human Resources Development—was released, producing a feeding frenzy among neoliberal think tanks, business groups, and political parties (notably the Reform Party). This seems to have tipped the balance within the cabinet, in favor of the minister of finance and other elements keen on tax cuts to "improve the business climate."

51. Beginning in January 2001, the program has clearly been identified as the first step toward a comprehensive child care program equivalent to Quebec's. On the latter, see Jenson, in this volume.

52. The minister refused to specify the amount, but the papers estimate that it is in the $300–500 million range; (Toronto) *Globe and Mail*, August 6, 2000.

53. The provinces and territories have to agree to spend the money on support for prenatal nutrition and infant care, improving parenting skills, and early childhood development and learning. The latter could include head start programs instead of child care. It is also up to the provinces and territories to decide how to apportion the funds. Presumably they could put the whole amount into other programs that fit the categories and ignore child care entirely.

54. For an analysis of the impact of the CCED, see Vincent and Woolley (2000).

References

Atkin, Wendy. 1998. "'Babies of the World Unite': The Early Day-Care Movement and Family Formation in the 1970s." In *Family Matters: Papers in Post-Confederation Canadian Family History*, ed. L. Chambers and E.-A. Montigny. Toronto: Canadian Scholar's Press.

Bach, Sandra, and Susan Phillips. 1998. "Constituting a New Social Union: Child Care Beyond Infancy?" In *How Ottawa Spends 1997–1998: Seeing Red: A Liberal Report Card*, ed. Gene Swimmer. Ottawa: Carleton University Press.

Baker, Maureen. 1995. *Canadian Family Policies: Cross-National Comparisons*. Toronto: University of Toronto Press.

Bashevkin, Sylvia. 1998. *Women on the Defensive: Living through Conservative Times*. Chicago: University of Chicago Press.

Beach, Jane, Jane Bertrand, and Gordon Cleveland. 1998. *Our Child Care Workforce: From Recognition to Remuneration*. Main Report for the Child Care Sector Study Steering Committee. Ottawa: HRDC.

Boismenu, Gérard, and Jane Jenson. 1998. "A Social Union or a Federal State? Intergovernmental Relations in the New Liberal Era." In *How Ottawa Spends 1998–99: Balancing Act: The Post-Deficit Mandate,* ed. L. Pal. Ottawa: Carleton University Press.

Burt, Sandra. 1986. "Women's Issues and the Women's Movement in Canada Since 1970." In *The Politics of Gender, Ethnicity and Language in Canada*, ed. Alan Cairns and Cynthia Williams. Toronto: University of Toronto Press.

CCCF (Canadian Child Care Federation). 1995. "Federal Policy on Child Care."

CCSD (Canadian Council on Social Development). 1999. *Work, Family and Community: Key Issues and Directions for Future Research*. Available online at http:www.ccsd.ca.

CLC (Canadian Labour Congress). 2000. "Analysis of UI [Unemployment Insurance] Coverage for Women." Ottawa: CLC. Available online at http://www.clc-ctc.ca/woman/index/html.

Canning, Patricia, and Shawn Irwin. 1992. "Nova Scotia." In *Canadian Child Care,* ed. A. Pence, vol. 2.

Cooke, Katie. 1986. *Report of the Cooke Task Force on Child Care*. Ottawa: Status of Women Canada.

Desjardins, Ghislaine. 1992. "Quebec—Historical Overview." In *Canadian Child Care,* ed. A. Pence, vol. 2.

Dobrowolosky, Alexandra. 2000. *The Politics of Pragmatism*. Toronto: Oxford University Press.

Doherty, Gillian, Martha Friendly, and Mab Oloman. 1998. *Women's Support, Women's Work:*

Child Care in an Era of Deficit Reduction, Devolution, Downsizing and Deregulation. Ottawa: Status of Women Canada.

Esping-Andersen, Gøsta. 1999. *Social Foundations of Postindustrial Economies*. Oxford: Oxford University Press.

Federal/Provincial/Territorial Ministers Responsible for Social Services. 1999. *The National Child Benefit Progress Report: 1999*. Ottawa: Minister of Public Works and Government Services Canada.

Findlay, Sue. 1987. "Facing the State: The Politics of the Women's Movement Reconsidered." In *Feminism and Political Economy: Women's Work, Women's Struggles*, ed. Heather Jon Maroney and Meg Luxton. Toronto: Methuen.

Finkel, Alvin. 1995. "Even the Little Children Cooperated: Family Strategies, Childcare Discourse and Social Welfare Debates, 1945–1975." *Labour/le travail* 36: 91–118.

Friendly, Martha. 1994. *Child Care Policy in Canada: Putting the Pieces Together*. Don Mills: Addison-Wesley.

Glassman, Marc. 1992. "Newfoundland." In *Canadian Child Care*, ed. A. Pence, vol. 2.

Griffen, Sandra. 1992. "BC Report." In *Canadian Child Care*, ed. A. Pence, vol. 1.

Haddow, Rodney. 1993. *Poverty Reform in Canada, 1958-1978*. Montreal: McGill-Queens University Press.

Humphrey, Mary. 1992. "Manitoba." In *Canadian Child Care*, ed. A. Pence, vol. 1.

Iversen, Torben, and Anne Wren. 1998. "Equality, Employment and Budgetary Restraint: The Trilemma of the Service Economy." *World Politics* 50: 507–46.

Jenson, Jane, and Susan Phillips. 1996. "Regime Shift: New Citizenship Practices in Canada." *International Journal of Canadian Studies* 14: 111–36.

Jenson, Jane, and Mariette Sineau, eds. 2001. *Who Cares? Women's Work, Childcare and Welfare State Redesign*. Toronto: University of Toronto Press.

Jenson, Jane, and Sharon Stroick. 1999. *What Is the Best Mix for Canada's Children? A Synthesis Report*. Ottawa: CPRN.

Jenson, Jane, with Sherry Thompson. 1999. *Comparative Family Policy: Six Provincial Stories*. Ottawa: CPRN.

Kyle, Irene. 1992. "Ontario." In Pence, ed. *Perspectives*, vol. 1.

Lero, Donna. 1992. "Historical Overview of Child Care in Ottawa." In *Canadian Child Care*, ed. A. Pence.

Little, Margaret. 1998. *No Car, No Radio, No Liquor Permit: The Moral Regulation of Single Mothers in Ontario 1920–1997*. Oxford: Oxford University Press.

LO (Swedish Trade Union Federation). 1996. *Barnomsorg, forvarvsarbete och jamstalldhet. Ett faktmaterial om forhallandena vid 1990 talets mitt* (Child Care, Employment and Gender Equality: A Fact Sheet about the Situation in the Mid-1990s). Nr. 29.

Mahon, Rianne. 2000. "The Never-Ending Story: Canadian Feminist Struggles for Universal Child Care in the 1970s. *Canadian Historical Review* 81, no.4: 582–615.

McCain, Margaret, and Fraser Mustard. 1999. *The Early Years Study*. Paper commissioned by the Government of Ontario. Toronto: Queen's Printer.

McKeen, Wendy. 1998. "The Canadian Poverty Debate: The Shaping of Feminist Political Interests, 1970 to 1995." Ph.D. diss., Carleton University, Ottawa.

Myles, John, and Paul Pierson. 1997. "Friedman's Revenge: the Reform of 'Liberal' Welfare States in Canada and the United States." *Politics and Society* 25: 443–72.

Noël, Alain. 2000. "Without Quebec: Collaborative Federalism with a Footnote?" *Policy Matters* 1, no. 2.

Nykyforuk, Jean. 1992. "Saskatchewan—Historical Perspective." In *Canadian Child Care,* ed. A. Pence, vol. 1.

O'Connor, Julia, Ann Orloff, and Sheila Shaver. 1999. *States, Markets, Families: Gender, Liberalism and Social Policy in Australia, Canada, Great Britain and the United States.* Cambridge: Cambridge University Press.

Pence, Alan R., ed. 1992a. *Canadian Child Care in Context: Perspectives from the Provinces and Territories,* 2 vols. Ottawa: Statistics Canada.

Pence, Alan R. 1992b. "Introduction." In *Canadian Child Care,* ed. A. Pence, vol. 1.

Phillips, Susan. 1991. "How Ottawa Blends: Shifting Government Relationships with Interest Groups." In *How Ottawa Spends 1991–1992: The Politics of Fragmentation*, ed. F. Abele. Ottawa: Carleton University Press.

Pierson, Paul. 1998. "Irresistible Forces, Immovable Objects: Postindustrial Welfare States Confront Permanent Austerity." *Journal of European Public Policy* 5, no. 4: 539–60.

Prentice, Susan. 1988. "'Kids Are Not for Profit': The Politics of Child Care." In *Social Movements/Social Change*, ed. Frank Cunningham, Suzanne Findlay, Martene Kadar, A. Lennan, and E. Silva. Toronto: Between the Lines.

_____. 1993. "Militant Mothers in Domestic Times: Toronto's Postwar Childcare Struggle." Ph.D. diss., York University, Toronto.

Prince, Michael J. and James J. Rice. 2000. *Changing Politics of Canadian Social Policy.* Toronto: University of Toronto Press.

Provincial/Territorial Council on Social Policy Renewal. 1995. *Report to the Premiers.* Ottawa: Provincial/Territorial Council on Social Policy Renewal.

RCSW. 1970. *The Report of the Royal Commission on the Status of Women of Canada.* Ottawa: Government of Canada.

Rothman, Laurel, and Jamie Kass. 1997. "Still Struggling for Better Child Care: The Role of Labour in the Canadian Child Care Movement." Paper prepared for the Eighth Conference on Canadian Social Welfare Policy, University of Regina, June 25–28.

Smiley, Donald. 1976. *Canada in Question: Federalism in the Seventies,* 2d. ed. Toronto: University of Toronto Press.

Soja, Eduard. 1989. *Postmodern Geographies: The Reassertion of Space in Critical Social Theory.* London: Verso.

Varga, Donna. 1997. *Constructing the Child: A History of Canadian Day Care.* Toronto: Lorimer.

Vincent, Carole, and Frances Woolley. 2000. "Taxing Canadian Families: What's Fair, What's Not." *Choices* 6, no. 5: 3–37.

Women's Bureau. 1958. *Survey of Married Women Working for Pay*. Ottawa: Government of Canada.

_____. 1964. "Day Care Services for the Children of Working Mothers." *Women's Bureau Bulletin* XI, January.

CHAPTER 9

Child Care in Britain, or, How Do You Restructure Nothing?

Vicky Randall

Introduction

The Labour government that came to power in Britain in 1997 had pledged in its electoral manifesto to develop a national child care strategy and, more specifically, to increase and improve child care provision. In May 1998, in pursuance of this commitment, it published a green paper, *Meeting the Childcare Challenge* (Department for Education and Employment 1998). To judge by the speed and vehemence of subsequent accusations that mothers of young children were being forced out to work and the importance of their mothering role correspondingly belittled, one might suppose that there already existed a superabundance of child care assistance and provision.

In fact in Britain the reverse has always been the case. Apart from the periods during the two world wars (especially World War II), government involvement in child care provision has been quite minimal. Thus, in 1988, publicly provided and funded day nursery places were available for less than 1 percent of children under five years of age in England and Wales. Publicly regulated child minders accounted for a further 5 percent (Cohen 1990, 3). It is notoriously difficult to compare forms and degrees of provision from one national context to another, but on any reckoning British public child care provision was way down on the European scale (European Commission Child Care Network 1990).

Much of the original explanation for this lack of government interest lies in the character of the postwar British welfare state—its (partial) incorporation of a liberal philosophy of government and strong male breadwinner assumptions. Partly as a consequence of the dominance and institutionalization of a welfare or custodial conception of child care, organized pressure and support for the expansion of state funded or sponsored child care provision was also slow to emerge. And it was almost immediately overtaken by the perceived imperatives of welfare-state retrenchment.

The terms *restructuring* and *retrenchment* are often used interchangeably. I shall argue that they do have rather different implications, and both tendencies have been apparent in Britain at different times and even simultaneously. Further, we shall see that the consequences of retrenchment/restructuring have not been purely negative for child care. First, given the paucity of public child care provision in the first place, there has been limited scope for actual cutback or retrenchment in the narrow sense. Second, restructuring itself has been propelled not simply by the desire or perceived need to expand the scope of the market, within the context of increased global economic competition. It has also in varying degree but perhaps increasingly over time been a response to internal pressures associated with important demographic changes and gendered shifts in employment patterns. That is to say, there has been no single, unanimously accepted formula for refashioning the welfare state. It constitutes a broad and imprecise goal, leaving plenty of room for dispute over strategies for its achievement. In Britain, under the Labour government, child care may be acquiring a new strategic importance in the context of a "welfare-to-work" approach, although given the legacy of earlier policies and the general resource constraints it has set itself, there will be major difficulties in translating this into actual increased provision.

The remainder of this chapter will develop the arguments outlined here. It is necessary first, however, briefly to establish what is to be meant by "child care" in this context. It will refer to forms of care for children under school age provided outside their home. In practice, in the British context this has meant primarily day nurseries, whether run directly by the local authority, on a voluntary basis, as a commercial undertaking or—though this is still relatively unusual—at the workplace. Second, it has comprised child minders, whether registered or unregistered. But, to the extent that they cater for children part of the day, it also covers nursery schools and classes, which are generally run on a part-day basis, and play groups, which are both part-day and typically offered only a couple of days a week. The relationship between child care and nursery education has been especially important and at the same time ambiguous. Not only is nursery education a form of child care; it is increasingly accepted that child care should include an educational dimension. At the same time, nursery education as currently provided cannot on its own cater for working parents' needs for child care throughout the day and during school holidays. Government and others have (opportunistically?) compounded the confusion, at certain times holding the distinction sacrosanct, at others conflating the two. The particular focus of interest in this chapter is the role of the (welfare) state in provision. Potentially the state is involved not only as a direct provider, but also through subsidies to the suppliers or customers for child care and through regulation of private and voluntary provision. Recently there has also been an emphasis on the role of the state as "coordinator" of child care provision.

Child Care Provision Prior to Retrenchment

In order to comprehend and evaluate the impact of retrenchment, we must first describe the pattern of provision in the mid- to late 1970s, when policies of retrenchment, never entirely absent, began to take firmer hold. Within government, responsibility for child care was still institutionalized along lines first adopted in 1918. There was no national child care strategy as such, but at the national level responsibility for an implicit child care policy was divided between different ministries, most significantly between the Ministries of Health and Education. The Ministry of Health oversaw local authority day nurseries and the system of registering child minders, while the Ministry of Education oversaw nursery schools and classes. Implementation was left largely to the discretion of local authorities, again internally divided along departmental lines. This was then a pattern of institutionalization based, first, on the perceived functional distinction we have already noted between child care and nursery education. Second, it embodied fundamental assumptions about the respective roles of mothers and of the state in child care. That is, public child care was depicted almost entirely as a welfare service for children in special need, whose mothers absolutely had to go out to work or whose caretaking was seriously inadequate in some other way.

The marginality of child care as a national policy priority was reflected in the status, pay, and conditions of child care workers, who were overwhelmingly female and engaged in what was seen as an extension of their "natural" mothering role. Worst off were child minders and workers within the growing play group sector, but those within state institutions were also affected. Typically day nurseries were headed by a "matron" who had been trained in child health; the bulk of the other nursery workers were unqualified. Myra Garrett (1975), who found that most of these nursery workers were young working-class women often recruited at age sixteen directly after leaving school, commented on the generally hierarchical relations at work and observed, "What goes on in the nursery is 'women's work' par excellence, and the workers are treated accordingly—undervalued in their work, underpaid, required to work longer hours than other council workers, cleaning toilets and polishing basins, feeding, washing, entertaining, educating up to 20 children for eight hours at a stretch" (6). Although the status and pay of nursery school teachers were higher than for other nursery workers, they were lower than for teachers of older children and associated with very limited career opportunities.

Although child care provision expanded dramatically during the war, in its aftermath, under pressure from the Ministry of Labour, the "war nurseries" were rapidly wound down. The Ministry of Health resumed prime responsibility at the national level while provision in practice was once more at the discretion of the local authorities. By 1963, thirteen (out of forty-eight) county councils and thirteen (out of seventy-nine) county boroughs had no day nursery places at all. The situation regarding nursery education was, in theory at least, rather different. Support had been steadily growing for the principle of nursery education and had received an additional boost during the war. The 1944 Education Act required local education authorities to "have regard to the need for" nursery education. In practice, other claims on education budgets took priority and indeed there was an increasing trend from full- to part-time modes of attendance.

As Denise Riley (1983) has demonstrated, it would be misleading to suggest that there was no public protest against the winding down of the nurseries. Nor, as might sometimes be implied, did employment opportunities for women suddenly dry up after the war. Although the employment rate for married women fell in the late forties, it was already 26 percent by 1951 and 35 percent by 1961 (Bruegel 1983). The postwar growth in female employment was to a large extent due to the expansion in part-time work. Moreover, overall employment rates for mothers with dependent children were much lower, on one estimate still only around 11–12 percent in 1961 (Tizard, Moss, and Perry 1976). This might be taken to imply that there was no urgent need for expanded child care provision.

In the 1960s, however, growing need was reflected in the dramatic expansion of private day nurseries and of childminding, both registered and unregistered. In addition, from 1960 a play group movement began to grow, with five hundred groups in place by 1965. Although play groups could not directly meet working parents' need for daylong child care provision, the movement constituted a recognition that small children also had needs that could not all be met at home.

If by the early 1970s both the scale and the diversity of child care provision were growing, there was also a modest but significant increase in public support for expanded state provision, especially in nursery education. On the one hand, an eclectic assortment of groups and interests—voluntary groups concerned with children, poverty or both, local authority associations, sections of the trade union movement, child-oriented professionals—increasingly pressed for better provision for those under five, while disagreeing among themselves on the form it should take. Feminist groups featured among them. Despite the fact that the first women's liberation conference in 1970 had identified "twenty-four-hour nurseries" as one of their four central demands, in practice activists' take up of this cause tended at this stage to be sporadic and local (Randall 1996). On the other hand, government itself commissioned a series of reports on tangentially related questions—primary education, organization of the social services, one-parent families—whose eventual recommendations included some expansion in public child care and nursery education, together with improved coordination between the two. In 1972 a ministry of education white paper—the minister in charge was Margaret Thatcher!—announced a major new initiative to expand nursery education until by 1982 it catered for all demand from parents of three- and four-year-olds. In the same year, and following reorganization of local authority social services, the Department of Health and Social Security (DHSS) required the new local social service departments to submit ten-year development plans, itself setting a new target of eight day-nursery places for every 1,000 children under five. However, public expenditure cutbacks, as early as 1974 and under a Labour government, effectively nipped these relatively modest plans in the bud.

Restructuring the Welfare State

In summary, by the mid- to late 1970s, and despite the last-minute surge of public support for state provision, such provision, whether in the form of child care or even part-time nursery education, was meager in the extreme. It can and has been argued, most notably in Mary Ruggie's pioneering comparative analysis of policies toward working women in Britain and Sweden (1984), that this situation was in no small measure the outcome of Britain's "liberal" state welfare tradition. The more recent elaboration of the notion of the "liberal" welfare state and feminist criticisms of it have been discussed in the introduction to this volume. There is no doubting their relevance here, although the characterization of Britain as "liberal" may understate both the strength of a social democratic tradition and the degree of state centralization. (For a fuller discussion of these qualifications, see Randall 2000.)

At any rate, in these circumstances, and with respect specifically to child care, one might be tempted to ask, What was there to "restructure"? This is, however, to take child care out of its wider actual or potential policy context, most especially its implications for employment and social security. While some government policies seem designed to reduce still further the state's direct responsibility for child care, in practice these intentions have been complicated by the need to achieve other objectives.

A substantial international literature has developed on the imperative of welfare state restructuring or retrenchment, in the wake of the two oil crises of the 1970s and in the face of internal demographic changes coupled with increasingly global economic competition. As already observed, the terms *retrenchment* and *restructuring* are sometimes used interchangeably and when they are distinguished there is no necessary consistency from one author to another. At face value, however, they do suggest different things and the British case seems to provide a good illustration. From the mid-1970s on, the Labour government embarked on a phase of retrenchment, but these expenditure cutbacks in government programs tended to be understood as regrettably necessary departures from originally sound policy plans. The incoming Conservative government from 1979 was largely identified with a neoliberal project whose faith in the market mechanism could be seen as a return to the tenets of classical liberalism. Much more actively and creatively than the outgoing Labour government, it embraced the opportunities for reshaping policy associated with expenditure cutbacks, in a way that accords more closely with the concept of "restructuring."

No welfare state has been immune from these pressures; all have seen some degree of adjustment. Nonetheless, a kind of consensus seems to be emerging among academic policy analysts that in practice internal political constraints have greatly limited state leaders' scope for cutting back. As Paul Pierson argues, "retrenchment is a difficult and distinctive exercise. Retrenchment advocates must operate on a terrain that the welfare state itself has fundamentally transformed" (1994, 1–2). The growth of constituencies—clients, employees, professionals, and suppliers—around welfare institutions together with the logic of competitive party politics have conspired to hem the politicians in. It is sometimes suggested that the British case, at least under Thatcher, may be somewhat deviant. Gøsta Esping-Andersen (1999) singles out Britain, together only with New Zealand, as exceptions to the general rule, of welfare state adaptation through marginal adjustments. While there might therefore be grounds for expecting overall welfare state retrenchment or restructuring to be more radical and far-reaching in Britain than elsewhere, perhaps the majority of studies conclude that change has been less than radical.[1] Given the continuing need for public and especially electoral support in a broadly competitive democratic system, British political leaders faced constraints similar to those facing other retrenching governments. As Pierson writes, "Even a government like Margaret Thatcher's, possessing centralized political authority and confronting a weak and divided opposition, had to acknowledge the potential for widespread popular disapproval of significant reforms" (1994, 2).

Restructuring and Child Care: Varying the Scope for Retrenchment

If the preceding discussion helps to place our analysis in broad theoretical context, it sheds only limited direct light on the specific case of child care. To understand what has happened in the child care field we need to extend the analysis, drawing in part on the more detailed argument of this welfare state restructuring literature. In the first place, it has been pointed out that the relative balance of retrenchment and resistance has varied between and even within policy areas. Thus, Pierson suggests that retrenchment measures have been most successful where supporting interest groups were weak or government found ways of preventing them from mobilizing. This is of great relevance to the case of child care, where the primary groups affected as "consumers"—mothers and children—lack political organization or leverage. Moreover, to the extent that actual clients of a public service form a potential constituency with a vested interest in its preservation, in this instance the clients were very few in number (though waiting lists for state-provided child care places have always been sizable) and, since child care was provided largely as a welfare function, among the most socially disadvantaged. Likewise, associated professional groups were generally low in status, especially nursery nurses but also nursery teachers compared to other members of the teaching profession.

This made it easier, to the extent that there was anything to cut back in the way of child care provision, for government to do so without major public outcry. In fact, it was less a case of directly cutting back existing government spending— although the number of local authority child care places in England did actually fall, from 28,437 to 27,039 between 1980 and 1991. Rather, all plans for expansion were dropped and there was a new emphasis on the role of private provision, which, as Peter Taylor-Gooby (1996) and others have argued, can be seen as cutting back in a different form. The official government view was now that child care should be "primarily a matter of private arrangement between parents and private and voluntary resources except where there are special needs."[2] During the 1980s, the principal government measure to promote child care provision was a series of "Under-5s Initiatives," in which the DHSS aimed to work directly with voluntary agencies involved in services to younger children, to an extent bypassing the local authorities. The first and biggest scheme ran from 1983 to 1987, followed by an interim small-grants scheme, and then a second initiative from 1989 to 1992. The sums involved were small, intended to be primarily short-term and "pump priming"; only some of the schemes were specifically concerned with child care provision and they were increasingly targeted on families identified as having special needs (Edwards 1992; van der Eyken 1987).

We have seen that from the 1970s on, a somewhat eclectic assortment of voices and organizations had been pressing for greater child care provision; during the 1980s such voices tended to grow, partly as a consequence of increasing feminist mobilization directly around the issue and within the contexts of local government and trade unions. Such voices generally carried little political weight under Thatcher, however. It was only toward the end of the decade, with the eruption of dire warnings of the coming "demographic time bomb," that pressure grew on government to be seen to be doing something about child care. Officially collected statistics seemed to indicate a fall of nearly one-third in the number of children who left school between 1988 and 1993, and though after that numbers were predicted to rise, it would not be to their original levels. Many concluded that both government and employers would need to persuade mothers of young children, and especially those with skills in short supply, to take up paid work. Employers in particular added their voice to pressures on government to take more of a lead on the child care question. In these circumstances, government announced a five-point program in March 1989, designed "to pave the way for the provision of child care which meets the needs of the family" (Cohen 1990, 31). Even then this was largely a symbolic policy gesture: rather than representing a major concession, the actual measures specified were already in effect or planned for. In any event, the demographic scare soon died down with the onset of recession.

Nursery education, it has been suggested, can be seen both as a component of child care and as a quite distinct activity. Although it has always tended to be in the situation of poor relation to the primary, secondary, and tertiary education sectors, nursery education has enjoyed more public support than child care. It is ideologically more compatible with social liberalism and its theme of equal opportunities. At the same time, nursery education provision has catered for the children of middle-class as well as working-class parents. All this might suggest that in the 1980s government would have had less scope for retrenchment with nursery education than with public child care. In fact, under the Thatcher government, although national plans to expand nursery education were rapidly abandoned, there was no additional cutback as such. Indeed, although the 1985 white paper envisaged no growth in provision, in practice numbers of places grew from 130,997 in 1980 to 177,863 in 1991, or an increase of 36 percent. Even so, this was only a modest addition, most of it part-time. There was concern among official inspectors and others at the number of four-year-olds being placed in primary school reception classes, to make up numbers and where the education provided was not necessarily suitable.

Revealingly enough, in 1991 the then secretary of state for education, Kenneth Clarke, described Thatcher's original commitment in 1972 to universal provision of nursery education as a "mistake" (Pugh 1992, 17).

These limits on expansion at a time when nursery education was increasingly in demand by middle-class parents and championed by prestigious experts might appear to lend support to the suggestion cited above that the British state at this point enjoyed an unusual degree of freedom in pursuing its restructuring agenda. It was only subsequently, in the context of heightened party competition—during the 1992 general election campaign both the Liberal and the Labour Parties committed themselves to universal nursery education provision for three- and four-year-olds—that John Major, as the new Conservative prime minister, rather suddenly announced in December 1993 that his government would also set itself the goal of universal provision.

Even then, New Right ideologues, based in the No. 10 policy unit[3] and associated "think tanks," fought a furious rear-guard action. Against the advice of Secretary of State for Education Gillian Shepherd, they succeeded in forcing the adoption of the nursery voucher scheme. This scheme did entail some new government expenditure: it was intended to combine £545 million that would otherwise have gone in grants that local education authorities had the option of using for nursery education with £165 million new funding. It can also be seen very much as part of a drive to restructure the welfare state, in that by subsidizing *demand* for nursery education rather than *supply*, it aimed to increase consumer choice, create more of a competitive market in provision and, to that extent, stimulate the private sector at the expense of the public. Under the scheme, parents of all four-year-olds were to receive vouchers worth £1100 to go toward the cost of nursery education, which, in theory, they could choose to spend on places in state nurseries or in private nurseries or play groups, provided they offered suitable education.

If the adoption of the nursery voucher scheme represented the political forces for restructuring fighting back, the sequel was much more in keeping with the broader Esping-Andersen/Pierson thesis of the difficulties—certainly in the longer run—of imposing cutbacks. Here the problems were above all at the level of implementation. By now the Conservative government was in any case running very scared, in the face of devastating opinion polls and an impending general election. Conservative control of local authorities had been steadily dwindling. The plan had been to launch a series of pilot schemes in twelve local authorities in February 1996, following which the policy would be fully implemented a year later. In any event, the deadline initially set for local authorities to volunteer to take part in the pilot had to be extended and even then only four authorities (three of them Conservative Party members) could be induced to sign up.

The experience of the four pilot projects was studied avidly and for the most part highly critically (AMA 1996; House of Commons Education and Employment Committee 1997). Although this experience was so brief and the policy was soon after abandoned, it is of interest for the present analysis to note some of their findings. The scheme was criticized for being costly to administer, and serious doubts were raised about the feasibility of inspection arrangements to ensure that educational standards were maintained. Most crucially, we have seen that a more or less explicit intention behind the scheme was to encourage private and voluntary providers. State educational institutions, both nursery schools and primary schools currently providing nursery education, certainly feared that they would lose the money the government was holding back from the local government grant; parents would choose to spend the vouchers into which this money had been converted on other forms of provision, especially since the value of the voucher, at £1100, was insufficient to cover the full cost of a state nursery place. In fact, early indications were that between 67 and 75 percent of the amount deducted from the SSA (Standard Security Assessment, the local authority grant) was redeemed in the form of vouchers by maintained (state-funded) schools; this might not satisfy the state-based institutions, but on the other hand it was hardly reassuring to the private sector, where providers were equally afraid of being at a disadvantage. Registered child minders were not normally considered eligible for the scheme. Representatives of the private nurseries accused the primary schools of modifying their admissions policies where necessary and ruthlessly "hoovering up" all the four-year-olds, who were eligible for vouchers, into reception classes.[4] Play group coordinators felt particularly vulnerable, as they lost their four-year-olds to the state sector, struggled with the complexities of administering the vouchers and were judged deficient on academic grounds.

In Britain, then, child care is one area where—to the extent that there is anything to cut back or hive off—government has been able to retrench or restructure with relative impunity. Rather than being an illustration of the general autonomy of the Thatcher government in comparison with governments elsewhere, this says more about the variable room for government maneuvering between different policy areas. Child care has been particularly vulnerable because of the weakness of countervailing interests. The case of nursery education is more equivocal: the Thatcher government did appear able to resist middle-class pressures for increased provision for some time, but under Major it had to yield ground, even though it was under the rubric of nursery education that the most audacious New Right–inspired reform was attempted.

Restructuring the Child Care Policy Context

So far I have concentrated on what could be seen as more direct and immediate ways of achieving retrenchment. But governments can also, in the longer run, seek to alter the *context* of policy: Pierson (1994) calls this "systemic" retrenchment. Most germane to the present discussion, through amendments to both policies and institutional arrangements, governments can modify the form and pattern of policy demands, including the relative strengths of different interests and voices involved in the policy process and the language and terms in which policy debate is framed.

The most obvious instance of this, which has already been touched on, is the way in which the trade unions and the local authority associations, which had both increasingly championed the cause of child care from the early to mid-70s, were demoted as players in the policy process. The trade unions, weakened by attrition of their membership, the showdown with miners in 1984, and a series of constraining acts of Parliament, were also soon being edged out of processes of government consultation (Marsh 1992). The Thatcher government likewise attacked the local councils as another bastion of the Left, reducing their powers, diminishing their financial independence (as described further below), and actually abolishing some of the largest urban authorities including the Greater London Council, which, under the leadership of Ken Livingstone, had incidentally sponsored an unprecedented expansion of public child care provision. The political clout of local authority associations declined in tandem.

A second aspect of this indirect restructuring, then, involved modifying the role of local authorities as child care providers themselves, in what effectively constituted, at least as far as government was concerned, a process of increased centralization of an already centralized system. Traditionally, while the Department of Health issued "guidelines" on the allocation of child care places, central government provided a substantial share of overall funding for local authorities but no earmarked funding for child care services, thereby tending to leave decisions on levels of provision to the authorities' discretion. Within the considerable overall constraints outlined, therefore, there was striking variation in actual rates of provision among the authorities (Moss 1991b). Although during the Thatcher/Major years the powers of local authorities to regulate private provision were strengthened (see below), the effect of some other changes was to chip away at their role in direct provision. By far the most important and increasing constraint was indirect, the steady growth of central control over local government expenditure as a whole. In fact, by 1995–96, according to one source, local authority discretion to deviate from a centrally controlled budget was down to less than 5 percent (Wilding 1997). In these circumstances it became increasingly difficult, even in the most well-disposed local councils, to maintain, let alone expand, funding for child care in the face of so many competing claims on resources.

But the policy context changed in more subtle ways. Under the Conservative Party government, from 1980 to 1991, the number of private nurseries increased more than threefold. While not directly a result of government policy, this increase can be attributed to a growth in demand, in the absence of subsidized publicly provided child care. Play group numbers also grew, though much less dramatically. Furthermore, the emphasis in government child care policy statements on the importance of the private sector's actual and potential contribution enhanced the respectability of these private organizations and helped to legitimate a more prominent policy role for them.

In 1989 Parliament passed the Children Act. This was primarily a much-needed and long-awaited systematization of laws surrounding the respective rights and duties of parents and of the state toward children, but it incorporated and updated measures regarding local authority registration of private nurseries and child minders previously legislated in 1948. Because of the expectations raised in the context of the demographic time-bomb alarm that government would take a stronger lead on child care, the act included more stringent registration and enforcement provisions. Under Section 19, local authorities were now obliged to register and inspect private child care services (where before it had been optional), and new, stricter staff-child ratios were specified. It was largely in response to this development that two new organizations were established representing private nurseries. The Childcare Association, which represented the more affluent end of the market, saw itself primarily as a professional association, emphasizing staff professionalism together with effective commercial management; it lasted only a few years. The National Private Day Nursery Association (NPDNA), which operated more like a conventional interest organization and representing its larger and more heterogeneous membership, is still going strong. Partly as a result of its pressures both direct and through the agency of sympathetic members of Parliament (MPs), between passage of the Children Act and issuance of government guidelines in 1991, and likewise between the guidelines and an official memorandum on their implementation in January 1993, requirements for registration and, in particular, the specified staff-child ratio, were weakened. The NPDNA also protested a couple of years later the anticipated effects of the nursery vouchers scheme; although the scheme was ostensibly designed to encourage private enterprise, the NPDNA argued that in practice it gave the state sector an unfair advantage.

The changing political conjuncture also seemed to favor the Pre-school Playgroup Association. Despite the growth in child minding and in private nurseries and the fact that the number of play groups was leveling off, by the end of the 1980s, they still cared for more children than any other category of provision. In the early 1990s, the government increased its play group subsidy. Thus encouraged, the association began to argue that play groups held the answer to the national child care shortage and, as the focus of government concern shifted from child care to nursery education, in 1994 the association issued a booklet, *The Way Forward*, promoting play groups as the way to realize the new nursery education targets. Subsequently, of course, the association—now renamed the Pre-school Learning Alliance—felt betrayed by the nursery voucher scheme. It successfully resisted a government proposal that play groups should receive voucher money at only half the rate of other providers; nonetheless, full implementation of the scheme would have hit play groups hard.

If government policies helped weaken some child care interests, strengthen others, and spawn yet new ones, they also exacerbated friction among the immensely heterogeneous groupings that made up the "under-fives" lobby. The successful campaign of the NPDNA to dilute nursery registration requirements under the 1989 act enraged other child care groups, as did the claims made in the Pre-school Playgroup Association's *The Way Forward*. Divisions might have been still more damaging had not the nursery voucher scheme helped to unite all groups in opposing it.

It can be argued that restructuring Conservative governments succeeded in changing the policy context in a further significant way, one whose effects have been most enduring. They managed to shift the terms of the debate. Back in the early 1970s, when public pressure for the expansion of child care was growing, this was envisaged largely in terms of increased state (local authority) provision, but by the 1990s not only the feasibility but even the legitimacy of this option was being widely questioned. Here it must be said that, while there were exceptions, the Conservative government as a collective did not directly challenge arguments about working mothers' needs for child care. To that extent, when the National Childcare Campaign (NCC) spoke of "tremendous pressure . . . being exerted on women to make them feel they should remain at home and take the major responsibility for the care of their children," this was quite misleading.

As Julia O'Connor, Ann Shola Orloff, and Sheila Shaver (1999) underline in general terms, while reinvoking some of the economic tenets of classical liberalism, neoliberalism has tended to move beyond its "traditional" family model, which had lingered in social liberalism, to a more consistent, ostensibly "gender-blind" emphasis on individual autonomy. This is partly a consequence of the actual changes in women's economic roles. In Britain, the Thatcher government recognized that the continued growth in the numbers of mothers of young children taking up paid work was a function partly of the decline in male employment and partly of the growing availability of part-time jobs. As time went by, and especially in the wake of the demographic time-bomb panic, government utterances were positively supportive of working mothers. When the issue was (almost unprecedentedly) discussed in the House of Commons in 1994, both Stephen Dorrell (national heritage secretary and later minister of health) and another young Conservative MP, Matthew Carrington, who had recently become fathers, declared that their wives would not be giving up paid employment. Carrington was largely correct in his observation: "The importance of child care is not in dispute in the House. We all accept that we must ensure a diversity of available child care which will become more important as our society develops."[5]

What the Conservative government regularly emphasized, however, was that child care arrangements were essentially a *private* matter, the responsibility of parents, and that private and voluntary agencies should play the central role in providing child care. Although this did not directly challenge working mothers, in a society in which daily life was still largely built around the assumption that mothers rather than fathers would be primarily responsible for child care, and in which the number of lone mothers was steadily growing, it certainly had conservative implications for gender relations and roles, especially in the case of working-class women who simply could not afford to pay for child care at unsubsidized rates. Nonetheless, throughout the 1980s it was increasingly accepted—as a result both of the appeal of neoliberal thinking in a national context in which, as we have argued, liberal values, in a broader sense, remained influential, but also one in which a pragmatic adjustment to what seemed to be the new reality—that the state could not be expected directly to solve growing child care problems through increased public provision, although expectations remained that the state would be the central provider for nursery education.

To illustrate this point, we can trace the shifting terms within which feminist child care demands were voiced over this period. We saw that feminist take-up of the issue was initially fragmentary, but by the early 1980s a more effective national-level campaign was emerging. Among feminists concerned with child care, there were disagreements between those who believed it to be the state's responsibility and those who deeply mistrusted the state and favored some form of community-based provision (even then, if possible, with some state subsidy). Neither tendency would have contemplated child care provision as a for-profit, commercial undertaking. They were indeed uncomfortable about private child minding, which, they rightly recognized, tended to exploit working-class women. They were even resistant for a long time to the idea of workplace nurseries. The NCC, set up in 1980, demanded uncompromisingly "comprehensive, flexible, free, democratically controlled child care facilities funded by the state."

Yet, reflecting the growth of market assumptions, the Working Mothers Association, organized in the mid-80s, was posited more on the notion of consumer choice than any commitment to public provision. The Workplace Nurseries Campaign, initiated at the same time as and closely linked with the trade unions, espoused the notion of a "mixed economy" of child care. It aimed to encourage employers to set up nurseries at the workplace, though subsequently and with the benefit of experience it became more insistent that employers could not be expected to do so without more state support. The more "liberal" Equal Opportunities Commission increasingly recognized the salience of child care in any effective equal opportunities strategy; its discussion paper *The Key to Real Choice* again envisaged a range of providers (Equal Opportunities Commission 1990). Not only did these new, or newly energized, organizations represent the shift in assumptions about the state's child care role, the position of the NCC itself evolved. Together with the Childcare Trust, which it had set up as a charity in 1986, the NCC soon abandoned the demand for free nursery care and came to accept the case for workplace nurseries.

Child Care and Alternative Restructuring Strategies

So far the discussion has tended to focus on child care almost as a self-contained issue, unrelated to wider policy concerns. Child care provision (as opposed to nursery education) was certainly subject to pressures for retrenchment, in the ways described above, under Conservative governments, especially during the Thatcher years. Under Major, however, there was already evident an alternative construction of the child care question, one in which it became a means to help realize other broader restructuring objectives to do with unemployment and welfare dependency. Under the Labour government from 1997 on, this construction, or more precisely a particular "New Labour" rendering of it, has come to influence child care policy and paradoxically to point to the possibilities of significant expansion in provision.

A central objective of the Thatcher government was to reduce welfare dependency, because of its supposed harmful moral effects and, more crucially, as part of the drive to cut back public expenditure. Initially the Government's emphasis, as reflected in the focus of the social security review conducted in the mid-1980s, was on such possible areas of retrenchment as unemployment benefit and pensions. Only toward the end of the decade, and partially influenced by the American polemicist Charles Murray, did government begin to target the growing contingent of lone mothers. Not only were there proportionately more women in this category in Britain than in any other European country, but the percentage of such women in paid employment actually declined from 45 in 1981 to 39 in 1993–94. Legislation in 1990 set up the Child Support Agency (CSA), whose mission was to oblige absent fathers to contribute their share of child maintenance, thus relieving the state coffers. From government's point of view the CSA has been a continuing disaster.[6]

In this context, in 1994, a new child care "disregard" or discount was allowed for low-income families who were already receiving an in-work income supplement (Family Credit). This meant that where parents (mothers or fathers) were in low-paid work and received Family Credit as an in-work benefit to supplement their income, they would be allowed to disregard up to £40 per week spent on child care from their earned income. This was of special relevance to lone mothers, since they figured disproportionately among Family Credit recipients. In keeping with the government's general approach, this measure was designed to increase effective *demand* for child care while leaving questions of *supply* to nongovernment initiative. Its effects were modest in terms of both the sums discounted and the number of families eligible. Nevertheless, it was cautiously welcomed by the child care lobby. The main point being made here, then, is that already under the Conservative government an alternative approach to child care policy, in which child care became an instrument of broader restructuring objectives, was discernible. Although the Labour Party in opposition was critical, in office it extended the disregard—or child care allowance—policy.

Elsewhere in Europe, where child care policies have been seen as an integral element of more strategic national policies having to do with employment, the family, or social equality, governments have pursued more active policies. In Britain, however, the state has hitherto been most prepared to intervene in child care provision only when there was an actual or anticipated shortage of labor, and getting mothers into paid employment was identified as part of the solution, most obviously in the First, and especially the Second, World Wars. The demographic time-bomb scare, threatening labor shortages, triggered government activity, although this was more show than substance. But the present policy context of government interest in child care provision is rather different. It is about *restructuring,* but in a wider sense than that term is sometimes employed—that is, as a response not only to exogenous pressures of economic competition but to internal changes and dysfunctions, including, notably, changes in household composition (the rising number of lone mothers) and patterns of employment (not just fewer traditional "male" jobs, but more women seeking work). In his most recent book, Esping-Andersen has described these changes in the labor market and in households as "revolutionary" (1999, 5). At any rate, in Britain, increasing government recognition of the scale and irreversibility of these domestic changes has had implications for social and economic policy, and thus for child care policy.

While this trend in child care policy was discernible in the last few years of Conservative rule, under Labour it has undergone further development. First, child care has assumed a much more central place in the government's policy statements; or, as Lisa Harker expresses it, there has been a sea-change in the way that child care is positioned as an issue under Labour. As early as July 1997, Chancellor of the Exchequer Gordon Brown declared in his budget speech that henceforth child care would be "an integral part of our economic policy" (quoted in Harker 1998, 459). Second, although the present government, like the last, is anxious to reduce welfare dependency, under New Labour this is articulated in different terms. New Labour tends to reject arguments for increasing equality through greater redistribution which were, up to a point, associated with "old" Labour. Yet it also sharply differentiates itself from the Conservative position. The emphasis now is on the need for equality of opportunity and for social inclusion rather than exclusion. The keys to these objectives are identified as education and, above all, paid work. As Harriet Harman, then minister of social security, declared, "[W]ork is central to the government's attack on social exclusion. . . . Work is not just about earning a living. It is a way of life" (quoted in Lister 1998, 219). Associated with this approach has been the "welfare-to-work" program, a range of policies designed to reduce "welfare dependency" and combat social exclusion through paid work, usually combined with in-work social security benefits, and promoted as a series of "New Deals" for different social groups. The New Deal for single mothers in particular has included the commitment to ensure access to affordable child care provision.

It must be said that government attention to the question of child care is not simply a function of its policy toward lone mothers, or even restructuring more broadly understood. The last general election returned a record number of women MPs to the House of Commons, including 101 Labour women. Child care is an issue whose importance women activists within the Labour Party have long underlined. In the New Labour government, Harriet Harman was not only made minister of social security, she was also appointed as minister for women, chairing a new cabinet subcommittee on women's issues, with administrative underpinning provided by a women's unit. Child care was identified as one of the key issues to be addressed by this unit, which Harman was happy to describe as "feminist." While many have detected more recently a tendency for government to distance itself from any kind of *explicitly* feminist agenda, there has been steady pressure—from women MPs, from trade unions, even from Cherie Blair, the prime minister's wife—to promote a range of more family-friendly employment policies such as paid parental leave.

The 1988 green paper *Meeting the Childcare Challenge* began by insisting that child care "has been neglected for too long," and depicted improved child care as both a means of promoting greater equality of training and employment opportunity, especially for mothers, and an essential component of measures to support the family and children, by helping parents who have to juggle paid work and family responsibilities. Thus it went beyond a narrow welfare approach to include a more generous conception of equality of opportunity, together with the needs of children.

The new importance attached to child care in government policy statements, and the way in which it is portrayed as potentially making a vital contribution to welfare-state restructuring à la New Labour, appear to provide a major new opportunity for expansion of the child care services. Yet the details of the green paper were less impressive or reassuring than were the statements of principle. There was, for instance, a welcome recognition of the need to raise the status of child care workers (though this need has been acknowledged for some time), but the chief means envisaged—apart from instituting a national minimum wage—was through establishing a national framework of training qualifications. The government no longer proposed leaving the determination of child care entirely to the private sector; rather, there would be *partnership* among national and local public bodies and a whole range of private or voluntary agencies. The implication was that the public authorities, as "enablers" and "facilitators," would take the lead. Even so, funding arrangements to back up these proposals indicated distinct limits to the government's contribution. The bulk of funds earmarked directly for services themselves were to go to the after-school schemes. There was commitment, whose problematic implications for child care are discussed further below, to ensure and fund nursery education for all four year olds. Building on the Conservative government's approach, provision for younger children would mainly be stimulated from the demand side. A new working families tax credit scheme, providing child care tax credit that is more generous and extends to families further up the income distribution than under previous child care disregard arrangements, actually became operative in October 1999 and has been augmented since.

Local child care "partnerships" have been set up to review provision and need in their area and submit forward-looking plans. These partnerships include representatives of the full range of local providers, though, as noted, in practice the local authority tends to take the leading role. One objective that appears to have met with some success has been to encourage the different providers to work together, in contrast to the disharmony sown by the Conservatives' voucher scheme.

From the standpoint specifically of child care, however, a complicating issue has been the parallel development of nursery education policy. As noted, the Labour government, while renouncing "vouchers," has sustained the Conservative pledge, and indeed the funding commitment, to provide nursery education for all four-year-olds. As early as June 1997, local education authorities (that is, the education departments of the local authorities) were being asked to establish Early Years Partnerships with agencies in the voluntary and private sector, in order to produce Early

Years Development Plans that would demonstrate how all four-year-olds in their area could be provided with a half-day nursery place by September 1998. While no longer taking the form of a voucher provided to parents but rather allocated directly to providers via the local education authority, the sum of £1100 was still to be available for the nursery education of each child of eligible age. The local authorities got to work with alacrity (many had already made a start in anticipation of the voucher scheme) and so successful was this policy in meeting its target that the minister for education, David Blunkett, announced that the next stage would be to expand nursery education to cover three-year-olds. When the new child care policy was launched in March 1998 it was in a sense grafted onto this Early Years policy. The existing local partnerships were now expanded so as to constitute Early Years Development and Childcare Partnerships. Generally this meant that, within the local authority, child care was brought under the auspices, if it was not located there already, of the education departments—in itself not such a bad thing since social service departments tended to see child care in strictly welfare terms—but was again in danger of being tacked onto an up-and-running and moreover, mandatory, nursery education policy.

The first partnership child care plans were submitted to government early in 1999, but as yet no overview of these plans has been made available. It is too early, then, to say for sure what difference the new national child care policy can make. There is no doubting the commitment of a number of the politicians and officials involved in driving the policy, but given the existing fragmentation and poverty of provision and government's very limited funding intentions, they have their work cut out for them.[7]

Conclusion

While welfare-state restructuring in Britain has had implications for child care policy, the relationship is not a simple or singular one. In the mid-1970s, when the Labour government was faced with a public expenditure "crisis," the very modest plans to expand both public child care and nursery education provision were among the first casualties of retrenchment. Rather than being rationalized as a new policy departure, this was presented as an unfortunate postponement of a fundamentally sound policy. Under Thatcher, there was a more concerted attack on the principle of public preschool provision, through reduced public funding, through an insistence upon the essentially private character of child care arrangements to be determined by the interplay of parental preferences, the market, and the voluntary sector and, less directly or immediately, through the effects of government policy on the articulation and organization of political interests around the child care issue. Although much of this policy momentum persisted under Major, growing pressure to extend nursery education, combined with the government's greater vulnerability, contributed to a new nursery education initiative from 1995, even though this then became the opportunity for the supremely market-oriented voucher experiment. Beginning under the Conservatives, however, child care was also taking on a new significance within a wider restructuring strategy of reducing welfare dependence in a context of changing employment patterns. New Labour's approach clearly differs from the redistributive politics of "old" Labour; it is, implicitly at least, reconciled to the need for restructuring, but rejects the "residualist" project of the Conservatives in favor of a new emphasis on empowerment and social inclusion. The intention seems to be for child care, largely supplied by the private and voluntary sectors, though with some indirect state funding through selective subsidising of demand, to play a much more central role in enabling mothers to go out to work. The goal is worthy, but one fears its realization may founder on the rocks of practicality.

Notes

1. Other examples include Glennerster (1992) and Le Grand (1990), both cited in George (1996), 13.

2. John Patten, *Official Report* (*Hansard*), February 18, 1985. London, House of Commons; cited in Moss (1991a, 133).

3. The No. 10 Policy Unit is made up of selected civil servants at 10 Downing Street, the prime minister's residence, who advise the prime minister.

4. These are intended for "rising-fives" children who are beginning primary school but are not yet five years old.

5. The debate on child care was initiated by then Labour front-bench spokeswoman, Harriet Harman, in the context of amendments to the 1994 Finance Bill. See Commons debate, *Hansard*, 19.4.94.

6. The CSA was set up too quickly, with insufficient staff and training and quite unrealistic targets.

7. For a fuller discussion of some of these issues, see the final chapter of Randall (2000).

References

AMA (Association of Metropolitan Authorities). 1996. *Education Vouchers for Early Years: The State of Play*. London: AMA.

Bruegel, Irene. 1983. "Women's Employment, Legislation and the Labour Market." In *Women's Welfare, Women's Rights*, ed. Jane Lewis. London: Croom-Helm.

Cohen, Bronwen. 1990. *Caring for Children: The 1990 Report*. London: Family Policy Studies Centre.

Department for Education and Employment. 1998. *Meeting the Childcare Challenge*. Cmnd 3959. London: The Stationery Office.

Edwards, Rosalind. 1992. *Beginnings: The Department of Health's New Under-Fives Initiative 1989–1992*. London: National Children's Bureau.

Equal Opportunities Commission. 1990. *The Key to Real Choice*. Manchester: EOC.

Esping-Anderson, Gøsta. 1996. "After the Golden Age?" In *Welfare States in Transition*, ed. G. Esping-Andersen. London: Sage.

_____. 1999. *Social Foundations of Postindustrial Economies*. Oxford: Oxford University Press.

European Commission Child Care Network. 1990. "Child Care in the European Communities 1985–1990," *Women of Europe*, supplement no. 31.

Garrett, Myra. 1975. "Girls and Boys Come Out to Play." *Red Rag* 8: 6–8.

George, Vic. 1996. "The Future of the Welfare State" In *European Welfare Policy,* ed. Vic George and Peter Taylor-Gooby. London: Macmillan.

Glennerster, Howard. 1992. *Paying for Welfare: The 1990s*. Hemel Hempstead: Harvester Wheatsheaf.

Harker, Lisa. 1998. "A National Child Care Strategy: Does It Meet the Child Care Challenge?" *Political Quarterly* 69: 458–63.

House of Commons Education and Employment Committee. 1997. *The Operation of the Nursery Voucher Scheme*. London: Stationery Office.

Le Grand, Julian. 1990. "The State of Welfare." In *The State of Welfare*, ed. J. Hills. Oxford: Oxford University Press.

Lister, Ruth. 1998. "From Equality to Social Inclusion: New Labour and the Welfare State." *Critical Social Policy* 55: 215–25.

O'Connor, Julia S., Ann Shola Orloff, and Sheila Shaver. 1999. *States, Markets, Families*. Cambridge: Cambridge University Press.

Marsh, David. 1992. *The New Politics of British Trade Unions: Union Power and the Thatcher Legacy*. Basingstoke: Macmillan.

Moss, Peter. 1991a. "Day Care in the UK." In *Day Care for Young Children*, ed. Edward C. Melhuish and Peter Moss. London: Routledge.

_____. 1991b. "Day Care Policy and Provision in Britain." In *Current Issues in Day Care for Young Children*, ed. Peter Moss and Edward Melhuish. London: HMSO.

Pierson, Paul. 1994. *Dismantling the Welfare State?* Cambridge: Cambridge University Press.

Pugh, Gillian. 1992. "An Equal Start for All Our Children?" Times Educational Supplement/ Greenwich Lecture.

Randall, Vicky. 1995. "The Irresponsible State? The Politics of Child Care Provision in Britain." *British Journal of Political Science* 25: 327–48.

_____. 1996. "Feminism and Child Care." *Journal of Social Policy* 25: 485–505.

_____. 2000. *The Politics of Child Care in Britain*. Oxford: Oxford University Press.

Riley, Denise. 1983. *War in the Nursery*. London: Virago.

Ruggie, Mary. 1984. *The State and Working Women: A Comparative Study of Britain and Sweden*. Princeton, N.J.: Princeton University Press.

Taylor-Gooby, Peter. 1996. "The United Kingdom: Radical Departures and Political Consensus." In *European Welfare Policy*, ed. Vic George and Peter Taylor-Gooby. London: Macmillan.

Tizard, Jack, Peter Moss, and Jane Perry. 1976. *All Our Children: Pre-school Services in a Changing Society*. London: Temple Smith for New Society.

Van der Eyken, W. 1987. *The DHSS Under-Fives Initiative 1983–1987: Final Report*. London: DHSS.

Wilding, Paul. 1997. "The Welfare State and the Conservatives." *Political Studies* 45: 716–26.

CHAPTER 10

More Can Be Less:
Child Care and Welfare Reform in the United States

Denise Urias Levy and Sonya Michel

In the United States today, child care provision is divided into two distinct sectors, public and private. Such an arrangement is not, of course, surprising in a welfare state regime that has been categorized as "liberal" (Esping-Andersen 1990). Nor should it be surprising to discover that this dual system has produced deep inequities in the quality, accessibility, and affordability of child care services. What is perhaps unexpected is that, despite the overall inadequacy of the system, the rate of full-time labor-force participation among American women, including mothers, is currently one of the highest in the Organization for Economic Cooperation and Development (OECD) countries.[1] This can be explained by a congeries of factors, including the demand for labor produced by the general upsurge in the U.S. economy (a trend that may now be reversing), relatively well-enforced antidiscrimination legislation in the area of employment, and, since 1996, a shift in public assistance policy "from welfare to workfare" that has pushed thousands of low-skilled women into the labor force. The fact that the majority of U.S. mothers, including those with very young children, are employed outside the home should *not*, however, be taken as an indication that, despite its flaws, the American child care system "works." Rather, it suggests that wage-earning parents at all income levels have learned to "make do"—to cope with the everyday stresses and long-term consequences of inadequate provisions, but at a significant toll on the quality of their private lives and the lives of their children (Hochschild 1997).

In both the public and private sectors, several different types of services may be available, ranging from in-home care to formal child care centers,[2] but the methods of payment differ. In the private sector, middle- and upper-income parents choose and pay for services directly, while in the public sector, poor and low-income parents must find child care centers or family day care providers that will accept state-issued vouchers to be reimbursed at fixed rates, or they may, in some instances, receive reimbursement for individual arrangements with kith or kin. While it appears that the private sector is wholly self-supporting, in fact it, too, is subsidized indirectly by the federal government through a dependent care tax credit and incentives to employers who establish child care services. Perhaps the more salient difference is that in the private sector, the state supports the independent, freely made decisions of parents to place their children in child care in order to seek paid employment or pursue educational or vocational goals, while in the public sector, the state subsidizes child care as part of a mandatory system of job training and employment (workfare) for parents seeking public assistance. In this instance, child care is used as a lever of a compulsory public policy.

This chapter will first briefly review the history of child care policy that preceded recent developments, highlighting public and private developments and the relationship between early childhood education and child care. The chapter goes on to analyze the politics of the linkage between child care and workfare and the ongoing opposition to universal policy. In the final sections, we examine in detail the deployment of contemporary public policy within the context of welfare reform, focusing on its impact on poor and low-income mothers and children and the implications for universal provisions.

American Child Care: A Very Brief History

The current arrangement of child care in the U.S. is the outcome of a long and vexed history of social provision characterized, as Sonya Michel has argued elsewhere (1999), by a strong man-as-breadwinner orientation (Lewis 1992), and both fueled by and constitutive of the policy logic typical of a public/private, liberal, or "residual" welfare state regime. Throughout its history, child care—like much of American social policy—has also reflected deep racial and class divisions. Beginning with the charitable day nurseries of the nineteenth century, child care in the U.S. has almost always been targeted toward the poor as a means of "helping them help themselves." Although the federal government took responsibility for providing services during periods of national crisis—first for the children of the unemployed during the Great Depression and then for children of defense workers during World War II—these policies did not lead to permanent public, universal provisions. For several decades after the war, the issue of state-sponsored child care lay more or less dormant. It was not until the 1960s and 1970s that it once again appeared on the public agenda, this time in conjunction with efforts to reform public assistance. In a series of amendments to the Social Security Act, the U.S. Congress foreshadowed the linkage between public provisions and mandatory employment that would become law in 1996.

The lack of public child care notwithstanding, the postwar decades witnessed a significant rise in employment among mothers, including those with preschool children, which in turn prompted the growth of market-based child care services. This trend was aided by several federal measures, including the child care tax deduction passed in 1954 (and converted to a child care tax credit in 1972), as well as a variety of incentives to employers to set up or sponsor services for their employees, beginning in 1962. Market-based services were of several types: while all charged fees, some were commercial enterprises, while others were run by voluntary or non-profit organizations (often denominational), many of which transformed existing part-day nursery schools into full-day child care centers in response to community demand.

The place of nursery schools in this history bears further explanation. Nursery schools, along with kindergartens, followed their own trajectory in the United States, one that was (in contrast to some of the other cases discussed in this volume) quite distinct from that of child care—and deliberately so (for a full discussion, see Michel 1999, chaps. 1–3). As part of the early childhood education/child development movement, nursery school and kindergarten innovators, advocates, and practitioners were among the first groups of American women who self-consciously sought to professionalize, and as such did not want their movement to become tainted with the odor of charity and poverty that clung (literally, in some cases) to the day nurseries. With their impetus, early childhood education forged ahead in the early twentieth century, leaving child care behind. As kindergartens were incorporated into the public school system and nursery schools (mostly fee-based) became the darlings of the middle class, day nurseries and child care centers gained a reputation for being "custodial warehouses" that only the poor would use as a last resort.

Early childhood educators believed that children of all classes should have the benefits of nursery schools, and in the 1930s they convinced New Deal policymakers to create a network of federally supported Emergency Nursery Schools for the children of the unemployed; these were, however, dismantled when the Depression was over. It was not until the mid-1960s that reformers were finally able to establish a permanent public program of early education for the poor: Head Start. The most successful and enduring of President Lyndon Baines Johnson's Great Society programs, Head Start has repeatedly demonstrated its educational value, but because of the way it was conceived and funded, it has not, until quite recently, been considered part of the public *child care* system. As we shall see below, the fact that it had its own funding stream has, no doubt, helped preserve Head Start, but this has also created problems of coordination with other public programs for young children.

Linking Child Care and Workfare

The 1960s saw several initiatives to reform public child care, all of which grew out of political concerns about the sharp rise in—and changing racial composition of—the welfare rolls. Because of deeply entrenched practices of racial segregation and discrimination throughout the country but especially in the south, the federal public assistance program Aid to Families with Dependent Children (AFDC) had, since its establishment in the 1930s, served primarily white families—a profile that hardly reflected the racial composition of America's poor (Bell 1965, pt. 1). But starting in the late 1950s, impoverished African Americans, as a result of a series of court cases brought by the strengthening civil rights movement, began to gain access to the assistance to which they were entitled by federal law (the following discussion is drawn from Michel 1999, 243–47; see also Mink 1998, chap. 2, and Kornbluh 2000, pt. 2). Between 1960 and 1967, the proportion of AFDC recipients had shifted from 86 percent white to 46 percent nonwhite.

AFDC had initially been based on the principle that the state should support mothers whose families lacked a male breadwinner so that they could remain at home caring for their children—a principle that fit well with America's general adherence to the "male-breadwinner" logic. As long as the majority of AFDC recipients were white, the policy proceeded without challenge.[3] But as the racial balance shifted, many politicians, especially those from the south, bridled at the idea that African-American women—who had "always" worked—were now going to receive public support to remain "idle." Not coincidentally, a new congressional consensus began to form around the idea that mothers should now be encouraged to become "self-sufficient"[4] and that child care would be a critical element of any policy designed to free mothers to pursue work or job training.

Congressional initiatives to link child care and welfare first produced the Social Security Amendments of 1962, which provided grants-in-aid to state welfare agencies for the development and support of licensed child care agencies (the following discussion is drawn from Levy 2000, chap. 3). Notably, these measures were intended to "encourage" welfare recipients to become self-sufficient, but they did not make work mandatory. Not so the 1967 amendments that created the Work Incentives program (WIN), granting child care funding to states that expelled welfare recipients who rejected job offers—including mothers, regardless of the age of their children. Despite the harsh tone of this legislation, Congress soon became aware that there were nowhere near enough child care facilities to serve every mother who was supposed to work—regardless of how much funding was made available. This fact emboldened liberal opposition to requiring mothers of young children to work or enroll in job training and led to a de facto abandonment of the program.

In 1969 a new approach to poverty emerged from the administration of Richard Nixon: the Family Assistance Plan (FAP) (Levy 2000, 18–19; Michel 1999, 249–51; Kornbluh 2000, chap. 3). This bill was intended to replace WIN with a guaranteed annual income and significantly expand job training and child care facilities. Simultaneously, congressional Democrats proposed a series of measures, including the Comprehensive Child Care Development Act of 1971, designed to increase and improve child care provisions for *all* American families. Nixon, while clearly favoring child care for the poor, opposed the liberals' universal proposal and vetoed the bill when it reached his desk. In the meantime, the FAP foundered in Congress because of disagreements over the principle of a guaranteed income and the amount of funding it would entail.

For the next two decades, the administration's bifurcated stance cast a long shadow over child care initiatives. Child care legislative initiatives were muted for most of the 1970s and suffered in the 1980s from growing disagreement about the role of government in family life. These disagreements prevented passage of comprehensive or universal child care legislation and continued to restrict federal support for child care to policies that served as work-incentive instruments within the context of welfare reform. Even those, however, fell short of their potential because state and local bureaucrats failed to implement them by drawing down federal funds and organizing adequate services (Michel 1999, 251–59).

The link between child care and welfare reform was further reinforced in 1988, when President Ronald Reagan signed into law the Family Support Act (FSA). This measure rephrased the principles underlying public assistance by articulating the view that welfare should be based upon a "social contract" that emphasized the mutual obligation and responsibility of both poor parents and the government. Under this contract, parents would be primarily financially responsible for their children, but the government would assist by granting benefits (cash subsidies, health insurance) to low-income, two-parent families while channeling the adults into the Job Opportunities and Basic Skills (JOBS) program.

The JOBS program reinstated the principles underpinning the ill-fated WIN program but attempted to make them work by emphasizing education and training and expanding support services like child care to facilitate participation. It also extended WIN's reach to new groups of recipients by *mandating* the participation of mothers with children aged three to five and of all teenage mothers, irrespective of the age of their children, who had not completed high school and had no work experience (these two groups had previously been exempted from most work mandates). On paper, the new program implied significant new commitments to provide child care to AFDC recipients who pursued education or training designed to improve their employability.

Two programs were created to fulfill these commitments: AFDC-Child Care and Transitional Child Care (TCC). The first required states to guarantee child care to any AFDC recipient who participated in state-approved education or training activities or who accepted or retained employment. The second required states to guarantee child care for up to twelve months to families who had received AFDC and its child care benefits in the past but were no longer eligible due to increased hours of employment or earnings. Although there was evidence at the time that these commitments could not be met within the existing structure of child care services, legislators supported the FSA as an alternative to a more comprehensive piece of child care legislation then pending in Congress, the Act for Better Child Care (ABC, discussed below). Indeed, later studies showed that both programs in many ways failed to live up to the commitments made in the law.

By the mid-1990s, only about 13 to 15 percent of the eligible children of adult enrollees in JOBS were being served—although three-fourths of the programs claimed to be providing child care subsidies or helping to arrange child care for all or almost all participants who needed assistance (U.S. General Accounting Office 1995a and 1995b). This was in part due to parents' difficulties in finding child care providers who were accessible (given the shortage of public transportation) and available during nontraditional hours of work, or flexible enough to accommodate part-time JOBS participation hours (most child care centers operate—and charge fees—on the assumption that slots will be filled full-time). The shortage of facilities led to the creation of long waiting lists which, in some states, included thousands of children (U.S. General Accounting Office 1995b). Also, because funds were scarce, states in practice often exempted welfare recipients from work requirements or limited participation in training programs to parents with school-aged children or those who could easily find free child care.

The Opposition to Universal Child Care

The problem of child care in the late 1980s was not, however, limited to the welfare population. By this time, the proportion of mothers with children under fifteen participating in the labor force had grown to 60 percent. In 1988, more than 10.5 million children under age six, including nearly 6.6 million infants and toddlers under age three, had wage-earning mothers. Yet the supply of child care remained small and the range of options limited, with cost a constraint affecting both factors. For low-income two-earner families who were not eligible for public subsidies, child care for just one child could consume more than a quarter of their total household income, 43 percent if they needed full-time infant care. This in turn limited parental options. While 31 percent of mothers of higher socioeconomic status were likely to enroll their children in a child care center or preschool, only 18 percent of low-income parents turned to such services. Within this latter group, relatives (other than one of the parents) were the most common source of care, which meant that a large percentage of children were in unlicensed home settings, often under inadequate conditions of safety, and with limited educational and developmental opportunities (Hayes, Palmer, and Zaslow 1990, 159–62; Michel 1999, 259–64).

Since the late 1960s, child care advocates had been trying to make a case for comprehensive child care legislation as the adequate response to these trends, and to convince policymakers that the care and education of all young children—not just the poor—should become a public responsibility. They attempted to explain that the existing system was inadequate to meet the needs of all parents, including those who could afford to pay more for child care. Some Congressional leaders were responsive to these concerns,[5] and many governors began to take an interest in child care issues, including then governor Bill Clinton of Arkansas, who was chairman of the National Governors' Association (Hofferth 1993).

Despite the visibility of and interest in child care issues in the late 1980s, proposals for comprehensive legislation could not gain the necessary traction in Congress. For example, in 1987, supporters introduced the ABC bill; this was debated well into 1988, even after the FSA was passed, and although it had the endorsement of more than 135 national groups, it met with fierce opposition from legislators, who remained divided about creating a new federal program—especially after President George H. W. Bush threatened to veto any child care law envisioning such an action.

If passed, the ABC bill would have dramatically shifted the political rationale for public child care by defining eligibility for subsidies on the basis of earnings rather than enrollment in welfare, using the state median income as a cutoff with a sliding fee scale. In addition, it would have established a federal funding stream for child care while preserving parental choice regarding the type of provision and offering a diverse delivery system using grants, contracts, and vouchers; and maintaining Social Services Block Grant funding for child care. The bill also mandated federal child care standards and required each state to develop its own child care plan, coordinate resources, establish an interagency committee of all bodies concerned with child care, and strengthen basic health and safety protections.

At the root of much opposition to the bill were political differences about the proper approach to funding child care programs. Democrats wanted to create federal grants to states to subsidize low-income families while improving child care for *all* families, while Republicans favored a combination of tax credits and vouchers, with benefits being targeted at low-income families only. In addition, some Republicans preferred policies that encouraged (nonwelfare) women to stay home with their children, at least while the children were very young. Finally, Democrats wanted to create national standards for child care, while Republicans argued that standards should remain a state responsibility.[6]

After two more years of introducing and debating dozens of competing child care bills without finding common ground, legislators were able to settle on a compromise child care package that retained many aspects of the original ABC bill but accommodated Republican demands for devolution to the states. The winning legislation, finally passed in 1990, had four major components: in addition to expanding funding for Head Start, it established a new entitlement program that expanded child care assistance under Title IV-A for families "at-risk" of falling into welfare dependency (At-Risk Child Care, or ARCC); expanded the Earned Income Tax Credit to low-income families (to alleviate the burden of their child care costs); and initiated a new program called the Child Care and Development Block Grant (CCDBG).

CCDBG allocated states the funds to create child care for eligible children, subject to a sliding scale based on family income.[7] Although all children under thirteen in families with incomes below 75 percent of the state's median income were *eligible* for services, they were not *guaranteed*. Indeed, funds were relatively modest. While the original ABC bill had envisaged resources on the order of $2.5 billion per year, Congress authorized only $750 million for 1991. Funding rose to $925 million in 1993, but the scope of the program remained limited. In 1991, only 571,095 children were being served, whereas an estimated ten million or more children under age thirteen were living below the federal poverty level (Levy 2000, 27), and millions more at the upper end of the sliding scale might have benefited from child care services.

The legislative process that produced CCDBG underscored two important lessons about U.S. politics. First, it showed that attempts to create comprehensive federal programs for child care outside the scope of welfare reform would lead to profound and irreconcilable controversies among the two parties; but second, it revealed that a block grant approach could provide a framework to accommodate this conflict. By giving states the responsibility for making difficult policy decisions, with outcomes that could be thought of as best reflecting local preferences, the act still allowed for an incremental move toward universal provisions.[8]

Child Care and Welfare Reform

While the 1990 legislation temporarily slowed debates over child care and welfare, it fully addressed neither issue. Thus both returned to the congressional agenda in 1996, with child care presented as part of the larger effort to reform public assistance. In passing the Personal Responsibility and Work Opportunity Reconciliation Act (PRWORA) in 1996, the United States initiated a major restructuring of its principal program of social assistance for lone mothers and low-income parents, Aid to Families with Dependent Children (AFDC). Instead of supporting such families to care for their own children at home, as AFDC had done, the new program requires a majority to seek paid employment within a specified length of time and sets a lifetime limit for receiving public assistance.[9] Following the trend toward "federalism" or devolution to the states initiated by President Reagan and exemplified in measures like the CCDBG, the measure provided funding through two major block grants to the states, one for temporary (cash) assistance to needy families (TANF), the other for child care (the Child Care and Development Fund, or CCDF).

In crafting the legislation, Congress was at first reluctant to confront the unprecedented demand for child care that would inevitably be generated by PRWORA's employment mandates. When "workfare" mandates become fully operational in 2002, an estimated one million children (in addition to the 3.3 million low-income children already being served under previous laws) will require subsidized services (Long and Clark 1997, 5 and 10, table 3; U.S. Bureau of the Census 1998). But after President Clinton twice vetoed the bill for lacking adequate funding for child care, Congress added $4 billion over five years to the child care block grant. Despite the additional funding, however, the new child care system has proven to be less than workable. There are a number of reasons for this: in addition to a lack of sufficient funding, there is wide variation in the bureaucratic practices that determine access to child care at the local level; inadequate compensation and benefits for child care providers, coupled with minimal support for improving program quality; and difficulties in coordinating child care with other public programs for early childhood education. We will examine each of these in turn.

Funding

Even with the additional spending authorized by Congress, there is not enough money in the system to care for all the children in low-income families who are by law *eligible* for, if not *entitled* to, subsidized child care. According to the law, all children under age thirteen in families with incomes below 85 percent of the state's median income are eligible for services. Currently, states can offer services to only a fraction of those who are eligible. According to one recent estimate, although current federal expenditures have climbed to nearly $12 billion, this amount is only about half of what is needed to meet the full demand (Democratic Staff 2001).

Under the terms of PRWORA, several preexisting sources of federal funding for child care for poor and low-income families were consolidated into one block grant to individual states—the CCDF. Although the CCDF potentially makes available more child care funding than all previous federal sources combined (the $2.97 billion appropriated for this fund in 1997 represented an increase of $600 million, or 27 percent, over the total federal child care funding for the previous year),[10] it is designed in such a way that a significant portion of the funds are controlled by state-level politics. Funds are divided into three categories: mandatory, matching, and discretionary, with $1.2 billion apportioned among the states based on their previous federal (Title IV-A) funding (see n. 3), $0.77 billion based on states maintaining their previous Title IV-A matches (the so-called maintenance-of-effort or MOE requirement), and an annually appropriated amount of discretionary spending ($1 billion for 1997), which is distributed according to states' economic and demographic features.[11]

In such a structure, state-level decision making becomes the key determinant of how much child care will be available and how it will be distributed. A number of factors—all of which vary from one state to another—come into play. For example, two analysts of child care policy argue that these decisions depend on level of need (which is related to child poverty), fiscal capacity (ability to tax; per capita income), and fiscal effort (willingness to devote resources to a service such as child care)—in other words, political climate (Douglas and Flores 1998). Denise Urias Levy (2000) points to a cluster of "policy levers" used with great flexibility by states that determine the distribution of provisions among poor and low-income families and also affect the shape and content of public child care overall.

A full understanding of all the state or subnational political contexts that determine child care funding decisions requires discussion of a large body of empirical research that is beyond the scope of this chapter, since each one is unique (for detailed analysis, see Levy 2000, chap. 5). We can, however, offer a few generalizations. A state's political disposition enters the formula at two points, one historical, one current. This means that to a certain extent a state's current funding status may be delimited or "contained" by its previous funding history. Levy (2000) has found that, to some extent, current levels reflect historical trends regarding social spending: states that have tended to be liberal (in the North American sense) in the past, such as those of the northeast, midwest, and far west, and those of a more conservative bent, such as those of the southeast, have (with a few notable exceptions) generally both remained true to type on this issue.[12]

Yet, prior history is not all-determining, and current conditions can still have telling effects. For example, most states, by refusing to spend their own money for child care, stand to lose a significant proportion of their potential federal funding as well, thus reducing their total budget for child care.[13] At the same time, *every* state stands to gain by maximizing its matching funds, with an average increase of 50 percent (Long and Clark 1997, 3). In many states, however, this would require increasing its own child care funding by 70 percent or more—something their funding histories suggest they may well be reluctant to do. In 1994, for example, twenty states fell short of allocating sufficient matching funds to draw down their maximum Title-IVA funding (Long and Clark 1997, 9–10, table 2), while twenty-one allocated enough to draw down the full amount (Adams and Poersch 1996).

Whatever its political predilections, a state's current fiscal capacity and the level of child care need also come into play. As Toby Douglas and Kimura Flores (1998) point out, "many of the states with higher rates of child poverty tended to have low fiscal capacities" (2). Thus states like Mississippi, Louisiana, New Mexico, and West Virginia, which rank 50th, 49th, 48th, and 47th, respectively, in terms of child poverty, also rank low in terms of per capita personal income (50th, 40th, 47th, and 49th). Three of these states also rank low or medium-low in terms of "fiscal effort" (willingness to tax): Louisiana (44th), Mississippi (29th), and West Virginia (28th). In sharp contrast, New Mexico ranks 5th on this scale (reflecting the political strength of its prominent Latino/a contingent). To take a somewhat different example, New York state, which is 40th in child poverty, ranks very high (4th) in terms of per capita income and *first* in fiscal effort (Douglas and Flores 1998, 8, table 2). Taken together, these three factors can either reinforce one another (as in the cases of Louisiana, Mississippi, and West Virginia) or offset one another (as in New Mexico and New York), but if fiscal capacity is too low, as in New Mexico, the effect of even high fiscal effort is minimized.

An accounting of total allocations, however, tells only part of the story. As Levy (2000, chap. 4) has discovered, states can, by manipulating certain policy levers, fine-tune the amount and quality of child care available, and how and to whom it is distributed; indirectly, these three levers can affect parental choice and access to quality child care. The levers themselves comprise income eligibility limits, parent copayments, and maximum payment rates to providers. According to the law, families earning incomes up to 85 percent of the state median income (SMI), whose heads are working or preparing to work, are eligible for child care assistance under the CCDF.[14] States may lower the income ceiling, thus reducing the number of families to be served. About half of the states have adopted a level equal to or lower than 65 percent of the SMI (in twenty-one, it falls between 40 and 59 percent). Of the remainder, about half set it between 65 and 80 percent, and only eight at the maximum rate of 85 percent (Levy 2000, 43). In calculating these ceilings, many states sought rough equivalency with the federal poverty level for a family of three, which was generally considerably lower than the SMIs.[15]

States' discretion to "manipulate" this policy lever and adjust it to their own needs and preferences has also been shown to be greater with the 1996 reform. The great autonomy granted by the reform led to a broader spectrum of choices. Of particular interest is the variety of approaches taken by states to deal with the insertion of very low-income families into the new program. Moreover, there has been an increased dispersion in eligibility limits established by states as well as a general decline of such limits in several states (Levy 2000, 46–51).

With regard to copayments, the law states that each family is supposed to contribute to the cost of child care services, although this requirement may be waived for families at or below the federal poverty level, or under special circumstances. All but eight states have some sort of waiver in place, but regulations vary widely. Thus, in three states, a single parent with a child in center-based care, earning $12,000 a year, would pay nothing, while in six others, she would pay more than $100 per month (Levy 2000, 52–56).[16] Here, too, there is considerable variation in the approaches taken by states when they designed their child care copayment policies, with a clear indication that copayment levels are used as a lever to limit the number of families served by the system. The higher the level of copayments, the more money available for child care and thus the wider the distribution of services over the eligible population. If the level of copayments is too high, however, eligible families will be unable to meet it and instead will seek alternative—and often lower-quality—forms of care.

The third policy lever, maximum payment rates to providers, affects the supply, accessibility to needy families to subsidized child care, and quality of services. High rates are likely to help in making more centers—and centers of better quality—available to children. However, given budgetary constraints, they may limit the number of children served, since the cost per child is likely to be higher. Under previous public programs, states were required to set payment rates at 75 percent of the local market rates for services, based on biannual surveys. The current law grants states flexibility to establish whatever payment rates they consider "fair" and conducive to equal access, and, until 1998, did not require regular surveys (Levy 2000, 64). In 1998 more than half the states failed to meet the 75th percentile standard as calculated for 1996 (Greenberg, Lombardi, and Schumacher 2000, 7). While the regulations now mandate regular surveys, they set no specific level for minimum (or maximum) payments; rates can thus range from less than $300 per month in the lowest five states to more than $600 in the highest five. Presumably, higher rates of compensation will promote the creation of centers and ensure their quality, but, given budgetary constraints, they may end up limiting the number of children being served, since the cost per child will be higher. By the same token, however, lower payment rates allow states to stretch child care dollars over a larger number of children, but they may also lower the supply of child care by deterring existing centers from opening up slots to subsidized children and discouraging individuals from becoming home-based providers. In addition, they depress staff salaries and benefits, leading to high turnover and lower quality overall.

States have another policy lever in the area of work requirements; that is, they can ease their own child care burden as well as that of TANF families by offering more latitude to parents with newborns and infants. Infant care is not only scarce but costly (because adult to child ratios are supposed to be quite high—normally no more than two infants to one adult), and some states have reasoned that it is cheaper to exempt the parents of newborns from mandatory employment or training rather than pay for infant care (providing, in effect, a form of paid maternity or parental leave, which is otherwise not mandated by law in the United States). Federal law allows states to provide such exemptions until a child reaches the age of one, but here again, states vary, with some interpreting long-term exemptions as a form of encouragement to poor families to have additional children.[17] Thus, although a few states offer the maximum exemption for *each* child, others allow only the minimum—thirteen weeks or three months—and some also set a lifetime limit of twelve months for the parent (Waller 1997, 6).

A final area of leverage affects the eligibility of families at different stages in their relationship to public assistance. As noted above, current law combines four previous programs—CCDBG, AFDC-Child Care, At-Risk Child Care, and Transitional Child Care—into a single block grant—the Child Care and Development Fund. Three of those programs guaranteed services to all families that fit specific criteria—AFDC-CC, for parents who were receiving aid who were working or participating in training or education; TCC, which provided services for 12 months to those no longer eligible for AFDC; and ARCC, for low-income parents who were "at-risk" of requiring public assistance. Moreover, funding for these programs was open-ended; that is, while states were required to put up matching funds in order to draw down federal dollars, there was no maximum for how much they could access. Under PRWORA, these separate funding streams have disappeared and the programs' constituencies have become absorbed into the larger group of those who are *eligible* for benefits under federal law but not *entitled* under state regulations. Each of the three groups must, in effect, compete for a share of limited child care funds, and while each presents a compelling case, one or more groups is inevitably granted lower priority. Most often, that group is the welfare "leavers."

States have the option of providing twelve months of transitional child care and shifting unused TANF funds from direct public assistance to child care as welfare rolls fall. About three-fourths of the states have done so (Schumacher and Greenberg 1999, 4), but recent studies of former recipients have found that in many states, fewer than half of those responding were receiving child care subsidies. The reasons they gave included lack of information about eligibility or a feeling that it was "too much trouble to apply" (Schumacher and Greenberg 1999, ii). While a majority of those without subsidies turned to relatives or neighbors, this type of care is not always reliable, making it difficult for former recipients to retain their hard-won employment.

Although PRWORA directs states to coordinate services for all categories of low-income families under one "lead agency," the practice of prioritizing one group over another can often create discontinuities in child care as families exhaust their TANF benefits and/or begin earning wages that exceed state-set income maxima for publicly supported child care. The irrationality of such arrangements becomes evident if we look at an individual case. In 1997, Christine Ferguson, a Wal-Mart cashier in Union Township, Ohio, found that her earnings of $6.80 an hour put her above the state's income maximum (which was set at 125 percent of the federal poverty level). When her county ran out of funds for child care, Ferguson and 109 other low-income parents were summarily cut off, and her child care costs jumped from $65 to $400 a month—an amount she simply could not afford. Reluctantly pulling her child out of care, Ferguson deplored her plight: "I'm really glad [President] Clinton wants to do this welfare reform—I think it's time. But you're going to send someone back to welfare if you take their child care" (quoted in Waller 1997, 1).

Ferguson's situation was the result of her state's interpretation of federal welfare requirements. Unlike most of its neighbors, Ohio had decided *not* to reallocate TANF funds to child care for low-income families as the number of TANF recipients fell, but instead lowered matching funds in order to reduce taxes.[18] Thus, Ferguson's county did not have enough funds to provide child care for all of its low-income, non-TANF families. In some states, former recipients are compelled to go back on TANF in order to receive child care benefits, thus keeping their "clocks" running and coming ever-closer to the five-year limit for benefits—precisely the course Ferguson was reluctant to take.

Bureaucratic Impediments and Local Conditions

Whatever the funding levels and priorities for their allocation, access to subsidized child care is ultimately determined at the local level, where widely varying bureaucratic practices can determine who receives services and who does not. Under previous "workfare" measures, states had an "affirmative responsibility" to provide services to all eligible families, and when these were not available, work requirements were waived for the families affected. Under PRWORA, this relationship is somewhat different; lone parents must still receive an exemption from work requirements if child care is not available for any child under the age of one, but states are no longer mandated to provide services (for the politics of this, see Levy 2000, 28–39). In order to receive an exemption, recipients must demonstrate that they cannot obtain child care "for one or more of the following reasons: a) unavailability of appropriate child care within a reasonable distance from the individual's home or work site; b) unavailability or unsuitability of informal child care by a relative or under other arrangements; c) unavailability of appropriate and affordable formal child care arrangements" (Greenberg 1998, 2–3). Although states themselves can be penalized for refusing to grant exemptions in these instances (risking a loss of up to 5 percent of their CCDF block grants), this rule does not serve as an effective deterrent, since those who administer the rules arbitrarily or improperly are not directly affected—while their clients are.

The attitudes of local officials and their willingness to extend themselves on behalf of their clients can determine access to child care and clients' prospects for success under the mandatory work program. Take, for example, Illinois. From a "macro" perspective, the state appears to be strongly committed to providing child care for its poor and low-income residents. It drew down 100 percent of its federal funds in 1994 (for a total child care budget of over $149 million), and from 1997 to 2000 its governors have consistently requested and won significant increases in state appropriations for child care (12 percent for 2000) on the basis of projected growth in the number of children requiring services (*Illinois Welfare News* 2000a, 6).[19] In turn, these triggered increased allocations from the federal government. The present governor has also consistently shifted TANF monies from employment and training services to child care (Schumacher et al. 2001, 35), suggesting that, at least in the state of Illinois, welfare reform is moving in the direction intended by PRWORA's architects, with funding following need as recipients move from welfare to work.

If we look beyond these state-level indicators, however, we find anecdotal evidence to suggest that child care funds and services may not be reaching needy families in a timely fashion, thus preventing TANF applicants and recipients from complying with work requirements. Further, clients are being sanctioned—unfairly—as a result. Welfare rights advocates have found repeated instances in which caseworkers summarily deny benefits to such individuals, even though this practice is specifically prohibited by federal law. In Illinois, caseworkers are required by state welfare policy to refer all TANF applicants and recipients to child care referral agencies and arrange for payments to be made as soon as an appropriate slot has been located. But instead, according to *Illinois Welfare News* (2000b), caseworkers are, in effect, telling clients, "Getting someone to watch your kids so you can go to work is your problem and not mine" (6). While this is technically true under federal statutes, its outcomes defy the spirit of PRWORA. To take just two examples:

> A Bloomington, Illinois, TANF applicant was unable to attend a job interview at a fast food employer on the day she applied for TANF because, as she informed her intake worker, she had no one to watch her three small children during the job interview. The intake worker deemed this a refusal to comply with job search requirements and denied her benefit application.

> After telling her caseworker that she could not find anyone to care for her special-needs child, a Chicago-area TANF applicant never got a referral to a child care resource and referral agency for help in finding child care. (*Illinois Welfare News* 2000b)

Thus what we might call *negative administrative orientation* prevents what appears—on the surface, at least—to be adequate child care funding from reaching its intended recipients.[20] While it is difficult to know precisely how widespread such practices are, variations in child care availability, coupled with other regulations, the vicissitudes of the job market, and the complexities of the lives of the poor, would suggest that they occur not infrequently (for a vivid example, see Bernstein 2001).

In other states, different problems crop up as the result of local variants in regulations. In North Carolina, for example, state regulations prohibit reimbursement for child care provided by "kith and kin." For rural African-American mothers, however, this is often the only kind of care that is available or readily accessible, given a lack of public transportation. Moreover, given the racial dynamics of their state, it is the only kind they feel they can trust. Many of these women thus try to defer employment until their children reach school age, and then they limit themselves to part-time jobs that will allow them to be home when their children reach school age (Sinclair 2001; Uttal 1998).

Inadequate Compensation

To make matters worse, several features of the new system have actually reduced the amount of care available for children from poor and low-income families. For instance, TANF's work requirements have weakened the informal networks that low-income women, particularly those in urban neighborhoods, typically depended upon for care not only for their children but for elders, the chronically ill, and other dependents needing regular assistance (Oliker 2000).[21] Such networks comprised kin, friends, and neighbors who were similarly situated economically and more or less available to provide services for one another.[22] Some of these women relied on public assistance, while others held jobs that did not pay enough for them to afford formal services. Before TANF, they could turn to their networks to arrange care for those for whom they were responsible, either on a regular basis, if they took employment outside the home, or occasionally, in order to accomplish other tasks (such as dealing with the welfare bureaucracy). TANF, however, has had an ambiguous impact on such practices. Though federal regulations permit child care payments to be made to kith and kin, TANF's mandatory work regulations have removed many of the women who had previously been available to offer care, leaving tattered support networks in their wake (Waller 1997, 1).

A second feature of TANF that has reduced the capacity of the existing system to care for poor and low-income children is the level and manner in which providers are reimbursed. As noted above, states may set their own rates for reimbursement and these are often below market rates; moreover, many states are slow to pay, forcing providers who accept vouchers or certificates in exchange for services to wait months for payments. This places a particular hardship on small independent and individual family providers, many of whom are already on the margins financially and can ill afford to offer places at a discount or extend credit to the state. Since providers are not mandated by law to reserve slots for poor and low-income children, many have simply refused to or stopped doing so, with the result that in some locales the number of subsidized slots for poor and low-income children has simply declined (Children's Defense Fund 2001).

A third factor feeds into the paradox that, despite an apparent abundance of child care funding, the supply is not keeping pace: this is due, in part, to low salaries and poor benefits typically offered to providers. The Children's Defense Fund has documented that, year after year, child care workers are paid less than amusement park attendants and garbage collectors, while other studies have shown that child care providers are less likely than other workers to receive needed benefits such as health care and pensions (Gallagher and Clifford 2000). For example, in 1997 in Champaign County, Illinois, the average annual salary of a lead teacher in a child care center was $13,770—only $440 above the federal poverty level for a family of three, and approximately half the average salary for all female workers in the United States with "some college education"—$26,747 (University of Illinois Extension 2001, 2). As a result, in the recent climate of near-full employment, child care centers have found it increasingly difficult to attract and retain qualified employees, and women who might become independent home-based providers choose other occupations. Under CCDBG, states were required to set aside 25 percent of their funding for "activities to improve the quality of child care and to provide . . . early childhood development services"; current law reduces this to 4 percent. Using these funds, however limited, and sometimes augmenting them with state money, at least eleven states have initiated programs to encourage child care workers to obtain more training and then reward them for doing so (see, e.g. T.E.A.C.H. Early Childhood Illinois, n.d. [2001]; for an overview, Blank and Poersch 1999),[23] while one state, Rhode Island, subsidizes benefits for child care workers. Such measures are, however, few and far between; they do little to raise the status of child care as an occupation or address the attendant issues of working conditions and quality.

Some welfare reformers have suggested that child care would be ideal occupation for TANF recipients seeking employment, and indeed, PRWORA singles it out for special mention (Greenberg 1996). Accordingly, TANF-related jobs programs also promote this type of employment (Little 1999), but such training does not adequately prepare recipients for working in centers (many of which require at least an associate's degree in early childhood education from a community college), or give them the wherewithal to overcome the many practical obstacles to starting a home-based service, such as lack of suitable housing, insurance and equipment costs, and so on. Moreover, child care analysts warn that not all women are, simply by gender, qualified to become child care providers. As one put it, "No public policies at the federal or state level should push or require people to care for children if they do not want to be providers" (Galinsky et al. 1994, 6). Thus the welfare-to-work program cannot, in itself, produce enough child care workers or providers to meet the increased need TANF itself has generated.

Quality and Coordination

The supply of child care is, of course, closely linked to its quality, and vice versa. When the supply is low and/or the variety of settings limited, parents may be compelled to settle for provisions with which they do not feel comfortable, that do not suit their child rearing preferences, or leave them feeling uneasy for any number of reasons. When, in addition, parents lack purchasing power, as do TANF recipients restricted by low rates of state reimbursement, their choices become even more limited. As noted above, prior to 1996, the quality of child care varied widely, with poor and low-income children more likely to be placed in low-quality settings.

More recent studies confirm that this is still the case, particularly for former welfare recipients who no longer receive child care subsidies (Fuller and Kagan 2000; Schumacher and Greenberg 1999).

Again, the paucity of federal funds for improving quality is partly responsible for this situation, but other factors feed into it as well. For example, child care facilities receiving TANF funds may have difficulty tapping into other funding streams or coordinating their services with those offered through other federal or state programs. The most obvious example of this problem is Head Start. Many low-income children participate in Head Start, the federally funded program of "compensatory" preschool education that had been in place since the mid-1960s. Beginning in 1990, appropriations for this program more than tripled, from $1.235 million in 1989 to $3.981 million in 1997, and enrollments nearly doubled, from 451,000 in 1989 to 794,000 in 1997 (U.S. House of Representatives 1999, 395, table 637). Explicitly designed to emphasize cognitive, social, and emotional development, Head Start programs are generally high in quality according to prevailing early childhood educational standards. But they usually run for only part of the day and thus cannot fully meet the child care needs of parents who work full-time or on irregular or night shifts. Moreover, income ceilings for Head Start families are extremely low—below what a parent might earn working full-time in a minimum-wage job. Thus, although both funding and enrollment in Head Start have increased since the implementation of TANF, the program is not ideally situated to address the new child care needs created by this policy.

Child care centers seeking to access Head Start funding or expose their charges to the benefits Head Start has to offer must not only meet cumbersome requirements but may also find that some of their families exceed income eligibility limits. In an effort to take advantage of Head Start for those of their children who do qualify, some centers transport them to Head Start classrooms for part of the day and offer "wrap-around services" during the remaining hours. Such plans are, however, awkward for staff and disruptive for the children involved. Centers attempting to coordinate their services with state-initiated prekindergarten programs for children of low-income families encounter similar problems. As of 1998–99, forty-two states had such initiatives, with a total of $1.7 billion in funding, but these served only about 725,000 children—approximately one-third of those eligible (Blank, Schulman, and Ewen 1999).

A final quality issue has to do with the lack of federal standards for federally funded child care. Long a bone of contention among child care advocates and their opponents (see Michel 1999, chap. 7), this issue predictably raised the hackles of proponents of devolution and never made it into the final legislation. Moreover, because policymakers' primary goal was moving welfare recipients into employment, they were not concerned when quality issues fell by the wayside. While licensed child care providers and centers must comply with state regulations, these vary widely, and weak enforcement often renders them virtually meaningless (Blank and Poersch 1999).

Conclusion

Although more public funding is available than ever before, the gap between the supply of child care and demand for it is, if anything, widening as the number of TANF applicants and recipients continues to grow, and rates of employment among moderate to high-income mothers remain steady or even climb (Children's Defense Fund 2001).[24] The obvious conclusion to be drawn is that while more funding is necessary, it will not be sufficient to carry out the task of meeting these new needs (though less funding would obviously make it even more difficult). States must be willing to loosen regulations, rationalize the organization of child care and facilitate access to it, and spend more of their own money in order to draw down maximum federal funds. While this last decision depends specifically on states' own fiscal capacity, all of these moves require a generally favorable and constructive attitude toward poor and low-income citizens. State-level decision making often founders on the paradox that the very political forces that are intent on reducing welfare rolls (primarily conservative Republicans[25]) are also opposed to both expanding government services *and* encouraging maternal employment. It is thus difficult to mobilize political support and funding for the very programs that are needed to make workfare succeed even in its own terms.

At worst, the supply of child care will continue to fall short of demand, causing TANF recipients to renege on their employment and training responsibilities. Under pressure from state bureaucracies and politicians to meet quotas, caseworkers will deny or terminate benefits rather than place blame where it belongs—on the child care crisis—and join clients in calling for appropriate responses. Only slightly better will be a kind of "gray" solution in which parents and children seeking child care circulate in a maelstrom of irregular, ad-hoc provisions, settling for arrangements that may be inadequate or shifting children around in an attempt to find better provisions and maximize child care dollars, while providers themselves cycle in and out of business, quitting when they can no longer afford to subsidize the state with their own labor and capital and/or when they find more lucrative jobs. Both scenarios are exacerbated by the fact that states are more or less on their own in setting criteria and regulations for most aspects of public child care, and that parents' employment status, rather than children's needs for developmental and educational services, have become the paramount factors in setting policy.

To move beyond either scenario, the federal government must itself be willing (or must give states incentives) to improve the quality and supply of child care and the working conditions of those who provide it. Obvious measures might include offering or earmarking funds for start-up costs for new child care centers; setting minimum salaries and funding mandated benefits for workers; and creating packages of liability insurance and benefits for independent providers, coupled with much more stringent regulations and oversight for such provisions.[26] States might make it more feasible for TANF recipients and other low-income individuals who *want* to go into child care (and this option should by no means be imposed on them) to receive training by providing tuition money, adequate living stipends, and benefits (including child care, of course) while they are preparing themselves.[27] In addition to sufficient funding, all of these measures require political predisposition and administrative capacity. While administrative capacity is probably best (and perhaps only) built up at the subnational (state) and local level, federal incentives, standards and regulations will undoubtedly be required to overcome local impediments and provide the necessary momentum when political predisposition is lacking.[28]

There is, of course, always the danger that such measures will tranform something that has usually been considered a social good—a boon to both parents and children—into an instrument of punitive control over women. In the feminist view, child care is an essential element of social citizenship; along with paid parental leaves and other policies allowing "time to care," it should be part of any social structure that allows women to choose freely whether to work or pursue education *or* care for family members. But feminists also believe that child care should *never* be used to compel women to work.[29] One is reminded of Jane Addams's comment, made in 1905, that the day nursery (as child care centers were called then) "is a 'double-edged implement' for doing good, which may also do a little harm. . . ." (quoted in Michel 1999, 72). Indeed, today's public child care system may be used to do more than a little harm to poor mothers, but in the current political climate, there seems to be little hope of turning back policymakers' commitment to workfare, at least not for the time being. Perhaps the best that feminists can hope for— and certainly what they should work toward—is a greatly improved system of public child care, one that provides poor and low-income families with convenient, affordable, high-quality care of the types they prefer. Only with such a system in place will TANF applicants and other women who must work outside the home be able to avoid making a Solomonic decision between leaving their children in questionable circumstances in order to comply with work requirements or staying at home to care for their children and sacrificing the wages and benefits they need to support them. And perhaps with the addition of federal standards and an extended sliding scale, such a system could come to constitute the basis for a universal system of provision in the United States. But this may be too optimistic.

Notes

1. In 1999, the U.S. rate was 60 percent, compared to 59 percent in Canada, 48.9 percent in Japan, and 58.5 percent in Sweden (van der Lippe and van Dijk 2001).

2. In theory, consumers of both public and private provision have "free choice" as to the type of child care they access for their children, but in fact, in both sectors, parents are constrained by what is available and what they can afford; poor and low-income parents generally have the fewest "choices."

3. As Jennifer Mittelstadt (2001) has recently shown, the idea of using public policy to

help poor women become self-sufficient actually had its roots in legislation passed in 1956, but implementation did not really get underway until the 1960s.

4. For a cogent critique of this term, see Young (forthcoming).

5. These included the Children's Caucus, led by Senator Christopher Dodd (D-Connecticut) and the Select Committee on Children, Youth and Families, led by Representative George A. Miller (D-California).

6. Another controversy arose around the issue of funding child care that included religious instruction. Republicans opposed any provision that would *not* fund child care sponsored by religious institutions, arguing that since most of the existing nonprofit centers fell into that category, excluding them from federal funding limited the available supply of child care and restricted parental choice.

7. Seventy-five percent of the funds was to be used for this purpose, while the remaining 25 percent was to be spent on quality improvement activities (5 percent), development of early childhood education (18.75 percent), and other quality-related activities (1.25 percent).

8. An alternative, less optimistic, interpretation is that devolution facilitates resolution by significantly reducing the power of diffuse interest groups such as poor families (Winston 1999).

9. The maximum time allowable is five years, but states have the option to reduce this, and many have.

10. Had PRWORA not been passed, maximum allocations for 1997 would have been $1.4 billion for the Title-IVA programs and $935 million under CCDBG (Long and Clark 1997, 2).

11. These include, for each state, the proportion of children who are under five, how many children receive free or reduced-rate school lunches, and the average per capita income. Thus, both overall wealth and the gap between rich and poor are taken into consideration.

12. For example, in 1994, Massachusetts, Connecticut, the District of Columbia, and Washington state all drew down 100 percent of their federal funds, while Louisiana drew down none, Mississippi 5 percent, and Tennessee 27 percent. Alabama, however, received 95 percent of its maximum.

13. For example, by failing to appropriate child care funds for 1997, only Arkansas, Mississippi, and New Mexico would end up with *more* money for child care than they had in 1995, while in most states, the amounts would range from 23 to 50 percent less (Long and Clark 1997, 4).

14. In 1997, the average SMI was $38,370, but this varied from just under $25,000 in West Virginia to just over $52,000 in Connecticut.

15. In 1997, the federal poverty level for a family of three was $13,330 ($1110.80 per month) in all states except Alaska and Hawaii, where it was $16,670 and $15,330 respectively.

16. Consensus has formed around the idea that "affordable" child care should take up no more than 10 percent of a family's total annual income; this percentage is, of course, far more onerous for a family earning $12,000 per annum than one earning $50,000 or more.

17. Many states already attempt to discourage additional births through the use of "family caps" that deny benefits to children born to parents while they are receiving assistance.

18. It should be noted that in 2000, Ohio finally decided to reallocate funds, transferring more than $77 million, or 11 percent of its TANF funds, to CCDF.

19. These projected increases in need were paralled by equivalent, if not greater, *decreases* in the TANF caseload; for fiscal year 2001, for example, Governor George Ryan requested an additional $66 million to cover a projected 12 percent increase in child care need, while calculating that the state would save $76 million from a projected 16 percent decrease in caseloads, a savings of $10 million. Other indicators, however, contradict the aforementioned signs of Illinois' generosity; according to Douglas and Flores (1998), the state is 33rd in child poverty, 8th in per capita income, and only 35th in fiscal effort (8, table 2). Indeed, for 2002, Ryan has drastically reduced his budget request for child care (Day Care Action Council 2001).

20. Negative administrative orientation has been flagrant in other areas of Illinois' welfare bureaucracy, as *Illinois Welfare News* (2000c) has demonstrated consistently since TANF went into effect. Its March 2000 column "Let's Get It Right" documented in detail one case of application delay and one of improper processing of appeals. *Illinois Welfare News* is published by the National Center on Poverty Law, which works with the Legal Assistance Foundation of Chicago and Prairie State Legal Services to advise TANF clients and assist them in making appeals.

21. The classic study of such arrangements is Stack (1974).

22. Assuming this was their preference; many women in these neighborhoods preferred placing their children in the care of coethnics rather than in formal centers that they perceived as sterile or culturally alien (Uttal 1998). For a historical perspective on this, see Lemke-Santangelo (1996).

23. The Illinois program requires the sponsoring child care program as well as the recipient to pay part of the cost; the sponsoring program must also provide release time and "agree to award the recipient either a bonus or raise at the end of the scholarship year." Students pay up to 20 percent of expenses; in return, they must "agree to remain at the sponsoring center, or continue to operate their center or home, for at least one year after the term of the scholarship and remain in the early childhood field in Illinois for an additional year" (T.E.A.C.H. n.d., 3–4).

24. It is not yet clear what impact, if any, the economic downturn of 2001 will have on these trends.

25. Indeed, many conservative women, with the support of their menfolk, have mobilized a back-to-the-home or mothers-at-home movement which is, among other things, adamantly opposed to child care (Michel 2000).

26. Americans might look to the French system for an excellent model of family child care, in which providers are linked into a local or neighborhood center that they visit regularly for advice and assistance with "problem" children, bringing their charges along with them to be supervised while they are attending sessions. Centers also loan toys, equipment, and other supplies (Richardson and Marx 1989).

27. As of March 2001, Democrats on the Senate Finance Committee, which oversees

welfare and child care legislation in that body, were considering proposing legislation to accomplish just these goals (Democratic Staff 2001).

28. Indeed, the history of federal programs like certain parts of Social Security should have taught us that certain states cannot be relied upon to make fair and equitable provisions for all of their citizens (Mettler 1998, 6–7 and passim).

29. Consider, for example, calls for nighttime child care to enable women to work the "swing" or "graveyard" shift. (This often becomes necessary because office cleaning, one of the few occupations open to unskilled entrants to the job market, is usually done at night.) On the one hand, such services enable women to take jobs, but on the other, they also disrupt children's routines and probably lead to exhaustion for mothers who have no time to rest during the day. See also Arlie Hochschild's (1995) comments about "hot" and "cold" modern relationships between work and family.

References

Adams, Gina, and Nicole Oxendine Poersch. 1996. *Who Cares? State Commitment to Child Care and Early Childhood Education.* Washington, D.C.: Children's Defense Fund.

Bell, Winifred. 1965. *Aid to Dependent Children.* New York: Cambridge University Press.

Bernstein, Nina. 2001. *The Lost Children of Wilder: The Epic Struggle to Change Foster Care.* New York: Pantheon.

Blank, Helen, and Nicole Oxendine Poersch. 1999. *State Child Care and Early Education Developments.* Washington, D.C.: Children's Defense Fund.

Blank, Helen, Karen Schulman, and Danielle Ewen. 1999. "State Prekindergarten Initiatives, 1998–1999." Executive Summary, *Seeds of Success.* Washington, D.C.: Children's Defense Fund.

Children's Defense Fund. 1996. *America's Children.* Washington, D.C.: Children's Defense Fund.

_____. 2001. "New Investments for Child Care Needed." Available online at http://www.cdfactioncouncil.org/New%20Investments.htm.

Day Care Action Council of Illinois. 2001. Press release, March 8.

Democratic Staff, U.S. Senate. 2001. Personal communication with the author. March 20.

Douglas, Toby, and Kimura Flores. 1998. "Federal and State Funding of Children's Programs." Washington, D.C.: Urban Institute. Available online at http://newfederalism. urban.org/html/occa5.html#appe.

Esping-Andersen, Gøsta. 1990. *The Three Worlds of Welfare Capitalism.* Princeton, N.J.: Princeton University Press.

Fuller, Bruce, and Sharon Kagan. 2000. *Remember the Children: Mothers Balance Work and Child Care Under Welfare Reform.* Berkeley and New Haven: Growing Up In Poverty Project, University of California-Berkeley and Yale University.

Galinsky, Ellen, Carolle Howes, Susan Kontos, and Marybeth Shinn. 1994. *The Study of Children in Family Child Care and Relative Care: Highlights of Findings.* New York: Families and Work Institute.

Gallagher, J., and R. Clifford. 2000. "The Missing Support Infrastructue in Early Child-hood." *Early Childhood Research and Practice* 2, no.1. Available online at www.ecrp.uiuc.edu/ v2n1/gallagher.html.

Gordon, Linda. 1994. *Pitied But Not Entitled: Single Mothers and the History of Welfare, 1890–1935.* Cambridge, Mass.: Harvard University Press.

Greenberg, Mark. 1996. "A Summary of Key Child Care Provisions of H.R. 3734, The Personal Responsibility and Work Opportunity Reconciliation Act of 1996. Washington, D.C.: Center for Law and Social Policy (CLASP). Available online at http://www.clasp.org/pubs/childcare/clkccp.html.

_____. 1998. "The Child Care Protection Under TANF." Washington, D.C.: CLASP. Available online at http://www.clasp.org/pubs/childcare/childcareprotect.htm.

Greenberg, Mark, Joan Lombardi, and Rachel Schumacher. 2000. "The Child Care and De-velopment Fund: An Overview." Washington, D.C.: Center for Law and Social Policy. Available online at http://www.clasp.org.

Harrington Meyer, Madonna, ed. 2000. *Care Work: Gender, Labor and the Welfare State.* New York: Routledge.

Hayes, Cheryl D., John L. Palmer, and Martha J. Zaslow. 1990. *Who Cares for America's Chil-dren? Child Care Policy for the 1990s.* Washington, D.C.: National Academy Press.

Hochschild, A. 1995. "The Culture of Politics: Traditional, Postmodern, Cold-Modern, and Warm-Modern Ideals of Care." *Social Politics* 2: no. 3, 331–46.

_____. 1997. *The Time Bind: When Work Becomes Home and Home Becomes Work.* New York: Metropolitan Books.

Hofferth, Sandra. 1993. "The 101st Congress: An Emerging Agenda for Children in Poverty." In *Child Poverty and Public Policy*, ed. Judith A. Chafel. Washington: Urban Insti-tute.

Illinois Welfare News. 2000a. "Child Care Increases As Income Assistance Declines in Gover-nor's Revised 2000 Spending and 2001 Budget." March: 1, 6.

_____. 2000b. "TANF Applicants and Recipients Not Getting the Child Care Assistance They Need and Are Being Penalized." March: 6–7.

_____. 2000c. "Let's Get It Right! Undue Delays in Processing Benefits and Appeals." March: 11.

Kornbluh, Felicia. 2000. "A Right to Welfare? Poor Women, Professionals, and Poverty Pro-grams." Ph.D. dissertation, Princeton University.

Lemke-Santangelo, Gretchen. 1996. *Abiding Courage: African American Migrant Women and the East Bay Community.* Chapel Hill: University of North Carolina Press.

Levy, Denise Urias. 2000. "Child Care Policies in America: Inter-State Differences and the Progress of Devolution." Ph.D. diss., University of Illinois at Chicago.

Lewis, Jane. 1992. "Gender and the Development of Welfare Regimes." *Journal of European Social Policy* 2, no. 3: 37–55.

Lippe, Tanja van der, and Liset van Dijk, eds. 2001. *Women's Employment in a Coroprate Perspec-tive.* New York: Aldine de Gruyter.

Little, Deborah. 1999. "Independent Workers, Dependable Mothers: Discourse, Resistance, and AFDC Workfare Programs." *Social Politics* 6, no. 2: 161–202.

Long, Sharon K., and Clark, Sandra J. 1997. "The New Child Care Block Grant: State Funding Choices and Their Implications," no. A-12, "New Federalism: Issues and Options for States." Washington, D.C.: Urban Institute. Available online at http://newfederalism. urban.org/html/ anf_a12.htm.

Mettler, Suzanne. 1998. *Dividing Citizens: Gender and Federalism in New Deal Public Policy.* Ithaca, N.Y.: Cornell University Press.

Michel, Sonya. 1999. *Children's Interests/Mothers' Rights: The Shaping of America's Child Care Policy.* New Haven, Conn.: Yale University Press.

_____. 2000. "Having the Right to Care—and Not to Care." In Harrington Meyer, ed., *Care Work.*

Mink, Gwendolyn. 1998. *Welfare's End.* Ithaca, N.Y.: Cornell University Press.

Mittelstadt, Jennifer. 2001. "'Dependency as a Problem to Be Solved': Rehabilitation and the Liberal Consensus on Welfare in the 1950s." *Social Politics* 8, no. 3: 228–57.

Oliker, Stacie. 2000. "Examining Care at Welfare's End." In Harrington Meyer, ed., *Care Work.*

Richardson, Gail, and Elisabeth Marx. 1989. *A Welcome for Every Child.* New York: French-American Foundation.

Schumacher, Rachel, and Mark Greenberg. 1999. "Child Care After Leaving Welfare: Early Evidence from State Studies." Washington, D.C.: CLASP.

Schumacher, Rachel, Mark Greenberg, and Janellen Duffy. 2001. "The Impact of TANF Funding on State Child Care Subsidy Programs." Washington, D.C.: CLASP.

Sinclair, Charlene. 2001. Personal communication with the author.

Stack, Carol B. 1974. *All Our Kin: Strategies for Survival in a Black Community.* New York: Harper and Row.

T.E.A.C.H. Early Childhood Illinois. n.d. [2001]. "Scholarship and Compensation Project." Glen Ellyn, Ill.: T.E.A.C.H.

U.S. Bureau of the Census. 1998. "Primary Child Care Arrangements Used for Preschoolers by Families with Employed Mothers, Selected Years, 1977 to 1994." Available online at http://www.census.gov/population/socdemo/child/p70-62/tableA.txt.

U.S. General Accounting Office. 1995a. *Welfare to Work: Child Care Assistance Limited: Welfare Reform May Expand Needs.* GAO/HEHS-95-220, September. Washington, D.C.: Government Printing Office.

_____. 1995b. *Child Care: Recipients Face Service Gaps and Supple Shortages.* GAO/T-HEHS-95-96, March 1. Washington, D.C.: Government Printing Office.

U.S. House of Representatives, Committee on Ways and Means. 1999. *1999 Green Book.* Washington, D.C.: Government Printing Office.

University of Illinois Extension. 2001. "Child Care in Champaign County." Available online at http://www.aces.uic.edu/-CCRSCare/champstats.htm.

Uttal, Lynet. 1998. "Racial Safety and Cultural Maintenance: The Childcare Concerns of Employed Mothers of Color." In *Families, Kinship and Domestic Politics in the U.S.: Critical Feminist Perspectives,* ed. Anita Garey and Karen Hansen. Philadelphia: Temple University Press.

Waller, Margy. 1997. "Welfare-to-Work and Child Care: A Survey of the Ten Big States."

September 26. Washington, D.C.: Progressive Policy Institute. Available online at http://www.dlcppi.org/texts/social/ccare.htm.

Winston, Pamela. 1999. "The Devil in Devolution: Welfare, the Nation, and the States." Ph.D. diss., Johns Hopkins University.

Young, Iris. Forthcoming. "Autonomy, Welfare Reform, and Meaningful Work." In *Philosophical Approaches to Dependency*, ed. Eva Feder Kittay and Ellen Feder. Lanham, Md.: Rowman and Littlefield.

preserving/creating universalism

CHAPTER 11

Danish Child Care Policy: Continuity Rather than Radical Change

Anette Borchorst

Introduction

Welfare restructuring was introduced into state planning and political decision making by Social Democratic governments in Denmark in the early 1970s. Confronted with a severe economic crisis and high unemployment as a consequence of increasing oil prices, child care services became the object of cutbacks in the mid 1970s. Yet, the rhetoric of welfare retrenchment was stronger than the political practice. This was also the case during the reign of bourgeois governments in the 1980s, despite the fact that they launched a comprehensive modernization of the public sector, aiming at making it less costly and more effective. The issue of retrenchment reappeared on the political agenda in the 1990s under the Social Democratic governments. A major break with the previous passive approach to unemployment was adopted, and activation was launched as the primary policy goal. Claimants of social assistance became obliged to participate in job training, education, or sheltered employment. In relation to child care, steps toward encouraging more individualistic and private solutions of child care—for instance, in the form of parents caring themselves and contracting out—have been taken. Still, the distinctive features of Danish child care policy have not been challenged.

The main pillars of this policy may be summed up as follows: Danish child care policy is above all characterized by a comparatively high public commitment to child care services. This commitment was inaugurated in 1919. For children from birth to three years of age, Denmark currently has the highest coverage rate of publicly funded child care among the European Union (EU) member countries, covering half of this group. More than 80 percent of the age group three to six are accommodated. This is, however, less than in countries like France, Belgium, and Italy, which provide school-based activities for almost all children from ages four and five (Europa Kommissionen 1998). Another distinctive feature of Danish child care policy is the universalist character of policy efforts and the transformation of human needs into individual entitlements. The policy was initially of a residual nature, since two-thirds of the children accommodated had to come from poor families, but in the mid-1960s universalism became the core principle of the legislation. Furthermore, child care services are based on "social pedagogic" ideas. In Danish, this term is neither old-fashioned nor does it have a negative connotation as it does in English. The term signals that activities for children under six should be related to socialization rather than to educational activities. Historically, the social pedagogic ideas embedded in policy efforts marked the integration of care and education, which laid the foundation for the abandonment of a two-track, class-based policy.

Danish child care policy may be seen as part and parcel of the social democratic welfare state model. Social democracy has undoubtedly played an important role in the formation of the Danish welfare state, but it is noteworthy that major national decisions on child care policy throughout the twentieth century have been consensual. Decentralization should also be added as a distinctive feature. Since the rise of child care facilities, local initiatives have been decisive in establishing, running, and financing services, but regulation during the first part of the twentieth century was predominantly centralized at the national level. This changed in the 1970s, when decentralization became the dominant governing principle. Municipalities gained more influence on number, form and pricing of provisions, allowing for considerable variation across the country. In subsequent decades, decentralization became even more pronounced.

The final feature of Danish child care policy to be noted is that gender equality has underpinned the overall objectives. Child care provisions have undoubtedly contributed to the economic independence that women have gained over the past three decades. Yet, it is significant that the policy is child centered, since the legislation defines services as a right of the child.

As indicated above, a number of the features that characterize Danish child care policy were shaped relatively early or developed gradually throughout the twentieth century. In this chapter I use a historical approach to elucidate some causal mechanisms for the robustness of the Danish child care model, and I discuss why it has been characterized by continuity more than by change. First, I explain how child care policy is related to the social democratic welfare state model and highlight inter-Scandinavian differences in relation to policies influencing the balancing of work and child care. I then analyze the historical legacy of the universal, social pedagogical child care services in different phases, focusing on political decisions, policy outcomes, effects and the role of actors, and discuss the implication for gender equality. The chapter concludes by focusing on future scenarios.

A Social Democratic and Weak-Breadwinner Welfare State

The so-called power resource school includes the Danish welfare state in the social democratic cluster of welfare regimes. In such regimes, the state plays a major role in securing the welfare of individuals, and rights are to a large extent based on citizenship. Benefits serve to decommodify individuals or lessen their dependency on the market much more than benefits in the liberal and the conservative-corporatist models, and class-based stratification is also less pronounced (Esping-Andersen

1990). The power resource school has improved the understanding of similarities and differences among Western welfare states, yet it needs clarification in several regards. The conclusions about the decisive role of social democracy for the development of the welfare state require some modification. The Danish Social Democratic Party has certainly played a central role in the development of the welfare state; however, it should also be taken into account that liberal and conservative parties to a certain degree also have supported universalist principles and extension of welfare benefits. Many of the welfare policies of the 1960s and 1970s were passed as the result of a broad consensus among the political parties and, as I will demonstrate, the major decisions regarding child care service have been mutually agreed upon throughout the twentieth century. This reflects the fact that political parties have not advocated fundamentally different ideologies of motherhood.

The redistributive character of Scandinavian welfare policies may be ascribed to the influence of peasant and working-class movements on politics, nationally as well as locally. Gender equality has to some extent also been considered a central goal of public policies, due, in part, to the political influence of women's organizations and movements. This factor has largely been ignored by the power resource school, which has analyzed the issue of coalition building from the point of view of social class only. A final criticism is that since this approach has failed to consider the role of care and unpaid work, it has not paid attention to the fact that child care services have served to commodify women rather than the opposite. Recent contributions have, however, highlighted the significance of public services for gender equality in the Scandinavian countries, yet without identifying the causal mechanisms behind this development (Esping-Andersen 1996).

Numerous feminist scholars have focused on the analytic inadequacies of the power resource school, highlighting the gendered stratification in welfare and suggested new typologies. With reference to the typologies of Jane Lewis (1992), Lewis and Ilona Ostner (1994), and Diane Sainsbury (1996), the Scandinavian welfare states may be included among the "weak breadwinner" or "individual" welfare states. That is, in these societies, familism has not been a guiding principle for public policies since the 1970s, and women, like men (and to some extent also children), are by and large addressed as individuals in social legislation. In addition, universalism has neutralized the influence of marriage on social rights. The three countries never developed a tradition of employing women as a reserve army of labor during the two world wars because the countries were not actively engaged in warfare. This also explains why public policymaking began to emphasize gender equality relatively early on. The gendering impact of welfare states may also be gauged by the criterion of whether they enable women to form autonomous households (Orloff 1993). By this measure, the relatively low poverty rates of lone mothers in Scandinavian countries indicate a relatively high level of gender equality.

Along this line, some scholars have concluded that the Scandinavian welfare states have a woman-friendly potential fostered by the interaction between a broad mobilization of women from below and response in the form of institutionalized gender equality from above (Hernes 1987). Spurred by their similar cultural and political background, the three countries engaged in a common process of "policy learning" during the first part of the twentieth century. This was particularly true with regard to gender equality, which was enhanced by quite similar legislation (Rosenbeck 2000).

Notwithstanding these similarities, a closer look reveals distinct differences, throughout Scandinavia, among gender profiles and the specific interplay between forces from above and below (Bergqvist 2000b). Also with regard to family policy, there are similarities as well as differences among the three countries. In comparison to other Western European countries, they all spend a considerable amount on family benefits, but they have adopted different policies in terms of who cares for the children. This becomes visible when child care services, care benefits, parental leave and other leave schemes are considered together. Sweden and Denmark have emphasized public solutions to the question of who should provide the care, and they have stressed women's entitlements as workers more than Norway, where women have acquired more rights as mothers (Leira 1989; Sainsbury 1996; Bergqvist 2000a). The overall picture is that Norwegian policies have favored cash benefits and family-based solutions more than Danish policies, which have emphasized public services and integration in paid work more. Sweden falls in between, with a relatively high level of services at the same time as the country has been at the forefront in terms of extending parental leave and entitling fathers to leave. Sweden also has the most flexible arrangement in terms of splitting the leave and involving both fathers and mothers. Despite the fact that Swedish family polices did suffer cutbacks during the early 1990s (see Bergqvist and Nyberg, this volume), the overall picture is one of enhancing parental options more than Norwegian and Danish policies. The latter have tended to encourage mothers either to stay at home or to engage in paid work.

The question remains why Denmark, where social democracy has played a weaker role than in Sweden and Norway, and where the political culture has had a stronger touch of liberalism, nevertheless has been at the forefront in terms of institutionalized child care.

The Rise of Danish Child Care Policy

As in most countries, the momentum for establishing child care facilities in Denmark came from the industrialization process. Because this process took off later in Denmark, child care initiatives came much later than in countries such as Britain and Germany. As in these countries, a two-tiered, class-based system was established, emphasizing care for working-class children and education for upper-class children. Private philanthropists organized shelters or asylums for children of working-class families in order to alleviate some of the most disastrous consequences of the extension of factory work; the first was established in 1828. These institutions were financed by charity, since most working class parents could not afford to pay. Conditions in the asylums were poor; typically they enrolled from 130 to 250 children, with only two or three adults looking after them. Needless to say, pedagogical and educational objectives were restricted, while the daily regime highlighted, above all, discipline and cleanliness (Munck 1981).

Some decades later, another type of facility for young children was introduced, inspired by the German pedagogue Friedrich Fröbel, who advocated a child-centered pedagogy based on the idea that early development was stimulated through play. The first "Fröbel kindergarten" was established in Denmark in 1870. Fröbel kindergartens were part-time institutions financed by parental fees that only upper-class families could afford, and they were staffed with trained professionals. The earliest kindergartens were intended to serve educational but not necessarily child care functions. But around the turn of the century, on the initiative of leading Danish Fröbelian pedagogues, a new type of institution, named the people's kindergarten, emerged, integrating care and educational objectives. Such facilities became the cornerstone of Danish child care policy for the rest of the century. Services were targeted mainly at working-class children and staffed with trained professionals as well as laypersons; they accommodated much smaller groups of children than the asylums. However, most of the facilities struggled financially, since the parents paid a small fee or nothing at all, if they could not afford it.

Within this context, Fröbelian pedagogues and influential Social Democrats in Copenhagen formed a strategic alliance with the aim of gaining public subsidies for the people's kindergartens. Social Democratic politicians submitted a proposal for subsidies to the parliament in 1919, which was passed unanimously in both chambers. It granted DKK250,000 to child care facilities and was administered by the Ministry of Education. The political parties saw the law as a preventive measure against children becoming criminals and being removed from their families. Thus, the policy was conceptualized as preventive child welfare (see Rigsdagstidende 1918–19: 4308–4730), and it was directed mainly toward poor families. Still, the facilities which obtained state support were allowed to accommodate a minor part of their children from better off families (Munck 1981; Kolstrup 1996). State subsidies for child care facilities were maintained and even increased during the following years, and several Social Democratic municipalities also supported child care facilities financially. Private, nonprofit initiatives based on pedagogical principles such as the Montessori or Fröbelian ideas played a major role in the expanding child care programs, and were crucial for the survival of the facilities during the coming years.

Institutionalization of a Residual Policy

In the 1930s, the state extended its oversight and support of child care policies, but in doing so, institutionalized the principle of residualism. In 1931, the health provisions in child care services came under regulation for the first time, and in 1933, child care was included in the first comprehensive social legislation (Socialreformen), with services placed under the authority of the Ministry of Social Affairs, which was established at this time. The legislation laid down conditions for state funding of people's kindergartens, which had expanded since 1919, and as a new phenomenon, stipulated that 50 percent of the costs of establishing facilities could be subsidized. To obtain support for running an institution, two-thirds of the children accommodated had to come from poor families. Child care facilities were far from abundant during those years. In the early 1930s, about three hundred institutions were concentrated in Copenhagen, and a few in other major towns, and local initiatives were still decisive in establishing services. Meanwhile, the drastic decline in fertility provided the impetus for the adoption of family benefits. Inspired by the ideas of Alva and Gunnar Myrdal, two leading Swedish social democrats, reformers suggested improving the social conditions of families. A population committee was formed to focus on the limited number and economic problems of child care facilities. The committee report recommended an expansion of child care facilities (Betænkning 1936), but due to economic constraints during the following period, no major change occurred. The size of public subsidies did not increase, and the maximum level of subsidies for establishing facilities was rarely granted.

On the whole, the status quo was maintained during the Second World War. Unlike their counterparts in the belligerent nations, Danish women were not pulled into the labor force in significant numbers, and thus the number of child care facilities remained flat. In 1945, the state increased the subsidies for child care facilities to relieve their economic problems. The state could now finance 40 percent of the running costs, provided that the municipalities paid 30 percent. Again, the decisions in both chambers were consensual (Rigsdagstidende 1945: Folketinget 860; Landstinget 582).

In 1949, a universal element was introduced in the law with the support of all political parties in both chambers. From now on, facilities accommodating children from well-off homes could also obtain state funding. This change was among other things suggested by the organization of professionals working in the child care facilities, who wanted to encourage the establishment of part-time facilities. One of the objectives was to accommodate children from different backgrounds in the same facilities (*Rigsdagstidende* 1948–49; *Folketinget* 3969–3974; *Landstinget* 838–645). Still, the number of part-time services did not increase significantly. In 1951, the public commitment was strengthened when the parliament unanimously decided that municipalities were obliged to support the running of child care facilities (*Lovtidende* 1950–51: no. 92).

It was also during the 1950s that the state began to establish and run schools for child care professionals. The dominant paradigm for training at this time was hygiene, because cleanliness was considered crucial for securing the health of the children. The prevailing pedagogical ideas were founded on what was termed "the three Rs": "ro, renlighed, and regelmæssighed"—that is, tranquility, cleanliness, and regular routines for eating, sleeping, and playing. In 1950, suggestions were made to increase the number of facilities in order to, among other things, enable lone mothers to support themselves and their families (Betænkning 1950). Some years later, a commission was set up to recommend policies to facilitate a large-scale integration of women in the labor force, and suggestions were made to rationalize housework and increase state commitment to child care (Betænkning no. 57, 1954). These commissions' proposals never materialized, since the cold war climate and the economic crisis radically changed the course of events. Instead, cost reduction was recommended, and more children were accommodated in the facilities. Toward the end of the 1950s, around seven hundred services for preschool children had been established, covering 10 percent of the three- to six-year-olds and less than 5 percent of those under three (PPII 1973).

During this decade, the male breadwinner/female homemaker family model spread to the working class, and by the late 1950s, three-fourths of married women were housewives. This implied that the breadwinner-homemaker model became dominant for the first time in Denmark, but as we shall see, it constituted a historical parenthesis, since family structures changed radically in the following decade.

The main force driving politicians to focus on child care during the initial phases of Danish child care policy came from individuals who were connected to pedagogical ideas and schools like those of Fröbel and Maria Montessori. They formed organizations committed to improving the situation of children and, together with Social Democratic politicians, put the issue on the political agenda. The Social Democrats managed to get support from the other political parties at the national level. Women played a role as professional pedagogues and as philanthropists, some of whom were mobilized in women's organizations. These organizations were actively engaged in promoting welfare services such as school meals, health visitors, and benefits for lone mothers and housewife substitutes, but they did not play a prominent role in the establishment of child care facilities (Borchorst 1985b).

Universalist Child Care Policy

The most radical change in Danish child care policy in the postwar period was triggered by an initiative by one of the major women's organizations. In 1959, the National Council of Women in Denmark, an umbrella organization of women's rights groups, organized a public hearing in Parliament. They wanted to highlight the need for part-time child care services, because the feminist organizations saw part-time solutions to child care and women's paid work as optimal. The initiative prompted the minister of social affairs to ask two committees consisting of child care professionals and civil servants to develop policy recommendations for extending part-time child care facilities in particular. Their almost identical recommendations were submitted to Parliament (Betænkning no. 326, 1963; Betænkning no. 337, 1963). The legislation stipulated universalism as the overall objective, and obliged the pub-

lic sector to provide child care facilities. In keeping with the recommendations, programs previously termed "preventive child welfare" (*forebyggende børneforsorg*) were
now referred to as "social pedagogical measures" (*socialpædagogiske foranstaltninger*).
Thus, a completely new terminology was launched with this law, though services
remained under the authority of the minister of social affairs, thereby signaling that
their objective was not predominantly educational. A number of different incentives
laid the foundation for this change. The increasing demand for labor, the wish to
strengthen child-centered ideas, and the objective to foster women's economic autonomy. In this way, the prosperity and new concepts of the role of the welfare state
provided the necessary momentum for activating ideas that had been fostered during previous decades, but had been regarded as economically unrealistic at the time.

The law was passed in 1964 with the support of all political parties in Parliament,[1] who agreed that this initiative could facilitate the integration of married
women into the labor force (*Folketingstidende* 1963/64: 1889–1896; 2201–2239;
5474–5498). It was decided that operating costs for child care facilities should be
equally divided between the state, municipalities, and parents. Under these conditions, the number of full-time child care facilities grew steadily during the late
1960s and early seventies. By 1970, 254 crèches, 102 day care mothers, and 1,210
kindergartens were receiving public funds. Growth was especially dramatic for full-
time facilities staffed predominantly by trained professionals, but part-time facilities
never gained ground in Danish policies. Regulation and subsidies for day care in private homes were included in the legislation for the first time, but such provisions
did not expand as quickly as crèches and kindergartens.

Nevertheless, supply never caught up with demand, since demand kept increasing. Priority was given to children of parents working outside the home, but the objective of supporting children at risk was still underlined, and a certain number of
these children had priority in enrollment. From the mid 1960s on, the activity rates
of married women increased sharply; by 1970, half of all married women were in
the labor force. It is noteworthy that this increase by and large covered the demand
for labor; as a result, unlike the situation in many other European countries during
this period, the number of immigrant workers only grew modestly.

In 1969, the education of professionals for these institutions was extended to
three years, and the social pedagogical aspects of the education were strengthened.
The number of trained professionals rose significantly, as did the number of employees in child care facilities. This, in turn, became one of the major female-dominated
sectors of the labor market. Social pedagogical ideas still prevailed, yet in the middle of the 1960s, a voluntary preschool educational program was launched in connection with primary schools on an experimental basis. It became quite successful
and was later made permanent. The preschool activities were not fundamentally different from what was going on in the kindergartens, but the program accommodated a lot more children in each group, and the daily routines resembled school
activities and also took place in classrooms.

The most prominent actors in bringing about radical change were the progressive pedagogues. Their organizations had not yet developed into proper unions, and they saw the cause of children as a vocation. Among politicians, Social Democrats and left-ists were the most supportive of the development, though bourgeois politicians also accepted the extension of public responsibility for child care. They were, however, more inclined to subsidize child minders caring for children in family settings.

During this period, women's organizations became more visible as actors, but they were still not as prominent in motivating politicians to expand child care as they were in pushing for initiatives to promote education of women and integrating them into the labor force. They were well represented in a commission that was formed to develop policies to facilitate the integration of women in the labor force; it recom-mended child care provisions for all children (Betænkning no. 715, 1974, 101).

Thus the consolidation of a universalist, pedagogically-based child care system in Denmark occurred in two stages. First, the establishment of people's kindergartens early in the twentieth century laid down the principle that care and pedagogy were not separate functions but must be combined in programs for young children. While these early institutions gained widespread public support, they were nonetheless framed as preventive measures and, mainly directed at low-income families, thus to some extent carrying a stigma in the public mind. All major decisions were consen-sual, and some politicians saw this first stage as a way to promote a social liberal state that would be responsible for the caring of small children as well as the educa-tion of children above the age of seven. The second major stage was marked by a shift toward universalist provisions, somewhat tentatively in the mid-1950s but de-cisively in the 1960s. This shift was based on political consensus regarding the inte-gration of women into the labor force and also regarding cost-sharing among the state, municipalities, and parents. With these principles as a foundation, the Danish child care system was well positioned to withstand the forces of retrenchment that arose in the ensuing decades.

The Rhetoric of Retrenchment

In the late 1960s and the early 1970s, public expenditures grew steadily as a conse-quence of the decision to expand the welfare state. The Social Democratic govern-ment now launched attempts to introduce unified planning for financing the public sector in order to control the level of expenditures. In a report from 1973, econo-mists provided a cost-benefit analysis of child care facilities and recommended that expenditures be controlled by raising the parents' payments and reducing the staff. The report also proposed a modular system entitling each child to one module of three hours of pedagogy each day. Additional modules would depend on the par-ents' employment. For children not entitled to full-time care, the report suggested less costly arrangements such as day care minders—part-time working women and housewives taking care of a group of children by turns—to supplement public facil-ities (PPII 1973, 524ff). These suggestions challenged some of the fundamental ped-agogical and child-centered ideas of Danish child care policy, implying, for instance, that some children would be cared for in two or three different settings a day, and thus met strong criticism from experts, professionals and parents.

Shortly after, the country was confronted with increasing oil prices and a severe economic crisis. As a consequence, between 1970 and 1980, unemployment rose from 1 to 7 percent and remained high for several years. The subsequent fall in tax revenues and increase in public expenditures put pressure on Danish welfare policies. The government anticipated the situation would be only temporary; meanwhile, admission of part-time workers into the unemployment insurance system and the enactment of a special extension measure served to keep the long-term unemployed—both men and women—in the workforce.[2] The rules linking access to child care to the labor market were tightened, but the child-centered legislation implied that the children of the unemployed should not lose their places in child care facilities. The government allowed some municipalities to force unemployed parents to take care of their children themselves, but only a limited number adopted this practice, and they had to guarantee that the children could return to the child care facilities once the parents were reemployed. In this way, the social pedagogic philosophy, stressing the needs of the children, served to lessen the negative impact of the economic downturn and unemployment on the daily situation of children.

After the so-called landslide national election in 1973,[3] the political climate changed radically, sparking an intense debate on whether the welfare state needed restructuring. Two parties formed in the beginning of the 1970s seriously questioned the public commitment to child care. One was an extreme right-wing party, the Progress Party, which above all presented itself as an antitax party. This party, which gained 16 percent of the parliamentary seats, launched a massive campaign targeted at child care professionals, whom they accused of indoctrinating the children in Marxism. The second group, the Christian People's Party, had been formed in reaction to the liberalization of pornography and abortion. This party, which gained 4 percent of parliamentary seats, ascribed great importance to family policies, arguing that children should be cared for in the family by one of their parents.

Faced with the economic downturn, the center and right wing parties decided to reduce public expenditures. The most extensive cut, of DKK119 million, passed in 1975, was targeted at staffing in child care facilities. This prompted a heated conflict and numerous protest demonstrations supported by professionals, parents, and left-wing politicians. Pedagogues working with small children had formed a proper union in 1973. It was quite leftist and adopted an extreme wagework philosophy, which above all was aimed at advocating the interests of the professionals. Although the unions did not welcome parents' interference in their daily work, the two groups often joined forces against cutbacks. The new feminist movement formed in the late 1960s mobilized a large number of young women to participate in those actions, especially at the local level (Dahlerup 1998). Considering the strong opposition to the previous policy voiced by the new political actors and the modest changes that were enacted, the model proved to be rather resistant. The socialist parties, some of the center parties and the Conservative People's Party still defended the public sector's commitment to child care, and they prevented major changes in the area.

In 1974, the regulation of child care facilities was integrated into the new Social Assistance Act ("Bistandsloven"), scheduled to take effect in 1976. It confirmed the basic decisions of the 1964 act, but assigned a more important role to the municipalities in accordance with decisions from the early 1970s to decentralize social policy. This increased the municipalities' latitude in determining the level of coverage, the balance between institutions and day care solutions, prices for services, and level of staffing. However, Parliament would still set the terms for funding, staffing, and parents' fees. Neither the extreme right nor the extreme left voted for the legislation, but only the extreme right was motivated by a wish to reduce the level of public commitment to child care (*Folketingstidende* 1973–74: 1269–1273; 7834–7836).

During the same period, the child-centered perspective on Danish family policy, which was framed as a children's policy,[4] gained ideological strength. In 1975, a commission on children formed by the Social Democratic government asked for a broad evaluation of the situation of children. In its report, the commission, which consisted of a small group of politicians and experts committed to children's well-being, warned that the children were paying a high price for the past decades' developments, among other things because some children spent many hours a day in child care facilities. The commission recommended shorter working hours, prolonged maternity leave, policies encouraging fathers to participate in child care, and more child care services to meet the demand. At the same time, however, it maintained that gender equality should be regarded as a central objective of Danish policies and recommended no policies encouraging women to leave the work force (Betænkning no. 918, 1981, chap. 8). While the actual success of the commission was limited, it did have a certain impact on the discourse on family structures and policy objectives.

In 1982, a bourgeois government took power and managed to stay in office until 1993. This was a unique situation, since the country, with very few exceptions, had been governed by Social Democratic minority coalitions for a very long period. In light of the second oil crisis, in 1979–80, and an unemployment rate of about 9 percent, the new government introduced cost-efficiency measures and launched programs to modernize the public sector. At the same time, proposals to encourage the responsibility of families and social networks suggested by the Social Democratic minister of social affairs in 1980 were intensified, yet retrenchment remained mainly rhetorical. Apart from upgrading day care in private homes and allowing more children to be accommodated in child care centers, no significant changes were made.

In 1987, earmarked funding for social measures was replaced by block grants calculated on the basis of demographic and social criteria, and municipalities were allowed further autonomy. In this way, another step toward decentralization was taken. The state could, however, provide supplementary funding for specific purposes. Thus, despite the fundamental restructuring of the political landscape and the economic situation, the bottom line was that the main pillars of the child care model remained intact and public commitment was even increased.

Toward More Private Solutions

In the 1990s, the restructuring of the welfare state reappeared on the political agenda. Under the bourgeois government, private and family-based solutions to child care gained momentum in several ways. Experiments with more flexible and private solutions to child care were introduced, and the political parties increasingly focused on cost efficiency and allowing choice among different types of child care arrangements. The bourgeois parties in particular argued for rethinking solutions to child care, whereas the Left and the Social Democrats were more reluctant. Within these parties, there was strong resistance to contracting out public care services and especially to allowing for-profit care arrangements. The role of mothers in caring for the youngest children was extended by enactment of a child care leave act in 1992–93. This scheme became quite popular; in the period 1994–96 one-fourth of all mothers of children under three had taken child care leave. Private solutions were also encouraged through the so-called pool arrangements, passed in 1990 with the support of all parties. These provided subsidies for child care or groups of children either in family settings or on business premises. While the number of pool arrangements accepted was modest (about two hundred obtained funding in 1994–96, only a few on business premises), they represented a shift in ideas about responsibility for organizing and providing care. The organization of these arrangements was put in the hands of the parents, who also had to find the physical location themselves. During the same period, decentralization of child care services was enhanced by the introduction of "user" boards of parents, which gained influence on issues like spending and hours of operation.

In 1993, a Social Democratic government took over, and shortly after, kick-started the economy, which over the next few years entered a relatively good period, with unemployment falling from 12 percent in 1993 to 6 percent in 1999. Subsequently, a historical turn in relation to income maintenance occurred, and access to unemployment benefits and social assistance became contingent on claimants to engage in job training, education, or sheltered employment. This move from passive to active measures did not, however, influence child care services, which were regarded as a means of meeting governmental policy goals, in terms of both employment and family structures. When the prime minister announced a child care guarantee planned to take effect by the end of 1995, pressure on the municipalities to meet the demand for child care increased. Some municipalities, however, reacted against this, and when national politicians barred municipalities from increasing parents' fees, conflicts arose between the national and local levels. Toward the end of 1999, a compromise was reached: starting in 2000, municipalities would be allowed to increase parents' fees from 30 to 33 percent of the expenses over three years, provided that they had implemented a child care guarantee. In the fall of 2000, almost 90 percent of all municipalities had implemented the guarantee.

When the social legislation was amended in 1997 (Lov om Social Service, implemented in 1998), the choice between private and public solutions to child care was enhanced. The legislation still contained the same formulations regarding the public sector's obligation to provide child care, but leeway to contract out child care was enhanced, though only to a limited degree and on special conditions. The legislation also included a free-choice scheme, which had been granted on an experimental basis since 1994. The scheme, which was targeted at parents who had already been offered a place in a service but could now choose to receive money to purchase child care from others, was optional for the municipalities.

During this period, market principles found their way to the public sector, and several attempts to enhance cost efficiency in the child care sector were considered. Recommendations to link the price of care to the actual use in order to increase the parents' incentive to spend more time with their children have been made, but are not yet implemented (Kommunenes Landsforening et al. 1999).

Quality has become a dominant issue in the child care debate, and it has been discussed whether there has been a trade-off between quantity and quality. Investigations into the rate of trained staffing indicate that levels have remained stable for crèches, kindergartens, and age-integrated services, but total expenditures seem to have declined. Recently, there has been more attention to the limited reading and writing abilities of Danish children; as a result, schools are now allowed to enroll children below six, and some kindergartens have decided to emphasize the role of educational activities. Yet the social pedagogical ideas are still considered the key objective of preschool activities.

Thus, on the whole, there is little evidence that the main pillars of Danish child care policy have been undermined by restructuring (Borchorst 2000). While the number of private child care initiatives has clearly increased, the supply of kindergartens and crèches has remained stable, and the number of age-integrated facilities for children under six has grown. Universalism was preserved, if not strengthened, by the implementation of the child care guarantee, and social pedagogic ideas are still regarded as the main objectives of the policy. Since the 1970s, policies have become less consensual, since the Left is critical of privatization in terms of both marketization and increasing the caring role of the family. By contrast, the bourgeois parties seek to enhance both. In the final analysis, however, it is clear that a majority of parties have supported the introduction of new solutions at the same time as they defend the existing model.

The Resilience of the Danish Child Care Model

The question remains as to why the Danish child care model has been characterized by continuity more than by change, even in periods of economic and political turmoil. One possible explanation is that the main pillars of Danish child policy were consolidated relatively early through a two-stage process emphasizing pedagogy and universalism, and this has generated a certain irreversibility. The absence of prominent actors working to roll back the public commitment and the presence of a number of actors seeking to promote it are, presumably, also significant factors. Initially, it was a strategic alliance between progressive pedagogues and Social Democratic politicians in the 1960s that placed child care on the political agenda, but in the decades that followed, the major decisions on child care were consensual. This may be explained as a political necessity, since the country has only rarely been governed by majority coalitions; yet the level of consensus on this issue has been remarkable, even by Danish standards. During the first half of the twentieth century, support for social pedagogical ideas was linked to preventive objectives, but during the prosperous 1960s, child-centered motives became conjoined with an interest in meeting the need for labor and support for gender equality. The principles of pedagogy and gender equality persisted through the periods of austerity in the 1970s and 1980s, when the policy remained relatively stable.

While it has been decisive that different actors have joined forces to protect or expand the model, it should be noted that the configuration of actors has changed over time. Toward the end of the 1960s, the progressive pedagogues who had been influential in the previous periods disappeared, and in the early 1970s, child care employees established proper unions, which initially adopted a very strong wage work philosophy. They constituted a vested interest that sought to maintain public institutions as the core of child care solutions. During the past decade, the wage work philosophy has been downplayed, and the unions have developed an occupational policy combining the demand for proper working conditions with child-centered arguments. Professionals have often joined forces with parents against the municipalities to protest cutbacks in child care services. While the parents represent a strong pressure group locally, decentralization has weakened the role of national protests, such as those held in the mid-1970s. Still, the parents constitute a large and visible voter group for the political parties, which have lost their traditional class-based constituencies. Most of the parties appeal to this group during election campaigns and are aware of the fact that a large number of families with small children depend on the availability of child care. From an institutional point of view, it has been crucial that child care services have remained under the auspices of the Ministry of Social Affairs. This has served to maintain the social pedagogical policy objectives as a major policy goal.

The Implications for Gender Equality

Beyond any doubt, the extension of child care services has facilitated the reconciliation of motherhood with paid work. The difference between the activity rates of men and women today is less than 10 percentage points (in 1999, it was 82 percent for men, 74 percent for women), and the two genders exhibit the same generational profile with high labor market activity throughout the life course. The emphasis on providing full-time services through the social system rather than part-time services through the educational system (as is the pattern in several other EU countries) has supported the extension of full-time work for women. In 1999, only 19 percent of Danish women worked part-time.

The question remains to what extent this radical extension of women's paid work has fostered more gender equality. A number of studies have demonstrated that Danish (and Scandinavian) women have acquired a well-developed citizenship in terms of the right to receive care (Lewis 1993; Leira 1989; Knijn and Kremer 1997). This has nurtured their autonomy in relation to husbands and marriage and weakened the male breadwinning features of the Danish society. It is, however, questionable whether Danish women have had the option to choose *not* to engage in paid work, since their right to time for care has been relatively restricted (Knijn and Kremer 1997). Feminist scholars have argued that women's control over their choices is crucial to their interests (Hernes 1987; Jónasdóttir 1991); according to this argument, gender equality is enhanced if women's options in relation to reproduction and care are improved. However, the question of which circumstances afford people real options and free choices is an intricate one. Choices are often restricted by a number of conditions of which people may not be aware or able to anticipate the long-term effects. A gender-differentiated division of care and breadwinning may for instance increase gender inequality in terms of social benefits. Furthermore, the relatively high divorce rate implies that a care/breadwinning split may have more serious consequences for women in the long run.

From this perspective it is problematic that during the 1990s gender did not occupy a central role in Danish policy debates beyond policies of equal opportunities. The debate over changes in child-care leave illustrate this point well. While the use of the leave has been extremely gendered, politicians have largely ignored the impact of this factor on the decision-making process (Borchorst 1999). Furthermore, a neoliberal discourse seems to have gained ground in public discussions: the division of care and breadwinning is being interpreted as a consequence of women's own preferences, while there is a strong notion that the battle for gender equality has been won.

Expansion of the care sector has above all triggered a shift from private to public responsibility, but the gendered division of care has by and large remained intact. Paid care work is highly segregated, and as mentioned earlier, Danish policies have been less effective than those of Sweden and Norway in encouraging fathers' participation in parenting by improving their social rights to provide care. This raises the question of whether women's dependency on husbands and marriage has merely been replaced by a dependency on the state. However, it is crucial to focus on variations in dependency attached to different roles vis-à-vis the state, and related to different types of welfare states and welfare systems (Hernes 1987). There is a huge difference between being dependent as a client on social welfare, with public assistance as one's only source of income, and being dependent as a consumer of a public service offered as a universal benefit. The latter, of course, enhances access to market income and actually reduces one's dependency as a client (Borchorst 1998). Furthermore, the situation as a client is often combined with social control and stigmatization, albeit with great variations among different welfare states. Consequently, I argue that the development of child care has generated some unquestionable gains for women, even though forces pulling towards both increased gender equality and reproduction of gendered patterns of care and breadwinning may be identified.

Future Scenarios and Dilemmas of Danish Child Care Policy

It is still not clear whether Danish child care policies will be subject to radical changes in the foreseeable future. Exogenous factors such as the European integration process and globalization have put pressure on governments to reduce the overall level of public expenditures in order to be competitive. The opening of borders and increasing calls for the harmonization of structural policies in EU member states may result in reduction of tax revenues in countries with a very high level of taxation, such as Denmark.[5] However, services will presumably be less vulnerable than cash benefits, which EU citizens may bring to other member states. Furthermore, almost all Organization for Economic Cooperation and Development countries face similar problems in terms of aging populations; within the EU, the European Council regards integration of women in the labor force as the major solution to this problem. At the same time, child care provisions are regarded as a means to facilitate this integration (cf. the Lisbon summit, in March 2000).

The most probable scenario is that pressure to provide child care will continue in all countries. Since Denmark has been at the forefront in terms of enlarging the female labor force and providing services for preschool children, it is less likely that the country will feel pressure to redesign its child care policy, at least as far as availability of services is concerned. However, the tax-financed universal Danish model based predominantly on public institutional solutions will probably not become predominant in Christian democratic and liberal countries, which are more likely to increase child care through a mix of private and public solutions to issues such as qualifications, organization, and financing of care. By the same token, the trend toward a proliferation of types of care, including both for-profit services and care in family settings, will undoubtedly also continue to grow. This development is likely to increase diversity in the care of children according to their social background. In terms of gender equality, a realistic scenario is that the caring role of fathers will be strengthened, but parental choice, which some bourgeois parties wish to enhance even further in terms of cash for care by the parents themselves, will probably also increase care by mothers. This may particularly affect less educated women and those who are marginal to the labor market. On the other hand, a majority of political parties will probably resist a fundamental restructuring of the Danish model.

Therefore a situation of continuous adaptations and increasing diversity is the most likely future scenario.

Notes

1. The upper chamber was abolished in 1953.

2. The rate of insured women in the labor force increased from 22 percent in 1973 to 56 percent in 1979; the corresponding figures for men were 45 and 61 percent (Bonke 1997).

3. Three new parties managed to get elected, and two regained representation. Together, the five parties occupied one-third of the seats in Parliament, thereby seriously challenging the role of the four old political parties, which had occupied 90 percent of the seats before the election.

4. The term *family policy* has not occupied a central position in Danish politics. Family benefits have been administered as part of social policy, and the country had a minister of family affairs for only a year and a half in the mid-1960s. Thus, from a conceptual point of view, it is precise to characterize Danish family policies as implicit, as some of the major comparative studies have done (Kamerman and Kahn 1978). This is, however, not accurate for policy efforts and level of spending, since the country's expenditures on family benefits have been comparatively high.

5. Indeed, the Danish welfare state today has the largest share of tax-financed benefits among the EU countries.

References

Bergqvist, Christina. 2000a. "Child care and Parental Leave Models." In *Equal Democracies? Gender and Politics in the Nordic Countries,* ed. Christina Bergqvist, Anette Borchorst, Ann-Dorte Christensen, Viveca Ramstedt-Silén, Nina C. Raaum, and Audur Styrkársdóttir. Oslo: Scandinavian University Press.

Bergqvist, Christina, et al., eds. 2000b. *Equal Democracies? Gender and Politics in the Nordic Countries,* Oslo: Scandinavian University Press.

Betænkning. 1936. *Foreløbig Betænkning vedrørende Børnehavespørgsmålet* (Interim Report on the Kindergarten Issue). Copenhagen: Befolkningskommissionen.

_____. 1950. *Betænkning vedrørende børneforsorgsinsitutionernes økonomi m.v.* (Report on the Economy, etc., of Child Welfare Institutions). Copenhagen: Udvalg om forebyggene børneforsorg og opdragelseshjemmene.

_____ no. 57. 1954. *Fællesanlæg til lettelse af hjemmets arbejde* (Common Facilities for Relief of Work in the Home). København: Boligministeriets udvalg vedrørende kollektive anlæg.

_____ no. 326. 1963. *Revision af Loven om Børne-og Ungdomsforsorg* (Revision of the Law on Child and Youth Welfare). Copenhagen: Revisionsudvalget.

_____ no. 337. 1963. *Om børnehaveproblemer* (About Kindergartens). Copenhagen: Børne-og Ungdomsforsorgens Pædagogiske Nævn.

_____ no. 715. 1974. *Vedrørende kvindernes stilling i samfundet* (Regarding Women's Position in Society). Copenhagen: Kommissionen Vedrørende Kuindernes stilling: Samfundet.

_____ no. 918. 1981. *Børnekommissionens betænkning* (The Child Commission's Report). Copenhagen: Børnekommissionen.

Bonke, Jens, ed. 1997. *Levevilkår i Danmark* (Living Conditions in Denmark). Copenhagen: Socialforskningsinstituttet, Danmarks Statistik.

Borchorst, Anette. 1985a. "Velfærdsstat og bøornepasniine: ligestilling, pasning eller pædagogik?" (Welfare State and Child Care: Equality, Care, or Pedagogies?). *Kritiske Historikere* (Critical History) 1: 32–56.

_____ . 1985b. "Barnomsorgspolitik och kvinnokrav" (Child Care Policy and Women's Demands). *Kvinnovetenskaplig tidskrift* 6 no. 3: 30–43.

_____ . 1998. "Feminist Thinking about the Welfare State." In *Revisioning Gender*, ed. Myra Marx Ferree, Judith Lorber, and Beth Hess. Thousand Oaks, Calif.: Sage.

_____ . 1999. "Den kønnede virkelighed—den kønsløse debat" (The Gendered Reality—The Nongendered Debate). In *Den demokratiske udfordring* (The Democratic Challenge), ed. Jørgen Goul Andersen, Peter Munk Christiansen, Torben Beck Jøorgensen, Lise Togeby, and Signild Vallgårda. Gylling: Hans Reitzels Forlag.

Borchorst, Annette, and Jørgen Elm Larsen. 2000. "Enlige mødre—velfrærdsstatens kritiske målestok?" (Single Mothers—the Critical Yardstick of the Welfare State). In *Kontinuitet & forandring—kontinuiteter og forandringer i samfundets differentierings-og interationsformer* (Continuity and Change: Continuities and Changes in Societal Forms of Differentiation and Integration), ed. Jørgen Elm Larsen, Jens Lind, and Iver Hornemann Møller. Gylling: Samfundslitteratur.

Dahlerup, Drude. 1998. *Rødstrømperne. Den danske rødstrømpebevægelses udvikling, nytænkning og gennemslag 1970–1985* (The Redstockings: The Development of the Danish Redstocking Movement, Innovation and Breakthrough), vols. 1 and 2. Haslev: Gyldendal.

Esping-Andersen, Gøsta. 1990. *The Three Worlds of Welfare Capitalism*. Princeton, N.J.: Princeton University Press.

_____ . 1996. *Social Foundations of Postindustrial Economies*. New York: Oxford University Press.

Europa Kommissionen. 1998. *Mulighederne for at forene arbejde og familieliv i Europa* (The Possibilities of Combining Work and Family Life in Europe). Brussels: Directorate-General, Employment and Social Affairs.

Folketinget. (Debates in Lower House of Parliament).

Folketingstidende. (Final legislation). Copenhagen.

Hernes, Helga. 1987. *Welfare State and Woman Power*. Oslo: Norwegian University Press.

Jónasdóttir, Anna. 1991. *Love, Power and Political Interests*. Kumla: Örebro Studies 7.

Kamerman, Sheila B., and Alfred J. Kahn. 1978. *Family Policy, Government and Families in Fourteen Countries*. New York: Columbia University Press.

Knijn, Trudie, and Monique Kremer. 1997. "Gender and the Caring Dimension of Welfare States: Toward Inclusive Citizenship." *Social Politics* 4 no. 3: 328–61.

Kolstrup, Søren. 1996. *Velfærdsstatens rødder fra kommunesocialisme til folke-pension* (The Welfare State's Roots from Local Socialism to Old Age Pension). Viborg: SFAH.

Kommunenes Landsforening (National Association of Municipalities) et al. 1999. *Fleksibilitet og betalingssystemer inden for dagtilbud til børn* (Flexibility and Payment Systems in Daytime Services for Children). Copenhagen: Socialministeriet.

Landstinget. (Debates in Lower House of Parliament).

Leira, Arnlaug. 1989. *Models of Motherhood: Welfare State Policies and Everyday Practices: The Scandinavian Experience.* Oslo: Institute for Social Research.

_____. 1998. "Caring as a Social Right: Cash for Child Care and Daddy Leave." *Social Politics* 3, no. 3: 362–78.

Lewis, Jane. 1992. "Gender and the Development of Welfare Regimes," *Journal of European Social Policy* 2, no. 3: 169–83.

_____, ed. 1993. *Women and Social Policies in Europe.* London: Elgar.

Lewis, Jane, and Ilona Ostner. 1994. *Gender and the Evolution of European Social Policies.* Zes-Arbeitspapier no. 4. Bremen: Universität Bremen.

Lovtidende. (Final legislation).

Munck, Agnete. 1981. *Asyler, frøbelbørnehaver og folkebørnehaver i København 1828–ca. 1920, set fra en klassetilgangsvinkel* (Asylums, Fröbel Kindergartens and Public Kindergartens in Copenhagen 1828–ca. 1920, Seen from a Class Perspective). Aarhus: Specialeopgave, Institut for Statskundskab, Aarhus Universitet.

NOSOKO (Nordic Social-Statistical Committee). 1999. *Social tryghed i de nordiske lande* (Social Protection in the Nordic Countries). Copenhagen: NOSOSKO.

Orloff, Ann Shola. 1993. "Gender and the Social Rights of Citizenship: the Comparative Analysis of Gender Relations and Welfare States." *American Sociological Review* 58: 303–28.

PPII (Perspektiv redegørelse [Long Term Report]). 1973. Copenhagen.

Rigsdagstidende. (Parliamentary records before 1953). Copenhagen.

Rosenbeck, Bente. 2000. "Modernization of Marriage in Scandinavia." In *Women's Politics and Women in Politics.* In Honour of Ida Blom, eds. Sølvi Sogner and Gro Hagemann. Bergen University: Cappelen Akademisk Forlag.

Sainsbury, Diane, ed. 1996. *Gender Equality and Welfare States.* Cambridge: Cambridge University Press.

CHAPTER 12

Welfare State Restructuring and Child Care in Sweden

Christina Bergqvist and Anita Nyberg

Introduction

The 1990s was one of the most critical periods for the Swedish welfare model. The employment rate fell dramatically and unemployment soared to levels unthinkable since the 1930s.[1] The situation began to improve only as the decade came to an end. The employment crisis, in turn, produced an accelerating public sector deficit, with revenues plummeting and public expenditures skyrocketing.[2] In addition to the economic crisis, there were also other factors that constituted a challenge to the stability of the traditional Swedish welfare state. First, the Social Democratic Party lost its historically dominant position, which opened the way for neoliberal ideas of marketization and privatization. The internationalization of capital markets and financial transactions, plus Sweden's participation in the European integration project, also posed new challenges.

Given the unemployment situation, the financial strains, globalization, and the spread of neoliberal ideas, it is reasonable to assume that serious attempts to transform the Swedish welfare state might have been undertaken. The aim of this chapter is to analyze the characteristics of this restructuring and to determine whether retrenchment did indeed take place in the Swedish welfare state in the 1990s. We will do this through the lens of public child care. The Swedish welfare state has as a political goal included the provision of high quality child care since the 1970s.[3] It was intended as a vehicle to promote gender equality and full employment, as well as equality between different kinds of families and equal provision of care and education for preschool children (Leira 1993; Hirdman 1998; Bergqvist 1999).

As Paul Pierson has argued, retrenchment involves more than cuts (1996, 157). In addition to expenditure cuts, changes in policies and program structure must also be examined. Our investigation accordingly relies on a combination of data on expenditures and qualitative analysis of the child care sector. We examine Swedish child care in relation to five important characteristics associated with the Swedish welfare state: (1) generous public spending; (2) high quality in social services; (3) limited scope for the private sector in social services; (4) universalism; and (5) egalitarianism (Esping-Andersen and Korpi 1987; Pierson 1996; Esping-Andersen 1999, 78–81; Sainsbury 1999, 259). By analyzing whether and how these characteristics have changed in the 1990s, we assess where the Swedish welfare state is heading.

The Historical Legacy and Development of Child Care Policies

The Social Democratic regime, for which Sweden is often the exemplar, is typified by universal benefits, a level of compensation and quality of service high enough to meet middle class expectations, and a strong commitment to equality and full employment (Esping-Andersen 1990). While Gøsta Esping-Andersen has focused on the relationship between the state, market, and class, feminist researchers have emphasized the importance of including the family and gender relations (Sainsbury 1994). The move from the male-breadwinner to dual-breadwinner norm has been one of the biggest social changes of the last thirty years, and the social democratic regime has tended to be more supportive of this change than other models (Hernes 1987; Borchorst 1994; Siim 1997). This is especially visible in Sweden's child care policies.

Although small public grants for child care institutions have been available since the 1940s, the demand for public child care has always been greater than supply. For example, in 1965, only 3 percent of all preschool children were in public child care. At the same time, nearly 36 percent of the mothers of preschool children were employed. The majority of parents arranged child care in the informal sector and this was common well into the 1980s (Nyberg 2000). It was, however, in the 1970s that public child care, together with the transformation of maternal leave into an income-related parental leave, became important characteristics of the "new" Swedish welfare and gender equality model.

The introduction of a National Preschool Act in 1975 imposed on local authorities the obligation to expand public child care. The municipalities were now required to provide all six-year olds with at least 525 hours of free preschooling—that is, at least part-time child care for six-year olds.[4] For younger children, however, eligibility for a place in public child care was linked to parent's employment (or study) status. Exceptions were made primarily for children in need of special support. The demand for public child care was always greater than supply. In 1985, the Social Democratic government increased its efforts to make good on its commitment to working parents, aiming to ensure places in public child care for all children between one and a half and six years of age whose parents worked or studied (Bengtsson 1995; Ministry of Education and Science 1999).

As a result, the number of children enrolled in different forms of publicly subsidized child care increased substantially. The most common form of service is the child care center, but family child care units and preschools remain important. In 1975, only 17 percent of all children between one and six were enrolled in one of these forms of child care. By 1990 the number had risen to 57 percent (see table 12.1). The use of public child care has to be seen in relation to the age of the child and the length of the paid parental leave. Today, hardly any children under the age of one are enrolled in public child care because of the long parental leave period, which increased from around six months to over a year in the mid-1970s.

Between the 1970s and 1990s the expansion of public child care services was generally an accepted policy objective (Gustafsson and Antman 1996). Two of the three bourgeois parties certainly remained in favor of a care allowance and were critical, in principle, of too much state involvement. Nevertheless, even when they formed the government in the latter part of the 1970s, they refrained from introducing any significant changes. During the 1980s, however, a debate, embedded in a discourse of "choice," arose over whether to increase for-profit alternatives. The social democratic government opened up the possibility for public support to centers not run by the municipalities but continued to exclude private for-profit child care, which prompted severe criticisms from the opposition, but also from some social democrats (Bengtsson 1995; Mahon 1997).

Choices and Challenges in the 1990s

Throughout the 1980s, the nonsocialist parties intensified their promotion of neoliberal alternatives that stressed choice, decentralization, markets, and privatization. In addition to questioning the rule prohibiting public subsidies for commercial child care, it was argued that parents did not have a real choice between staying at home with children or working. Introduction of a care allowance—long favored by the Conservative, Center (agrarian), and small Christian Democratic Parties—was again touted as a means for providing such choice. With the election in 1991 of a bourgeois coalition government, headed by Carl Bildt of the Conservative Party, a child care policy in line with neoliberal and conservative ideas was on the agenda. Interestingly enough, while the Bildt government introduced elements of a bourgeois policy, it also expanded the social democratic/liberal line of earlier child care policies.

Thus the care allowance was introduced in July 1994, just as new elections were approaching. The aim of the allowance was to make it possible for one of the parents to stay at home for a longer period than parental leave, which lasts for about a year with income compensation plus three months with a flat-rate benefit. This version of care allowance was, however, designed more as a child care check than as a mother's wage. The parents could use the money to enable one parent to stay at home or for child care. Parents could also choose between public and private forms of child care, both of which were eligible for public subsidies.[5]

TABLE 12.1: CHILDREN ENROLLED IN PUBLICLY SUBSIDIZED CHILD CARE CENTERS, PRESCHOOLS, AND FAMILY DAY CARE UNITS, 1975–1990
(IN PERCENT OF THE POPULATION BY AGE)

	1–2 YEARS OLD	3–6 YEARS OLD	1–6 YEARS OLD IN TOTAL
1975	16	17	17
1980	31	38	36
1985	45	55	52
1990	44	64	57

SOURCE: Skolverket (1998).

The government coalition, however, also included the Liberal Party, which continued to favor the right to institutionalized child care and a more equal division of labor between women and men in the family. In particular, the Liberal minister for social affairs and gender equality, Bengt Westerberg, was a driving force behind two important developments—a new Act on Child Care, and what is popularly known as the "daddy month," a measure designed to get fathers to take a greater share of parental leave (Bergqvist, Kuusipalo, and Styrkarsdóttir 1999).

The Act on Child Care was introduced as part of a move from detailed state regulation of the municipalities towards a general decentralization of authority and responsibilities to the municipalities. This process involved a tightening and clarification of municipal obligations to provide child care without unreasonable delay for children between the ages of one and twelve. The main criteria remained, however, that the parents were working or studying or that the child had special needs. The municipalities were also given more freedom. During the phase of expansion in the 1970s and 1980s, public child care had been part of centralized government funding. Gross costs of child care were divided in such a way that the state and the municipalities each covered about 45 percent of the costs and parents' fees the rest. In 1993, program-specific state grants to the municipalities for child care were replaced by block grants (Ministry of Education and Science 1999; SOU 2000: 3; Oberhuemer and Ulich 1997). The municipalities thus have a higher autonomy today as to how these funds should be expended and how child care should be run and organized. At the same time, the act required the municipalities to provide child care "without unreasonable delay."

To summarize, the family policies of the bourgeois government were grounded on a contradictory mixture of traditional family values, neoliberal ideas of privatization and of gender equality. It would thus be erroneous to conclude that a radical shift towards a new model was taken. The basic components of the parental leave legislation were maintained and the right to child care was strengthened. The care allowance, moreover, became but an historical parenthesis. The Social Democratic government that took office in the fall of 1994 abolished it while retaining the "daddy month," the Act on Child Care, and the opening to public funding for commercial child care centers. Public responsibility for child care remained strong throughout the 1990s, even though the state had assumed a new role. Authority and responsibilities had been decentralized and, at the local level, the provision of child care became more diversified.

Public Expenditure on Child Care[6]

One criterion to distinguish types of welfare states is the level of expenditure on social services. In Sweden, a large proportion of national income is devoted to the goal of provision of high quality services for all. In terms of child care, the provision of accessible, high-quality child care services is understood to contribute to a good start

in life for children from all social backgrounds, as well as supporting parents, especially mothers, in managing the tension between paid work and caregiving responsibilities. The proportion of public resources spent on child care can thus be seen as an
indication of the extent of the state's commitment to the two-breadwinner models
and to equal opportunities for parents and children from different backgrounds.

The most common way of measuring the extensiveness of the public sector is
the cost of social services as a share of gross domestic product (GDP). In this respect, public child care has become an increasingly important sector in the Swedish
economy. The contribution of public child care to GDP increased from 0.2 percent
around 1970 to 1.68 percent in 1980 and 2.4 percent in 1990. This contribution is
larger than that of agriculture and comparable in size to the chemical industry
(Kjulin 1995 III, 2; Edebalk, Ståhlberg, and Wadensjö 1998, 134; SCB 2000). This
reflects the high priority attached to public support for child care, at least until the
beginning of the 1990s when Sweden entered a severe economic crisis.

Given the state of the economy, the unemployment level, the increasing social
expenditure, and the worsening of the public finances one might have expected calls
for cost cutting and retrenchments in public child care. The costs of child care as a

FIGURE 12.1: COSTS OF PUBLIC CHILD CARE AS A SHARE OF GDP, GROSS COSTS
FOR PUBLIC CHILD CARE, NUMBER OF CHILDREN IN PUBLIC CHILD CARE, AND
COST PER CHILD (INDEX 1991 = 100)

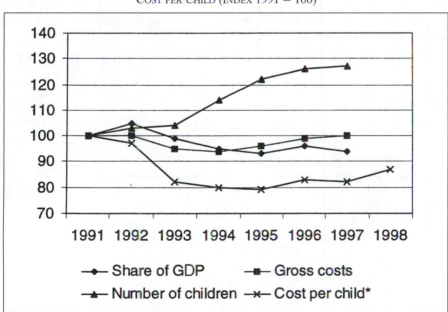

*Costs per hour (1991–1995) and costs per child full-time (1996–1998) in public child care centers.
Unfortunately, due to changes in the statistics in 1998 it is not possible to make comparisons with the
years after 1997 in the other measurements. Until 1997 preschool covered one- to six-year olds, in
1998 one- to five-year olds.

SOURCES: SOU (2000 3, 115); SCB (2000); Skolverket (1999a, diagram 5).

share of GDP did decrease somewhat between 1991 and 1997 (see fig. 12.1). This provides, however, a rather crude measure of public commitment to child care provision, for it is affected by changes in the GDP as well as resources devoted to child care. If instead we look at the development of total gross costs in fixed prices, we find that the amount was the same in 1997 as it was in 1991, with a dip in between. This suggests that public child care remained a high priority.

When we take the number of children in child care into consideration, we get a somewhat different picture. Around 188,000 more children were in public child care in 1998 than in 1990. In other words, fewer resources were spent per child. In fixed prices the decrease was about 14 percent per child between 1991 and 1998 (SOU 2000: 3, 113ff). Moreover, parents have been contributing a rising share of the costs. In 1990 parents paid 10 percent of the total gross costs of child care in direct child care fees but by 1998 this proportion had increased to 17 percent. As the total gross costs for public child care remained the same, the total amount, as well as the amount per child, of "public" money spent on child care has diminished.

This development should not, however, be seen as a result of changed political priorities and restructuring, but as a "temporary" retrenchment. Harsh economic circumstances combined with increased demand for child care as a result of a high rate of fertility increased the strains on the system. Toward the end of the decade, the economy improved while fertility rates fell.[7] The resources used for child care—independently of how it is measured—increased again. Due to new reforms, described in the next section, more resources will in the future be dedicated to the child care sector.

Public Child Care and Universalism

Social rights and benefits are usually classified as universal, labor market related, or income/needs tested. *Universalism* in a strict sense of the term means that all citizens or individuals in a specific category (e.g., a particular age group) get the same bene-

TABLE 12.2: DEMAND AND SUPPLY OF PUBLIC CHILD CARE 1980–1996.
NUMBERS IN THOUSANDS AND PERCENT OF ALL CHILDREN. PRESCHOOL-AGE
CHILDREN (3 MONTHS TO SIX YEARS)

YEAR	DEMAND		SUPPLY		DIFFERENCE	
	NUMBER	PERCENT OF ALL CHILDREN	NUMBER	PERCENT OF ALL CHILDREN	NUMBER	PERCENT OF ALL CHILDREN
1980	348	49	211	30	137	19
1986	374	58	299	47	75	12
1990	400	57	337	48	63	9
1993	443	56	386	49	57	7
1996	494	62	444	55	50	7

SOURCES: SCB (1994 and 1997).

fits and same rights without any restrictions based on need or labor-market status. The flat-rate child allowance for all children up to fifteen years of age is an example of a genuinely universal benefit and primary and secondary education are provided as a universal social service. As a concept, universalism is not always used in this way. In the Scandinavian context it is often used for social insurance and services that are widely available and apply to large segments of the population or all wage earners (Anttonen and Sipilä 1996).

From a comparative perspective, Swedish policies can perhaps be considered universal, but many programs have indeed been tied to employment status (Clayton and Pontusson 1998). More specifically, the main social programs usually consist of a flat-rate universal component, based on citizenship or residence, and a more generous component dependent on one's labor-market participation. In the case of parental leave insurance this means that citizens and permanent residents who become mothers or fathers are entitled to parental leave for the same length of time and everyone is entitled to a low flat-rate benefit. When one has been employed during the last eight months before the child is born, one receives the more generous income-related benefit. As long as almost everyone—including women—is employed, the vast majority of citizens are eligible for the richer benefits. When unemployment grows, however, as it did during the 1990s, a growing number of citizens are forced to rely on the flat-rate benefit (SOU 2000: 3).

As we have seen, the right to child care has never been universal in the same sense as education. Except for some hours of preschool for six-year-olds, the right to public child care has in practice been restricted to children whose parents are in paid work, or to children with special needs. That is, labor-market participation or need have formed the basis for eligibility to publicly financed child care. Moreover, supply has never matched demand, so even employed parents have been unable to find the child care they need, as table 12.2 shows.

In times of cuts in public spending, moreover, one might expect a tightening of eligibility rules as one way to save money. This has not, however, been the route taken in Sweden. In fact, more children than ever had access to child care institutions in the 1990s. As can be seen from table 12.2, both demand and supply increased substantially between 1980 and 1996. In 1980, the gap was 19 percentage

TABLE 12.3: CHILDREN ENROLLED IN PUBLICLY SUBSIDIZED CHILD CARE CENTERS, PRESCHOOLS, AND FAMILY DAY CARE UNITS, 1990–1997
(PERCENT OF THE POPULATION BY AGE)

	1–2 YEARS OLD	3–6 YEARS OLD	1–6 YEARS OLD IN TOTAL
1990	44	64	57
1992	46	65	59
1994	48	70	63
1996	57	76	70
1997	59	78	73

SOURCE: Skolverket (1998).

points but by 1995, when the new Child Care Act came into effect, it had shrunk to 7. In that same year, 55 percent of all preschool children had a place in publicly financed child care. Of the remaining 45 percent, parents on parental leave took care of a large majority of the children. Overall, as table 12.3 indicates, the percentage of children from one to six increased considerably from 1990 to 1997.

Contrary to what might have been expected, then, universalism has been strengthened. This process of universalization and integration of child care and education reflects, in part, the commitment to "life-long learning." The goal of public child care is not only to serve working parents but also to educate and support the development of preschool children. This is, of course, not possible if eligibility is tied to the parent's status on the labor market. Of particular concern here are the children of families where the parents are unemployed. These children do not get the same support and early childhood education as those whose parents work and who therefore are eligible for a place in public child care.[8]

As a step toward a more universal preschool system, responsibility for child care at the national level was moved from the Ministry of Health and Social Affairs to the Ministry of Education and Science in July 1996, with the aim of strengthening the pedagogical profile of child care. This inaugurated a process of integrating child care and school into the same legislation. In the public documents the term *child care center (daghem)* has been replaced by references to preschool and preschool activities.[9] Legislation for the whole child care sector has been brought into the School Act and the National Agency for Education has the supervisory responsibility.

Thus, contrary to what might have been expected in times of economic restraint, on the aggregate level universalism has been strengthened. Supply has increased, but so has demand. In 1998, 95 percent of the municipalities could offer a place within three or four months after application (Socialdepartmentet 1999: 53, 26).

In addition, the social democratic government has put on the agenda new reforms that move child care further in the direction of universalism. These include child care for the children of the unemployed, a universal and free preschool for all four- and five-year-olds, and the imposition, by the national government, of a maximum parental fee (Socialdepartmentet 1999, 53; Proposition 1999/2000, 129). In November 2000 the Swedish Parliament decided to implement the suggested reforms during the coming three years. The Social Democratic Party got support from the Left Party and the Green Party for these reforms. The four bourgeois parties in opposition did not support the reforms and instead suggested a lump sum (child care account) to all parents with preschool children, and the right to tax deductions of child care costs.

The Quality of Public Child Care

Cuts in public costs in child care have not been translated into fewer children in child care, which might suggest that quality has deteriorated. Quality in child care is not easy to measure but changes in child/staff ratios and group size provide a rough indication. As figure 12.1 shows, the number of children in child care has expanded while gross costs and costs per child initially decreased, then rose somewhat during the latter part of the 1990s. This is reflected in the development of the child/staff ratio, with a lag. Until 1991, the number of children and the number of staff increased at about the same pace. Thereafter the number of children rose, but not the number of staff. While staff-child ratios were the same in 1980 and 1990 (see table 12.4), after that the number of children per staff rose rapidly such that by 1998 each staff member was taking care of 1.5 children more than in 1990.

Also, if quality is measured by group size, we find that quality has deteriorated. In 1990 the average group size was 13.8 children but by 1998 it was 16.5 children. There was, however, some improvement after 1997 (SOU 2000: 3, 116; Skolverket 2000a, 18).[10]

More children per group and per adult can be interpreted as a deterioration of the quality in child care, but it can also be associated with an increase in productivity. That is, it is possible that the municipalities are producing as high quality child care with fewer resources. It is difficult to assess whether lower costs mean lower quality or higher productivity. The large variation in child care costs among municipalities can be seen as evidence that productivity gains are possible.[11] It does not seem unreasonable to suggest that decentralization and increased coordination between child care and school have increased productivity. That the municipalities have increasingly substituted family day care for child care centers and, within the centers, child minders for preschool teachers, might have raised productivity.[12] There are, however, no systematic studies of how quality is affected by changes in resources over time (Svenska Kommunförbundet 1998).

It is hard to give a straightforward answer on the question of changes in the quality of Swedish public child care over the last decade. However, a recent investigation concerning the quality of nine different sectors in the economy found that child care was rated highest while local traffic companies and insurance services were rated lowest (Konsumentverket 2000).

TABLE 12.4: THE DEVELOPMENT OF THE AVERAGE NUMBER OF CHILDREN
PER ANNUAL WORKER IN CHILD CARE CENTERS

YEAR	NO. OF CHILDREN/ANNUAL WORKER
1980	4.2
1985	4.3
1990	4.2
1992	4.9
1994	5.2
1996	5.5
1998	5.7
1999	5.4

SOURCES: Välfärds Bulletinen (1994); Skolverket (1999a); Skolverket (2000a).

Also, an Organization for Economic Cooperation and Development (OECD) evaluation of public child care in various countries notes that Swedish staff have been under increased pressure to provide services to greater number of children (1999, 38). At the same time, the report found the preschool system outstanding and waxed eloquent about the Swedish child care system, noting that "it is said that the merit of any nation may be judged by how it treats its children—particularly the poor and needy. If that adage is true, then Sweden surely sits at an international pinnacle. Nothing honors Sweden more than the way it honors and respects its young" (OECD 1999, 43).

Privatization of Child Care

One dimension of variation between different welfare-state regimes is the role of the market in relation to the public sector. The characteristic of the Swedish welfare state has been to offer "high-quality public services that obviated the need for supplementary private solutions" (Mahon 1997, 385). During the last decades of the twentieth century, a political trend towards privatization has swept over the world. This has not left Sweden untouched, and this is visible in the production of social services such as child care.

Private solutions can be of different kinds. Child care can be purchased from profit-making enterprises or nonprofit organizations or it can by provided by the family. The implications of privatization will be different depending on whether privatization means expanding the role of commercial enterprises, nonprofit organizations, and/or the family. During the 1990s, the bourgeois government introduced a care allowance as a way of trying to privatize to the family.[13] Upon their return to office, the Social Democrats abolished the care allowance.

Privatization to for-profit or nonprofit organizations was more successful. Such privatization can be divided into three aspects: provision, financing, and regulation. Swedish child care today is, even when it is "private," publicly regulated, and financed. Private—meaning not provided by the municipality—child care is nothing new in Sweden. Private child care centers have existed for a long time.[14] The most common form of private child care in Sweden, as in other countries, until the 1990s was privately arranged (and paid for), unregistered family child care. In the 1980s, nonmunicipal child care centers became eligible for public subsidies, as long as they met certain requirements. The center had to be run by a nonprofit organization, such as a parents' cooperative, or offer a special form of pedagogy or other similar grounds. In 1991, when the bourgeois parties were in power, the law was changed to include child care centers run by personnel cooperatives, the Swedish church, and for-profit organizations. Parental fees had to be kept on a "reasonable" level, so as not to diverge too much from the parental fees in the municipally run child care (Nyberg 2000).

In 1990, there were some privately run, but publicly regulated and financed, child care centers. The proportion of children in private nonprofit and commercial child care centers rose from 5 percent in 1990 to 15 percent in 1999 (SOU 2000, 3; Skolverket 2000a). Most of the private child care centers are run by nonprofit organizations. The most common form is parental cooperatives. In 1998, parental cooperative child care centers provided places for 47 percent of all children in private child care centers. This form of child care offered in the 1970s and 1980s parents who could not get a place in a public child care center a chance to bypass the often long queue for public child care (Antman 1996, 150). In this form of child care, parents employ the personnel and often themselves participate on a rotating basis in the work at the child care center. Cooperatives run by staff and voluntary associations each accounted for an additional 10 percent of children in privately run child care centers (Skolverket 1999a, 21, table 1.2).

The ideological difference between social democrats and the bourgeois parties has not concerned child care centers run by nonprofit organizations such as parental cooperatives, but for-profit, company-run child care centers. The bourgeois parties opened the way for public subsidies to for-profit child care centers at the beginning of the 1990s. The Social Democrats did not reverse this decision when they came back into power. In 1998 commercial child care accounted for around a quarter of the privately run child care centers.

Another way of privatizing child care is to increase and restructure the fee system. During the 1990s a majority of the municipalities raised the level of fees and, to a greater extent, relied on time- and income-related fees to control demand and keep costs down. The difference between different municipalities is substantial.[15]

The general impression is that the private sector in child care has grown. This can, however, be contested. The proportion of children in private child care of all children in child care is smaller today (16 percent) than in the 1980s (40 percent).[16] Private child care is also less "private" today since it is now publicly regulated and financed. In other words, the big difference between the 1980s and today is that the need for unregulated child care, organized and financed privately by the parents, has been crowded out by publicly financed child care. The great majority of child care is today run by the municipalities. At the same time, the way has been opened for public subsidies to nonprofit and for-profit child care.

More or Less Egalitarianism?

According to Esping-Andersen, "The social democratic model and egalitarianism have become basically synonymous. To many, the egalitarian element is simply the practice of universalism: everybody enjoys the same rights and benefits, whether rich or poor. To others, it refers to the active promotion of well-being and life chances—perhaps no more evident than for women. Still others equate egalitarianism with redistribution and the elimination of poverty" (1999, 80). Public child care has contained all three of these elements. Here we examine how the increase in number of places in publicly financed and regulated child care has affected the distribution of public child care among different groups in society.

Lone and Cohabiting Mothers

It could be argued that the aim of early child care centers in Sweden was to enhance women's "capacity to form and maintain an autonomous household," to use the phrase of Ann Orloff (1993). The concern that women would be able to support themselves and their children, had little, however, to do with gender equality at that time. Child care was seen as a way to alleviate poverty by making it possible for poor mothers to work for pay and to be self-sufficient. Lone mothers have long had access to public child care to a greater extent than cohabiting mothers have. In 1966, 46 percent of the children in child care centers were children of lone mothers, which is well above their proportion of the population. From the 1970s through the 1990s, this proportion decreased. In 1994 only 16 percent of the children in public child care were children of lone mothers. This reflects the very substantial increase in the number of children of cohabiting/married mothers in public child care rather than a decline in access for lone parents. Access has, in fact, improved for the children of lone parents, too. In 1975, 56 percent of the preschool children of lone mothers were in public child care, but by 1994, 74 percent had places (Antman 1996, 148). Lone parents working full-time normally have their children in publicly subsidized child care and they make use of it—as always—to a higher degree than cohabiting parents (Prop. 1999/2000, 1).[17] In 1996, 83 percent of cohabiting, employed parents had their children in public child care as compared to 91 percent of lone parents (SCB 1997, Översiktstabell 6).

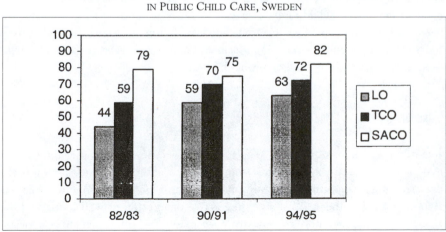

FIGURE 12.2: PROPORTION OF CHILDREN TWO TO SIX YEARS OF AGE
IN PUBLIC CHILD CARE, SWEDEN

SOURCE: LO (1996).

Workers and the Professional Classes

In the first half of the twentieth century, full-time child care was clearly linked to poverty relief, and child care centers did not enjoy a good reputation as long as their main role was to mind the children while their mothers, of necessity, worked. When their role was expanded to stimulate and educate the children too, middle-class parents became interested. This was reflected in a rapid increase in the share of middle-class children and a concomitant decrease in the share of working-class children among the children in public child care in the 1960s and 1970s. By the beginning of the 1980s, 18 percent of the children of parents organized by unions belonging to the blue-collar umbrella organization, LO (Swedish Trade Union Federation), had a place in a public child care center. The corresponding share was 26 percent among children of white-collar workers belonging to TCO (Swedish Confederation of Professional Employees), the largest umbrella organization for white-collar workers, and 43 percent of preschool children of professionals, organized by SACO (Swedish Confederation of Professional Associations).[18] If public family child care is included, the proportion was 44 percent of LO children, 59 percent of TCO children, and 79 percent of SACO children (see Figure 12.2).

In the 1980s, part of the controversy surrounding child care policy stemmed from the fact that not all children of appropriate ages had placements in public child care, either because they did not demand it or because they were locked out due to rationing of scarce spaces. The heavy subsidization of some, but not all, families with young children can be regarded as unfair. To make matters worse for a Social Democratic government, the children of high-income parents were the main beneficiaries. Contrary to the original intention of Social Democrats and their blue-collar union partners, public child care was contributing to enhanced differences between parents and children from different classes. As public child care expanded in the 1990s, however, the proportion of LO children with access to public child care increased faster than the other two categories. By 1994/5, the distance between the groups had appreciably diminished, as figure 12.2 shows.

The main reason for the difference between blue-collar and white-collar and professional workers' access to child care is the difference in mothers' working time. Public child care is primarily used by families where both members work for pay on a full-time basis. Today almost all children of parents working full-time have a place in child care and the difference between those with higher and lower education levels is small (98 percent for higher educated, full-time working parents versus 87 percent for those with the lowest levels of education). The same picture emerges when the socioeconomic status of parents is examined. Around 97 percent of all children of higher-paid employees have a place in public child care, compared to 91 percent of children of full-time blue-collar workers (Prop. 1999/2000, 1 Bilaga 1).

In the 1990s, however, attitudes toward part-time child care began to change. Child care centers were originally thought of as full-time care. Families who did not need full-time child care were not given the same priority. The municipalities did not want part-time children in child care since they reduced state grants and the families themselves often avoided child care since the fee was high relative to the time needed. The grant system was reorganized at the end of the 1980s, however, and in many municipalities, more flexible fee schedules were introduced (Antman 1996).

The Unemployed and Immigrants

In Sweden, egalitarianism has traditionally been discussed in terms of class, and later, gender. Today the concern to promote equality has widened to include employment status and ethnic background. The two are related. When parents are working outside the home, children of immigrants are as likely to have a place in public child care as other children (Ministry of Education and Science 1999, 43; Socialdepartmentet 1999, 53, 29). Immigrants, however, today experience a higher rate of unemployment than Swedes and a greater share work part-time.

A recent study shows that in 40 percent of the municipalities, children lose their place in child care if a parent loses her job. Another 49 percent offer child care for a limited number of hours to children with unemployed parents and a few municipalities offer separate, short-term child care to unemployed parents to assist them in their job-seeking efforts. This means that it is already vulnerable groups are shut out of public child care. It should be observed that the number of children with unemployed parents today is a bigger group than the number of children with an "at-home mother." The Social Democrats have, however, proposed that the children of the unemployed be given a right to a place in public preschool.

Differences between Municipalities

In the 1980s, under the mantle of decentralization and democratization, new arrangements began to be worked out between the state and the municipalities designed to allow the latter greater latitude in adapting national legislation to local conditions. Some regarded this as a way of introducing more of a market orientation into the public sector, while others spoke about user influence and power of the citizens. During the 1990s, decision-making power was increasingly transferred from the state to the municipalities. This has led to a situation where child care, which once operated according to the same rules across the country, can vary substantially across municipalities.[19] The question is, does child care in municipalities run by bourgeois governments differ from that provided by social democratic municipalities? Is public child care more universal, egalitarian and less oriented towards private provisioning in social democratic municipalities than in those where the bourgeois parties are in majority?

There are indications that this is the case. Universalism and egalitarianism seems to be a more common aim in Social Democratic municipalities than in bourgeois municipalities. An example of this is that, in 1998, the share of municipalities where the children of unemployed parents could keep a place in public child care, was considerably higher in municipalities with a Social Democratic/Left Party majority (58 percent) than in municipalities with a bourgeois majority (39 percent) (Skolverket 2000b, 9). Private child care—and, it is argued, freedom of choice—is higher in bourgeois than in socialist municipalities. In 68 percent of the Social Democratic municipalities, as compared to 86 percent of the bourgeois, there was an alternative to municipal child care (estimated from data from Skolverket 2000a).[20]

The partisan cast of government is also connected to the size of parents' fees and their tax levels. Municipalities with a socialist majority on average have higher local taxes than municipalities with bourgeois majority and are more likely to have lower parental fees than municipalities with bourgeois majority. The connection is strongest with regard to single parents' families, which is the family type with the lowest incomes. Of the quarter of municipalities with the lowest fees on average for single parents, 64 percent had a socialist majority and only 7 percent bourgeois majority. Of the quarter with the highest fees, 56 percent had bourgeois majority and 17 percent socialist majority (Skolverket 1999b, 10). On average, staff ratios tend to be somewhat lower in bourgeois governed municipalities than socialist municipalities (Asker and Kehnberg 1999). A maximum fee in publicly financed child care can be seen as a strategy for the Social Democratic government to retain some of the power from the municipalities.

Conclusions

As the 1990s unfolded, some were prepared to declare the Swedish model of the welfare state dead. Comparative welfare research has however found that most social programs enjoy a surprising durability (Pierson 1996; Stephens 1996). Our analysis of Swedish child care suggests that Sweden is no exception in this respect. This does not mean that no restructuring has taken place. We found that restructuring has, on the one hand, served to strengthen several of the core features of the Swedish model. This becomes evident if one takes into consideration the decisions taken in 2000 about a maximum fee, the right of children of the unemployed and of four- and five-year-olds to preschool, proposed at the end of the 1990s. On the other hand, new features have also been introduced.

Certainly there was a modest reduction in the resources devoted to child care on a per-child basis in the 1990s, yet this is partly the result of changes in the number of children demanding child care. A "mini baby boom" around 1990 temporarily increased the demand for spaces. This also happened at a time when municipalities were trying to cope with sharper fiscal constraints while meeting an obligation to provide spaces for all children who need it, within a reasonable amount of time. This development probably affected the quality of the care, as each child care worker has more children to care for. There is, however, also some evidence of gains in productivity. The decisions taken in 2000 also mean that more economic resources will be devoted to publicly financed child care in the future.

The 1990s have witnessed a general trend toward a decentralization of responsibilities from the state to the local level and this has affected child care. State grants for child care and other social services now come in the form of block grants. In addition, regulation by central state authorities has become less detailed. As the system becomes more decentralized, it has also become more differentiated between municipalities concerning things like rules of eligibility, parental fees, and the share of private child care. At the same time, however, the 1995 Act on Child Care clarified the municipalities' obligation to provide child care for all who need it.

Another new element is a move toward greater privatization. The number of children in child care run by for-profit organizations remains small, yet the basic principle of private service delivery—within the framework of public financing and public regulations—has been accepted. In addition, the basic rationale of trying to improve performance by exposing public service production to market disciplines has become a key part of public management reforms, including the provision of child care. The idea is that by strengthening market elements, gains in economy and efficiency will be made at the same time as higher-quality service and greater choice can be offered.

At the same time, on aggregate, inequalities between different social groups have not increased. Today public child care provides places for a larger share of preschool children than it did in 1990. Those who earlier found it harder to get access to child care—particularly blue-collar workers—have found it easier to do so, reducing the "class gap" highlighted in the 1980s debates. The norm today is that children are in publicly financed child care except when parents are on parental leave. Nevertheless, the right to a place in public child care does not apply to children of unemployed parents in about half the municipalities. This has become an important issue as unemployment affected more people and as it became apparent that immigrants constitute a disproportionate share of the unemployed. However, from the year 2001 on, children of unemployed parents will have a right to at least three hours per day or fifteen hours per week of preschool.

In the 1990s we saw a higher degree of diversity at the local level, but during the second half of the decade there was also a trend toward a more universalistic system. This could be seen in the shift from a focus on child care as a service for working parents and children in need to a right for all preschool children to preschool education. Responsibility for child care has been transferred from the Ministry of Social Affairs to the Ministry of Education. In line with this, the Social Democratic government, with the help of the Green Party and the Left Party, have decided to create a universal (but not obligatory) preschool for all four- and five-year olds.

In the debate over the fate of the traditional Swedish welfare state some would argue that globalization and neoliberalism has put Sweden under pressure to reduce social standards and that profound retrenchment and restructuring is taking place. Others counter that the social system shows a high degree of path dependency and that the traditional Swedish welfare state still is strong. Our conclusion is that it is not a question of *either/or* but one of continuity *and* change—or, perhaps, continuous change. Generous public spending, high quality in social services, universalism and egalitarianism are retained, while change is seen in increased marketization and privatization.

Notes

1. The employment rate was 85 percent for men and 81 percent for women in 1990 and 75 percent for men and 71 percent for women in 1999. The unemployment rate was 1.7 percent for men and 1.6 percent for women in 1990 and 5.9 percent for men and 5.2 percent for women in 1999 (SCB 1999).

2. In 1990 the central government budget showed a surplus of almost SEK19 billion. In 1993 the deficit amounted to almost SEK210 billion and in 1994 close to SEK200 billion. In 1998 there was again a surplus, this time slightly more than SEK20 billion (SOU 2000: 3, 40).

3. We use the term *child care* in a broad sense, including parental leave and care allowances as well as child care institutions and the like. The child care system can be seen as comprising a broad variety of different resources for caring for children. In this chapter, however, we mainly analyze child care institutions and preschools.

4. Children used to start regular school at age seven, but today it is also possible to start at six.

5. The care allowance was given to all children between ages one and three, and the amount was 2000 Swedish crowns a month, which is far from sufficient to be able to support oneself. In practice the reform meant that the ninety flat-rate days in the parental leave were replaced with a care allowance lasting until the child was three (Lag 1994: 553, om rätt till vårdnadsbidrag [Law 1994: 553, concerning the right to a care allowance]).

6. Public child care included publicly regulated, financed, and provisioned child care, but also publicly regulated and financed, but privately provided, child care centers.

7. The total fertility rates were: 1988: 1.961; 1990: 2.137; 1992: 2.090; 1994: 1.890; 1996: 1.606, and 1998: 1.504 (Statistisk Årsbok 2000, table 68).

8. There are no national rules for how the children of unemployed parents should be treated, and regional differences are substantial. Some municipalities offer child care for children of the unemployed but others do not. These differences will be analyzed later.

9. Preschool activities include what is now called preschool (*förskola*), which is part-time, and child care centers, family day care homes (*familjedaghem*), and open preschools, where parents can go together with their preschool children if the children are not attending any of the other activities.

10. The staff in Swedish public preschool child care fall mainly into two categories: preschool teachers and qualified child minders. Almost 98 percent of personnel working in preschool child care are trained to work with children: 60 percent of staff are university-trained preschool teachers, while the remaining staff are qualified child minders (Oberhuemer and Ulich 1997). In family day care services, over 70 percent of day care mothers have been trained to work with children, having either earned a children's nurse certificate or

participated in special training provided by the municipality (Ministry of Education and Science 1999, 33). Up until 1990, child minders predominated in public child care, but today university-trained preschool teachers form the biggest category (VälfärdsBulletinen 6, 1994; Skolverket 1998).

11. In eight of ten municipalities, the cost of care per full-time child varies between SEK84,400 and 129,900, a difference of 50 percent (Skolverket 2000a, 18). Various studies report productivity increases in public child care centers (ESO 1988, 1994; Socialstyrelsen 1997; Svenska Kommunförbundet 1998).

12. The number of children in family day care decreased throughout the 1990s and continues to do so. Since 1990 the number of children has been halved. In 1999 11 percent of all children between one and five were in family day care (Skolverket 2000c, 12).

13. There has also been discussion about subsidized domestic services in the home similar to those in France, but no such policy has as yet been adopted (Nyberg 1999).

14. The highest *proportion* of private child care centers was found in the first half of the twentieth century, when it reached almost 100 percent. The highest *numbers* before the 1990s were found in the 1950s. In the 1960s and 1970s, however, private child care centers almost disappeared altogether. One important reason for this was changes in the rules for state grants. Of almost 9,000 child care centers in 1981 only sixty-four—less than 1 percent—were run by nonmunicipal organizations (Nyberg 2000).

15. A family with two children and an average income can pay as little as SEK1,300 and as much as 3,400 per month in different municipalities (Socialdepartementet 1999: 53, 4). These differences will diminish greatly with the introduction of a maximum fee to be implemented in 2002.

16. Calculated from SCB (1994 and 1997).

17. Traditionally the employment of single mothers has been higher than cohabiting mothers. Today, however, single mothers have a higher unemployment rate than married/cohabiting mothers. Single mothers have greater difficulties supporting themselves through paid work, and they have lower earnings than cohabiting mothers (Nyberg 1997).

18. The categorization is based on the union to which the interviewed parent belonged. It should be pointed out that a very high proportion of the employees in Sweden are members of unions.

19. In 114 municipalities, the Social Democrats/Left Party is in the majority; in 92 the bourgeois parties are in majority and in 83 there is no majority.

20. Sixty-four out of 289 municipalities only had municipally-run centers.

References

Antman, Peter. 1996. *Barn och äldreomsorg i Tyskland och Sverige. Välfärdsprojektet. Sverigedelen* (Child Care and Elder Care in Germany and Sweden. The Welfare Project: Sweden). Stockholm: Socialdepartementet.

Anttonen, Anneli and Sipilä, Jorma. 1996. "European Social Care Services: Is It Possible to Identify Models?" *Journal of European Social Policy* 6, no. 2: 87–100.

Asker, Anna, and Ola Kehnberg. 1999. "Alltfärre vuxna i skula och daghem" (Fewer and Fewer Adults in Schools and Child Care Centers). *Svenska Dagbladet* (Swedish Daily), January 14: 8.

Bengtsson, Hans. 1995. *Förskolereformen. En studie i implementering av svensk välfärdspolitik 1985–1991* (Preschool Reform: A Study of the Implementation of Swedish Welfare Policy 1985–1991). Lund: Political Studies.

Bergqvist, Christina. 1999. "Child Care and Parental Leave Models." In *Equal Democracies? Gender and Politics in the Nordic Countries,* ed. Christina Bergqvist, Anette Borchorst, Ann-Dorte Christensen, Viveca Ramstedt-Silén, Nina C. Raaum, and Audur Styrkásdótti. Oslo: Scandinavian University Press.

Bergqvist, Christina, Jaana Kuusipalo, and Audur Styrkarsdóttir. 1999. "The Debate on Child Care Policies." In Bergqvist et al., eds. *Equal Democracies?*

Borchorst, Annette. 1994. "The Scandinavian Welfare States—Patriarchal, Gender Neutral or Woman-Friendly?" *International Journal of Contemporary Sociology* 31, no. 1: 45–67.

Clayton, Richard, and Jonas Pontusson. 1998. "Welfare-State Retrenchment Revisited: Entitlement Cuts, Public Sector Restructuring and Inegalitarian Trends in Advanced Capitalist Societies," *World Politics* 51: 67–98.

Edebalk, Per Gunnar, Ann-Charlotte Ståhlberg, and Eskil Wadensjö. 1998. *Socialförsäkringarna: ett samhällsekonomiskt perspektiv* (Social Security: A Social Economic Perspective). Stockholm: SNS.

ESO (Expert Group on Public Finance). 1988. *Kvalitetsutvecklingen inom den kommunala barnomsorgen: rapport till ESO—Expertgruppen för studier i offentlig ekonomi* (The Development of Quality in Public Child Care). (Ds Fi 1988:1). Stockholm: Allmänna förlaget.

————. 1994. *Den offentliga sektorns produktivitetsutveckling 1980–1992: rapport till Expertgruppen för studier i offentlig ekonomi* (The Development of Productivity in the Public Sector 1980–1992). (Ds 1994: 24). Stockholm: Fritzse.

Esping-Andersen, Gøsta. 1990. *The Three Worlds of Welfare Capitalism.* Cambridge: Polity Press.

————. 1999. *Social Foundations of Postindustrial Economies.* Oxford: Oxford University Press.

Esping-Andersen, Gøsta, and Walter Korpi. 1987. "From Poor Relief to Institutional Welfare States." In *The Scandinavian Model:Welfare States and Welfare Researcy*, ed. Robert Erikson et al. New York: Sharpe.

Gustafsson, Rolf Å, and Peter Antman. 1996. "Välfärd på entreprenad" (Tenders on Welfare). In *Generell välfärd. Hot och möjligheter?* (Universal Welfare: Threat or Possibilities?), ed. Joakim Palme and Irene Wennemo. Stockholm: Socialdepartementet.

Hernes, Helga. 1987. *Welfare State and Women Power.* Olso: Norwegian University Press.

Hirdman, Yvonne. 1998. *Med kluven tunga* (With Forked Tongue). Stockholm: Atlas.

Johansson, Susanne. 2000. *Genusstrukturer och lokala välfärdsmodeller. Fyra kommuner möter omvandlingen av den offentliga sektorn* (Gender Structures and Local Welfare Models: Four Municipalities and the Transition of the Public Sector). Regionstudier nr 40. Uppsala: Uppsala Universitet.

Kjulin, Urban. 1995. *Economic Perspectives on Child Care.* Nr 56 avhandling (dissertation).

Ekonomiska studier utgivna av Nationalekonomiska institutionen (Economic Studies published by Economics Dept.). Göteborg: Handelshögskolan vid Göteborgs universitet.

Konsumentverket. 2000. *Tjänste bra? Marknad, kvalitet och klagomål—konsumenter om nio tjänstebranscher* (Is It Good? The Market, Quality and Complaints—Consumers about Nine Service Sectors). Rapport 2000: 20. Stockholm: Konsumentverket.

Leira, Arnlaug. 1993. "The Woman-Friendly Welfare State? The Case of Norway and Sweden." In *Women and Social Policies in Europe,* ed. Jane Lewis. Aldershot, Eng.: Edward Elgar.

LO. 1996. *Barnomsorg, förvärvsarbete och jämställdhet. Ett faktamaterial om förhållandena vid 1990-talets mitt* (Child Care, Employment and Gender Equality: A Fact Sheet about the Situation in the 1990s). Nr 29. Stockholm: LO.

Mahon, Rianne. 1997. "Child Care in Canada and Sweden: Policy and Politics." *Social Politics* 4, no. 3: 382–418.

Ministry of Education and Science. 1999. *Early Childhood Education and Care Policy in Sweden. Background report prepared for the OECD Thematic Review of Early Childhood Education and Care Policy.* Stockholm: Ministry of Education and Science.

Nyberg, Anita. 1997. *Women, Men and Incomes. Gender Equality and Economic Independence, SOU 1997: 87.* Stockholm: Fritzes.

_____.1999. "Hemnära tjänster—kvinnornas befriare?" (Domestic Services—The Liberator of Women?) *Kvinnovetenskaplig tidskrift* (Women's Studies Journal) 3: 31–48.

_____. 2000. "From Foster Mothers to Child Care Centers: A History of Working Mothers and Child Care in Sweden." *Feminist Economics* 1, no. 1: 5–20.

Oberhuemer, Pamela, and Michaela Ulich. 1997. *Working with Young Children in Europe: Provision and Staff Training.* London: Paul Chapman.

OECD. 1999. *OECD Country Note: Early Childhood Education and Care Policy in Sweden.* Paris: OECD.

Orloff, Ann. 1993. "Gender and the Social Rights of Citizenship." *American Sociological Review* 58: 303–28.

Pateman, Carol. 1988. "The Patriarchal Welfare State." In *Democracy and the Welfare State,* ed. Amy Gutmann. Princeton, N.J.: University Press.

Pierson, Paul. 1996. "The New Politics of the Welfare State." *World Politics* 48:143–179.

Prop. 1999/2000: 1 Bilaga 1. *Fördelningspolitisk redogörelse* (A Report of the Distribution). Stockholm: Inansdepartementet.

Prop. 1999/2000: 129. *Maxtaxa och allmän förskola m.m.* (A Maximum Fee and Universal Preschool, etc.). Stockholm: Inansdepartementet.

Sainsbury, Diane, ed. 1994. *Gendering Welfare States.* London: Sage.

_____. 1999. *Gender and Welfare State Regimes.* Oxford: Oxford University Press.

SCB (Statistiska Centralbyrån—Statistics Sweden). 1990, 1999. *AKU Arbetskraftsundersökningarna* (Labor Force Surveys). Stockholm: SCB.

_____. 1994. *Barnomsorgsundersökningen 1994* (The Child Care Investigation 1994). Stockholm.

_____. 1997. *Barnomsorgsundersökningen,* Hösten 1996 (The Child Care Investigation, Fall 1996). Stockholm: Hela Riket.

_____. 2000. *Kommunernas finanser, Nationalräkenskaper* (The Finances of the Municipalities, National Accounts). Örebro: SCB.

Siim, Birte. 1997. "Dilemmas of Citizenship in Denmark: Lone Mothers between Work and Care." In *Lone Mothers in European Welfare Regimes,* ed. Jane Lewis. London: Jessica Kingsley Publishers.

Skolverket. 1998. *Barnomsorgen i siffror* (Child Care in Numbers). Rapport nr 152. Stockholm: Skolverket.

_____. 1999a. *Barnomsorg och skola i siffror 1999. Del 2—Barn personal, elever och lärare* (Child Care and Schools in Numbers 1999. Part 2—Children, Personnel and Teachers). Rapport nr. 167. Stockholm: Skolverket.

_____. 1999b. *Avgifter i förskola och fritidshem 1999* (Parental Fees in Preschools and Leisure Homes). Rapport nr. 174. Stockholm: Skolverket.

_____. 2000a. *Barnomsorg och skola. Jämförelsetal för huvudmän. Resurser* (Child Care and School. Comparisons between Providers). Rapport nr. 172. Stockholm: Skolverket.

_____. 2000b. *Skolverkets årsredovisning för budgetåret 1999* (Annual Report of the Board of Education 1999). Stockholm: Skolverket.

_____. 2000c. *Barnomsorg och skola. Jämförelsetal för huvudmän. Del 1 Organization—Personal—Resultat* (Child Care and School: Comparative Numbers for Providers. Part 1: Organization, Personnel—Results). Rapport nr 183. Stockholm: Skolverket.

Socialdepartmentet. 1999. Ds 1999: 53. *Valfrihetsrevolutionen i praktiken* (The Revolution of Choice in Practice). Stockholm: Socialdepartementet.

Socialstyrelsen. 1997. *Social service, vård och omsorg i Sverige 1996* (Social Service and Care in Sweden 1996). Stockholm: Socialstyrelsen.

SOU (Government Official Reports) 1996:169. *Förändrinsmodeller och förändringsprocesser i kommuner och landsting* (Models and Processes of Change in Muncipalities and County Councils). Stockholm: Fritzes.

_____. 2000:3. *Välfärd vid vägskäl. Utvecklingen under 1990-talet* (Welfare at the Crossroads. The Development during the 1990s). Stockholm: Fritzes.

Statistisk Årsbok (Statistical Yearbook). 2000. Stockholm: SBC.

Stephens, John D. 1996. "The Scandinavian Welfare States: Achievements, Crisis, and Prospects." In *Welfare States in Transition: National Adaptations in Global Economies,* ed. Gøsta Esping-Andersen. London: Sage.

Svenska Kommunförbundet. 1998. *Förändringar av kvalitet och produktivitet i barnomsorg, skola och äldreomsorg* (Changes in Quality and Productivity in Child Care and Elder Care). Stockholm: Svenska Kommunförbundet.

Uddhammar, Emil. 1993. *Partierna och den stora staten: en analys av statsteorier och svensk politik under 1900-talet* (The Parties and the Big State: An Analysis of Theories of State and Swedish Policy during the 1990s). Stockholm: City University Press.

VälfärdsBulletinen (The Welfare Bulletin) 6. 1994. Stockholm: SCB.

CHAPTER 13

Against the Current: Child Care and Family Policy in Quebec

Jane Jenson

In 1997 the government of Quebec legislated a new family policy. It provided, among other things, three innovative programs. First is a family allowance targeted to low-income families and set at a level sufficiently high to recognize the basic needs of a child. The second is universal educational child care at a very low cost, with parents paying full fees at only five dollars per day. The third is the promise of a paid parental leave, including a portion reserved to fathers, which would be longer, more comprehensive, and at a higher replacement rate than the limited leaves already in place in Canada.

These three innovative steps identify Quebec's strategy as being very different from that of many European countries and certainly its neighbors in North America, whether other Canadian provinces or the United States. Where many European countries have been moving in the direction of encouraging a diversification of services and expanding the range of choice, in part by encouraging and even financing informal care (Jenson and Sineau 1998, chap. 10; 2001, chap. 9), Quebec is rowing against that current. It simply eliminated the tax deductions for informal care and noneducational care, which had been in place for two decades, and poured the savings into the creation of regulated spaces providing developmentally focused professional child care. It was moving, in other words, if not toward a one-size-fits-all model, certainly in the direction of inducing parents to use either center-based care or family child care linked to the new Early Childhood Centers. At the same time, by eliminating the universal Family Allowance, the government was signaling that it did not consider such benefits were meant to compensate parents who chose to provide their own child care. Moreover, while the parental leaves would be extended, they were by no means the "long leaves" of several years that some European jurisdictions have been instituting in order to reduce demand for services for those under three years of age.

Even more dramatic was Quebec's divergence from the liberal welfare-state model of North America. The first difference was the dramatic recommitment to universality. This engagement with a value that is rapidly losing what little legitimacy it ever had in liberal welfare states has been strengthened in Quebec. Recently, the highest-ranking civil servant responsible for Quebec's family policy listed as its first goal "to ensure fairness by offering universal support to families."[1] The low-cost child care services, as well as a range of universal tax credits and the implementation of full-day kindergarten for five-year-olds, all express this commitment to maintaining solidarity via universality. By promising that middle-class families could, at a reasonable price, gain access to quality services, the province was rejecting the liberal welfare state's long-standing form of targeting, which subsidizes licensed care for poor families, while in the name of "choice" sending middle-income families into a market in which they confront hard decisions about trading off quality and dependability against affordability.[2]

Second, although since 1997 family allowances have been targeted to low-income recipients, no strings are attached. As with a similar benefit paid by Ottawa, the only condition is the presence of a dependent child under eighteen. But in addition in Quebec, the level of benefits depends on the number of adults living with the child; single-parent families receive more generous benefits, as well as particular tax advantages.[3] The design decisions, in other words, reflect nothing of the "moral panic" about lone mothers characterizing some liberal welfare states in the years of welfare reform. Nor do they reproduce the neutrality of programs that do not take into account the particular difficulties faced by lone parents.

In these ways, then, we can see that Quebec is moving against the current. Is this simply because Quebec is continuing down a path that has always been "distinct," it being the only North American jurisdiction that has had an explicit "family policy" for two decades? Here the answer is negative. While Quebec has been distinct, the policies and programs put into place since 1997 do not support a story of path dependency.

The new policy marked a break with past practices in at least two ways. It banished an increase in the birth rate from the list of goals of family policy, despite the fact that previous governments, both Liberal Party and Parti Québécois, had made natalism a principal axis of concern, as we will see below. Second, while this family policy, like previous ones, arises from a concern with fostering social solidarity, the ways selected to do so have been quite simply reversed. In the past universal family allowances and income redistribution were the preferred instrument for expressing solidarity, and child care was a program essentially targeted to working parents, with subsidies going to those "in need." After 1997, rapidly rising government investments in educational child care have become the symbol of societal cohesion, while family allowances serve as the instrument for assuring cross-class equity.[4]

Given this flip-flop with respect to Quebec's own history and the "lone ranger" quality of several of its actions, we need to seek an explanation in factors other than the path dependency of liberal welfare regimes, the category into which Quebec has been slotted in the past. This example is a fascinating case study, because these different policy choices were instituted explicitly in order to confront the same challenges as those in other liberal welfare regimes: globalization, the transformation of women's economic activity and family forms, and especially the poverty trap in which so many lone parent families find themselves. The policy recognizes that labor markets have been restructured and—most important for the comparison to other liberal welfare regimes—it is also seen as part of a strategy to promote employability.

As the civil servant quoted above told his audience, "We decided that we had to increase our support to families. . . . As a result we put in place a number of structural measures for the society of the year 2000, the harmonious functioning of which centers on employment" (Boisvert 2000, 3). And, as the Ministry of Child and Family Welfare puts it bluntly,[5] "Poverty is less present in families with full-time jobs. This is why the government has chosen to fight against it not only through providing financial support to the poorest families but also in the field of employment by offering parents conditions making it easier to balance family and job responsibilities."[6] Even the educational emphasis in child care and the extension of school to younger children is justified as much in terms of avoiding costly school failures by promoting school readiness, as it is in terms of the development of the child.

The Quebec story is not, it should be clear from the start, one of social democratic progressivism forging ahead in the face of neoliberalism found everywhere else. Its reform of social assistance, begun in the mid-1980s, has been widely criticized for being coercive, instituting "workfare" even before the word was well known in English (Bouchard, Labrie, and Noël 1996, 94). Coupled with this coercion have been, however, what Gérard Boychuk (1998) terms market-performance features. These programs reward efforts to enter and stay in the labor force (88). The combination has generated a social assistance regime that includes both sticks and carrots. The reformed family policy fits into this mixed regime, albeit falling more on the market-performance side, as we will see.

Already however, it should be clear that Quebec is not following some "golden age" welfare regime tradition; its eye is clearly on the twenty-first century and the needs of this small society in which many actors harbor hopes of becoming independent and being able to go it alone in the era of globalization. Thus, as this chapter will argue, we need to seek the explanation for the specifics of this program in the balance of political forces that created it, the goals the various actors sought to achieve, the compromises they worked out among themselves, both for family policy and the broader economy, and always with an eye on the effects for the political future of Quebec in Canada.

The Roots of the System—Ideas, Institutions, and Actors

Quebec's Summit on the Economy and Employment in October 1996 brought together employers, unions, and a broad selection of popular sector groups to reflect upon plans for the medium-term future of the province. At the end of the summit, Premier Lucien Bouchard announced a fundamental revision of family policy that eventually culminated in the three programs described above. Maligned by students because he refused to freeze tuition fees, under pressure from antipoverty activists to embrace the goal of *appauvrissement zéro* (zero poverty) rather than striving to achieve a "zero deficit," Bouchard might be accused of searching for a theme that would unite rather than divide.[7] But the decision to announce a major reform of family policy, with universal and affordable child care at its center, was much more than an effort to get out of a sticky political situation. It represented the victory of a coalition of activists and officials seeking to address the needs of families and children within Quebec's societal strategy (*projet de société*).

Indeed, the summit was only one moment, albeit a crucial one, in a decades-long controversy about family policy. By the mid-1990s positions were aligned, in part, with reference to the government's Third Family Action Plan (1995–1997). Elaborated after broad public consultations in the 1995 International Year of the Family, the plan focused on prevention (including measures to prevent spousal abuse and encourage greater participation of fathers in child rearing), balancing work and family (including more child care and teaching adolescents about the importance of both parents sharing family responsibilities), financial support for parents, and improving the environment of families (including housing, valuing solidarity across families, and emphasizing the family dimension in all services).[8] This list represents the compromise arrived at among feminists, the family movement, antipoverty activists, social workers, and experts on development and early childhood education, as well as municipal government and the provincial public sector.

Family policy has never been a policy domain apart from the great issues agitating Quebec politics. By 1996 it had become a part of a broader process of welfare-state redesign, touching on social assistance and labor market policy. The multidimensional reform, laid out at the summit, sought to (1) improve parents' capacity to balance work and family life; (2) provide child care services which were both financially accessible and developmentally sound, in particular for facilitating school readiness; and (3) induce parents with low incomes or on social assistance to find employment or better jobs.[9] Given this strategic location in the process of modernizing social policy, it is not surprising that the announcement of the new family policy garnered a huge amount of attention. Nor did this abate over the next months. In January 1997 the government published a white paper, *Les enfants au cœur de nos choix* (Children at the Heart of Our Choices), and legislated the following July.

Family policies can set a number of priorities. They might seek, for example, to promote children's development, to maximize equality of opportunity and condition among all types of families, or to advance gender equality (Jenson and Stroick 1999, 2–3 provides one such list). Quebec's family policy over the last decades has always had a range of goals, as the Third Action Plan described above well indicates. Nonetheless, promoting parental employment has recently risen to the top. But this is not surprising. The institution responsible for family policy, the Ministère de la Famille et de l'Enfance (Ministry of Child and Family Welfare) was created in 1997 by amalgamating the Family Secretariat, the Office des Services de Garde à l'Enfance (Office of Child Care Services, or OSGE) responsible for regulating and licensing child care, and the Ministère de la Securité du Revenu (Ministry of Income Security).

This has not always been the case. The use of the state to encourage parental labor-force participation, as well as the provision of public services, is a relatively new phenomenon. As Yves Vaillancourt (1988, 144) says, Quebec is the Canadian province that had the most privatized social services (before 1970) and the most public ones (after 1970). Quebec's social services were altered fundamentally by the wave of reforms initiated after 1960. Services had been provided either by the Catholic Church (to Catholic Quebecers) or via a network of charitable and non-profit agencies (to the non-Catholic communities). This changed dramatically as a new team of reformers, based in both the Quebec Liberal Party and the Parti Québécois, took the reins of power in the next decades. Modernizing politicians, bureaucrats, and other experts have had a major influence over the shape of policy since 1960, but they have also had to contend with a mobilized civil society that has sometimes had different assessments of the best direction for change. The 1960s thrust to reform also intersected with initiatives from Ottawa that were setting all the provinces down some new paths.

In Quebec, the combination of internal and external forces for change was dramatic. The Social Assistance Act of 1969 was Quebec's response to the 1965 Canada Assistance Plan (CAP), while the Health and Social Services Act (1971) established Quebec's universal health care system. Both pieces of legislation followed in the tracks of the Castonguay-Nepveu Commission, a major investigatory body that framed the terms of debate about health and social services for several decades. Its work had involved most of the thinkers about social policy in the province, both conservative and reformist, and it had heard from almost every sector of Quebec society (Lesemann 1981).

Despite a new social assistance regime that adopted an individualized approach to social security and was noncategorical (Boychuk 1998, 84), there was a concomitant concern about families. One result was a provincial family allowance regime, put in place in 1969, that did not share with Ottawa the distrust of large families that had shaped federal family allowances since 1946 (Bergeron 1997, 261–68). These Family Allowances, altered at each moment of reform over the last decades, remain a key pillar of Quebec's family policy.

The Castonguay-Nepveu Commission was very critical of private services, whether nonprofit or commercial; it clearly put the accent on public services (Vaillancourt 1988, 147–49; 151). Nonetheless, opposition to nonprofit provision was somewhat tempered because, in the 1960s and continuing today, Quebec civil society was traversed by a dense network of community groups, agencies, projects and popular initiatives whose political project was and remains to provide services "differently." From the early 1960s, citizens' committees were actively intervening in the social policy domain. They were critical of the individualistic "case work" approach of social workers as much as the charity-based religious orientations. They sought instead to provide collective solutions and services that would build local leadership and develop community capacity. While they turned to local governments, as well as to Quebec and Ottawa, for funding and support, their take on social services was never statist. By the late 1960s these popular sector groups' (*groupes populaires*) political project was quite explicit. Rather than lobbying for public services, they mobilized self-help groups and community action through legal aid, literacy training, help with family budgeting, child care centers and people's clinics (Bélanger and Lévesque 1992, 715–24). Unions were also active participants, for example by backing local self-help groups intended to promote financial independence among low-income groups, including by setting up food, child care, or other cooperatives.

This mobilization, both in cities and rural areas, might have gone the way of comparable collective action throughout North America at the time—that is, toward obscurity—if it had not been institutionalized in important locales, two of which are of central importance to this chapter. A central action of the popular sector movement involved establishment of child care centers (*garderies*), the first of the two institutions. These were incorporated as nonprofit organizations run by councils of parents and staff which embraced both democratic and child development goals.

Such services had also been a major goal of the second wave of the women's movement since its appearance in the mid-1960s. The Fédération des femmes du Québec (Federation of Quebec Women, or FFQ) had state-provided child care on its list of six demands at its founding in 1965, and continued to agitate for child care, for example, in its brief to the Royal Commission on the Status of Women, or RCSW (Collectif Clio 1992, 464). The Confédération des Syndicats Nationaux (Confederation of National Unions, or CSN) also presented a brief to the RCSW centered on child care. Taking things in their own hands, women's and other popular sector groups accessed the funds of the federal Local Initiative Program (LIP) to set up nonprofit, democratically and parent-managed centers in disadvantaged and other neighborhoods (Desjardins 1991, chap. 3; Lamoureux 1992, 699). These first politicized child care centers have been reclaimed as the model for today's central institution for child care and development: the early childhood centers (ECCs) created by the 1997 reform.[10]

A second important institution created at this time was the *centre local de services communautaires* (local community service center, or CLSC). Modeled on the people's clinics, the CLSC serves as a point of entry to the healthcare system—providing home care (including postpartum services for multiple births), perinatal care, parenting support, and so forth—and is supposed to be a pivotal actor in community development projects.[11] The CLSC was in many ways an institutionalized expression of a community-based progressive approach to health and social services, one that was suspicious of "medical" solutions, professionals, centralization, and commercialization. Employing social animators as well as social workers and health care professionals, the CLSC has official responsibility for liaison with the voluntary sector and the community (Roy 1987). The CLSC remains a key partner in virtually all programs for children and families. The local CLSCs have become a crucial link in the family policy chain, working closely with early childhood centers in their catchment areas.

For its part, the government of Quebec did not move very quickly onto the child care field (Baillargeon 1996). Its first formal involvement was in 1974, when the temptation of the shared-cost CAP program led the government to institute (as did all other provinces) subsidies for low-income parents using licensed child care.[12] New legislation in 1979 continued subsidies to low-income parents, established direct subsidies to centers, and created an allowance for the care of children with disabilities. The regulatory and licensing body, the OSGE, was created at the same time.

Over these same years, despite the philosophy and rhetoric privileging nonprofit and community groups, the commercial private sector was not at a standstill, in part because of governmental foot-dragging. It, too, expanded when the supply of services could not keep up with demand (Vaillancourt 1988, 161). The mix was always an uneasy one, however, with ministers frequently expressing an aversion to commercial expansion and even seeking to halt it.

By the end of the 1970s, a child care system was in place that looked very much like those of the other Canadian provinces. Just as elsewhere, child care services were a mixed bag, including regulated day care centers and family day care, as well as unregulated "nursery schools" and drop-in centers, and school-based child care under the jurisdiction of the Ministry of Education (Childcare Resource and Research Unit 1997, 25). Nonprofit groups delivered most of the licensed services, but a commercial sector also existed. This system had been built by a variety of actors involved in the family policy network. Alongside bureaucrats there were activists and "femocrats" from the women's movements, and community development activists who sought to change society from the bottom up. They sought to facilitate the balancing of work and family responsibilities, but also to use democratically governed child care centers as a locus for community empowerment.

In this mix, the one factor that did distinguish Quebec from the rest of Canada was the active presence of a mobilized family movement. As the next section will make clear, this actor became more important in the next decade, as a family policy was redesigned to meet a set of new challenges. The sharp drop in the birth rate that coincided with the Quiet Revolution increased the fragility of the French language and culture in North America, at the same time as the governments were going through the first of their neoliberal "cures."

Juggling Purposes and Multiple Instruments: Family Policy in the 1980s

There has never been full consensus on family policy in Quebec. Debates range over the types of services, to be sure. Some vaunt nonprofit groups while others argue for a level playing field for commercial services. Some claim public financing is sufficient while others believe services must also be publicly delivered. Beyond these controversies, there is always the issue of the birthrate, and whether public policy should be pronatalist in its goals. The continued predominance of concerns about the birthrate is hardly surprising, given the fact that in the single decade from 1961 to 1971, the average size of a Quebec family fell from four to two children, while in the mid-1980s the birthrate dropped to 1.4 (Dandurand 1992, 368).

The new economic and cultural concerns of the 1980s, which had a significant demographic content, meant that while the actors remained the same, the balance of forces was different. Thus, the women's movement—by the 1970s supported by femocrats within several ministries as well as the Conseil du Statut de la Femme (Council on the Status of Women)—was there. But demographers and the family movement also were influential actors, as were bureaucrats in a range of social and economic ministries and outside experts.

In 1979, three years into its first term in office, the Parti Québécois (PQ) government launched what would become a long and vibrant debate about family policy, one that continued through the terms of the succeeding Liberal government, to culminate in 1987–88 in a new family policy and two new institutions, the Conseil de la Famille (Council of the Family, a parapublic body responsible for advising the minister) and the Secrétariat à la Famille (Family Secretariat).[13] It started as a discussion of economic growth, including the population size needed to sustain a growth model. This was prompted by the PQ government's economic strategy statement *Bâtir le Québec* (*Building Quebec*, 1979), a document that reasoned from a heavy dose of demographic fears and was natalist in its prescriptions. Soon there was a wholesale public debate about families, equality and social equity.

The next step was a policy document explicitly addressing family policy. Nonetheless, it is important to understand the context surrounding the Green Paper, *Pour les familles québécoises* (For Quebec Families), issued by the government in 1984, because it framed the debate and positions adopted by the major actors. In 1984 the PQ government was already actively considering tax reform and strategies for protecting the French language and Quebec culture in the face of a declining birth rate. The tax reform process was tending in the direction of favoring two-parent and working families, while an important parliamentary commission, headed by Richard French and reporting in 1985, had a mandate to analyze the demographic situation in the context of cultural policy. It proposed a dualistic approach of increased immigration and fostering a higher birthrate.[14]

Seeing both these policy developments emerging, women's groups were anxious. Despite Quebec's 1975 Charter of Rights and Liberties guaranteeing gender equality, and a progressive policy to advance equality between the sexes put into place in 1978, the province appeared to be moving back toward traditionalism, via the tax treatment of families and in order to deal with cultural challenges (Dandurand 1987, 353). Therefore feminists, coming from both the FFQ and the more traditionalist Association Féminine d'Éducation et d'Action Sociale (Women's Association for Education and Social Action, or AFEAS) actively intervened in the consultations organized by the consultative committee on the green paper that toured Quebec throughout 1985–86. Women were optimistic that their voices would be heard, because one member of the consultative committee, Nicole Boily, was a feminist who had worked with the FFQ, and another, Christiane Bérubé, had just ended her term as President of AFEAS.

In addition to tax reformers, natalists, and feminists, debate was engaged with professionals who had a stake in establishing clear new norms and gaining additional resources for social work, psychology, health and so on (Dandurand 1987, 355). And last but never least, the family movement was actively involved. This movement of individuals or groups promoting healthy families and family life has been an important actor for decades. Renée B-Dandurand (1987, 355–56) describes its two wings. There is a conservative and Catholic one, very close to the Church. But there is also a liberal wing, which looks to the state to support families in their diverse needs and their diverse situations. The third member of the consultative committee, the author Maurice Champagne-Gilbert, was associated with this second branch of the family movement, as well as being a well-known human rights advocate.

The consultative committee's reports came down strongly in favor of the principle of shared responsibility between parents and the community;[15] they recognized the variety of situations in which families live, and they downplayed natalism. More generally, the committee argued that there was no "crisis of the family." The real challenge was to institute new forms of solidarity between the sexes. In its recommendations, the committee sought to avoid supporting natalist policy, proposing higher levels of spending and more coherent support for families, as well as improved parental leaves, conditions of part-time employment and family allowances. It was strangely silent on the matter of child care, making only the recommendation that the current regime be better organized and that everyone, including employers, do their part. However, it did recommend retaining the existing subsidy for low-income families using services.

With the Quebec Liberal Party in government by the time the second report was issued, some adjustments to expectations were inevitable. However, the change from one party to another did not mark a major policy reorientation. The statement on family policy issued by the Ministry of Health and Social Services in 1987 stood on four principles, most of which reflected the general thinking of the consultative committee. The fourth was, of course, the exception to that generalization. The four principles were: providing public support for the costs of child rearing, fighting poverty, encouraging parents to seek employment, and supporting a higher birthrate (Lefebvre 1998, 221).

The second and third principles provided the rationale for needs-based subsidies for child care, tax credits, recurring funding to child care centers, and generous maternity and parental leave packages, as well as allowances for young children and income support for working parents. Thus, 1988 saw the creation of the Parental Wage Assistance Program, known as APPORT in French. This provides a wage supplement to families with even a tiny amount (now $100 per month) of earned income and extra support for child care expenses, in order to draw them into the labor force (Beauvais and Jenson 2001, appendix A, table 11).

Principles one and four generated four types of family allowances. One was universal. Others addressed the particular needs of young children and the disabled. Perhaps the best known was the birth allowance (*prime à la naissance*), whose amount increased to very generous levels for third and higher children.[16] The birth allowances favoring "the third child" never had unanimous support, and controversy over them touched on all the central issues of Quebec politics. As had occurred throughout the 1980s, the issues ranged from economic development to the role of the state, immigration, and linguistic assimilation. Demographers debated feminist demographers, proponents of social spending confronted neoliberals, and natalists verbally sparred with familialists and feminists. The controversy shook the National Assembly, government agencies such as the Secrétariat à la Famille, parapublic bodies (for example, the Conseil du Statut de la Femme, as well as the Conseil de la Famille), the press, and intellectuals.

The post-1987 system was coherent in the sense that it stood on the four principles listed above, but it was complicated, with a wide variety of different programs. Moreover, while other governmental goals were coherent in themselves, as an expression of the goals of family policy, the design did not always mesh well with them. Despite targeting low-income families and paying wage supplements, there were still problems linking family policy to employability measures; there was mounting concern about the "poverty trap" and intergenerational reliance on social assistance.

After its election in 1995, the PQ government, like its Liberal predecessor, undertook to reform social assistance programs. In a decade, Quebec had transformed its social assistance regime into one based on both income support and "employability" (Noël 1996). But because of the limited results obtained by training and other programs and because of rising rates of unemployment and welfare, a large debate on the subject opened. From the beginning, child benefits were part of this discussion, as was expanding child care, because of the place single mothers and other poor families occupied in policymakers' concerns.[17]

In preparation for reforming social assistance, the government asked a group of experts to make proposals for redesigning the system. Eventually, the majority (headed by psychologist Camil Bouchard, and therefore called the *Bouchard Report*) and the minority (headed by economist Pierre Fournier) reports were written, because the experts could not agree (Noël 1996). Nonetheless, despite their disagreements on a range of other matters, both groups did agree that "children should be removed from social assistance" and both recommended the creation of an integrated family allowance (Lefevbre 1998, 215–16).

The Estates-General of Education, which reported in 1996 after months of touring the province for consultations, also recommended increased, more accessible child care for the youngest children and extended preschool education services, in order to combat high drop-out rates and school failure in general. The Conseil Supérieur de l'Éducation (Higher Council of Education) did the same, as did the majority report of the expert group on social reform mentioned above. The experts reminded Quebecers that years ago the *Parent Report*, which had been the blueprint in the 1960s Quiet Revolution for secularizing and modernizing education, had recommended kindergarten for four- and five-year-olds.

The claims and proposals of these expert studies, consultations, and other groups addressing poverty and promoting gender equality all fed into the announcement at the Summit on the Economy and Employment in 1996 and especially into the white paper released the next January.

Toward a Family Policy with "Children at the Heart of Our Choices"

As we have seen throughout this chapter, changes to child care programs in Quebec have always been located in a broader set of family policies. The 1997 reform, known perhaps best for the five-dollars-per-day spaces, is no exception here. This shift in funding arrangements as well as the emphasis on universality and a developmentally appropriate curriculum, were all part of a much broader effort to reform social assistance, develop broad-based support for the PQ's political vision, promote gender equality, and demonstrate Ottawa's recalcitrance with respect to the federal principle. With such an all-encompassing agenda, it is not surprising that a number of actors considered the reform to be crucially important for them.

First into the lists were the fiscal conservatives, who wanted to achieve a zero deficit and saw in the universal family allowances and generous birth allowances a "waste" of state spending. Going as they did to families whether they "needed" them or not, those who shared with the minister of finance, Bernard Landry, an overwhelming fear of deficit spending (at least on social programs) were looking for a change. But because this was a PQ and not a Liberal government, certain intragovernmental compromises were necessary. Feminists and social democrats, such as Pauline Marois and Louise Harel, had risen to high cabinet responsibility, and femocrats were scattered throughout the bureaucracy. The women's movement was mobilized after the 1995 March for Bread and Roses and the President of the FFQ, Françoise David, was an important player at the Summit on the Economy and Employment. Movement women had ties to women within the state, but of perhaps equal relevance was the desire of the PQ to assure that no gender gap would interfere with its support in the next referendum on independence for Quebec.

Other crucial actors in this policy network, often providing the "glue" that held all the parts together, were child development experts. Camil Bouchard, for example, had published a formative document in 1991, *Un Québec fou de ses enfants* (Quebec, Mad about its Children) (MSSS 1991). It made the case that early childhood education was crucial to proper development and that poverty and disadvantage were the factors most likely to place children at risk for negative developmental outcomes. In the preparations of the 1997 white paper he helped to make the links across domains such as social assistance (recall he had signed the majority report coming out of the 1996 consultation of experts on reform of social assistance), early childhood education, and social solidarity.

The white paper was not preceded by any formal public consultation. It was written by the secretariat of the Committee of Priorities of the Executive Council and signed by one of its members, Marois, the minister of education.[18] The government deemed it was important to keep the process well under control for a number of reasons. First, the major lines of the reform had already been announced at the summit; the government knew what it wanted to do. Second, the direction of reform was not universally popular. The natalist wing of the family movement was not happy about the threat to the birth allowances. Commercial child care operators were also opposed to the reform. Indeed, part of the impetus for reform had come from Marois's concern about the rising importance of commercial providers of child care in the system and her decision immediately after the 1995 election to place a moratorium on new licenses. Therefore, the commercial sector knew its future was on the line. Third, the government was meeting resistance to its parallel reform of social assistance and it did not want to open up another line of attack. And fourth, the government as well as the bureaucrats and experts who supported the reform understood that it made sense *only as a package*. None of the pieces in and of itself was a compelling reform, but together they created a momentum for positive change. Therefore, it had to hold together, and be held together.

The white paper made this argument for coherence, presenting a strong case for "integration" across domains, including social, educational, and employment.[19] Family policy is now described as having four main objectives:

- to ensure fairness by offering universal support to families;
- to give more assistance to low income families;
- to facilitate the balancing of parental and work responsibilities;
- to foster children's development and equal opportunity.[20]

In the white paper the emphasis was somewhat more on promoting employment and equal opportunity. Despite such differences, however, the policy has a number of clear principles, some of which continue past practices, and others that break with the past:[21]

- An integrated family allowance, targeted to low-income parents, covering the estimated costs of raising a child from birth to age eighteen;
- universality in the tax regime, including a tax exemption for dependent children's basic needs and a nonrefundable tax credit for dependent children;
- insurance providing paid parental leaves to virtually all employed new parents;
- educational and developmental child care services organized by early childhood centers;
- accessible child care services, at fees of five dollars per day; reduced-cost child care for low-income working parents and 23.5 hours per week free

child care for social assistance recipients, in order to ensure that children at-risk use the developmental service;

- full-day kindergarten for five-year-olds; half-day kindergarten coupled with child care for four-year-olds in disadvantaged neighborhoods in Montreal.

The focus on equal opportunity, equity and solidarity across classes is expressed in the integrated family allowance, available to all low-income families with dependent children under eighteen. It replaces three family allowances,[22] and those parts of the social assistance regime that had been paid with respect to children. The amount varies according to the birth order of the child and whether two parents live with the child or not, as well as according to family income. The family allowance supplements the Canada Child Tax Benefit (CCTB), which Revenue Canada pays to Quebec families (Jenson 2001); in other words, it tops it up if necessary to arrive at Quebec's preferred level.[23]

The overall assessment of the effects of this unification of programs is that they keep low-income parents more or less where they were in terms of benefits, as long as they stay on social assistance (Rose 1998). However, because the benefits are neutral as to employment, there is a gain made by those who are working in a low-paying job. Therefore, reflecting the tie back to employability goals, there is an incentive to seek employment.

The major losers in this shift to a single, targeted family allowance were better-off families with more than two children. They no longer could count, for example, on a birth allowance injecting up to $8000 into the family treasury. While middle-income parents lost the previously universal family allowance, they acquired less costly child care. This was a gain for those who used the places, but not for families who cared for their own children or used informal care. Therefore, there has been some dispute about the fairness of the new system, and about whether it recognizes the diversity of family needs (IRPP 2000; Vérificateur Général 1999).

In contrast to the targeted family allowance, the emphasis on universality is evident in the fact that the 1997 reform maintained the tax exemption for dependent children, the nonrefundable credit for the first child of single parent families and the nonrefundable tax credit to all families.[24] This third credit is the only universal tax credit for families with children in the country (Clarke 1998, 13) and it is worth $598 for the first child ($897 for a single-parent family) and $552 for subsequent children. These tax advantages are a key expression of solidarity in the form of universality; the same principle underpins the child care programs, presented in more detail below.

The white paper also announced that the government would institute a program of parental insurance. This idea of redesigning parental leave, to extend coverage and unlink it from eligibility to unemployment insurance, had been promoted by the PQ for almost a decade. It was part of the 1981 election campaign. In addition, the Conseil du Statut de la Femme had also been pushing for such a change since

1988, when it published a detailed analysis of the gaps in coverage. Between 1997 and 2000 this became much more than a gender-equity measure. For the *indépendantiste* PQ government, promoting parental insurance became a way to reveal the intransigence of Ottawa vis-à-vis what the Quebec government described as its rightful area of constitutional competence. It was also presented as yet another piece of evidence of the greater generosity and progressiveness of Quebec governments toward the population.

The announcement of parental insurance continued the established tradition of Quebec having the most generous programs of paid maternity and unpaid parental leave in Canada.[25] The only paid leave available to Canadian parents (outside that provided privately through collective agreements) comes from the unemployment insurance (UI, but now called employment insurance) regime. That insurance program has never covered all workers. For example, it excludes the self-employed, and until 1997 it also excluded part-time workers. Second, in order to claim benefits, workers have to meet strict eligibility requirements based on the number of hours worked. Third, it does not replace lost wages, but only 55 percent of them up to a fixed limit. Therefore, it is a very partial program, covering at best about one of every two new mothers (Beauvais and Jenson 2001, 9).

Despite these limits, the federal government has recently accumulated much political capital by extending parental leaves, for those eligible, to fifty-two weeks. This is a formula competing with that proposed by Quebec's white paper, which hoped to break the link to employment completely. A new regime, based on earned income rather than weeks or hours of work, would make leaves available to any parent who earned at least $2,000 during the year prior to the birth. Management of the program would be transferred to the *Régie des Rentes* (government control of allowances) and the rate would be 75 percent of the previous year's income.[26] It also proposed a paternity leave of five weeks, with the rate calculated on the father's income. There would also be an adoption leave of twelve weeks (Lepage and Moisan 1998).

Parental insurance has not been implemented in Quebec, but it is on its way, the product of a go-it-alone strategy built on appeals to Quebec's "distinctiveness." The PQ promised to create a new regime both in the 1998 election campaign and at the March 1999 opening of the National Assembly. In May 1999 consultations with employers, unions, and family organizations on a go-it-alone strategy began, and in fall 1999 consultations with employers led by the ministry brought agreement, in principle—although with some change to the details (Quebec 2000, 133). The February 2000 Youth Summit endorsed a "made in Quebec" plan; included in the consensus were not only youth groups but also employers, unions, women's groups and so on. In the face of continued rejection by Ottawa, and a growing mobilization in Quebec, the minister of state, Pauline Marois, tabled Bill 140 on June 6, 2000, doing so in the name of the "historic demand of women's groups" and other socioeconomic groups, as well as the consensus expressed in the two summits, of 1996 and 2000.[27]

The history of this program illustrates well the capacity of the government to break with past practice and innovate, by using a strategy critical of constitutional arrangements and appealing to the "differences" of Quebec society, as well as to the need for adaptation in the face of new global realities and in the name of gender equality. In this context employers and unions were willing to pay the extra costs that the reform would bring.

Getting to Five Dollars-per-Day Child Care and the Early Childhood Centers

Of course a major dimension of family policy reform in 1997 was the redesign of child care delivery. In 1995, the licensing body, the OSGE, imposed a moratorium on new licenses because officials and the minister responsible were concerned that the commercial sector was taking too much of a place in the overall system. The 1997 reform ended that moratorium but, more importantly, it created a new institution, the early childhood center (*Centre de la petite enfance*).[28]

Once up and running as intended throughout the province, such centers will mark a major shift in thinking about young children, work and family, and the transition to school. They are governed by a nonprofit corporation, with a majority of parents on the governing council, and offer different kinds of child care, either center based or through family day care. In other words, incorporated under a single roof are both the traditional *garderies* (for at least seven children) and the supervisory responsibility for family day care.[29] The family day care option tends to be selected for infants (almost half of children under twelve months are in a family day care) and older children who are in kindergarten part of the day. Center-based care predominates among two- to four-year-olds (Québec 1999, 130). Centers may also take school-age children who do not have access to an after-school facility.

There are twenty centers operating in Aboriginal communities, and an agreement is being developed to transfer administrative responsibility for governing and oversight to the Kativik Regional Government. Services are also available as far north as Inuktitut (Boisvert 2000, 7).

Family day care providers have access to the resources and educational programs of the centers, which provide a variety of programs open to the community in collaboration with other agencies—particularly that other important local institution in Quebec, the CLSC.

Probably the best known part of the child care reform is the promise to phase in truly affordable child care by setting a standard rate, paid by all parents no matter their income, of five dollars per day, or twenty-five per week, for full-time day care up to ten hours a day. The province fills the gap between fees and operating costs with direct grants to the centers. The money for financing the program was found, among other places, in the decision to cancel the tax deduction for child care expenses. As sufficient low cost spaces become available, parents can no longer deduct child care expenses from their provincial income taxes. Nor can they claim the federal CCED because providers do not issue receipts.

Beginning in 1997, four-year olds were offered low-cost spaces, with three-year-olds and after-school care covered in September 1998. The aim was to reach newborns by the year 2001, but the calendar was actually sped up so that as of September 2000 the rate parents of any child in center care, family day care, or after-school care pay is five dollars per day (Québec 2000, vol. III, 132).

Parents on social assistance, with preschool children over two or children with a medical certificate prescribing attendance, have access to free child care for 23.5 hours a week in a center or in family day care. The goal here is clearly not to allow parents' exclusion from the labor force to hinder their child's development. The Ministry of Social Solidarity will pay for hours in excess of 23.5 for parents on social assistance participating in employability programs. Finally, parents who are eligible for the income supplement program, the Parental Wage Assistance Program, receive a three-dollars-per-day subsidy, so they only pay ten dollars per week.

The encouragement, by means of free or very low cost care, illustrates how child care policy is directly and unabashedly based on the principles of enabling even parents with low earning capacity to enter the labor force. All parents on social assistance with children older than two are now classified as "employable." Simultaneously, however, it provides strong inducements for such parents to use child care that is not only regulated but also has strong educational content.

Early childhood education and development is a clear focus of this reform, promoting school readiness for all children and seeking to overcome the learning disadvantages often associated with low income and poverty. Early childhood education is defined as the key program for successful integration of children into society, for school readiness, and for preventing problems later in life. Thus, early childhood centers have a strong educational mandate, based on a new and province-wide program. Tailored to different age groups, it is a play-based learning program.

Developmental priorities also underpin the extension of kindergarten to a full day for five-year-olds (schools extended their kindergarten services in September 1997). Compulsory schooling still begins at age six, and full-day kindergarten attendance is optional, but over 98 percent of children in the age category do attend. In addition, four-year-olds living in areas designated as "disadvantaged" on the island of Montreal have access to half-day junior kindergarten and educational child care.

The educational emphasis demanded some serious attention toward improving the credentials of child care workers and also raising their wages. The former was long overdue; Quebec's regulations for training and staff ratios are among the least demanding in the country. Moreover, in 1999, 23 percent of the early childhood centers did not meet the licensing requirements for trained workers (Vérificateur Général 1999, para 4.65). New training programs are being developed. For example, managers of child care facilities can take a program developed by the Université de Québec à Montréal, while family day care providers can now be trained in the province-wide educational program, via distance learning through Quebec's Télé-Université.

Wages have been raised, under pressure from workers who threatened to strike in the spring of 1999. Seeking to avoid the disruption such a strike would provoke, the government settled with the union, which was affiliated to the CSN, after a series of short stoppages and well-publicized threats. Wages have been improved by an average of 38 percent, and the ministry has allowed the early childhood centers to increase the income of family day care providers (Québec 2000, 132). Despite the hoopla, the starting salary of a child care worker with a CEGEP (junior college) diploma will only be $25,000 (currently it is $20, 293). Nevertheless, the ministry reports an increase of 56 percent in enrollments in such programs.[30]

Problems and Pressure Points

The new family policy, along with the child care component, has many supporters, not least of whom are its designers and promoters inside the state. However, there is also a good deal of popular support for it. During the 1998 election campaign, the leader of the Quebec Liberal Party, Jean Charest, floated a critique of the five-dollars-per-day program as "not meeting the needs of all parents." In under thirty-six hours the item had disappeared from the campaign agenda, as negative reactions and objections swamped the Liberal leader.

This said, there are still critics. First, as everywhere else, are those parents who cannot get a space for their children. While any parent may use child care, centers still ration access, via waiting lists and the like, because there are not enough spaces to meet demand. In 1998–99, for example, the number of spaces increased by 17 percent overall. There were major differences across regions, however, with rural and peripheral regions benefiting particularly. Spaces in Montreal increased 6 percent, while those in the region Nord du Québec rose from 356 in 1996–97 to 712 in 1998–99, and fully 68 percent in the latter year. The same year, spaces in the Côte Nord increased by 35 percent.

Often parents with "atypical needs" still do not such their needs met, and they must resort to all the usual strategies of using unregulated care, including drop-in centers or unlicensed kindergartens. However, several pilot projects were announced in 2000 to provide services twenty-four hours a day for shift workers, a promise that had earlier been included in the white paper but was left aside until recently.

There is constant pressure to create new spaces. Waiting lists continue despite the increase of spaces. Indeed, the auditor-general reported a shortfall of 135,213 places in March 1999. Of the 229,323 children needing a space, only 94,110 had one (Vérificateur Général 1999, para 4.45). The government claimed in June 2000 to have added 34,000 spaces over the previous two years, or 300 a week in 1999–2000.[31] An additional target is 12,000 new jobs by 2005.

This juggling of numbers and targets represents, in part, the difficulty of predicting demand. The initial calculations that informed the white paper were based on a survey done under the old regime in 1993–94 (Vérificateur Général 1999, para 4.48); many more parents than anticipated appeared at the door of the early childhood centers, seeking to place their children in the educationally focused programs rather than the informal care or other arrangements they had been using.

Among the critical parents are those who are losers under this new program. They have not hesitated to make their voices heard. One group is those who saw their tax deductions disappear: parents employing nannies and in-home babysitters or using unregulated but receipted care could no longer deduct those expenses from their Quebec taxes (of course they retained the federal deduction). Parents also complain that, in this competitive market for spaces, centers are charging additional fees—for registration, for example—or hiding higher costs in "program fees." Therefore, the promise of fixed costs may in some cases be illusory.

A second important critic has been the auditor-general, who issued a damning report in 1999 that criticized the ministry for mismanagement as well as a lack of evaluation criteria of the central goals—that is, child development and school readiness. Beyond these somewhat accountant-like criticisms were others going to the heart of the matter. The auditor-general found an increased use of family day care—from 26 percent of spaces in 1996 to 34 percent in 1999, with an oversight by the ECC that is minimal, at best (Vérificateur Général 1999, para 4.53). The report also pointed out that Quebec still lacked the administrative capacity to license drop-in centers and private kindergartens, although this type of service is still providing a goodly amount of child care in order to fill the gap between supply and demand described above.

The ministry has responded to the criticisms about training, as described above, and has established a task force to investigate the "contribution" of drop-in centers (ministry press release, June 22, 2000). Nonetheless, there are still gaps in the capacity to regulate and to manage the system.

The third group of vociferous and long-standing critics are the other major losers under the new regime: commercial operators. They have difficulty making ends meet with the limited grants to which they are entitled, and the minister made no bones about preferring to see them play a more diminished role. The original white paper had suggested that commercial providers would be phased out, but after a major mobilization and a rising recognition that without them there would not be enough spaces available, a compromise was eventually struck. Existing licensed operators receive public funds, but at a lower rate, via an "agreement" in which the government "rents" spaces. Since 1997 there has been a five-year moratorium on new licenses. Owners have also been offered the possibility of being transformed into centers, by selling their businesses to nonprofit associations of parents that would become the governing bodies. The auditor-general was also critical of the ministry's mishandling of these transformations. The process is cumbersome and slow, and in the meantime the ministry is even closing its eyes to illegal operators because it cannot afford to lose the spaces (Vérificateur Général 1999, para 4.77 ff).

A fourth set of critics comes from within the family movement. These opponents of the 1997 design support state spending on children and families, but they would prefer to see the generosity that Quebec directs toward child care diverted to a universal family allowance recognizing the contributions of *all parents* to society. For example, the Institute for Research on Public Policy (IRPP 2000) reissued a report written by researchers close to the family movement documenting that three-fourths of families received less money under the new regime than the previous one. The authors were critical of the retreat from universal family allowances in favor of targeting low-income parents. They recommended, as in the traditional French system, generous and universal family allowances for all parents, in the name of horizontal redistribution across families, rather than vertical redistribution from better-off to low-income families. However, their recommendation with respect to child care was exactly the reverse. The authors claimed that it should *not* be universal but more market driven, allowing parents to chose whether to pay for care or provide it themselves, as well as to select the type they preferred.

These two positions are exactly opposite those adopted by the government in 1996–97, which seeks to build solidarity via universality and invest in children's development in the realm of child care while expressing a commitment to equity with its targeted family allowances. In part the divergence comes from differing assessments of two elements of the family policy mix. One is clearly the educational component of child care. The authors of the IRPP study (2000, 28–29) insist that "parents know best" about the quality of care, and that governments should not be in the business of establishing standards for credentials or programs.[32] The editor's note, signed by Carole Vincent of the IRPP, makes a plea not only for greater choice, but for revaluing parental care. She also writes, "Indeed it is difficult to argue that the benefits generated by daycare services exceed those generated by parental care" (IRPP 2000, 3). The government, in contrast, inspired by the literature on child psychology and early childhood development, has opted for another position: it seeks to overcome the threat to children that may come from their parents' circumstances, such as living in poverty, or from the failure to act quickly on a diagnosis—often begun by childhood educators—of developmental problems that children of any socioeconomic background may experience.

A second difference is in the attention to matters of equality, especially gender equality. Even if there has been a discernible decline in the rhetoric of gender equality in the post-1997 Family Policy as compared to its predecessors, it is still present. Therefore, the design of parental insurance, child care, and family allowances reflects, among other things, attention to gender inequalities in the labor market for all women, whether low-income lone mothers or professionals living in two-parent families. The IRPP report, in contrast, is virtually silent on matters of gender equality—never the strong suit of the family movement. In other words, this debate takes us back to the fundamental issues raised by women's movements and experts in child development for decades. While the issues are familiar, the responses of familialists and the current government of Quebec to the challenges are not the same. They have alternative models.

There are lessons to be drawn from this "mini-comparison" as well as from the longer history recounted in this paper. Even in a liberal welfare state, there is space to develop more progressive programs. Quebec shares with other liberal welfare states a concern with employability and fostering parents' labor-force participation; indeed, it was something of an "innovator" in the 1980s in implementing coercive forms of employability policies (Boychuk 1998, 87). Yet at the same time, it has developed universal social programs and avoided putting children at risk of poor-quality child care. Therefore, rather than a story of path dependency, this is a story of how a determined reform coalition sensitive to children's developmental needs as well as to gender and class equality can row against the neoliberal tide, saving some values in the general process of welfare-state redesign.

Notes

This research is supported by the Social Science and Humanities Research Council of Canada and Founds pour la Formation de Chercheurs et l'Aide à la Récherche.

1. See the June 26, 2000, speech by the highest-ranking civil servant of the Ministry of Family and Child Welfare, which lists four goals, of which this is the first (Boisvert 2000, 4). This list is not idiosyncratic by any means; see that provided in the ministry's presentation of family policy online at www.famille-enfance.gouv.qc.ca.

2. This is the Head Start model used in the United States and Aboriginal communities in Canada by the federal government, as well as the practice in all Canadian provinces as a legacy of the Canada Assistance Plan (CAP) since 1965 (Beauvais and Jenson 2001).

3. Quebec is not the only province to do so. A number of other provinces—including Manitoba, Saskatchewan, and recently Ontario—provide some additional benefits to lone-parent families (Beauvais and Jenson 2001, appendix A).

4. This inversion of priorities has not gone unnoticed or without criticism. For a well-argued defense of universal family allowances and targeted subsidies for child care see IRPP (2000).

5. The Ministère de la Famille et de l'Enfance choses to translate its name this way. Therefore, out of respect for self-naming, we will do the same.

6. This is a quote from "Family Policy—Financial Support," available online at www.famille-enfance.gouv.qc.ca.

7. The press at the time made such arguments. See, for example, Mario Cloutier, "Le sommet sur l'économie et l'emploi" (Summit on Jobs and the Economy), Le Devoir, November 1, 1996, and Donald Charette, "Les jeunes claquent la porte" (Young People Banging at the Door), Le Soleil, November 1, 1996.

8. For a description of this Action Plan see "Family Policy History," online at www.famille-enfance.gouv.qc.ca.

9. See the press at the time. For a recent review of the summit declarations, see the auditor-general's 1999 report (Vérificateur Général du Québec 1999, para 4.16), available online at www.vgq.gouv.qc.ca.

10. See Boisvert (2000, 5), who says of the new ECC, "I would be remiss if I failed to mention the beginnings of these child care centers. The current network was created out of parent-run day care centers and home day care providers who formed agencies responsible for their management. The collaborative spirit between educators and parents has been maintained, protected—I would even say made a priority. . . ."

11. The CLSCs resemble the "people's clinics" in many ways, especially in the emphasis on empowerment of communities through mobilization and action. Nonetheless, several of the groups running people's clinics (which were staffed by a mix of medically-trained personnel, social animators and volunteers) opposed Bill 65, which established the CLSCs because they saw them as excessively statist (Bélanger and Lévesque 1992, 721–22).

12. For the current situation across Canada, putting Quebec in comparative perspective, see Beauvais and Jenson (2001, appendix a, tables 5 and 6).

13. A Secrétariat à la Politique Familiale (Secretariat for Family Policy) was set up in 1984, but reorganized and renamed in 1988.

14. Academic demographers, always important actors in this policy network in Quebec, had been writing of demographic crisis for years. The parliamentary commission, reporting in September 1985, had a mandate to "study the cultural, social, and economic impact of current demographic tendencies for the future of Quebec as a distinct society" (Dandurand 1987, 354).

15. These were *Le soutien collectif réclamé pour les familles québécoises. Rapport de la consultation sur la politique familiale* (Collective Support Demanded for Quebec Families: Report of the Consultative Committee on Family Policy), 1985, and *Le soutien collectif recommandé pour les parents québécois. Rapport de la consultation sur la politique familiale* (Collective Support Recommended for Quebec Parents: Report of the Consultative Committee on Family Policy), 1986. The move from "families" to "parents" signals the shift in perspective that the committee was trying to provoke.

16. The *prime à la naissance* was profoundly natalist in design: $500 for the first and second births (which in 1989 became $1,000 for the second birth). In 1988, third births brought $3,000, in 1989 $4,500 and, until 1997, $8,000 spread over five years. Prior to the 1997 reform, the basic family allowances and young child allowance also rose with birth order.

17. Quebec was not alone in Canada in framing the debate about reforming social assistance and developing employability measures via policies directed toward families and children (Beauvais and Jenson 2001, 15–23).

18. Her executive assistant, and the chief negotiator, throughout this process was Nicole Boily, who had been a member of the 1984–86 consultative committee and who would subsequently be named president of the Conseil de la Famille.

19. For a description of the movement across Canada toward "integration" and the development of new machinery for breaking out of the traditional silos of policy categories, see Mahon (2001).

20. These three goals are constantly reiterated in a range of documents. This English version is from Boisvert (2000, 4). Sometimes, however, the first and second are merged, to

generate three main objectives (see, for example, "Family Policy: Main Measures and Objectives" available online at www.famille-enfance.gouv.qc.ca).

21. Current information about the programs can be obtained online at www.famille-enfance.gouv.qc.ca.

22. A separate allowance for children with disabilities is still available.

23. Quebec was among the eight provinces taxing back the CCTB going to families on social assistance, at least until 2000. When the federal government increased the amount paid out in the CCTB and its supplement in the 2000 Budget, Quebec decided not to tax back all the increase, as some said because it would remove their involvement with too many families.

24. There is also a range of other tax benefits for families with children. For details and comparisons to other provinces, see Beauvais and Jenson 2001, appendix 1, table 6.

25. In 1978 Quebec created a maternity allowance that provided coverage for the first two weeks of maternity leave *not* covered by federal unemployment insurance (now employment insurance, or EI). Quebec also had the most generous unpaid parental leave in Canada until 2000. In 1990, new parents, both by birth and through adopting, could access thirty-four weeks of unpaid parental leave; the unpaid leave was extended to fifty-two weeks in 1997. Ottawa decided to extend paid parental leave for those eligible under EI to a full year. The provinces have had to adjust their labor codes accordingly in order to give the right to leave.

26. This idea of a separate *caisse* (fund) for parental leave, as well as extended coverage, had been promoted by the PQ for a number of years. See "La cause des femmes selon Louise Harel" (The Women's Cause According to Louise Harel). *La Gazette des femmes*, July–August 1996: 16.

27. In addition to a paternity leave of five weeks, the draft bill sets out two options for parents: forty weeks at 75 percent replacement of the previous year's earnings or fifty weeks at 70 percent for the first eighteen and 55 percent for the rest. See the *communiqués de presse* of the Ministère de la Famille et de l'Enfance, June 6, 2000, and June 9, 2000, available online at www.famille-enfance.gouv.qc.ca.

28. The Ministry's documentation in English calls these "child care centers," but I believe "early childhood center" is a better translation, because it both marks a distinction from what has become the term in many places for *any* day care center, and makes the link to "early childhood development," which is a major part of their mission.

29. Family day care providers can care for up to six children, or nine if they have an adult assistant. For details about the early childhood centers, see *Les centres de la petite enfance* or the overview in "Family Policy—Educational and Child Care Services," both available online at www.famille-enfance.gouv.qc.ca.

30. See the *communiqué de presse* of the Ministère de la Famille et de l'Enfance, June 22, 2000, available online at www.famille-enfance.gouv.qc.ca.

31. The first figure is from Boisvert (2000, 7) and the second from the ministry's press release of June 22, 2000.

32. They concede a role for regulation of health and safety, however.

References

Baillargeon, Denise. 1996. "Les politiques familiales au Québec" (Family Policies in Quebec), *Lien social et Politiques—RIAC*, no. 36: 21–32.

Beauvais, Caroline, and Jane Jenson. 2001. *Two Policy Paradigms: Family Responsibility and Investing in Children*. Ottawa: CPRN F-12. Available online at www.cprn.org/publications.

Bélanger, Paul R. and Benoît Lévesque. 1992. "Le mouvement populaire et communautaire: de la revendication au partenariat (1963–1992)" (The Popular and Community Sector Movement: From Demands to Partnerships). In *Le Québec en jeu* (Quebec at Stake), ed. Gérard Daigle. Montreal: Presses de l'Université de Montréal.

Boisvert, Maurice. 2000. Speech to the World Summit on Social Development, Geneva, June 26, 2000. Available online at www.famille-enfance.gouv.qc.ca.

Bergeron, Josée. 1997. "Les frontiéres imaginaires et imaginées de d'l'État-Providence" (The Imaginary and Imagined Borders of the Welfare State). Ph.D. diss., Carlton University, Ottawa, Canada.

Bouchard, Camil, Vivienne Labrie, and Alain Noël. 1996. *Chacun sa part: Rapport de trois membres du comité externe de réforme de la sécurité du revenu* (To Each His Share: Report by Three Members of the External Reform Committee of Income Security). Montreal: Ministére de la Securité du Revenu.

Boychuk, Gérard William. 1998. *Patchworks of Purpose: The Development of Provincial Social Assistance Regimes in Canada*. Montreal: McGill-Queen's University Press.

Childcare Resource and Research Unit. 1997. *Child Care in Canada: Provinces and Territories 1995*. Toronto: Childcare Resource and Research Unit.

Clarke, Christopher. 1998. *Canada's Income Security Programs*. Ottawa: Canadian Council on Social Development.

Collectif Clio. 1992. *L'Histoire des femmes au Québec depuis quatre siècles* (The History of Women in Quebec for the Last Four Centuries). Montreal: Le Jour, 1992.

Daigle, Gérard. 1992. *Le Québec en Jeu* (Quebec in Play). Montreal: Presses de l'Université de Montréal.

Dandurand, Renée B-. 1987. "Une politique familiale: Enjeux et débats" (Family Policy: Stakes and Debates). *Recherches sociographiques* 28: 2–3.

_____. 1992. "La famille n'est pas une île" (The Family Is Not an Island). In Daigle, ed. *Le Québec*.

Desjardins, Ghislaine. 1991. *Faire garder ses enfants au Québec . . . une histoire toujours en marche* (Getting Child Care in Quebec . . . an Ever-Unfolding History). Quebec: Office des services de garde à l'enfance.

IRPP. 2000. "Quebec Family Policy: Impact and Options." *Choices* 6, no. 1.

Jenson, Jane. 2001. "Canada's Shifting Citizenship Regime: The Child as Model Citizen." In *The Dynamics of Decentralization: Canadian Federalism and British Devolution,* ed. Trevor C. Salmon and Michael Keating. Montreal: McGill-Queen's University Press.

Jenson, Jane, and Mariette Sineau. 1998. *Qui doit garder le jeune enfant? Le travail des mères dans l'Europe en crise* (Who Should Care for Young Children? Mothers' Work in a Europe in Crisis). Paris: LGDJ.

_____. 2001. *Who Cares? Women's Work, Childcare and Welfare State Redesign.* Toronto: University of Toronto Press.

Jenson, Jane, and Sharon M. Stroick. 1999. *What Is the Best Policy Mix for Canada's Young Children?* Ottawa: CPRN F-09. Available online at www.cprn.org.

Lamoureux, Diane. 1992. "Nos luttes ont changé nos vies. L'impact du mouvement féministe" (Our Struggles Have Changed Our Lives: The Impact of the Feminist Movement). In Daigle, ed., *Le Québec.*

Lefebvre, Pierre. 1998. "Les nouvelles orientations de la politique familiale du Québec: une critique de l'allocation unifiée" (New Trends in Family Policy in Quebec: A Critique of Unified Benefits). In Dandurand, Renée B., Pierre Lefebvre, and Jean-Pierre Lamoureux, eds. 1998. *Quelle politique familiale à l'aube de l'an 2000?* (What Family Policy at the Dawn of the Year 2000?). Pans and Montreal: Éditions l'Harmattan.

Lepage, Francine, and Marie Moisan. 1998. "L'assurance parentale: la nouvelle politique québécoise et les prestations réservées aux pères" (Parental Insurance: The New Quebec Policy and Benefits Reserved for Fathers). In Dandurand et al., eds., *Quelle politique.*

Lesemann, Frédéric. 1981. *Du pain et des services: la réforme de la santé et des services sociaux au Québec* (Bread and Services: Health and Social Service Reform in Quebec). Laval: Éds. Saint-Martin.

Mahon, Rianne. 2001. *School-Aged Children Across Canada: A Patchwork of Public Policies.* Ottawa: CPRN, F-11. Available online at www.cprn.org.

MSSS (Ministère de la Santé et des Services Sociaux). 1991. *Un Québec fou de ses enfants. Rapport du Groupe de travail pour les jeunes* (Quebec, Mad about Its Children. Report of the Working Party for Young People). Known as the "Bouchard Report." Quebec: MSSS.

Noël, Alain. 1996. "La contrepartie dans l'aide sociale au Québec" (Social Security Compensation in Quebec). *Revue française des affaires sociales* 50, no. 4: 387–99.

Québec. 1999. *Un portrait statistique des familles et des enfants au Québec* (A Statistical Portrait of Families and Children in Quebec). Quebec: Gouvernement du Québec.

Québec. 2000. *Budget de dépenses 2000–2001*, vol. 3, *Plans ministériels de gestion des dépenses* (Expenditure Budget 2000–2001, vol. 3, Ministerial Expenditure Management Plans). Quebec: Gouvernement du Québec.

Rose, Ruth. 1998. "Politiques pour les familles pauvres: supplément au revenu gagné et revenus minimums garantis" (Policies for Poor Families: Supplement to Earned Income and Guaranteed Minimum Incomes). In Dandurand et al., eds., *Quelle Politique.*

Roy, Maurice. 1987. *Les CLSC. Ce qu'il faut savoir* (CLSCs: What You Need to Know). Montreal: Éds. Saint-Martin.

Vaillancourt, Yves. 1988. "Quebec." In *Privatisation and Provincial Social Services in Canada,* ed. J. S. Ismael and Yves Vaillancourt. Edmonton: University of Alberta Press.

Vérificateur Général du Québec. 1999. *Rapport à l'Assemblée nationale pour l'année 1998–1999* (Report to the National Assembly for 1998–1999). Quebec: Gouvernement du Québec.

Dilemmas of Child Care

Sonya Michel

In the heyday of second-wave feminism, activists envisioned a world in which child rearing had become completely socialized, making traditional motherhood a thing of the past. More than three decades have passed since feminists first demanded free, twenty-four-hour-a-day child care, yet no society has come close to fulfilling such a utopian (some would say *dystopian*) vision. As the preceding chapters have documented, progress toward child care has been slow, the result of both restructuring and specific problems that appear to be endemic to the notion itself. At the same time, feminists' position on child care has also changed.

Child care is one of the most protean of social policies, one that may be deployed by different social actors to achieve a variety of ends. Although feminists, the group to whom child care is arguably the most meaningful, have declared child care to be an essential component of women's social citizenship, they have not always been its most effective advocates. This for at least two reasons: first, feminism itself has always been a volatile issue, one that often engenders strong backlash, and second, child care, unlike other items on the feminist agenda—say, antidiscrimination policies—involves not only women, but children too. In seeking to transform the way in which young children are reared, feminist child care advocates inevitably challenge fundamental social values and cultural traditions.

Not surprisingly, then, when it comes to child care, feminists have often found they can do more good if they remain in the shadows while other social actors lobby for child care on behalf of interests that are not explicitly feminist, such as child development, poverty reduction, labor shortages, or demographic crises. Such campaigns, however, produce mixed results, for the provisions they yield may be encumbered with conditions that are unpalatable to feminists (for example, pronatalism or mandatory employment) or not conducive to the kind of universal, high-quality, state-supported provisions that can engender long-term political support. This afterword will briefly examine some of these political complexities.

Let us turn first to coalitions, often the only option open to feminist advocates of child care but also a source of potential frustration. The terms of such alliances may require feminists to cloak their own support for child care in the rhetoric of another interest group (early childhood education, as we have seen, being the most common). In consequence, though the resulting provisions may well benefit certain groups of women and children, they may also do little to advance the cause of feminism. Moreover, the fruits of coalition politics are often impermanent or narrowly targeted. When child care is designed to address specific social or economic conditions, provisions become contingent upon those conditions and therefore politically unstable or not amenable to universalization. Nonetheless, there is always the possibility that limited policymaking will have unintended consequences; that is, in targeting child care to address a specific problem or social issue, states may inadvertently create a constituency that will seek to extend provisions more generally. At this point, however, because of the initial framing of the policy, feminists may lack standing on the policy and thus find it difficult to lend support.

Because of their closely overlapping interests, child care advocates have most frequently made common cause with early childhood educators, whose goals tend to appear more benign to wary publics. In societies where a strong partnership between the two fields took shape early on (Sweden, Denmark, France, and Australia, for instance), educators helped overcome objections to placing small children in child care by emphasizing the social, emotional, and cognitive benefits of group situations. By contrast, in societies where the fields remained separate, most notably the United States, child care has remained stigmatized, lacking in public and state support, and markedly low in quality. On a practical level, preschools, nursery schools, and kindergartens have often functioned as forms of child care, though not always as well as intentional child care services in certain respects (for example, they may offer fewer hours of service); they do, however, generally provide higher-quality, or at least more structured, services. In addition, as we have seen, early childhood educators have been in a better position to call for universalizing provisions by exposing the folly of limiting access to child care to those children whose parents are employed or pursuing education; if child care does indeed have educational and developmental benefits, they claim, then it should become available to *all* children.

Still, the partnership is not perfect. While professional pride encourages early childhood educators to showcase the benefits of their services, it can also lead them to denigrate the influence of the parents whose care they are replacing, particularly when those parents come from low-income, less-well-educated social strata (Solinger 2001, chap. 6).[1] When applied to child care, educators' insistence on maintaining high standards with regard to staff qualifications, staff-to-child ratios, curriculum, equipment, and other programmatic dimensions may have the unintended consequence of pricing child care out of the market; that is, neoliberal policymakers may be able to concede the importance of offering high-quality provisions but then claim that the state cannot afford to finance them, and that offering anything less would be harmful to children. Such arguments ultimately undermined deployment of a workfare policy in the Netherlands, but landed upon deaf ears in the United States and Canada, where the commitment to workfare has been more absolute.

Another dilemma arises in the area of care for very young children. Some early childhood educators flatly oppose this type of service on the grounds that it is emotionally and medically risky. Others believe it can be beneficial if proper safeguards are maintained. Most experts agree, however, that ensuring the health and development of those under three, and especially those under two, requires very high adult-to-child ratios (1:2 or 1:3 for infants; 1:4 or 1:5 for toddlers). Such care is, of course, very expensive. Thus, in several societies, policymakers have opted instead to provide paid maternity and/or parental leave.

Parental leaves, while admirable from the perspective of child welfare and undoubtedly preferred by many parents (especially newly parturient mothers), have ambiguous implications for women on the whole. Even though most policies stipulate that employees should be permitted to return to the same or equivalent jobs, such guarantees are not always honored, and extended absences almost invariably affect leave-takers' employment prospects and lifetime earnings potential by interrupting their career trajectories. The effects may be weaker for workers in lower employment rungs (which partly explains why women in such occupations are so eager to take leaves), but they undoubtedly contribute to occupational stagnation. Moreover, the pronounced trend toward increased take-up of maternity leave and extended parental leave among low-skilled and less-educated women workers documented in several of the cases discussed above (France in particular) constitutes a dilemma that is particularly troubling to feminists. Because take-up is much less common among fathers, parental leave continues to be associated with women, branding them as "unreliable" workers and barring them from more responsible, more lucrative jobs.[2] Finally, while presenting parental leaves as a boon to parents, states have, as several of our cases show, also used them as a form of labor-market policy—again, usually to the detriment of female workers.

The concentration of less-well-educated women in home-based child care provision is also a concern for feminists, particularly when much of their clientele consists of middle- and upper-class families. State support has undoubtedly improved working conditions for these providers (as well as the quality of their services), but niggling questions remain about how women come to "choose" this occupation. Monique Kremer argues in this volume that such a pattern of caregiving fits well with "ideals of care" in certain societies (e.g., Flanders), but this interpretation, while compelling, may be too complacent in its implicit functionalism. What educational and training opportunities have these women had? What other occupations are open to them? If these women had other options for employment, might they not challenge the values they now appear to accept? Such questions become all the more troubling when they are placed within the broader context of recent findings on the global division of labor with regard to caring work (Hondagneu-Sotelo 2000; Vachani 1995).

Because of such dilemmas, today's feminists have moved far from the radical child care demands of the 1960s. Indeed, taking a position that would have been unthinkable then,[3] many are now calling for the right to care—the right to time to care for children, elders, and other family members needing assistance, and, through acknowledgment of such activities as *work,* the right to receive state support for caregiving.[4] Though one might argue that the crisis of caregiving—the "care deficit"—perceived by many is in itself the result of inadequate child care provisions, the issues these critics raise cannot be easily brushed aside.

Within contemporary feminist discussions of caregiving, two separate discourses may be identified. Both begin by attributing the loss of the right to care to the increasing commodification (in Gøsta Esping-Andersen's sense of the term) of women, but they emphasize different aspects of this trend according to the nature of commodification—that is, whether it is self-chosen or coerced by the state. One discourse, drawing on the work of analysts like Nancy Fraser (1997), Trudie Knijn and Monique Kremer (1997), Arlie Hochschild (1995, 1997) and Jane Lewis (2001), focuses on the impact of forms of commodification that are more or less voluntary. These are rooted in the conjuncture between contemporary labor market needs and women's eagerness to follow through on second-wave feminism's demands for access to employment. But what began as an assertion of rights has now become a necessity. For married women, declining wages for men as well as women mean that two incomes are needed to sustain households, while for lone mothers, declining state support propels them into the labor market (Lewis 2001). Increasing hours of work, coupled with a lack of accommodation by either employers or the state (including a paucity of adequate child care), create a "care deficit" that deprives dependent family members of needed attention and puts pressure on those (usually women) who are expected to provide care as well as earn wages.

A second, more specific discourse, embedded in the work of analysts such as Gwendolyn Mink (1999), Rickie Solinger (2001), and Dorothy Roberts (1994), deplores the involuntary forms of commodification produced by mandatory welfare-to-work, or "workfare," policies that require low-income mothers (disproportionately women of color) to take employment outside the home as a condition of receiving public assistance. Under such regimes (of which the United States is the most extreme example), the care deficit becomes acute as women are forced to choose between using care services that may be less than adequate or losing their benefits. Picking up arguments made by welfare rights activists since the 1970s (Kornbluh 2000), these critics point to policymakers' cynical, perhaps deliberate, refusal to acknowledge the value of poor women's caregiving and compensate it as a form of work in itself.

Neither set of analysts would argue that child care per se has *caused* the commodification of women, but they would probably concur that it has *enabled* the phenomenon merely by its existence as a modern form of social provision and its availability (at least in theory, regardless of whether supply, quality, and/or support are adequate).[5] Moreover, with regard to workfare, as we have seen in the United States, child care has been specifically deployed as a policy lever. Thus while neither group would call for the elimination of child care, they are wary of its implications in the current political climate, and their support for child care policies has weakened as a result.

Given the variety of dilemmas engendered by efforts to construct and deploy child care provisions, to what extent can we attribute current inadequacies in this policy area to restructuring? Restructuring clearly fuels arguments against fiscal support for child care and discourages states from expanding bureaucracies in order to administer and oversee public provisions. Such counterrationales are not only powerful in themselves but also serve as convenient loincloths for less politically palatable objections to child care, such as those stemming from religious conservatism or blatant gender discrimination. But this does not mean that in the absence of restructuring child care policies would proceed apace, for the dilemmas also signal structural and ideological issues that have little to do with restructuring but must be resolved in any case.

Feminists' future role in such a process is unclear. At the moment, it seems likely that they will continue to give priority to the struggle around the right to care, for the care deficit is real and persistent, and the human costs palpable. Unfortunately, however, this orientation may well prevent feminists from seeing that one of the best ways to address this problem is by supporting universal child care, not eschewing it. As long as affordable, high-quality public child care provisions remain scarce and staff members must put up with poor working conditions, the care deficit will remain acute. But when children have the benefit of a nurturing and stimulating environment all day, parents will be less likely to feel the strain of having to provide compensatory attention at night; their concerns will be alleviated and their sense of conflict reduced, making their time on the job less stressful. By the same token, when child care workers are held to high standards but also well compensated and provided with adequate equipment and support, they will enjoy high status and perform their jobs more effectively, thus improving the quality of provisions. Child care that fulfills expectations for good services and good working conditions will attract both committed families and eager staff members, and, in turn, generate popular and political support for public provisions. This, in turn, will reduce the demand for market-based provisions, with all of the drawbacks these entail. Only with an adequate child care policy in place can women truly exercise their rights both to work and to care.

Notes

1. This effect may also occur in early childhood educators' interactions with preschool parents, but child care clienteles tend to embrace a broader class spectrum, with more families at the lower end.

2. For a historical perspective on the ambiguous implications of protective legislation, see Kessler-Harris, Lewis, and Wikander (1995).

3. *Almost* unthinkable, perhaps; there was, of course, the Wages for Housework campaign, a minor but significant strand running through second-wave feminist thought; see Dalla Costa and James (1975).

4. It should be noted that while these discussions signal a distinct rewriting of second-wave feminism's sometimes heavy-handed critique of marriage and motherhood, their awareness of the issues raised in that critique precludes reversion to the kind of unselfconscious embrace of caregiving roles for women that marked earlier maternalist thought.

5. The link between child care and poverty is not entirely new; as a number of the foregoing chapters note, the earliest forms of child care—nineteenth-century créches, or day nurseries—were also intended to "help poor women help themselves."

References

Dalla Costa, Mariarosa, and Selma James. 1975. *The Power of Women and the Subversion of the Community.* Bristol: Falling Wall Press.

Fraser, Nancy. 1997. "After the Family Wage: A Postindustrial Thought Experiment." In Fraser, *Justice Interruptus: Critical Reflections on the 'Postsocialist' Condition.* New York: Routledge.

Hochschild, Arlie. 1995. "The Culture of Politics: Traditional, Postmodern, Cold-Modern, and Warm-Modern Ideals of Care." *Social Politics* 2, no. 3: 331–46.

_____. 1997. *The Time Bind: When Work Becomes Home and Home Becomes Work.* New York: Metropolitan Books.

Hondagneu-Sotelo, Pierrette. 2000. "The International Division of Caring and Cleaning Work." In *Care Work: Gender, Labor, and the Welfare State,* ed. Madonna Harrington Meyer. New York: Routledge.

Kessler-Harris, Alice, Jane Lewis, and Ulla Wikander, eds. 1995. *Protecting Women: Labor Legislation in Europe, the United States, and Australia, 1880–1920.* Urbana: University of Illinois Press.

Knijn, Trudie, and Monique Kremer. 1997. "Gender and the Caring Dimension of Welfare States: Towards Inclusive Citizenship." *Social Politics* 4, no 3: 328–61.

Kornbluh, Felicia. 2000. "A Right to Welfare? Poor Women, Professionals, and Poverty Programs." Ph.D. diss., Princeton University.

Lewis, Jane. 2001. "The Decline of the Male-Breadwinner Model: Implications for Work and Care." *Social Politics* 8, no. 2: 152–69.

Mink, Gwendolyn. 1999. *Welfare's End.* Ithaca, N.Y.: Cornell University Press.

Roberts, Dorothy. 1994. "The Value of Black Mothers' Work." *Connecticut Law Review* 26: 871–78.

Solinger, Rickie. 2001. *Beggars and Choosers: How the Politics of Choice Shapes Adoption, Abortion, and Welfare in the United States.* New York: Hill and Wang.

Vachani, Nilita. 1995. *When Mother Came Home for Christmas.* Documentary video. Germany/Greece: ZDF (Das Kleine Fernsehspiel)/Film Sixteen.

Notes on Contributors

CHRISTINA BERGQVIST, a political scientist, is a researcher at the National Institute for Working Life, where she is affiliated with the research program on The Swedish Model in Transition. She was editor-in-chief of *Equal Democracies? Gender and Politics in the Nordic Countries* (Scandinavian University Press, 1999).

ANETTE BORCHORST teaches gender and social policy at Aalborg University in Denmark. One of the pioneers of gender studies in Denmark, she has published numerous articles on gender and welfare states in a comparative context.

DEBORAH BRENNAN is an associate professor in Government and International Relations at the University of Sydney. She has published widely on gender and family policy, welfare state history, and Australian politics. Her current research is on maternity and parental leave and the role of taxation in family policy, and her publications include *The Politics of Australian Child Care: From Philanthropy to Feminism* (Cambridge University Press, 1994). She was a founding member of the National Association of Community-Based Children's Services in Australia and has served on the Commonwealth Ministerial Advisory Council on Children's Services.

VINCENT DELLA SALA is an associate professor in the Department of Political Science at Carleton University, Canada. His research deals primarily with the political economy of European integration.

JACQUELINE HEINEN is Professor of Sociology at the University of Versailles Saint-Quentin-en-Yvelines and also lectures at IEP, Institut d'Etudes Politiques in Paris. She is director of *Cahiers du Genre*, a journal of the CNRS (Centre national de recherche scientifique), and a specialist on gender issues and social policy in Eastern and Western Europe. She is currently coordinator of a comparative study on women in local politics, "Gender and local management of change in seven countries of the European Union," a project funded by the European Commission, DG XII. Recent publications include *Chômage et devenir de main-d'oeuvre en Pologne* (Paris, 1995) and an edited volume (with Alisa del Re), *Quelle citoyenneté pour les femmes? La crise des Etats-providence et de la représentation politique en Europe* (What Citizenship for Women? The Crisis of Welfare States and Political Representation in Europe) (Milano Press, 1996).

JANE JENSON is professor of political science at the Université de Montréal, where she is also Director of the Institute for European Studies of the Université de Montréal and McGill University. She is Director of the Family Network of the Canadian Policy Research Networks, Inc. (www.cprn.org). She has written frequently on issues of social policy in Europe and Canada and is the author, with Mariette Sinuea, of *Who Cares? Women's Work, Child Care, and Welfare State Restructuring* (University of Toronto Press, 2001).

MONIQUE KREMER is a graduate student at the Univeristy of Utrecht, completing a Ph.D. dissertation entitled "Gender, Care, and the Welfare State: An International Comparison." She compares working and caring in four welfare states: Britain, Belgium, the Netherlands, and Denmark, all countries where she has either studied or worked. While at the Netherlands Institute of Care and Welfare (NIZW), she published on Danish employment policies and on caring and citizenship in an international perspective.

DENISE URIAS LEVY earned her Ph.D. in Public Policy Analysis at the University of Illinois at Chicago in 2000. Her thesis, "Child Care Policies in America: Inter-State Differences and the Progress of Devolution," analyzes child care policies for low-income families in the United States, with a focus on the cross-state variation of parameters regulating these policies in the aftermath of the 1996 welfare reform. Her research interests also include family law and women's employment. She is a native of Brazil, where she has also practiced law.

RIANNE MAHON is Director of the Institute of Political Economy and a professor in the School of Public Policy and Administration and the Department of Sociology and Anthropology at Carleton University, Canada. She has published various articles on the politics of child care in Canada and Sweden. She also works on labor market restructuring and union strategies, with a focus on these two countries.

SONYA MICHEL is currently Director of the Gender and Women's Studies Program and professor of gender and women's studies and history at the University of Illinois at Chicago. She is a founding editor of the journal *Social Politics: International Studies in Gender, State and Society* and author, most recently, of *Children's Interests / Mothers' Rights: The Shaping of America's Child Care Policy* (Yale University Press, 1999). As of September 2002, she will be professor of American studies and history at the University of Maryland, College Park.

KIMBERLY MORGAN is an assistant professor of political science at George Washington University. She received her Ph.D from Princeton University and has been a post-doctoral fellow at the Institute of French Studies at New York University. Her publications have appeared in *Comparative Politics* and *The Journal of Policy History*. Dr.

Morgan is currently a fellow in the Robert Wood Johnson Foundation's Scholars in Health Policy Research Program at Yale University.

ANITA NYBERG is professor of gender, work, and economy at the National Institute for Working Life in Stockholm. Her work has mainly dealt with women's, but also men's paid and unpaid work. Her most recent publications in English include "Women, Men and Incomes: Gender Equality and Economic Independence" (1997).

ITO PENG is currently an associate professor of social policy at the School of Policy Studies, Kwansei Gakuin University, Japan. Her main research interests are gender, welfare states, and east-west comparisons of social policy. She has published several articles and chapters on the Japanese welfare state and gender and social policies in Japan. She is currently writing a book on lone mother families in Japan, and co-authoring another, *Transforming East Asian Welfare States: A Comparison of Japan, Korea, and Taiwan*. As of July 2002, she will be an associate professor of sociology at the University of Toronto.

SUSAN PHILLIPS is an associate professor in the School of Public Policy and Administration and Director of the Centre of Voluntary Sector Research and Development at Carleton University in Ottawa, Canada. Her research interests focus on the relationship between the welfare state and voluntary organizations.

VICKY RANDALL is a professor in the Department of Government, University of Essex. She is the author of *Women and Politics: An International Perspective* (MacMillan, 1987) and *The Politics of Child Daycare in Britain* (Cambridge University Press, 2000), and co-author (with Joni Lovenduski) of *Contemporary Feminist Politics* (Oxford University Press, 1993).

CELIA VALIENTE is a lecturer in the Department of Political Science and Sociology of the Universidad Carlos III de Madrid, Spain. Her main research interests are in public policies and social movements in Spain, with a particular focus on gender. Her publications include *Políticas Públicas de Género en Perspectiva Comparada* (Public Gender Policies in Comparative Perspective) (Madrid: Universidad Autónoma de Madrid).

Index